Invention
&Design

Invention &Design

A Rhetorical Reader

Second Edition

Forrest D. Burt
E. Cleve Want
Texas A&M University

Random House
New York

Second Edition

98765432

Copyright © 1975, 1978 by Random House, Inc.

Library of Congress Cataloging in Publication Data

Burt, Forrest D   Comp.
Invention and design.

Includes bibliographical references and index.
1.   College readers.   2.   English language—Rhetoric.
I.   Want, E. Cleve, 1934-   joint comp.
II.   Title.
PE1417.B846   1978   808'.04275   77-17205
ISBN 0-394-32116-2

Manufactured in the United States of America.   Composed by Precision Typographers Inc., New Hyde Park, N.Y.   Printed and bound by R. R. Donnelley & Sons, Co., Crawfordsville, Ill.

Permissions Acknowledgments

We dedicate this book to our families: first to our parents, who have influenced us in ways beyond the comprehension of any of us; next to our wives, Veva and Jan, whose love, support, and willingness to rearrange family schedules around our projects are appreciated more than we can express with words; and finally to our children—Eileen, Bob, Lori, Julie, Cheree, Diane, Kevin, Ginger, and Cathy—who give us so much of our motivation for loving and working and so much in return for our efforts.

A Preface to the Teacher

In our experience of teaching composition and other courses that involve writing, we have found that students typically bring a combination of strengths and weaknesses to these courses. Student writing that is grammatically, mechanically, and structurally correct often lacks vitality, originality, and, above all, concreteness. Student writing that shows concreteness and imagination may, however, be incoherent and unintelligible because of deficiencies in grammar, mechanics, and structure. Separately, these types of writing are weak. But when the positive elements in both can be encouraged and combined through effective teaching, students benefit immeasurably in improving their ability to think and write coherently and clearly. This book is intended to aid both teachers and students by providing models of effective writing in a sequence that makes pedagogical sense, by stimulating intelligent analysis of the selections, and by encouraging the incorporation of the results of such analysis into progressively more sophisticated student writing.

Invention and Design was conceived out of the belief that the key rhetorical skills of inventing and designing are vital to the writing process. Furthermore, it grew and developed in the conviction that these skills should serve as controlling principles throughout the book, both directly and indirectly. By *invention* we mean the complex process of originating and discovering ideas, illustrations, comparisons, contrasts, and various forms of analysis through the working of reason and imagination upon the writer's accumulated knowledge—including personal experience, perception, reading, and education. *Design* is the equally complex process of selecting, ordering, and structuring the results of invention into a coherent and effective finished product.

A third major rhetorical concept should also be mentioned here: style. *Style* is the accumulation of choices the writer makes in wording, sentence structure, paragraphing, and overall design. These choices grow out of the writer's unique personality and his or her attitudes toward both the subject and the reading audience. The finer points of style can be more adequately treated in a composition/rhetoric textbook or handbook than in a reader. *Invention and Design,* however, discusses many stylistic concerns in its introductions; illustrates a wide variety of them in its selections; and features questions headed *Questions on Invention, Design, and Style* that help students to perceive such concerns and to analyze the bases of the choices the writer has made. Effective teaching can, of course, build on these materials to make direct applications to student writing.

The progression of selections and apparatus from simple to complex has been carefully thought out to help students integrate the various rhetorical modes into their own developing styles. The book is divided into four main sections: Illustration, Comparison and Contrast, Analysis, and Argument. Thus the book moves from relatively basic concepts to more complex ones, for comparison and contrast often imply pairs of illustrations; analysis implies an elaboration of comparison and contrast into further distinctions based on similarity and difference; and effective argument subsumes all the preceding categories. This progressive arrangement continues into the smaller divisions of the book as well, for each section is divided into subsections that in turn move from simple to complex, and the individual selections within each subsection are arranged in like manner.

The selections themselves have been chosen for their appropriateness to the section and subsection in which they appear, their excellence as models of good writing, their diversity of appropriate styles, and their average length—approximately the same as papers that the students will write. In addition, they have been chosen to illustrate a cross section of the richness and diversity of human experience in their subject matter and to exhibit a sensitive response to the human condition in their treatment of that subject matter. All of these selections have been trial tested by us or by others in freshman composition classrooms.

The apparatus of *Invention and Design* includes a primary table of contents arranged (like the book) by rhetorical types and an alternate table of contents divided into seventeen subject categories. "An Introduction to Writing" provides students with an understanding of the key rhetorical concepts in the book and, more important, guides them to applications of those concepts in actual writing situations. Four main section introductions explain the concepts of Illustration, Comparison and Contrast, Analysis, and Argument and relate them to student writing; twelve subsection introductions explain more detailed aspects of those categories with continued emphasis on their relevance for students.

Within the subsections, each selection is preceded by a headnote and followed by two categories of questions and a range of applications. The headnotes are intended to stimulate students' interest in each selection and direct their attention to the rhetorical principles present in it. The *Questions on Content* deal with content apart from interpretation and analysis. Some teachers will find them useful in motivating the kind of close, if literal, reading that is a necessary step toward more sophisticated reading and understanding. Other teachers may choose to ignore them or to recommend them to students as a self-check on their reading comprehension. The *Questions on Invention, Design, and Style* are intended to help students analyze the finished essays and the processes by which they came to be invented and designed. In general, they, like the selections themselves, become increasingly sophisticated in subsequent sections of the book. The *Applications* are writing assignments—at least two after each selection—that allow students to apply to their own writing the invention and design principles explained and analyzed in each subsection. The subject matter in these assignments grows out of the subject matter of the selections in each subsection and encourages students to draw from their own perception, personal experience, and memory for sources of invention.

At the end of the book are a Glossary of Terms and a list of Biographical Notes. The glossary includes definitions of all major rhetorical terms and often features more detailed discussions of them than is possible in the introductions earlier in the book. The biographical notes provide dates and other essential information about the authors of the individual selections. Some teachers may wish to make reading of the relevant biography automatic for each selection assigned.

The success of the first edition of *Invention and Design* has encouraged us to prepare a second edition that seeks to refine and improve on the first rather than alter it in any basic way. Consequently, the basic division of the book into four main sections and into various subsections is unchanged. One subsection from the first edition—Complex Illustration—has been eliminated because we and others found it introduced overly sophisticated concepts too early in the book. Also, the introduction to the subsection on classification analysis has been enlarged to include the principles of formal definition. In addition, the sequence of Reason in Argument and Emotion in Argument has been reversed to give greater prominence to the former. In all other respects, the subsections as well as main sections in the present edition are the same as in the first.

We have eliminated eighteen individual selections from the first edition on the basis of our, and others', experiences in the classroom. We have substituted nineteen new selections, also on the basis of classroom effectiveness and to provide models more nearly like what students will write in college and in their subsequent careers. In addition, we have reedited the selection by Rachel Carson in order to provide what we believe is an outstanding opening selection for the present edition. We have also made numerous shifts of individual selections from one subsection to another in order to give the overall movement of the book better coherence and consistency.

The apparatus of the book has also been extensively revised. "An Introduction to Writing" has been added so that the basic terms can be defined and main principles of writing introduced apart from the main section and subsection introductions. As a result, these specialized introductions in the present edition are much more complete and thorough in treating their specific subjects than the corresponding ones in the first edition. We have attempted here to define all our concepts more precisely, develop and illustrate them more fully, and demonstrate their applicability to student writing more clearly. Also, every head-note, question, and writing assignment from the first edition has been closely scrutinized and, in many instances, changed. The glossary at the back of the book is a new feature that we hope will be useful for quick reference to the terms included in it.

We have found our revision of *Invention and Design* to be a satisfying and highly instructive process. We believe that our own experience in using the first edition in the classroom has been enhanced by honest student reaction and by the candid suggestions of our colleagues at Texas A&M University and across the country. We wish to express our thanks to all these people—unfortunately, too numerous to mention by name—who have contributed greatly to what we believe is a distinctly improved book.

In addition, we wish to thank Professors Neil Nakadate of Iowa State University, James L. Kinneavy of The University of Texas at Austin, Jonathan N. Lawson of St. Cloud State University, David Skwire of Cuyahoga Community College, Betty Barnes of Spokane Community College, and Lois Cundiff of Jefferson Community College for their detailed and most useful responses to our prospectus for the second edition. We want again to thank Professor Richard Larson, of Lehmann College of the City University of New York, for his especially perceptive criticism and advice.

We cannot imagine more pleasant direction and assistance than we have received from Richard Garretson and Alice Solomon of Random House for this edition or from Pat Klossner and Helen Greer for the first edition. No doubt there are other members of the Random House staff whose names we don't know but whose contributions are gratefully acknowledged here.

To those administrators, faculty, and staff of Texas A&M University, especially within the Department of English, who have encouraged and actively contributed to this project, we express our deep and heartfelt thanks.

Finally, we thank our wives, Veva Burt and Jan Want, whose unfailing understanding and support have made this work possible.

F. D. B.
E. C. W.
College Station, Texas
September 1977

Contents

Part Three Analysis · 133

Classification Analysis and Definition · 139
Florence H. Pettit Woods for Carving · 142
Arnold J. Mandell A Psychiatrist Looks at Pro Football · 145
Warren S. Brown Left Brain, Right Brain · 151
Aaron Copland Listening to Music · 156
Bernard Rudofsky The Fashionable Body · 163
S. I. Hayakawa Reports, Inferences, Judgments · 171

Process Analysis · 180
Peter Elbow Freewriting · 183
Caroline Seebohm How to Change Your Point of View · 188
Robert Angus Good Keyboard Recording · 195
Roy C. Selby, Jr. A Delicate Operation · 200
Jessica Mitford To Bid the World Farewell · 206
Time Stars: Where Life Begins · 214

Causal Analysis · 223
X. J. Kennedy Who Killed King Kong? · 228
Sir James Jeans Why the Sky Looks Blue · 234
Lewis Thomas The Iks · 236
C. S. Lewis Why We Make Excuses · 241
J. Bronowski Human Sexuality · 247
Erich Fromm The Worker as Creator or Machine · 253

Part Four Argument · 261

Reason in Argument · 269
Thomas Henry Huxley Everyone Is a Scientist · 273
Andrew Marvell To His Coy Mistress · 281
Thomas Jefferson and Others Declaration of Independence · 284
Dorothy Z. Seymour Understanding Language Differences · 289
George Bernard Shaw Law Is Indispensable · 300

Emotion in Argument · 306
John Robinson The Bambi Syndrome · 308
Cleveland Amory Little Brother of the Wolf · 312
Anne Roiphe Confessions of a Female Chauvinist Sow · 319

Alternate Table of Contents by Subjects

Problem Solving

The Human Body

Law and Justice

① subordinator

An Introduction to Writing

[Thinking back to your own reading experience] try to recall a time when the book or article or letter you were reading was so compelling that you literally forgot where you were, forgot what time it was, forgot everything except the world created by the writer. If it was a story or novel, you might have felt you were actually observing the scene and characters and sharing the suspense or joy they were experiencing. If it was a letter, you might have felt you were meeting an old friend again and catching up on what he or she had been doing since the last meeting or communication. If it was an article, you might have felt an excitement at being shown a new perspective on an old idea like growing up or an interest at being told clearly how to make a better-quality tape recording.

On the other hand, we have all read material that had opposite effects. We became frustrated by our inability to stay interested in what the writer was saying, to grasp the point, or to see its significance. Our minds wandered to objects and ideas far from the printed page. The writer simply failed to get us involved in what was being said.

Consider for a moment the words we apply to writing that seems especially worth reading. Perhaps you can add to the following list:

interesting	exciting
believable	frightening
down-to-earth	clear
concrete	informative
easy to follow	funny
inspiring	sad
thought-provoking	important
convincing	moving

Contrast these to words we apply to writing that seems much less worthwhile. Again, you may want to add your own descriptive terms to the list:

dull	dead
lifeless	monotonous

repetitive	laborious
abstract	slow
pompous	trivial
confusing	phony
unrealistic	long-winded

Certainly the first group of terms suggests characteristics we recognize effective writing as having and points to the kind of reader response any writer aims for.   How can we achieve that kind of response rather than the one suggested by the second group of terms—in other words, how can we write effectively?

First of all, effective writers write for a clearly defined purpose or reason.   They want to change or influence their readers in a particular way. Sometimes writers aim to convince readers to believe the way they do on a specific issue or to take some specific action on a subject.   At other times, they may simply want to explain a subject or to provide readers with new information about a subject.   Always, though, the type of writing that influences us most involves a writer writing with a particular *purpose* in mind about a definite subject to a specific audience.

Of course, the purpose writers have is reflected in the *thesis* of the essay, a statement of their central idea, and is carried out in detail as they support that thesis.   One of our students, for instance, recently wrote an essay on appealing a parking ticket that she felt was undeserved.   Her *purpose* was to explain the process of effectively appealing a parking ticket.   Her *thesis* was stated clearly and simply: "A student unfairly accused of violating the parking regulations can win a case before the traffic judge by researching the subject thoroughly beforehand, observing several traffic court sessions, and explaining persuasively why receiving the traffic ticket was unfair."   In her essay she told how she had gotten the ticket, how she had contested it, and how the judge had reversed the decision and excused her from having to pay the fine.   And because she had had this personal experience, she spoke with considerable authority on the subject.   The finished essay was so original in its presentation of practical ways to appeal to the campus police, and it was so clearly ordered and well illustrated, that we can easily still remember how effective it was.   The student had a definite purpose for writing, knew the subject well, and successfully arranged her ideas on the subject so the reader clearly understood.

That, we have thought over and over again, is the type of writing students should do.   Above all, writing such as this parking ticket essay (1) makes it clear that the writer knows well what she or he is speaking of and (2) displays an organizational pattern that makes the writer's idea clear and meaningful to the reader.   These two writing strengths grow out of two processes central to effective writing: *invention* and *design*.

Invention in its broadest sense, Frank D'Angelo states, is "any mental activity that will bring to conscious awareness something previously unknown." [1]   By *invention*, we mean the process by which writers originate and discover ideas, illustrations, comparisons, contrasts, and ways of analyzing a subject through the working of reason and imagination upon their accumulated knowledge—including personal experience, perception, reading and education.   *Invention*, then, is a very practical, useful way for a writer to learn enough about a subject to write about it effectively.

Exactly how *invention* works for a writer can be illustrated by returning to the parking ticket essay mentioned above.   The student first of all drew from her *personal experience* of parking the car in what only the day before had been a space designated for student parking and then returning after class to find that she had received a ticket from the campus police.   She relied upon her *memory* to recall the details from this experience: how she had carefully parked the car, locked it, made certain that it was positioned within the marked lines of the parking space, and walked confidently to class.   She drew information from her *conversations* with fellow students concerning their experiences with the campus police and with the traffic panel and traffic judge.   The student drew also from her *reading* of the traffic regulations manual to determine the distinctions between reserve parking, random parking, and parking areas restricted to faculty and staff.   She even depended upon her own *observation* of an actual open hearing of a student appeal before

---

[1] *Process and Thought in Composition*, p. 27.

the traffic judge and the traffic appeal panel. From this source she was, of course, able to get a clearer idea of which approaches would be effective and which would not. Then, when she considered the unfairness of her receiving the ticket, she could begin to think of how to *illustrate* this belief—giving, for instance, accounts of actual conversations she had had with students and with the campus police. She could begin to think of how to *compare* this experience of being falsely accused with that of other, similar experiences—with, for example, an experience she once had in elementary school of being punished for someone else's wrong. Finally, she could begin to think of how she would analyze the experience of appearing before the traffic judge and traffic panel and successfully arguing for the unfairness of the ticket. In this way, *invention* became a useful and practical way for the student to learn about her subject and to generate ideas about that subject.

Essentially, then, *invention* is the systematic process by which a writer discovers a subject, probes it and its implications, and discovers ideas, illustrations, comparisons and contrasts, ways of analyzing, and so on, through such mental processes as memory, reason, brainstorming, imagination, and so on. The wide range of sources of invention available to the writer can be further illustrated by looking to the writers in this textbook. Larry McMurtry (p. 18), for instance, draws from personal experience, including a conversation with a waitress to show how, for him, the present is tied to the past. Langston Hughes (pp. 20–22) depends upon his memory of a childhood experience and conversations in that experience to involve the reader in a moral dilemma of crucial importance to him. And Earl Shorris (pp. 23–29) relies on his careful observation of the problems of American Indians through an actual interview with one of them to inform the reader of the difficulty of their life in modern times.

The result of the invention *process* is a *product,* like the essays in this text. What this means to the student writer is that as you analyze the essays or products, you come to understand more fully the very nature of the invention process the writers used to generate their ideas. It is through analysis and the application of what is learned from this analysis that you as a writer will be able to gain the reader responses mentioned above—interesting, exciting, believable—rather than the unfavorable responses of dull, trivial, dead.

Likewise, learning how writers design these products or essays is a second key to your learning what effective writing is and how it is achieved. By *design* we mean the process by which writers give form and order to the ideas that they have invented on a particular subject; it is the process by which writers arrange their ideas in a manner appropriate to the subject and effective for the audience addressed.

If we look once more at the example of the parking ticket essay, we can understand more fully how a writer arranges or designs his ideas on a subject, for a particular purpose, and for a specific audience. As the student determined her purpose of explaining the process of appealing a parking ticket and as she began to consider ways of arranging all that she knew and wanted to say about the subject, she found the rhetorical skill of designing both useful and necessary. Knowing her purpose was to explain the process of appealing a parking ticket and knowing the audience was fellow students guided her in selecting, out of all that she knew about the subject, what could be effectively included and what could not.

This purpose offered her the chance to use a similar order to that which she had followed in exploring the subject: a chronological, step-by-step account of the process by which, ideally, one can appeal a parking ticket. The *introduction* to the paper introduced the subject, introduced the writer and her position on this issue, and established the *tone* of the essay—the writer's distinctive attitude toward the subject and the reader. She introduced her subject of "appealing a parking ticket." She revealed herself as a person who had had experience with this subject and was therefore knowledgeable and as a person who believed that innocent people can win in a traffic court. And the *tone* of the introduction, while being highly serious, was nevertheless a personal one. As she developed the essay, her *writing style*—the choices in wording, sentence structure, and paragraphing and the overall pattern of the writing—not only was appropriate to the subject, but became a concrete means of achieving her purpose. Undoubtedly, these writing choices were grounded in the writer's personality and reflected her attitude toward both the subject and the readers—being consistent with the tone set in the introduction.   Then, after developing the subject as outlined above, the student gave her paper a *conclusion*.   In so doing she restated her thesis and summed up the main points of the process in light of all that she had presented on appealing parking tickets.   The particular type of paper that she was writing, a process analysis, required that she follow a fairly definite pattern of organization (see pp. 180–183)—one that gives order and clarity to the writing.   The dynamic and creative nature of the writing process was clearly manifested in this student's work; for while she gained her knowledge of this subject through invention, as she designed and ordered that knowledge to fit her purpose and audience she continued to discover and invent new dimensions to that subject.   The result was truly an effective piece of writing.

In other words, then, *invention* and *design* are both distinct stages of writing and overlapping processes in writing.   The *invention* stage of writing, often called *prewriting*, precedes and takes place before the writer writes.   And the *design* stage of writing follows and is an outgrowth of the *invention* stage.   But as processes they overlap.   As writers invent, they are beginning to give order and form to their ideas; some arrangement is inherent in the ideas and the discovery of those ideas.   And as they design and order their thoughts they are often stimulated by the organization of those thoughts to discover dimensions of the subject that had previously escaped them. In fact, if we understand this dynamic nature of writing, we can easily understand why many writers consider all writing to be creative.

Consider also how essayists Bruce Catton (pp. 98–103) and Aaron Copland (pp. 156–161) have designed their ideas.   Bruce Catton writes of a new awareness of life and death that came to him as a result of two strikingly different personal experiences. Understandably, then, the design of his essay takes the form of a two-part structure: first, an account of one experience, and then, an account of the contrasting experience.   Aaron Copland, on the other hand, analyzes the process of listening to music.   The form that his writing takes is a three-part design, a division of listening to music into three levels, or planes. Thus, the ideas in these essays are arranged appropriately for the subject and the purpose the writers have for writing—the first, to explain the nature of Catton's vision, and the second, to explain the levels on which we listen to music.

But although both essays illustrate how the designing process leads to the product of a finished piece of writing, these essays also illustrate how interrelated the invention and design processes actually are. Through the ordering of his two experiences and the contrasting of them, Catton probes his subject and discovers a view of life that he had not known before, much of it no doubt unknown to him until he actually began to contrast the two. Similarly, Copland's use of the term *planes* to represent levels of listening not only gives order to the essay Copland is writing, but also opens up ways of viewing the subject of listening to music that the author—as well as the reader—may have missed otherwise. Therefore, by examining these two essays in this way, we see that *invention* and *design* can be viewed separately or as interrelated processes that cooperatively generate and form the finished product we call effective writing.

Since both invention and design are fairly complex processes, this book is arranged to move from relatively basic applications of them to relatively more sophisticated ones. This movement from simple to complex is seen both in the four main sections—Illustration, Comparison and Contrast, Analysis, and Argument—and in the subsections into which each main section is divided. Introductions to the sections and subsections explain the subject matter in each and apply it to writing situations the student writer is most likely to face.

The individual selections are intended as models of effective writing, and the accompanying apparatus of headnotes, questions, and applications is intended to help teachers and students analyze those models so that the principles of invention and design in them can be understood and used in student writing.

Our hope is that this book will help students think and write with greater clarity and effectiveness, for we believe much is at stake here. The future of most students both in school and later will depend on their ability to communicate and to influence others through words.

Part one
Illustration

Illustration

Illustration is a characteristic of every piece of effective writing. It is essential to clear and interesting communication. An *illustration* is a unit of language—a word, phrase, sentence, paragraph, or an even longer unit—that stimulates the reader to imagine a sight (a cheerful smile), a sound (screeching tires), a touch sensation (soft, cool grass under bare feet), a smell (bread baking), or a taste (rich, hot coffee). In providing illustrations, the writer's aim is to *show* the reader what he is talking about—not simply to tell him in general terms.

Of course the writer does not literally "show" the reader by holding up a physical object or pointing to something the reader can actually see. He illustrates by using words that stimulate the reader to *imagine* concretely what the writer wants him to imagine. Indeed, the skilled user of words is like a movie director, except that, beside sights and sounds, he or she can also transmit touch sensations, tastes, and smells to the audience's nervous systems. The theater, with its projectors and other electronic devices, is each reader's imagination, connected to the five senses. The writer provides the film—with its visual, sound, touch, taste, and smell tracks—for the theater of the reader's imagination.

Suppose that you are a freshman in college writing a letter to an old friend from high school about a new acquaintance in your biology class. As you can't introduce the two in person,

3

you have to rely on written communication. You might begin,
"This guy in my biology class likes the same kinds of music
that you and I do, but he sure lives in a strange place."   Surely
this isn't enough, though, to *show* what the place is like; "a
strange place" could suggest to your old friend anything from
a penthouse apartment full of weirdly colored furniture and
paintings to a mildewed cellar where twelve people share one
room.   More likely, he or she will not be able to imagine anything very specific at all.   You have to supply enough concrete
details so that your reader can imagine specifically what you
mean.   Furthermore, you might share your own experience of
shock at your first visit to the new acquaintance's surroundings
and complete your sketch with an illustration of the new acquaintance himself.   A good way to get the invention process
started would be to think back to the experience and to select
those details that are most significant to you—the things you
have seen, heard, touched, smelled, and tasted.   Then you
might phrase your impressions as follows:

> This guy I met in my biology class likes the same kinds of music
> you and I do, but he sure lives in a strange place. Last week he in-
> vited me over to his place in an old, gritty frame boardinghouse next
> to the railroad tracks. He met me at the front door and led me up
> two flights of creaky stairs. The smells of stale tobacco smoke and
> decaying food made me want to throw up, but he kept urging me
> on. Finally we reached the door to his room, and I felt the dry paint
> crumble under my fingers as I helped him open it. I could hardly
> believe my eyes. The floor was littered with dust balls and cluttered
> with everything from dirty clothes to peanut hulls. He stumbled
> noisily over that mess to one corner of the room, and then I noticed
> the only two of his possessions that were clean and well cared for—
> an elaborate stereo set and an acoustic guitar with shiny strings.
> He pushed his long, rattail hair out of his face and grinned at me,
> showing two rows of cracked yellow teeth. He asked, "What d'ya
> wanna hear first?"

Certainly, your old friend from high school would have a far
clearer idea of your new acquaintance from this illustration
than from an abstract, unillustrated comment like "This guy I
met in my biology class sure lives in a strange place."   Also, he

Illustration   5

would be able to share your own insight into this new acquaintance's indifference to how his room looks, his seriousness
about music, and his eagerness to share that interest with you.
Illustrations have other purposes, though, than sharing personal experiences with an old friend.   Often they are used to
provide concrete *examples* (instances that make more general
terms understandable) of a subject under discussion.   For instance, psychiatrist Robert Coles uses the following illustration
in his essay "A Domain (of Sorts)" as an example of the mix
of health and sickness frequent in Appalachian children:

> At the edge of Logan County, West Virginia, by Rocky Creek, lives
> Billy Potter, age eight.   Billy is tall for his age, with blue eyes and
> black hair. He has a strong face. His forehead is broad, his nose
> substantial and sharp, his chin long. Billy is large-boned and al-
> ready broad-shouldered. He is thin, much thinner than he was
> meant to be. His teeth are in fearful condition, giving him pains
> in the mouth, and he suffers from dizzy spells; but his cheeks are
> red and he looks like the very picture of health.

While Coles does not describe every physical feature of Billy
Potter, he gives enough detail for the reader to imagine the
child concretely and to grasp Cole's main point—that Appalachian children exhibit both the advantages and disadvantages
of growing up where they do.   The careful selection and the
clear presentation of such details as height, broad shoulders,
sharp features, and red cheeks help to illustrate the effects of
healthy surroundings.   Thinness, bad teeth, pain, and dizzy
spells illustrate the effects of poor nutrition and medical care.
An illustration can also help a reader to *visualize an action*
that might be difficult or impossible to understand without it.
Surgeon Roy C. Selby, Jr., describes the process of brain
surgery in an essay entitled "A Delicate Operation," reprinted
later in this book.   In illustrating the process, Dr. Selby writes
of a "curved incision" in the forehead, extending "almost from
ear to ear"; of the scalp being "folded back to the level of the
eyebrows"; of a piece of skull being "pried loose and held out
of the way by a large sponge"; and of the exposed brain tumor,
"two-and-one-half inches behind the nose," as being "pink in

color" and "very fibrous and tough" to the touch.   The words and phrases are appropriate for an average reader (not just a fellow surgeon), for they are part of the vocabulary of most people and refer to familiar actions (curved, folded, pried), objects (eyebrows, sponge, nose), and concepts (inches and pink).   An especially vivid detail, one that helps the reader to imagine himself not only in the operating room but even in the role of the surgeon, is the statement about what the tumor *feels* like— "very fibrous and tough."

As the preceding examples demonstrate, one of the most important sources of illustrations is careful observation and experience of people, objects, and actions.   A genuine curiosity about the *looks* of things (and also the *smells, tastes, sounds,* and *touch sensations* of things) is an important asset to any writer, for it guarantees a world of potential material for illustrations. Another asset is a clear and active memory that serves as a storehouse of past observations and experiences of the kind just mentioned.   Each human being has a largely untapped hoard of material for writing and other forms of communication just waiting, perhaps itching, to be unlocked and used.   What makes each person's hoard of memories especially valuable is that it is unique—no other person has ever had precisely the same memories or ever will.

Still other important sources of illustrations are other people, books, and other media, which make it possible for each of us to add the observations, experiences, and memories of others to our own.   The writer who relies solely on his or her own resources operates at an obvious disadvantage.   Many selections in this book demonstrate how writers have successfully combined personal and secondary materials.

In addition, the writer must learn to analyze materials drawn from observation, memory, and secondary sources—to sort out, select, reject, develop, and put into a meaningful design the available raw materials so that they make sense to himself or herself and to the reader.   The selections in the first part of this book demonstrate the potential of illustrations for clarifying subjects, adding interest, and helping readers to perceive the writer's meaning.   The introductions to the subsections and the questions following each reading are intended to help the

Illustration 7

student writer to understand how the illustrations have been made effective through selection, development, and arrangement.

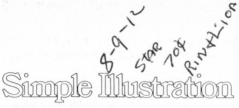

Simple Illustration

Images that stimulate the reader's senses: sight, sound, touch, smell, taste
Simple illustrations as parts of larger essays

Poets often use brief illustrations that stimulate a reader's imagination senses in a few vivid words. The following poem by Matsuo Bashō, for example, evokes a strong, immediate sense impression:

> How very cool it feels:
> taking a noonday nap, to have
> this wall against my heels.

Here the impression of touch is stimulated in the first and third lines by direct references to coolness and the feel of "this wall" against the heels. Less directly a feeling of contentment and relaxation is evoked also by the word "nap" and by the implied position of the speaker's body. Although the poem is 300 years old, it succeeds very well in accomplishing the poet's purpose—to share sensations with the reader.

In conversation and prose writing, a simple illustration is most often used to make the idea or point of a statement clear without burying it in words. For instance, if I tell you that there was a bad wreck on the freeway last night, you will have only a vague impression of the event. But, if I briefly illustrate the accident with a concise word picture of a bent steering wheel and a broken windshield splattered with large bloodstains, the event will become real to you very quickly.

In a much more subtle way, Rachel Carson's simple illustration of a starfish and its reflection in a pool enables her to share an experience of the "beauty of things that are ephemeral" with her readers. The effectiveness of the passage depends as much on its brevity and simplicity as it does on Carson's careful selection of words.

In "Seventy Cents" Imamu A. Baraka develops the idea that the word "money" means different things to different people. He shows what it means to *him* through the illustration of coins in his pockets and the notion of the quart of ale he could buy with them. The reader is easily able to imagine Baraka feeling the coins, to share the thought of the bottle of ale with him—and to grasp his point.

All illustrations are dependent upon clear and well-selected images for their effectiveness, and this is especially true of simple illustrations. *Images,* the basic components of any illustration, are the single words and phrases that stimulate one or more of the reader's five senses. Ordinarily, several images are used in combination to make up a complete illustration, for example, taking an antacid tablet:

visual image	She watched the tablet tumble slowly to the bottom of the glass . . .
sound image	and heard the faint sound of bubbles breaking on the surface of the water.
touch image	Then she felt the cold, smooth brim of the glass against her lips . . .
smell image	and winced slightly as she smelled the sharp, alkaline tang of the foam.
taste image	Finally she swallowed the sour liquid.

The following selections have been chosen as examples of the effective use of images. Although simple illustrations rarely serve as the bases for whole essays, these demonstrate how illustrations can operate, each in a sentence or two, to make abstract ideas like beauty, money, and death concrete.

The Starfish
Rachel Carson

Clarity of imagery is the prime feature of this excerpt by the late marine biologist Rachel Carson, in which she illustrated the beauty of short-lived scenes.

In the moment when I looked into the cave a little elfin starfish hung down, suspended by the merest thread, perhaps by only a single tube foot. It reached down to touch its own reflection, so perfectly delineated that there might have been, not one starfish, but two. The beauty of the reflected images and of the limpid pool itself was the poignant beauty of things that are ephemeral, existing only until the sea should return to fill the little cave.

Questions on Content

1. What two physical objects is the starfish touching?
2. Why is the reflection so clear that there seem to be two starfish rather than one?
3. Why will the scene in the cave be visible only for a short time?

Questions on Invention, Design, and Style

1. What details of the scene in the cave most effectively illustrate the "beauty of things that are ephemeral"?
2. What is gained by including the image "suspended . . . by only a single tube foot" in the illustration?
3. If Carson had written that the reflection of the starfish in the pool was not clear but broken by ripples, how would the meaning of the final sentence have been affected?

Applications

1. Think back to a time when something you observed—a spilled dessert, a broken toy, a dead animal, or the like—made a strong impression on you. In one paragraph share the experience with your reader, illustrating clearly what you saw and explaining the meaning it had for you.
2. Select a visual image that illustrates an idea that you have, and use that image to communicate the idea to your reader.

Seventy Cents
Imamu A. Baraka

One of the most frequent uses of illustration is to make general ideas concrete and thus more easily understandable to readers. In this brief passage from his essay "Expressive Language," Imamu A. Baraka uses sight and touch images to show what the word "money" means to different people.

1   *Money* does not possess the same meanings for the rich man as it does for me, a lower-middle-class American, albeit of laughably "aristocratic" pretensions. What possibly can "money" mean to a poor man? And I am not talking now about those courageous products of our permissive society who walk knowledgeably into "poverty" as they would into a public toilet. I mean, The Poor.

2   I look in my pocket; I have seventy cents. Possibly I can buy a beer. A quart of ale, specifically. Then I will have twenty cents with which to annoy and seduce my fingers when they wearily search for gainful employment. I have no idea at this moment what that seventy cents will mean to my neighbor around the corner, a poor Puerto Rican man I have seen hopefully watching my plastic garbage can. But I am certain it cannot mean the same thing. Say to David Rockefeller, "I have money," and he will think you mean something entirely different. That is, if you also dress the part. He would not for a moment think, "Seventy cents."

Questions on Content

1. Where does Baraka place himself on the social scale? With whom does he contrast himself?
2. Why does the poor Puerto Rican man watch Baraka's garbage can closely?
3. What might the word "money" mean to the poor Puerto Rican man?
4. What do you think "I have money" would mean to David Rockefeller?

Questions on Invention, Design, and Style

1. Who are the "courageous products" referred to in paragraph 1? Why does he term them "courageous"? What is Baraka's purpose in mentioning them?
2. What is gained by using the touch image in paragraph 2?
3. What larger idea is Baraka illustrating in this passage? How do the examples of the Puerto Rican man and David Rockefeller support and develop that idea?
4. Look again at paragraph 2, and tell where Baraka has drawn upon the following sources for his illustration: personal experience and observation, imagination, memory, general knowledge.

Applications

1. Using images that stimulate at least two of the senses, write a paragraph illustrating what one of the following means to you: success, cruelty, work, fun, boredom, truth, progress, difficulty, dream.
2. Drawing on your memory or imagination, write a paragraph in which you make a general idea concrete through the use of specific images.

A Rhinoceros and a Lion
Kaoru Maruyama

Through striking visual images, contemporary Japanese poet Kaoru Maruyama makes such abstractions as violence, death, and eternity concrete. As you read, let the scene form clearly in your mind.

A rhinoceros was running;
  A lion was clinging to his back,
    Biting.

Blood spouted up and, twisting his neck in agony,
The rhinoceros was looking at the sky.
The sky was blue and quiet.
The daytime moon floated in it.

5

It was a picture,
An accidental moment in a far country of jungles,
So the landscape was silent,   10
The two animals remained as they were.
Only in the stillness
The lion was, moment by moment, trying to kill;
The rhinoceros was, eternally, about to die.

Questions on Content

1. Without looking again at the poem, tell what happens in it.
   What impresses you most about the incident? What do you think
   impressed the poet most?
2. Why are the animals still and silent in this scene?
3. Why is the rhinoceros eternally about to die?

Questions on Invention, Design, and Style

1. What color images occur in the poem? How do they help establish a contrast between the struggle of the animals and the quiet
   of the sky?
2. How does each of the following images contribute to the picture
   Maruyama is painting: "rhinoceros was running," "lion was
   clinging to his back,/Biting," "blood spouted up," "twisting his
   neck," "looking at the sky," "blue and quiet," "daytime moon
   floated"?
3. Why has Maruyama chosen to restrict all the vivid imagery in the
   poem to the first seven lines? What would be the effect of ending
   the poem there?
4. How does the poet tie the last two lines of the poem together by
   his arrangement of words? What concept does he thus establish?

Applications

1. Look at pictures in magazines and books or at your own snapshots, and choose one of special interest to you. Describe the
   picture in a paragraph so that the reader can visualize it without
   actually seeing it. Avoid unnecessary detail and flowery language and avoid telling a story. Concentrate on vivid, concise
   images that will be meaningful to your reader.
2. Illustrate a violent scene you have witnessed personally or seen
   in a film or television program. Tell in a concluding sentence
   or two what meaning the scene has for you now.

Extended Illustration

Extended illustration as a series of images
Narration as illustration extended in time
Description as illustration extended in space
Determining how much narration and description
Determining how much quoted and summarized dialogue

Although a single simple illustration is appropriate when only a sentence or two is needed to clarify or explain a minor point, a more complex point requires an *extended illustration*—one that is developed more fully by means of a series of images arranged in order in time or space or, as is ordinarily the case, in a combination of the two.

An illustration extended in time is a *narrative*—an account of a series of events, usually in their chronological order, as in the opening two sentences of Thomas Carlyle's "The Irish Widow." In this passage, a series of events is told briefly in the most natural order—the order in which they occurred in time. The writer begins with one event (the death of the woman's husband) and recounts a series of events in chronological order, ending with the death of "seventeen other persons."

An illustration developed in space is a *description*—a word picture of an object, place, or person. A series of images is arranged in a spatial order, that is, in a sequence that progresses from one point in space to another. The earlier paragraph about the guitar player and his living quarters (page 4) is an example—beginning outside the boardinghouse, then moving inside, up the stairs, pausing at the door to the room, and then into the room, where it focuses on a few details, finally noting significant features of the guitar player (his hair and teeth).

Of course, narration and description seldom occur in their pure forms, unmixed. In the example of the guitar player, for instance, there is a chronological as well as a spatial order, for the paragraph begins when the writer is invited to the guitar player's room and continues until he or she enters it. Also, while the first two sentences of Carlyle's account of the Irish widow lack specific descriptions, they do imply settings such as the "Charitable Establishments" in which the imagined dialogue at the end of the selection takes place. After all, no event takes place in a vacuum—there is always a setting for it, whether implied or actually described.

The decision about how much narration and how much description an extended illustration should include is one that the writer must make according to the purpose of the writing and the audience being addressed. For instance, Robert Coles' illustration of Billy Potter, quoted on page 5, rightly emphasizes description over narration and effectively makes the point, in a brief space, that Appalachian children often exhibit the effects of both healthy surroundings and poor nutrition and medical care. A narrative that made the same point by recounting an incident would almost surely be much longer. In Carlyle's story of the Irish widow, however, the brief narrative in the opening two sentences effectively makes the point that the lives and health of the community are inescapably tied to the life and health of an individual. In this illustration, the point would only be blunted by descriptive touches that would slow the narrative. Capable writers know their subjects and audiences well enough to invent appropriate extended illustrations that contain the most effective mixtures of narration and description.

Another decision the writer must make about such illustrations is how much dialogue to include in direct quotations and how much to summarize. Direct quotation, which renders the exact wording of the speaker, is a form of sound imagery that suggests to the reader's imagination the actual sound of the speaker's voice. Indirect quotation, though often helpful in summarizing a long dialogue in a few words, makes a less dramatic impact. Consider, for instance, the words of the waitress in Larry McMurtry's "Dalhart": "I hope that steak's done enough. There ain't nothin' like steak when you're hungry, is there, son?" Much of the impression of a real person speaking would be lost if McMurtry had instead written, "She said she hoped the steak was done and remarked that nothing tastes so good to a person who is hungry." This is not to say that the writer should try to reproduce all dialogue as direct quotation; but direct quotation, when carefully selected, can contribute greatly to the vividness of an illustration.

The readings in this section demonstrate the use of narration and description in varying proportions. Thomas Carlyle leans heavily toward narration; Earl Shorris gives more emphasis to descriptions of Roger Stops and the settings in which he lives and works, in order to provide a powerful portrait of the frustrations of life on an Indian reservation. Larry McMurtry and Langston Hughes very skillfully combine narrative and descriptive elements in coherent designs.

These four readings also offer excellent examples of effective direct quotation—whether imaginary, as in "The Irish Widow," or apparently real, as in the other three selections. In each case, note how the writer holds back in using this device, thus achieving greater emphasis when it is used.

The Irish Widow
Thomas Carlyle

To illustrate how one person's well-being affects that of others, Thomas Carlyle narrates the story of an Irish widow who proved her sisterhood to her "fellow-creatures."

A poor Irish Widow, her husband having died in one of the Lanes of Edinburgh, went forth with her three children, bare of all resource, to solicit help from the Charitable Establishments of that City. At this Charitable Establishment and then at that she was refused; referred from one to the other, helped by none;—till she had exhausted them all; till her strength and heart failed her: she sank down in typhus-fever; died, and infected her Lane with fever, so that "seventeen other persons" died of fever there in consequence.... Would it not have been *economy* to help this poor Widow? She took typhus-fever, and killed seventeen of you!—Very curious.   The forlorn Irish Widow applies to her fellow-creatures, as if saying, "Behold I am sinking, bare of help: ye must help me! I am your sister, bone of your bone; one God made us: ye must help me!" They answer, "No; impossible; thou art no sister of ours."   But she proves her sisterhood; her typhus-fever kills *them:* they actually were her brothers, though denying it! Had human creature ever to go lower for a proof?

Questions on Content

1. What request does the Irish widow make of her "fellow-creatures" in Edinburgh?
2. Why do they ignore her plea?
3. Exactly how does she prove her sisterhood?
4. Why does Carlyle believe people like the Irish widow should be helped?

Questions on Invention, Design, and Style

1. Why does Carlyle say that "seventeen other persons" rather than "many other persons" died?
2. Identify Carlyle's main idea in this passage, and explain how the narrative illustrates it.
3. How does repetition of the Irish widow's story in the last third of the selection underline its significance?
4. Carlyle drew this story of the Irish widow from *Observations on the Management of the Poor in Scotland* by William Alison Pulteney, M.D.   What is the apparent source, though, of the dialogue in the last fourth of the passage?   What does the passage gain by the inclusion of this dialogue?

Applications

1. Write a short narrative, several paragraphs long, illustrating what can happen if one person is indifferent to another's need.
2. Using your imagination to enhance a story you have read or heard about, create a narrative, with dialogue, that makes a significant point.

Dalhart
Larry McMurtry

Contemporary novelist Larry McMurtry was born and grew up in west Texas. In this descriptive narrative, he tells of returning to a town that he associates with Texas' past and his own.

1   I curved back down to Dalhart through the wind the trail-herders bucked, and the last few miles, with the lights twinkling ahead of me on the plain, were among the best of the trip. It only remained to perform some *acte symbolistique* [1] to give the drive coherence, tie the present to the past.   I stopped at a cafe in Dalhart and ordered a chicken fried steak.   Only a rank degenerate would drive 1,500 miles across Texas without eating a chicken fried steak.   The cafe was full of boys in football jackets, and the jukebox was playing an odious number called "Billy Broke My Heart in Walgreen's and I Cried All the Way to Sears."

2   The waitress was a thin, sad-eyed woman with hands that looked like she had used them to twist barbed-wire all her life. She set the steak in front of me and went wearily back to the counter to get a bottle of ketchup.   The meat looked like a piece of old wood that had had perhaps one coat of white paint in the thirties and then had had that sanded off by thirty years of Panhandle sandstorms.

3   "Here," the waitress said, setting the ketchup bottle down.   "I hope that steak's done enough.   There ain't nothin' like steak when you're hungry, is there, son?"

4   "No ma'am, there ain't," I said.

Questions on Content

1.   Why does McMurtry order chicken fried steak in the cafe?
2.   Is McMurtry pleased or repelled by the steak the waitress sets before him?   How does he let you know this?

---

[1] Symbolic act.

Questions on Invention, Design, and Style

1. Point out at least four details in this selection that indicate Mc-Murtry's keen awareness of sights and sounds.
2. McMurtry includes only three details of the waitress' appearance. Are they enough to make you picture her clearly? If so, why? If not, why not?
3. How would the sense of the selection be changed if paragraph 2 were omitted? (Note especially the last sentence in the paragraph.)
4. Why does McMurtry use the French phrase *acte symbolistique* in paragraph 1 and the expression "No ma'am, there ain't" in paragraph 4? To whom is he speaking in each case?
5. Does McMurtry seriously believe he will be a "rank degenerate" if he does not order chicken fried steak? If not, why does he use this phrase?
6. McMurtry says he wishes to "tie the present to the past." Review the selection for instances in which he does so.
7. The selection can be viewed as having four parts. Discuss the function of
   a. the first four sentences, ending "without eating a chicken fried steak."
   b. the last sentence of paragraph 1, mentioning the boys in football jackets and the song playing on the jukebox.
   c. paragraph 2, describing the waitress and the steak.
   d. paragraphs 3 and 4, including the ketchup bottle and the dialogue between McMurtry and the waitress.

Applications

1. Describe a visit to a new city, the behavior of people who are strangers to you, or a situation in which you felt left out—an observer rather than a participant. Focus on three or four significant details that will help your readers visualize the place and people.
2. Visit a local restaurant you do not usually patronize. Study the waitress or waiter, the manager, and the other customers. Afterwards, evaluate the experience and come to some conclusions. Then, using what you have seen, heard, tasted, smelled, and so on, write an essay, narrating and describing the experience in such a way that the reader understands why you have drawn the conclusions that you have.

Salvation
Langston Hughes

**In the following scene and brief epilogue, the late American poet
Langston Hughes related an experience at a religious revival meeting. Hughes' skillful blending of description, narration, and dialogue helps the reader share his experience.**

1   I was saved from sin when I was going on thirteen. But
not really saved. It happened like this. There was a big revival at my Auntie Reed's church. Every night for weeks there
had been much preaching, singing, praying, and shouting, and
some very hardened sinners had been brought to Christ, and the
membership of the church had grown by leaps and bounds.
Then just before the revival ended, they held a special meeting
for children, "to bring the young lambs to the fold." My aunt
spoke of it for days ahead. That night I was escorted to the
front row and placed on the mourners' bench with all the other
young sinners, who had not yet been brought to Jesus.

2   My aunt told me that when you were saved you saw a light,
and something happened to you inside! And Jesus came into
your life! And God was with you from then on! She said you
could see and hear and feel Jesus in your soul. I believed her.
I had heard a great many old people say the same thing and it
seemed to me they ought to know. So I sat there calmly in the
hot, crowded church, waiting for Jesus to come to me.

3   The preacher preached a wonderful rhythmical sermon, all
moans and shouts and lonely cries and dire pictures of hell, and
then he sang a song about the ninety and nine safe in the fold,
but one little lamb was left out in the cold. Then he said:
"Won't you come? Won't you come to Jesus? Young lambs,
won't you come?" And he held out his arms to all us young
sinners there on the mourners' bench. And the little girls
cried. And some of them jumped up and went to Jesus right
away. But most of us just sat there.

4   A great many old people came and knelt around us and
prayed, old women with jet-black faces and braided hair, old
men with work-gnarled hands. And the church sang a song
about the lower lights are burning, some poor sinners to be

saved.   And the whole building rocked with prayer and song.

5   Still I kept waiting to *see* Jesus.

6   Finally all the young people had gone to the altar and were saved, but one boy and me.   He was a rounder's son named Westley.   Westley and I were surrounded by sisters and deacons praying.   It was very hot in the church, and getting late now.   Finally Westley said to me in a whisper: "God damn! I'm tired o' sitting here.   Let's get up and be saved." So he got up and was saved.

7   Then I was left all alone on the mourners' bench.   My aunt came and knelt at my knees and cried, while prayers and songs swirled all around me in the little church.   The whole congregation prayed for me alone, in a mighty wail of moans and voices.   And I kept waiting serenely for Jesus, waiting, waiting —but he didn't come.   I wanted to see him, but nothing happened to me.   Nothing!   I wanted something to happen to me, but nothing happened.

8   I heard the songs and the minister saying: "Why don't you come?   My dear child, why don't you come to Jesus?   Jesus is waiting for you.   He wants you.   Why don't you come?   Sister Reed, what is this child's name?"

9   "Langston," my aunt sobbed.

10   "Langston, why don't you come?   Why don't you come and be saved?   Oh, Lamb of God!   Why don't you come?"

11   Now it was really getting late.   I began to be ashamed of myself, holding everything up so long.   I began to wonder what God thought about Westley, who certainly hadn't seen Jesus either, but who was now sitting proudly on the platform, swinging his knickerbockered legs and grinning down at me, surrounded by deacons and old women on their knees praying. God had not struck Westley dead for taking his name in vain or for lying in the temple.   So I decided that maybe to save further trouble, I'd better lie, too, and say that Jesus had come, and get up and be saved.

12   So I got up.

13   Suddenly the whole room broke into a sea of shouting, as they saw me rise.   Waves of rejoicing swept the place.   Women leaped in the air.   My aunt threw her arms around me.   The minister took me by the hand and led me to the platform.

14   When things quieted down, in a hushed silence, punctuated by a few ecstatic "Amens," all the new young lambs were blessed in the name of God.   Then joyous singing filled the room.

15   That night, for the last time in my life but one—for I was a big boy twelve years old—I cried.   I cried, in bed alone, and couldn't stop.   I buried my head under the quilts, but my aunt heard me.   She woke up and told my uncle I was crying because the Holy Ghost had come into my life, and because I had seen Jesus.   But I was really crying because I couldn't bear to tell her that I had lied, that I had deceived everybody in the church, and I hadn't seen Jesus, and that now I didn't believe there was a Jesus any more, since he didn't come to help me.

Questions on Content

1.   Why does Hughes attend the revival?
2.   What appeals are made to convince the children they should be saved?
3.   Why does Westley go up to the platform?
4.   How does Westley's decision change the situation for Hughes? Why doesn't he immediately follow Westley?
5.   How does Hughes' response differ from Westley's?   What does this difference reveal about Hughes' character?
6.   What is the reason that Hughes couldn't stop crying the night after the revival meeting?

Questions on Invention, Design, and Style

1.   What essential information does Hughes give the reader in the first three sentences of this essay?   How do these sentences arouse the reader's interest in the subject of the essay?   Describe the relationship between the writer and the reader that is set up in these opening sentences—whether it is formal, serious, comic, informal, or the like.
2.   Paragraphs 1 and 2 provide a more detailed introduction to the revival scene and the epilogue (*paragraph 15*).   What specific points are introduced in these opening paragraphs that are necessary to help the reader understand the events that follow?
3.   Which details in paragraphs 3 and 4 illustrate the emotional pressures placed on the children to be saved?   Which sound and sight images help readers to imagine the scene as if they were present?

4. What new details in paragraphs 6 and 7 develop a further sense of conflict and urgency? How does the first sentence of paragraph 11 add to this sense?

5. Hughes provides a particularly vivid image of Westley in the second sentence of paragraph 11. How does this image help to explain why Hughes decides to lie and "be saved"?

6. Consider the reasons given in the last sentence of the essay for Hughes' inability to stop crying. How has Hughes prepared the reader for this conclusion?

7. Of all the many possible details which a writer could select from an experience or event, a setting or scene, a skillful writer like Hughes will select *only* that detail which is effective with his audience and relevant to the idea he is developing. Note, for example, that Hughes selects from all that was said and sung that night at the revival only the direct quotations found in paragraphs 3, 6, and 8–10. Why are these so effective?

Applications

1. Using an extended illustration, write an account of how you (or someone you know) learned that actions often do not reflect inner feelings.

2. Recall a time when you conformed to the expectations of others in order to be accepted. Write an essay, several paragraphs long, in which first you explain how the expectations of others can influence a person to behave in ways he or she would not otherwise behave and then you illustrate this idea with images from your own experience. Arrange the materials in such an order that the most important scene is saved for last, where it will have the greatest impact.

How 114 Washing Machines Came to the Crow Reservation
Earl Shorris

In this selection free-lance writer Earl Shorris introduces Roger Stops, a café and laundromat owner, as an illustration of the frustrations experienced on Indian reservations. To achieve this, Shorris

emphasizes physical details about Stops himself and his surroundings, rather than continuous narrative.

1   The problems of the Indian are the weights and measures of Roger Stops. He fills saucers with cigarette butts while contemplating them. During the day, he stands behind the counter of his café, drinking coffee, playing with his granddaughter, talking to her in Crow; sometimes he cooks a hamburger or sells bottles of soda pop or shouts to his wife or tells a kid that the jukebox is broken because he is not yet ready to hear it; the whole of his day is pocked with the problems of washing machines: change is needed, the rinse cycle has failed, a machine has spun itself into collapse, and then there are the dryers and children who make too much noise. Through it all, he smokes and schemes and practices the arts of exegesis and nostalgia on everything that touches his life. If only he had a little capital, enough for this machine, which is certain to . . .

2   His name is not Stops, but Stops-at-Pretty-Places; and it isn't Roger, not his Indian name; he is really Likes-to-Go-on-the-Warpath. He is a member of the Greasy Mouth clan on both sides, which is unusual for a Crow or any Indian, for it defies the function of the clan system. His wife is Mandan and Hidatsa, both of which are Siouan-speaking people, as are the Crow, but since Roger and his wife cannot easily speak to each other, the language in the home is almost always English. So Roger Stops speaks English to his wife and most of his customers, and Crow to his children and his friends.

3   He is a man of great bulk, more than six feet tall, wide at the shoulders and deep through the chest; after fifty-one years, his belly has begun to dominate: his shirt separates from his trousers when he stretches; he leaves his dapper brown shoes untied. On the Crow, Roger Stops is something of a celebrity because his brother died in combat in France during World War II. Roger believes that he survived Korea as well as World War II because the old men who gathered around to name him Likes-to-Go-on-the-Warpath said he would be safe in combat.

4   He achieved the rank of master sergeant, fighting without being injured, except for his teeth, which were knocked out by a comrade who jumped into his trench feet first. He tells of the

incident by way of apologizing for having no teeth now.

5   After the Korean War, he decided to stay in the Army until he was able to retire, but he became ill. The army doctors diagnosed his illness as cancer of the stomach, operated on him to remove the cancer, then discharged him as incurable. He returned to the reservation to die, his body shriveled and weak at 146 pounds. "I came back here and took sweat baths and prayed," he said, "and I cured myself in the Indian way." He keeps a medicine bundle in his house, but he hesitates when asked about it, saying that he is afraid it will only make white men laugh. "The things in a medicine bundle are things we see in visions," he said; "they have the power of God in them. They don't look like much, a stone or a feather or a piece of fur; whites wouldn't understand."

. . .

6   . . . He calls himself a "dumb savage," saying that he never really went to school, that he preferred to stay outside and play with his "bow and arrows." It is a bitterness befitting a man conceived by Dostoevsky, and in the night, when the café is empty, Roger Stops retreats to his Underground in a laundromat. He locks himself into a storeroom, sitting on a high stool behind a discarded display counter or reclining on a couch of raw board and rags, filling the room with smoke, sweetly stale, suspended on the steam that pours from the washing machines and dryers, and reading Indian history or law.

7   The room is further decorated with a single shelf of books, a typewriter on a high stand, and a calendar. Outside, the washing machines and dryers roar and grind, and children shout over them, playing, aware though unconcerned that Stops is in his office reading Felix Cohen's book on Indian law, battling the Bureau of Indian Affairs with bookmarks and underlining. It is a room adjacent to Hell, and in it, contemplative and powerless, Stops turns the pages with enormous and slow hands, seeking the little victories that allow him another day. . . .

. . .

8   The declared purpose of Roger Stops's reading, scheming, and contemplation is "to help my people," but there would

seem to be another purpose: the saving of himself. He works hard, two or three hours a day, on a Crow language project, thinking back on the old words, collecting them from his friends and customers, learning the structure and development of his own language, pleased to understand that the Crow words for dog and horse are actually "my horse" and "my real horse," and that they are linguistic proof of the history of domesticated animals among the Crow. He plans to translate the Bible into Crow, though he is not a Christian. There is no payment for the work, and it takes a subtle mind to understand how such an effort can be of help to his people. Though there is little doubt that Roger Stops is capable of such subtle thinking, it is also clear that the intellectual stimulation is a requisite of his own sanity, the lonely joy that sustains him through another day of overdue payments and lost customers.

. . .

9   Brooding and hopelessness are the occupations of Indians; the managed life allows little else: an Indian cannot plan his future, the BIA does that; he cannot decide what to do with his land, his crops, or his herd, the BIA has rules for that; he cannot even enjoy the prerogatives of power within his own tribe, the BIA superintendent has veto power. He is neither a free man nor a captive; weeping and dreaming have the same value in his life.

10   Roger Stops, soldier, truck driver, and entrepreneur, rejects the psychology of the managed life in his businesses and his attitude toward the BIA. But he cannot escape the reality of it: when he argued with a BIA official, the official was not unpleasant to him, nor did he do anything that could be considered a direct reprisal. Instead, the federal government quite suddenly purchased 114 washing machines and distributed them to the Crows. "I used to make $35 to $37 a day in the laundromat," said Stops, "good money. Now I can't meet my payments. I don't know what to do. The whole tribe is watching me, waiting to see if I make it."

11   He refuses to pay his water bill, citing an obscure passage in a treaty as his authority. It may cut back on his expenses for a while, but 114 free washing machines is more than he can cope with. He is thinking of turning his laundromat into a rec-

reation center for the young people on the reservation, something beyond the occasional movies shown by the churches and
the pinball machines and jukebox that now serve that purpose.
The problem is that such a place couldn't support itself.

. . .

12   So he schemes. He has a plan to make money from selling
a photographic gimmick to tourists. As a start on the scheme
he has built a darkroom in his laundromat. "You wouldn't
think a dumb savage could learn that all by himself," he said.
He smiles proudly and runs his hands through his hair, like
huge combs. It is a gesture of concern encroaching on the
pride. Everywhere he turns there are restraining enemies. "I
fight the BIA in my own way," he says. "I don't join any of
those organizations. But it's hard to fight them, because they
can always get you, like the guy with the washing machines.
I made trouble for him, so he ruined my business. You can't
go to the tribal council and complain because the chairman is
in on it. At the tribal fair not one Indian had a concession.
I wanted to run a concession, but they asked me for a payoff,
and I told them I wouldn't do it."

13   Even when the federal government seems to be helping, the
Indians are, in his view, somehow made to suffer. "I knew a
guy in Los Angeles," he says, "who wanted to get into a relocation program. He went to the Bureau, and they told him he had
to go back to the reservation to apply for relocation in Los Angeles. He didn't go; he couldn't." And then there is the new
Boy Scout camp. The tribe donated one hundred sixty acres
of land, and an Office of Economic Opportunity Community
Action Program supplied the money to build a fine camp on the
land. Stops describes the camp proudly, giving details of the
construction and operation. Then he shakes his head: "The
first year it was for Indian kids. Now they say the OEO rules
prohibit discrimination because of race. The camp has to be
opened up to white kids from Billings. By next summer there
won't be room for any Indian kids up there. Another hundred
and sixty acres is gone."

14   When there are visitors to his smoky office, they come with
serio-comic deference. Stops once participated in a land-leas-
ing negotiation which raised the rate per acre from ten cents to

sixty cents.   He once helped to get surplus commodities distributed on the reservation, about which he says, "Our people
didn't feel like it was charity.   They took it as a victory over the
white man.   They outsmarted him."   Those are his successes;
there have also been failures.   He is a sorcerer of dubious powers, poring over his ragged books, marking the possibilities,
making war on the white man with his own logic.

15   George Mad Bear, tidy in his windbreaker and cowboy hat
in contrast to the thorough dishabille of Stops, takes his wife
to the laundromat, visiting in the small office for the duration
of one complete washing-machine cycle.   He and Stops discuss
their victory over the state of Montana.   Mad Bear had been no-
tified by the state that he had to pay back taxes and interest for
three years during which he was employed by the federal government on the reservation.   The Legal Services office on the
reservation told him they could not take his case, because his
income was too high for him to qualify under the OEO rules.
The lawyer, however, did give him some advice: he told Mad
Bear to pay the taxes and the penalties, although he admitted
that he had no specific information on the subject.

16   Mad Bear had no knowledge of the law, but he did not understand why he had been singled out to pay state taxes.   He
took the problem to Roger Stops, who consulted his books and
determined that an Indian employed by the federal government
and living on a reservation was not obliged to pay taxes to the
state of Montana.   They wrote a letter to their U.S. representative, who confirmed the opinion.   A few weeks later, Mad Bear
walked by the Legal Services office.   The young lawyer called
out to him, "George, about those state taxes, you don't have to
pay them.   I got the information."   Mad Bear said, "Yes, I
know.   I had them send it to you."

17   The dissident sorcerer is not the only one who knows, but
he is an Indian, he is the one who cares.   Where else can those
who are governed without their consent turn for help?   The
enemy of power is surrounded by washing machines and soda
pop bottles.   His hair is grown long, reaching for his collar.
He has no connections among the college students who conduct sit-ins and make rage in the newspapers.   His fingernails
are thick and rimmed with black.   He does not tie his shoes.

He is toothless, and fat has begun to round away the character of his face.   But he is an ally against the BIA, the OEO, and the officials of the tribe.   He can say with them, "They tried to destroy us for five hundred years, and now we're destroying ourselves."   Dreams of freedom and self-determination are symbolized in his dissent.

18   Roger Stops understands his position in the tribe.   It is not what he expects of himself, but it is all he can do.   "This is the only culture I know," he said.   "Everything I do is trying to achieve a higher state in the Indian way.   But I was brought up in war, and now I fry hamburgers for a living.   I'm degraded in the eyes of my people."

Questions on Content

1.   How does Stops account for his having survived World War II and the Korean war?
2.   Why did he not die of cancer although army doctors had diagnosed his condition as incurable?
3.   What are Stops' two reasons for "reading, scheming, and contemplation"?
4.   How did the 114 washing machines come to the Crow reservation?
5.   How does Stops' physical appearance differ from that of Mad Bear?
6.   What is the significance of Mad Bear's response to the lawyer at the end of paragraph 16?
7.   To what extent are "dissident sorcerer" and "enemy of power" accurate descriptions of Stops?
8.   What does Roger Stops understand his position in the tribe to be?   In your opinion, is Stops' final statement about himself (*paragraph 18*) that of a failure or of a modest person?

Questions on Invention, Design, and Style

1.   In the description of Roger Stops, note Shorris' references in paragraph 1 to cigarette butts, speaking in Crow, cooking hamburger, bottles of soda pop, and washing machines.   Trace the expansion of these details later in the essay.   How does each contribute to your understanding of Stops?
2.   Why does the author repeat the description of Stops and his sur-

roundings (washing machines, soda-pop bottles, and frying hamburgers) in paragraphs 17 and 18?   (See also paragraphs 1, 3, and
4.)

3.   How do the 114 washing machines illustrate the relationship between the people on the reservation and the Bureau of Indian Affairs?   In this connection, what is the significance of the word
"collapse" in paragraph 1?

4.   Why does Stops lock himself in the storeroom?   Why is the room
described as "adjacent to Hell" and Stops in it as "contemplative," "powerless"?

5.   In paragraphs 6 and 7, note the physical details—of sight, sound,
and smell—that characterize Stops.   What do such details as the
locked door, abundant tobacco smoke and tobacco smell, steam
from the washing machines, the single shelf of books, sounds of
washing machines and of children indifferent to him, the bookmarks and underlining, and his turning "pages with enormous
and slow hands, seeking the little victories that allow him another
day" reveal about Stops, his work, and his relations with others?

6.   Shorris writes, "He [the Indian] is neither a free man nor a captive."   How does Stops illustrate this point?

Applications

1.   Recall an individual who made a deep impression upon you because he or she, while very much an individual, seemed to represent a whole group of people.   As Shorris has done with Roger
Stops, write a paper showing how that person is both unique and
representative.

2.   Describe an interesting, complex person you have known in relation to the physical setting in which that person lives or works.
Select a few details that both make the surroundings vivid and
also reveal the person's character and life style.   Use the details
and surroundings to introudce the person to the reader and to
provide a setting for the conclusion of the essay.

Multiple Illustration

Uses of multiple illustration
Determining an appropriate number of illustrations
Determining an appropriate sequence for illustrations

Another decision the writer must make is *how many* illustrations are needed to develop the subject or the point within a subject. Is one illustration more effective, or would *multiple illustration* (the use of two or more illustrations) work better? Rachel Carson, for example, might have chosen to include *several* simple illustrations of beautiful scenes at low tide, rather than one. Thomas Carlyle might have introduced other narratives of human brother- or sisterhood in addition to the one about the Irish widow; Earl Shorris might have told of frustrations on the Crow reservation, not only through his extended illustration of Roger Stops, but through equally extended illustrations of Stops' wife and George Mad Bear as well. As these examples show, illustration can involve two or more simple or extended illustrations. The same principles operate at either level.

Ray Bradbury's "The Impulse to Write" includes two illustrations of stories written out of anger and two of stories written out of love. All are brief, but the first one, about Bradbury's story "Sun and Shadow," is slightly extended, thus setting the stage for those that follow. Once the pattern is set, the writer does not have to repeat it in full each time.

In "Death in the Open," Lewis Thomas also uses very brief illustrations. As his subject is dead animals—a potentially repulsive topic—he does not dwell on the grisly details of the corpses. Indeed, some of his illustrations might be called multiple images ("... fragments, evoking memories of woodchucks, badgers, skunks ... sometimes the mysterious wreckage of a deer"). They are brief to avoid undue emphasis on

31

blood and bones and varied to suggest universality. Thomas' most extended illustration involves the unexpected and dignified care that elephants bestow on the dead of their species.

Nora Ephron's three illustrations in "Truth and Consequences" are extended more fully so that we can identify with the conflicts arising from her commitments both to journalism and to the women's movement. In each she explores the subject from a different, and significant, angle.

By far the most fully developed essay in this subsection is Robert Coles' "A Domain (of Sorts)," in which he portrays a whole region through multiple illustrations. Four families were selected, in order to include male and female children and adults and to depict a range of financial situations from extreme poverty to relative affluence. Through this selection of illustrations the reader can understand that, although the people of Appalachia are certainly individuals, they share some important basic experiences and attitudes about their region and way of life. A single illustration, no matter how detailed, would not convey quite the same sense of community.

Coles' essay, then, stands in contrast to Earl Shorris' "How 114 Washing Machines Came to the Crow Reservation" in the previous subsection, despite the fact that both depict relatively isolated societies that consider themselves different from mainstream America and both are roughly equal in length and complexity. Unlike Coles, Shorris shows life on the Crow reservation through a single example—that of Roger Stops, who is presented in many different settings and situations. Although he is not the typical or average member of the tribe, he does exhibit the frustrations of the reservation particularly well. In skillful hands, either single illustration or multiple illustration can communicate a subject, even the same subject, well. The effect will surely be different, however, as Coles' focus on community and Shorris' on individuality demonstrate. A good writer should, of course, master both techniques.

When multiple illustration is used, however, still another decision faces the writer: What is the best sequence or order for the illustrations?

If the different illustrations all support the same point, the best principle is to save the most emphatic and telling one for last, where it has the greatest impact and can lead to the strong conclusion most easily.   Nora Ephron's essay is a good example of this point, for her final illustration is the most serious one —it involves potential danger to human life.   Especially when there are more than two illustrations, the first one must also be effective (Ray Bradbury's illustration of the Puerto Rican man is probably his most striking one).   If any one of the illustrations is weaker than the others, it should be between the first and last ones, where it will receive less emphasis.

If the different illustrations support different points, the points themselves, of course, determine the order of the illustrations, as in Annie Dillard's "Learning to See."   The points of the essay can themselves usually be best arranged in the pattern suggested in the preceding paragraph: important, less important (perhaps several of these), most important.   Dillard, for instance, saves for last her most telling point—that as children we all perceived our surroundings as do people seeing for the first time after an eye operation, but that "learning to see" with understanding means losing visions of wonder and magic.

In considering *how many* illustrations will best achieve the purpose of a piece of writing, it is important to remember that it is just as possible to include too many as too few.   If the invention process has been thorough, the writer should have more than enough material at hand to do the job and must then select the best and discard the rest.   Annie Dillard, for instance, had at hand a whole book, as well as her own experiences, from which to draw illustrations; Robert Coles undoubtedly met and interviewed more people during his field work than he mentions in "A Domain (of Sorts)."   As you read the following selections, try to determine why the writers chose the particular illustrations they used.

The Impulse to Write
Ray Bradbury

To stress the invention process, science-fiction writer Ray Bradbury offers briefly illustrations of stories written with the zest of anger and of love. Although this selection was addressed to an audience of fiction writers, it offers good advice for composition students on the distinction between the first draft and the revision stage.

1   If you are writing without zest, without gusto, without love, without fun, you are only half a writer. . . . For the first thing a writer should be is—excited. He should be a thing of fevers and enthusiasms. Without such vigor, he might as well be out picking peaches or digging ditches. God knows it'd be better for his health.

2   How long has it been since you wrote a story where your real love or your real hatred somehow got onto the paper? When was the last time you dared release a cherished prejudice so it slammed the page like a lightning bolt? What are the best things and the worst things in your life, and when are you going to get around to whispering or shouting them?

3   Wouldn't it be wonderful, for instance, to throw down a copy of *Harper's Bazaar* you happened to be leafing through at the dentist's, and leap to your typewriter and ride off with hilarious anger, attacking their silly and sometimes shocking snobbishness? I did just that a few years back. I came across an issue where the *Bazaar* photographers, with their perverted sense of equality once again utilized natives in a Puerto Rican back-street as props in front of which their starved-looking mannikins postured for the benefit of yet more emaciated half-women in the best salons in the country. The photographs so enraged me I ran, did not walk, to my machine and wrote "Sun and Shadow," the story of an old Puerto Rican who ruins the *Bazaar* photographer's afternoon by sneaking into each picture and dropping his pants.

4   I dare say there are a few of you who would like to have done this job. I had the fun of doing it; the cleansing after-effects of the hoot, the holler, and the great horselaugh. Probably the editors at the *Bazaar* never heard. But a lot of readers did and cried, "Go it, *Bazaar;* go it, Bradbury!" I claim no vic-

tory. But there was blood on my gloves when I hung them up.

5 When was the last time you did a story like that, out of pure indignation?

6 When was the last time you were stopped by the police in your neighborhood because you like to walk, and perhaps think, at night? It happened to me just often enough that, irritated, I wrote "The Pedestrian," a story of a time, fifty years from now, when a man is arrested and taken off for clinical study because he insists on looking at un-televised reality, and breathing un-air-conditioned air.

7 Irritations and angers aside, what about loves? What do you love most in the world? The big and little things, I mean. A trolley car, a pair of tennis shoes? These, at one time when we were children, were invested with magic for us. During the past year I've published one story about a boy's last ride in a trolley that smells of all the thunderstorms in time, full of cool green moss-velvet seats and blue electricity, but doomed to be replaced by the more prosaic, more practical-smelling bus. Another story concerned a boy who wanted to own a pair of new tennis shoes for the power they gave him to leap rivers and houses and streets, and even bushes, sidewalks, and dogs. The shoes were to him, the surge of antelope and gazelle on African summer veldt. The energy of unleashed rivers and summer storms lay in the shoes; he had to have them more than anything else in the world.

8 So, simply then, here is my formula.

9 What do you want more than anything else in the world? What do you love, or what do you hate?

10 Find a character, like yourself, who will want something or not want something, with all his heart. Give him running orders. Shoot him off. Then follow as fast as you can go. The character, in his great love, or hate will rush you through to the end of the story. The zest and gusto of his need, and there *is* zest in hate as well as in love, will fire the landscape and raise the temperature of your typewriter thirty degrees.

11 All of this is primarily directed to the writer who has already learned his trade; that is, has put into himself enough grammatical tools and literary knowledge so he won't trip himself up when he wants to run. The advice holds good for the

beginner, too, however, even though his steps may falter for purely technical reasons.   Even here, passion often saves the day.

12   The history of each story, then, should read almost like a weather report: Hot today, cool tomorrow.   This afternoon, burn down the house.   Tomorrow, pour cold critical water upon the simmering coals.   Time enough to think and cut and rewrite tomorrow.   But today—explode—fly apart—disintegrate!   The other six or seven drafts are going to be pure torture.   So why not enjoy the first draft, in the hope that your joy will seek and find others in the world who, reading your story, will catch fire, too?

13   It doesn't have to be a big fire.   A small blaze, candlelight perhaps; a longing for a mechanical wonder like a trolley or an animal wonder like a pair of sneakers rabbiting the lawns of early morning.   Look for the little loves, find and shape the little bitternesses.   Savor them in your mouth, try them on your typewriter. . . .   Ideas lie everywhere, like apples fallen and melting in the grass for lack of wayfaring strangers with an eye and a tongue for beauty whether absurd, horrific, or genteel.

Questions on Content

1. According to Bradbury, what is the first thing a writer should be?
2. What enraged Bradbury so much that he wrote "Sun and Shadow"?   What is the story about?
3. What irritated Bradbury so that he wrote "The Pedestrian"?   What is the story about?
4. What points do the stories of the trolley car and the pair of tennis shoes illustrate?
5. What is Bradbury's formula for writing a story out of love or anger?
6. What distinction does Bradbury make between experienced and beginning writers?
7. How should the history of a story be like a weather report?
8. Make a list of the characteristics that Bradbury either states or implies about the two parts of the writing process.

Questions on Invention, Design, and Style

1. Why do you think Bradbury includes two illustrations of stories written out of love and two out of anger?   What would be the re-

sult of only one illustration of each? Of one illustration of one and two of the other?

2. Bradbury uses as illustrations four of his own stories and, in two instances, the personal experiences that led to his writing them. Why do you think Bradbury omits the personal experience in the last two illustrations? Why does he spend four paragraphs on the first pair and one paragraph on the second?

3. How does Bradbury's comparison of the writing process to a weather report illustrate the importance of writing with zest?

4. Evaluate paragraph 1 as an introduction. How does Bradbury introduce his subject in this paragraph? In what ways does he arouse the reader's interest? How fully does he establish the tone for the essay in this paragraph? Is it formal or informal, serious or humorous, and so on? Why is this tone appropriate to Bradbury's subject and purpose in this essay?

5. How do the questions in paragraph 2 further arouse the reader's interest and further introduce the subject of the essay?

6. Bradbury continues to use questions throughout—most often to mark transitions from one part of the essay to the next, as in the first sentence of paragraph 3, where he ties the introduction to his first illustration. What is the function of the two questions in paragraph 5 and the first sentence in paragraph 6? the first sentence in paragraph 7? paragraph 9? the last sentence in paragraph 12?

Applications

1. Think of several recent experiences in which you were irritated and upset by a friend, relative, or teacher. Write an essay in which you use several of these experiences to support an idea that you have formed about irritation or anger.

2. Invent a character who has had several experiences of frustration. Then write a brief sketch in which these experiences are summarized and effectively illustrated. Finally, use this character sketch to support a significant insight into the nature of frustration.

3. Think of movies that you have enjoyed seeing or books that you have enjoyed reading. What characteristics did they share that made them enjoyable to you? Write a paper telling what characteristics are most important to your enjoyment of movies or books, briefly illustrating those characteristics by reference to specific details in those works.

Truth and Consequences
Nora Ephron

Journalist Nora Ephron illustrates her own conflict between objectivity and involvement with three well-chosen and well-arranged narratives.

1   I read something in a reporting piece years ago that made a profound impression on me.   The way I remember the incident (which probably has almost nothing to do with what actually happened) is this: a group of pathetically naïve out-of-towners are in New York for a week and want very much to go to Coney Island.   They go to Times Square to take the subway, but instead of taking the train to Brooklyn, they take an uptown train to the Bronx.   And what knocked me out about that incident was that the reporter involved had been cool enough and detached enough and professional enough and (I could not help thinking) cruel enough to let this hopeless group take the wrong train.   I could never have done it.   And when I read the article, I was disturbed and sorry that I could not: the story is a whole lot better when they take the wrong train.

2   When I first read that, I was a newspaper reporter, and I still had some illusions about objectivity—and certainly about that thing that has come to be known as participatory journalism; I believed that reporters had no business getting really involved in what they were writing about.   Which did not seem to me to be a problem at the time.   A good part of the reason I became a newspaper reporter was that I was much too cynical and detached to become involved in anything; I was temperamentally suited to be a witness to events.   Or so I told myself.

. . .

3   Years pass, and it is 1972 and I am at the Democratic Convention in Miami attending a rump, half-secret meeting: a group of Betty Friedan's followers are trying to organize a drive to make Shirley Chisholm Vice-President.   Friedan is not here, but Jacqui Ceballos, a leader in N.O.W., *is,* and it is instantly apparent to the journalists in the room that she does not know what she is talking about.   It is Monday afternoon and she is telling the group of partisans assembled in this dingy hotel

room that petitions supporting Chisholm's Vice-Presidential candidacy must be in at the National Committee by Tuesday afternoon.   But the President won't be nominated until Wednesday night; clearly the Vice-Presidential petitions do not have to be filed until the next day.   I am supposed to be a reporter here and let things happen.   I am supposed to let them take the wrong train.   But I can't, and my hand is up, and I am saying that they must be wrong, they must have gotten the wrong information, there's no need to rush the petitions, they can't be due until Thursday.   Afterward, I walk out onto Collins Avenue with a fellow journalist/feminist who has managed to keep her mouth shut.   "I guess I got a little carried away in there," I say guiltily.   "I guess you did," she replies.   (The next night, at the convention debate on abortion, there are women reporters so passionately involved in the issue that they are lobbying the delegates.   I feel slightly less guilty.   But not much.)

4   To give you another example, a book comes in for review. I am on the list now, The Woman List, and the books come in all the time.   Novels by women.   Nonfiction books about women and the women's movement.   The apparently endless number of movement-oriented and movement-inspired anthologies on feminism; the even more endless number of anthologies on the role of the family or the future of the family or the decline of the family.   I take up a book, a book I think might make a column.   It is *Women and Madness,* by Phyllis Chesler.   I agree with the book politically.   What Chesler is saying is that the psychological profession has always applied a double standard when dealing with women; that psychological definitions of madness have been dictated by what men believe women's role ought to be; and this is wrong.   Right on, Phyllis.   But here is the book: it is badly written and self-indulgent, and the research seems to me to be full of holes.   If I say this, though, I will hurt the book politically, provide a way for people who want to dismiss Chesler's conclusions to ignore them entirely. On the other hand, if I fail to say that there are problems with the book, I'm applying a double standard of my own, treating works that are important to the movement differently from others: babying them, tending to gloss over their faults, gentling the author as if she and her book were somehow incapable of

withstanding a single carping clause. *Her heart is in the right place; why knock her when there are so many truly evil books around?* This is what is known in the women's movement as sisterhood, and it is good politics, I suppose, but it doesn't make for good criticism. Or honesty. Or the truth. (Furthermore, it is every bit as condescending as the sort of criticism men apply to books about women these days—that unconsciously patronizing tone that treats books by and about women as some sort of sub-genre of literature, outside the mainstream, not quite relevant, interesting really, how-these-women-do-go-on-and-we-really-must-try-to-understand-what-they-are-getting-at-whatever-it-is.)

5   I will tell you one more story to the point—though this one is not about me.   A year and a half ago, some women from the Los Angeles Self-Help Clinic came to New York to demonstrate do-it-yourself gynecology and performed an abortion onstage using a controversial device called the Karman cannula. Subsequently, the woman on whom the abortion had been performed developed a serious infection and had to go into the hospital for a D and C.[1]   One of the reporters covering the story, a feminist, found out about the infection, but she decided not to make the fact public, because she thought that to do so might hurt the self-help movement.   When I heard about it, I was appalled; I was more appalled when I realized that I understood why she had done it.

6   But I cannot excuse that kind of self-censorship, either in that reporter or in myself.   I think that many of us in this awkward position worry too much about what the movement will think and how what we write will affect the movement.   In fact, the movement is nothing more than an amorphous blob of individual women and groups, most of whom disagree with each other.   In fact, no amount of criticism of the movement will stop its forward momentum.   In fact, I am intelligent enough to know that nothing I write really matters in any significant way to any of it.   And knowing all this, I worry.   I am a writer. I am a feminist.   When I manage, from time to time, to over-

---

[1] Dilation and curettage: enlargement of the cervical canal and scraping of the uterine wall.

come my political leanings and get at the truth, I feel a little better. And then I worry some more.

Questions on Content

1. What impressed Ephron most about the story of the group who took the wrong subway? What disturbed her about it?
2. What did Ephron at first believe about a journalist getting involved?
3. What is one of the major reasons that she became a newspaper reporter?
4. What is Ephron's conflict at the Democratic convention? in writing about *Women and Madness*?
5. Why was Ephron appalled at the journalist/feminist in paragraph 5? Why was she appalled at herself?
6. What does Ephron think the future of the women's movement will be?
7. What is the final impression she gives of herself in the essay? In what way is the impression reflected in the title of the essay?

Questions on Invention, Design, and Style

1. The design of Ephron's essay is clear-cut and simple: a two-paragraph introduction, a three-paragraph body consisting of three narratives, and a one-paragraph conclusion. Examine the final sentence of paragraph 2 and the opening sentences of paragraphs 3, 4, 5, and 6, and show how each sentence serves as an effective transition from the previous point to the one that follows.
2. The introduction itself opens with an illustration—of the newspaperman who watched a group of people take the wrong train and reported the story, rather than telling them of their mistake. How do Ephron's reactions to this illustration prepare the reader for the entire essay that follows? How does it prepare specifically for Ephron's involvement as told in paragraph 3? Which sentence in paragraph 3 directly ties the two illustrations together?
3. What point about Ephron is illustrated in paragraph 3 that is not in paragraph 4 or 5? What further point about involvement and objectivity is illustrated in paragraph 4 more clearly than in paragraphs 3 and 5? Why is the story of the on-stage abortion told last, even though it is the shortest one and Ephron is not directly involved in it?
4. Examine the conclusion of the essay in paragraph 6. Why is it stated in more general language than the preceding three para-

graphs? What new positions does Ephron take here? What is
the position stated in the last six sentences?

Applications

1. Write your own essay on the conflict between objectivity and involvement. You may choose to use illustrations from your own
experience or from your reading or knowledge of the experiences
of others. Conclude with an observation on whether or not the
conflict can be resolved and, if so, how.
2. Focus on a subject about which you have conflicting feelings.
Write an essay illustrating these feelings with examples from
your own experiences, observations, reading, and so on. Draw
a conclusion about these feelings at the end of the essay.

Death in the Open
Lewis Thomas

**Using multiple illustrations both to introduce his subject and to clar-
ify his points, physician and medical researcher Lewis Thomas examines our natural tendency to evade the immensity of death and questions whether or not this attitude may change in the future.**

1   Most of the dead animals you see on highways near the cities are dogs, a few cats. Out in the countryside, the forms and
coloring of the dead are strange; these are the wild creatures.
Seen from a car window they appear as fragments, evoking memories of woodchucks, badgers, skunks, voles, snakes, sometimes the mysterious wreckage of a deer.

2   It is always a queer shock, part a sudden upwelling of grief,
part unaccountable amazement. It is simply astounding to see
an animal dead on a highway. The outrage is more than just
the location; it is the impropriety of such visible death, anywhere. You do not expect to see dead animals in the open.
It is the nature of animals to die alone, off somewhere, hidden.
It is wrong to see them lying out on the highway; it is wrong
to see them anywhere.

3   Everything in the world dies, but we only know about it as

a kind of abstraction.   If you stand in a meadow, at the edge of a hillside, and look around carefully, almost everything you can catch sight of is in the process of dying, and most things will be dead long before you are.   If it were not for the constant renewal and replacement going on before your eyes, the whole place would turn to stone and sand under your feet.

4   There are some creatures that do not seem to die at all; they simply vanish totally into their own progeny.   Single cells do this.   The cell becomes two, then four, and so on, and after a while the last trace is gone.   It cannot be seen as death; barring mutation, the descendants are simply the first cell, living all over again.   The cycles of the slime mold have episodes that seem as conclusive as death, but the withered slug, with its stalk and fruiting body, is plainly the transient tissue of a developing animal; the free-swimming amebocytes use this organ collectively in order to produce more of themselves.

5   There are said to be a billion billion insects on the earth at any moment, most of them with very short life expectancies by our standards.   Someone has estimated that there are 25 million assorted insects hanging in the air over every temperate square mile, in a column extending upward for thousands of feet, drifting through the layers of the atmosphere like plankton.   They are dying steadily, some by being eaten, some just dropping in their tracks, tons of them around the earth, disintegrating as they die, invisibly.

6   Who ever sees dead birds, in anything like the huge numbers stipulated by the certainty of the death of all birds?   A dead bird is an incongruity, more startling than an unexpected live bird, sure evidence to the human mind that something has gone wrong.   Birds do their dying off somewhere, behind things, under things, never on the wing.

7   Animals seem to have an instinct for performing death alone, hidden.   Even the largest, most conspicuous ones find ways to conceal themselves in time.   If an elephant missteps and dies in an open place, the herd will not leave him there; the others will pick him up and carry the body from place to place, finally putting it down in some inexplicably suitable location. When elephants encounter the skeleton of an elephant out in the open, they methodically take up each of the bones and dis-

tribute them, in a ponderous ceremony, over neighboring acres.

8   It is a natural marvel. All of the life of the earth dies, all of the time, in the same volume as the new life that dazzles us each morning, each spring. All we see of this is the odd stump, the fly struggling on the porch floor of the summer house in October, the fragment on the highway. I have lived all my life with an embarrassment of squirrels in my backyard, they are all over the place, all year long, and I have never seen, anywhere, a dead squirrel.

9   I suppose it is just as well. If the earth were otherwise, and all the dying were done in the open, with the dead there to be looked at, we would never have it out of our minds. We can forget about it much of the time, or think of it as an accident to be avoided, somehow. But it does make the process of dying seem more exceptional than it really is, and harder to engage in at the times when we must ourselves engage.

10   In our way, we conform as best we can to the rest of nature. The obituary pages tell us of the news that we are dying away, while the birth announcements in finer print, off at the side of the page, inform us of our replacements; but we get no grasp from this of the enormity of scale. There are 3 billion of us on the earth, and all 3 billion must be dead, on a schedule, within this lifetime. The vast mortality, involving something over 50 million of us each year, takes place in relative secrecy. We can only really know of the deaths in our households, or among our friends. These, detached in our minds from all the rest, we take to be unnatural events, anomalies, outrages. We speak of our own dead in low voices; struck down, we say, as though visible death can only occur for cause, by disease or violence, avoidably. We send off for flowers, grieve, make ceremonies, scatter bones, unaware of the rest of the 3 billion on the same schedule. All of that immense mass of flesh and bone and consciousness will disappear by absorption into the earth, without recognition by the transient survivors.

11   Less than a half century from now, our replacements will have more than doubled the numbers. It is hard to see how we can continue to keep the secret, with such multitudes doing the dying. We will have to give up the notion that death is catastrophe, or detestable, or avoidable, or even strange. We will

need to learn more about the cycling of life in the rest of the system, and about our connection to the process. Everything that comes alive seems to be in trade for something that dies, cell for cell. There might be some comfort in the recognition ... that we all go down together, in the best of company.

Questions on Content

1. What animals are most often seen dead on highways near cities? What animals are most commonly seen dead in the open countryside?
2. What, according to Thomas, is our reaction to the sight of a dead animal on the highway? in the open countryside? anywhere?
3. What would happen if everything living were not in the process of dying?
4. What are the estimates on how many insects there are hanging in the air over every temperate square mile?
5. In what sense is the privacy of death a "natural marvel"? What would happen if all dying were done in the open? How has man conformed to this secrecy about death? How has he extended this secrecy to the point that death has come to seem unreal, even avoidable?
6. According to Thomas' estimates, how many people will be living less than half a century from now?
7. What does Thomas think will and should happen to our ideas about death because of this number?

Questions on Invention, Design, and Style

1. Paragraph 1 of this essay provides a series of quick images of dead animals, and paragraph 2 records the human response to this sight. How do these two paragraphs gain the reader's interest immediately and introduce central ideas that are developed in the following paragraphs?
2. The opening sentence in paragraph 3 contains two parts: "Everything in the world dies" and "but we only know about it as a kind of abstraction." How is the first part illustrated in paragraphs 3, 4, 5, 6, 7, and 8? How is the second part illustrated in paragraph 10? How does paragraph 9 function as a transition between these two ideas?
3. What new attitude toward death is introduced in paragraph 11? How does this new attitude stimulate readers to continue thinking about the essay after finishing it?

4. How does Thomas' use of the word "replacement" in paragraphs 3, 10, and 11 help to prepare the reader for the final statements of the essay: "Everything that comes alive seems to be in trade for something that dies, cell for cell. . . . [W]e all go down together, in the best of company"?

5. How do the words "avoidably" in paragraph 10 and "avoidable" in paragraph 11 help to explain man's attitude and beliefs about the nature of death? Why are these words appropriate?

6. What material in the essay has been drawn from Thomas' personal experience? his observations? his general reading? his knowledge of biology?

Applications

1. Write an essay using multiple illustrations to develop an idea that you have formed about death, privacy, or sexuality.

2. Using multiple illustrations drawn from your experiences and observations or from your reading and reflections, write an essay showing how a previously abstract idea (honesty, boredom, kindness, or the like) came to have particular meaning for you.

Learning to See
Annie Dillard

Drawing her illustrations from books, personal experience, and memory, essayist Annie Dillard reflects on the fascinating subject of how infants and the newly sighted view the world. Rather than designing her essay around her illustrations, Dillard sets up a series of generalized observations and selects brief and telling illustrations to support them.

1   I chanced on a wonderful book called *Space and Sight*, by Marius Von Senden. When Western surgeons discovered how to perform safe cataract operations, they ranged across Europe and America operating on dozens of men and women of all ages who had been blinded by cataracts since birth. Von Senden collected accounts of such cases; the histories are fascinating. Many doctors had tested their patients' sense perceptions and ideas of space both before and after the operations. The vast

majority of patients, of both sexes and all ages, had, in Von Senden's opinion, no idea of space whatsoever. Form, distance, and size were so many meaningless syllables. A patient "had no idea of depth, confusing it with roundness." Before the operation a doctor would give a blind patient a cube and a sphere; the patient would tongue it or feel it with his hands, and name it correctly. After the operation the doctor would show the same objects to the patient without letting him touch them; now he had no clue whatsoever to what he was seeing. One patient called lemonade "square" because it pricked on his tongue as a square shape pricked on the touch of his hands. Of another postoperative patient the doctor writes, "I have found in her no notion of size, for example, not even within the narrow limits which she might have encompassed with the aid of touch. Thus when I asked her to show me how big her mother was, she did not stretch out her hands, but set her two index fingers a few inches apart."

2   For the newly sighted, vision is pure sensation unencumbered by meaning. When a newly sighted girl saw photographs and paintings, she asked, " 'Why do they put those dark marks all over them?' 'Those aren't dark marks,' her mother explained, 'those are shadows. That is one of the ways the eye knows that things have shape. If it were not for shadows, many things would look flat.' 'Well, that's how things do look,' Joan answered. 'Everything looks flat with dark patches.' "

3   In general the newly sighted see the world as a dazzle of "color-patches." They are pleased by the sensation of color, and learn quickly to name the colors, but the rest of seeing is tormentingly difficult. Soon after his operation a patient "generally bumps into one of these colour-patches and observes them to be substantial, since they resist him as tactual objects do. In walking about it also strikes him—or can if he pays attention—that he is continually passing in between the colours he sees, that he can go past a visual object, that a part of it then steadily disappears from view; and that in spite of this, however he twists and turns—whether entering the room from the door, for example, or returning back to it—he always has a visual space in front of him. Thus he gradually comes to realize that there is also a space behind him, which he does not see."

4   The mental effort involved in these reasonings proves over-whelming for many patients. It oppresses them to realize, if they ever do at all, the tremendous size of the world, which they had previously conceived of as something touchingly manage-able. It oppresses them to realize that they have been visible to people all along, perhaps unattractively so, without their knowledge or consen´ A disheartening number of them refuse to use their new vision, continuing to go over objects with their tongues, and lapsing into apathy and despair.

5   On the other hand, many newly sighted people speak well of the world, and teach us how dull our own vision is. To one patient, a human hand, unrecognized, is "something bright and then holes." Shown a bunch of grapes, a boy calls out, "It is dark, blue and shiny. . . . It isn't smooth, it has bumps and hol-lows." A little girl visits a garden. "She is greatly astonished, and can scarcely be persuaded to answer, stands speechless in front of the tree, which she only names on taking hold of it, and then as 'the tree with the lights in it.' " Another patient, a twenty-two-year-old girl, was dazzled by the world's brightness and kept her eyes shut for two weeks. When at the end of that time she opened her eyes again, she did not recognize any ob-jects, but "the more she now directed her gaze upon everything about her, the more it could be seen how an expression of grati-fication and astonishment overspread her features; she repeat-edly exclaimed: 'Oh God! How beautiful!' "

6   I saw color-patches for weeks after I read this wonderful book. It was summer; the peaches were ripe in the valley or-chards. When I woke in the morning, color-patches wrapped round my eyes, intricately, leaving not one unfilled spot. All day long I walked among shifting color-patches that parted be-fore me like the Red Sea and closed again in silence, transfig-ured, wherever I looked back. Some patches swelled and loomed, while others vanished utterly, and dark marks flitted at random over the whole dazzling sweep. But I couldn't sustain the illusion of flatness. I've been around for too long. Form is condemned to an eternal danse macabre[1] with meaning: I

---

[1] Dance of death, leading to the grave.

couldn't unpeach the peaches. Nor can I remember ever having seen without understanding; the color-patches of infancy are lost. My brain then must have been smooth as any balloon. I'm told I reached for the moon; many babies do. But the color-patches of infancy swelled as meaning filled them; they arrayed themselves in solemn ranks down distance which unrolled and stretched before me like a plain. The moon rocketed away. I live now in a world of shadows that shape and distance color, a world where space makes a kind of terrible sense. . . . The fluttering patch I saw in my nursery window—silver and green and shape-shifting blue—is gone; a row of Lombardy poplars takes its place, mute, across the distant lawn. That humming oblong creature pale as light that stole along the walls of my room at night, stretching exhilaratingly around the corners, is gone, too, gone the night I ate of the bittersweet fruit, put two and two together and puckered forever my brain. Martin Buber tells this tale: "Rabbi Mendel once boasted to his teacher Rabbi Elimelekh that evenings he saw the angel who rolls away the light before the darkness, and mornings the angel who rolls away the darkness before the light. 'Yes,' said Rabbi Elimelekh, 'in my youth I saw that too. Later on you don't see these things anymore.' "

7 Why didn't someone hand those newly sighted people paints and brushes from the start, when they still didn't know what anything was? Then maybe we all could see color-patches too, the world unraveled from reason, Eden before Adam gave names. The scales would drop from my eyes; I'd see trees like men walking; I'd run down the road against all orders, hallooing and leaping.

Questions on Content

1. How did the reading of Von Senden's book affect Dillard's own perceptions?
2. Why did one man call lemonade "square"?
3. For the newly sighted, how do shadows appear? Why are the perceptions of these people called "color-patches"?
4. Why do some of the newly sighted become depressed? Why do some enjoy the experience?
5. In the absence of sight, what other senses do the people mentioned in this essay seem to rely on most?

6. What can the newly sighted teach us about our own vision?
7. What distinction does Dillard make between "pure sensation" and sensation encumbered with meaning? With what two stages of life does Dillard associate these ideas in paragraph 6?

Questions on Invention, Design, and Style

1. Throughout the essay Dillard is enthusiastic and involved in her subject. Locate examples of this enthusiasm in paragraph 1. How is it also evident in the final paragraph? Does this enthusiasm seem warranted by her illustrations and the uses she makes of them in the body of the essay?
2. Locate the illustrations that Dillard has taken from *Space and Sight,* from her recent experiences, from her childhood, and from Martin Buber. How do the sources of each illustration match the two-part structure of the essay: the gaining of sight by the formerly blind (*paragraphs 1–5*) and the loss of sight as we move from childhood to adulthood (*paragraphs 6–7*)? How selective does Dillard seem to be in choosing her illustrations?
3. The design or structure of the essay follows closely Dillard's aims in the different parts of the essay. How has she designed the first paragraph around her aim of introducing the subject of learning to see? paragraphs 2–5 around the aim of illustrating how a formerly blind person reacts to a world seen for the first time? paragraph 6 around the aim of telling how the vision of those who *can* see becomes dull as they grow older? paragraph 7 around the aim of realizing what we might have learned about seeing from the formerly blind?
4. Note that Dillard also designs her material so that paragraphs 5 and 7 receive great emphasis. How does paragraph 4 prepare for paragraph 5? How does paragraph 5 function as a conclusion to all the preceding paragraphs? How do paragraph 5 and the preceding paragraphs prepare the reader for paragraph 7? How does paragraph 6 prepare the reader for paragraph 7?
5. Dillard makes several brief *allusions* (see "Glossary") to the Bible in the last two paragraphs. What does she mean when she says, in paragraph 6, that the "color-patches . . . parted before me like the Red Sea and closed again in silence"? What is the purpose of this reference? What story does she refer to when she speaks of eating "the bittersweet fruit" (*paragraph 6*) and Adam giving names (*paragraph 7*)? How is this story related to the loss of childhood sight? What biblical material is alluded to in the final

sentence? How is this material related to Dillard's central idea?
to her enthusiasm for her subject?

Applications

1. Interview someone who, because of a broken bone or illness, has
    recently been without the use of an arm or a leg. Then write an
    essay with multiple illustrations, drawn both from this interview
    and from your imagination, of what it must be like to have such
    an experience.
2. Scan articles in recent issues of such magazines as *Scientific
    American* and *Psychology Today*. Locate one article that you
    find especially appealing and worthwhile. Using Dillard's essay
    as a model of how to combine printed materials and personal
    experiences as sources of illustrations, write one of your own,
    based upon the subject matter of that article.

A Domain (of Sorts)
Robert Coles

**Psychiatrist Robert Coles draws on interviews and his own observa-
tions for multiple illustrations of Appalachian families and individuals. Although he adds description and commentary, most of this
essay is made up of direct quotations from the mountaineers themselves. Their differences give variety to the essay and give effective
emphasis to their areas of agreement.**

1   They live up alongside the hills, in hollow after hollow.
They live in eastern Kentucky and eastern Tennessee and in
the western part of North Carolina and the western part of Virginia and in just about the whole state of West Virginia. They
live close to the land; they farm it and some of them go down
into it to extract its coal. Their ancestors, a century or two ago,
fought their way westward from the Atlantic seaboard, came up
on the mountains, penetrated the valleys, and moved stubbornly
up the creeks for room, for privacy, for a view, for a domain of
sorts. They are Appalachian people, mountain people, hill
people. They are white yeomen, or miners, or hollow folk, or
subsistence farmers.

2   From the first months of childhood to later years, the land and the woods and the hills figure prominently in the lives of mountain children, not to mention their parents. As a result, the tasks and struggles that confront all children take on a particular and characteristic quality among Appalachian children, a quality that has to do with learning about one's roots, one's territory, as a central fact, perhaps the central fact of existence.

3   In Wolfe County, Kentucky, I became rather friendly with a whole hollow of Workmans and Taylors, all related to one another.* The Workmans had followed a stream up a hill well over a century ago, and Kenneth and Laura Workman are there today, in a cabin in Deep Hollow, so named because it is one of the steepest hollows around. Kenneth Workman is forty as I write this. He is now a small farmer. He used to dig for coal in the mines down in Harlan County, Kentucky, but he was lucky enough to lose his job in 1954. Many of the older men he worked with also lost their jobs around that time, when the mines were becoming increasingly automated, but they came back to Wolfe County sick, injured, often near death.

4   "If we're going to be good parents," Kenneth told me, "we've got to teach our kids a lot about Deep Hollow, so they can find their way around and know everything they've got to know. It's their home, the hollow is. People who come here from outside are not likely to figure out that we've got a lot of teaching to do for our kids outside of school, and it's not the kind they'll get in books. My boy Danny has got to master the hollow; that's what my dad used to say to me; all the time he would tell me and tell me and then I'd be in good shape for the rest of my life."

5   How does Danny get to master the hollow? For one thing, he was born there, and his very survival augurs well for his future mastery. Laura received no medical care while she carried Danny; the boy was delivered by his two aunts, who also live in Deep Hollow. Danny's first encounter with the Appalachian land took place minutes after he was taken, breathing and screaming, from his mother. Laura describes what happened:

---

* At the request of the people mentioned in this essay I have changed their names and some place-names.

"Well, as I can recall, my sister Dorothy came over and showed him to me, and then he was making so much noise we knew he was all right. His birthday is July tenth, you see, and it was a real nice day. She brought me a pail of blackberries that she'd picked and she said they were for later. When Danny was born Dorothy took him over and showed him the blackberries and said it won't be long before he'll be eating them, but first he'll have to learn to pick them, and that will be real soon. Then he was still crying, and she asked me if I didn't think he ought to go outside and see his daddy's corn growing up there, good and tall, and the chickens we have, and Spot and Tan, because they're going to be his dogs, just like everyone else's. I said to go ahead, and my sister Anne held me up a little so I could see, and the next thing I knew the baby was out there near Ken's corn, crying as loud as he could.

6 "Ken held him high over his head and pointed him around like he was one of the guns being aimed. I heard him telling the baby that here was the corn, there was the beets, and there was cucumbers, and here was the lettuce, and there was the best laying chicken we've got. Next thing he told the baby to stop the crying—and he did, he just did. Ken has a way with kids, even as soon as they're born. He told him to shush up, and he did, and then he just took him and put him down over there, near the corn, and the other kids and my sisters all stood and looked. Dorothy was going to pick him up and bring him back to me, but Ken said he was fast asleep and quiet, and let him just lie there and we should all go and leave things be for a while. So they did; and Ken came in and told me I'd done real well, and he was glad to have a red-haired son, at last, what with two girls that have red hair but all the boys with brown hair. He said did I mind the little fellow lying out there near his daddy's farm getting to know Deep Hollow, and I said no, why should I."

7 Shortly after each child of hers is born, the boy or girl is set down on the land, and within a few months he is peering out at it, moving on it, turning over on it, clutching at wild mountain flowers or a slingshot (a present from an older brother) or a spoon (a present from an older sister). Next comes crawling; and mountain children do indeed crawl.

They take to crawling and turning over and rolling down the grass and weeds.   They take to pushing their heads against bushes and picking up stones and rocks.   They take to following sounds, moving toward a bird's call or a frog's.   I have rarely seen mothers like Laura Workman lift up babies like Danny and try to make them walk by holding them and pulling them along.

    . . .

8   . . . At three, Danny had been all over his father's land, and up and down the hollow.   He would roam about with his older brother or sister, tagging after them, trying to join in with their work or play.   He had learned how to pick crops and throw a line into a stream and catch a fish.   He knew his way down the creek and up the hill that leads to the meadow.   He knew about spiders and butterflies and nuts and minnows and all sorts of bugs and beetles and lizards and worms and moles and mice—and those crickets making their noise.   He went after caterpillars.   He collected rocks of sizes and shapes: they were in fact his toys.   He knew which branches of which trees were hard or soft, unbending or wonderfully pliable.   He knew how to cool himself off and wash himself off and fill himself up—all with the water of a high stream.   At three, he had been learning all that for about a year.

9   At the edge of Logan County, West Virginia, by Rocky Creek, lives Billy Potter, age eight.   Billy is tall for his age, with blue eyes and black hair.   He has a strong face.   His forehead is broad, his nose substantial and sharp, his chin long. Billy is large-boned and already broad-shouldered.   He is thin, much thinner than he was meant to be.   His teeth are in fearful condition, giving him pains in the mouth, and he suffers from dizzy spells; but his cheeks are red and he looks like the very picture of health.

10   "If I had to choose a time of the year I like best," Billy told me one day when we were talking, "then I'd choose the winter. It's hard in the winter, and you're cold and you shiver, even near the fire; but the creek looks the best, and we all have the most laughing and fun then.   My daddy says he's in a better mood in winter than any other time, because there's no place to go,

and we just get buried in Rocky Creek, and we have the big sled we built and we go hunting, and it's a real job you have, fooling those animals and catching them, what with the snow and a lot of them hiding and some of them only out for a short time.   A lot of time there's no school, because you can't get in here and you can't get out.   We play checkers and cards and we take turns picking the guitar and we have the radio with all the music we want, except if there's a bad storm out there.   Daddy teaches us how to cut wood and make more things than you can believe.   Each winter he has a new plan on what I'm to make out of wood with my knife.   He says he's my teacher when there's no school.

11   "For me, this is the best place to be in the whole world. I've not been to other places, I know; but if you have the best place right round you, before your eyes, you don't have to go looking.   I hear they come from all over the country to look at the mountains we have, and Daddy says he wouldn't let one of them, with the cameras and all, into the creek, because they just want to stare and stare, and they don't know what to look for. He says they'll look at a hill, and they won't even stop to think what's on it—the different trees and the animals and birds. . . .

12   "If I left here and went to live in a city, I'd be losing everything—that's what I hear said by my father and my uncle and cousins.   We've been here so long, it's as long as when the country was started.   My people came here and they followed the creek up to here and they named it Rocky Creek; they were the ones, that's right.   In the Bible we have written down the names of our kin that came before us and when they were born and when they died, and my name is there and I'm not going to leave here, because there'd be no mention of me when I get married and no mention of my children, if I left the creek."

13   On the map, Martin County in Kentucky looks a short distance from Logan County, West Virginia, but ordinary maps tell little about high, nearly impassable hills and mountains and valleys that run north to south rather than east to west—and therefore form a barrier to someone moving across rather than up and down the Appalachians.   Marie Lewis is a seven-year-old girl who lives in Martin County, not too far from Inez, the county seat.   Marie's father is a good deal better off than

Billy's. Mr. Lewis has a full-time job as a bus driver and school custodian. He works for the county's school board, and considers himself extremely fortunate to do so. Jobs are short in the county, and a steady job makes one secure beyond the comprehension of outsiders. George Lewis's salary by national standards is low, very low; in 1969 it placed him among the nation's poor, among those who make less than $3,000 a year. Yet, as he himself put it: "When others see no money at all, and you get your check every week, you're doing pretty good."

14 Little Marie, as her father calls her, is almost a picture-book child. She has blond, curly hair, blue eyes, a round face with pink cheeks, and a sturdy body, though even at seven she carries herself like a lady—perhaps like the gentle, sensitive schoolteacher she wants to be. She has such a teacher in school, and she idolizes her. And if little Marie someday does become a teacher, she will substantially consolidate her father's rise in position or class or whatever. Her parents realize this. They see few if any jobs available for their sons, but Marie might indeed be able to become a teacher, unless she marries young, has children, and forgets the whole idea.

. . .

15 Marie lives in a modest bungalow, but . . . the house is luxurious compared to some of the cabins up the hollow, which rises and rises behind the Lewises' house. Still, the Lewis family is poor. They are not townspeople, but by their own description they are "people just lucky enough to get out of the hollow." They are *at* but not *in* the hollow. They enjoy electricity and a furnace and running water. They have a television set and a radio and a refrigerator and an electric stove. They don't have much money for furniture, nor do they drive a car. They will be paying off the house they have built for years and years and years, and it is all the property they have and hope to have.

16 Marie can be a little casual and even humorous as she talks about things up in the hollow, for all the sadness and misery to be found there. She can point out to her worried and pitying listener that schoolmates of hers, from homes as poor as any in America, nevertheless smile and laugh and jostle one another

and get fresh and nasty and tease one another and have fights, "good fights," she calls them, sometimes serious and fierce ones, then make up and become helpful and kind and thoughtful—to everyone, which certainly includes her: "I'd like to marry someone from this county. We have the best people in the world here. The boys can do anything. They can climb every hill, I know they can. They can hunt and fish better than people who live in other places. I know from what my father says. If you go to the cities in Ohio and states like that, you don't know what the people are like. They talk different and they think different. A lot of them don't go to church, and they're mean to you, unless you're in their family; and they don't help you out the way we do here to everyone who comes by, so long as he means well."

17   Like a good social scientist (not to mention a person with common sense), Marie talks about the social distinctions she observes, from the grossly apparent ones to others that are decidedly subtle: "The history book the teacher reads to us says our country is made up of different kinds of people, and they come from all over the world, but then in a book about Kentucky she read to us, it said we're mostly the same here in the mountains. I don't agree we're all the same here, and neither does my daddy, because if you look around in school and in church and if you go with my daddy on the bus when he picks everyone up, you'll see we're not the same.

18   "There's a girl Sally who doesn't want to be a teacher or a nurse or anything. She says she doesn't want to come to school, but her mother tells her she should go just long enough to read and write a little, but not too much. . . .

19   "Once the teacher called me over, and she said I was being real nice because I shared my cookies with the kids, and my mother packed me extra ones, because I told her I felt bad eating, when others have nothing to eat. I told her they're hungry from up there, and they need better clothes than they have. I give them the cookies, but they're not going to be saying thank you all the time, and I'm glad they don't! You have to keep your chin up, and not bow and scrape, and people don't like to be asking for favors all the time. Sally said her mother told her not to take anything for free and not to go asking favors of people,

and she should have her pride. Sally said her mother told her, 'To hell with people feeling sorry for us, because if they try, they'll get shot real fast around here.' "

. . .

20 Sally's parents live as far up the hollow as one can go. From their cabin one can see a truly splendid view of the Appalachians: the hills close by and far; the low-hanging white clouds and the higher gray clouds; the mist or the drizzle or the fog; and, near at hand, everywhere the green of the trees. The cabin is black, tar-paper black, and stands on four cement blocks. It lacks curtains but does indeed possess that old stove, the place where life-giving food is prepared and life-preserving heat is given off. Near the stove there are three beds with mattresses but nothing else. Ten human beings use the mattresses: Sally's grandmother, her parents, and the seven children in the family. The cabin possesses a table but only one chair to go with it, and two other old "sitting chairs," both of which are battered and tattered, with springs in each quite visible.

21 The children sit and eat outside under the trees, or inside on the floor, or near the house on the ground; or else they walk out in front of the house, in which case they often remain standing or hunch over their food. The children commonly use their hands to eat, or share a limited number of forks (four), spoons (five), and knives (seven) with their parents and grandmother. The children also share clothes: two pairs of shoes, both in serious need of repair, two ragged winter jackets, and three very old pairs of winter gloves. The children, let it be said, also share something else—the hollow: its hills and land, its vast imposing view, its bushes and shrubs and plants and animals and water and silence and noise, its seclusion and isolation, and also its people—for Sally a whole crowded, complicated, sustaining world.

22 What I have learned from Sally's life (and her words and her) does not require me to say that a good deal of it is unsatisfying—to her, never mind me. She does not need me to express her central longing that her family find a more coherent, valuable kind of existence. Sally and children like her made it very

clear to me that on the one hand they very much like certain things about mountain living, and on the other hand they are troubled and confused and even badly hurt (yes, they *know* they are hurt) by the hunger pangs they experience, the sickness that goes untreated, and, perhaps worst of all, the sight of what their suffering does to their parents.   Those Appalachian parents certainly do take notice of their children's suffering—partly because they are parents, and also because they are traditionally proud and defiant people.   Children notice their parents noticing, and Sally herself can talk about that kind of watching and counterwatching as it goes on among bruised and offended people, unwilling to let go of their sense of dignity and self-respect, and unwilling also to let go of their love for their ancestors, for their homes, their land, their conventions: "There's nothing that gets my daddy going worse than liquor.   Once he told my mother he was going to start drinking because he was upset as bad as he could be, because he'd been down the hollow and over to the welfare people and it was the first time he'd gone and it was going to be the last, even if he starved to death.   I guess they didn't give him anything.   They said they were sorry. They said there's no money for most people, and that's all they can do in the office there.

. . .

23   "I wouldn't want to live any other place.   What do you do if there's no hill you're on—if it's flat like they show you in the books in school?   If I could change anything I wanted, I'd tear down that place Daddy and his friends use to make the liquor. I'd just have the hill here, where we live, and the other ones, to go and look at.   I'd have us living in a different house, maybe like Marie's.   Then we'd all be happier, I know that.   Then I think my daddy might stop his drinking and never start again, like he'll promise us each time that he's going to do."

24   Mountaineers look upon life as a sort of stalemate, in which there is plenty of good as well as plenty of bad, plenty to hold onto as well as plenty to wish for, and, as a result "an awful lot of plenty" to be high-strung about, unsettled about, feel torn about.   Faced with such thoroughly mixed feelings, mountaineers stand fast and try to persist.   In the words of

Marie's father, they "stick it out, last it out." Stick out and last out what, one wonders? Does he mean the obvious lack of material things and opportunities? That, yes; but more is at stake than some of us on the outside realize. Marie's father says, "As I see it, up there in the hollow it's real bad—yes, with Sally and her people. But there's plenty they just don't want to lose, an awful lot of plenty, I'll tell you. People come in here and they don't know that. I heard on the TV a man saying we're supposed to be suspicious up in the mountains, and we don't trust no one, except ourselves. What a lot of hooey he had in his mouth, saying that. Sure we're not going to like someone if he comes in here and tells us we're a bunch of damn fools, and we should do this and that and everything they want us, and then we'll be all right.

. . .

25   "Sure, we need more, a hell of a lot more, and you must have figured that out by now. But no one's going to get us feeling kindly by coming on first thing with a lot of that lousy pity stuff you hear on the TV—about the poor people of Appalachia! Hell on that! Hell on it! They start with that and the next thing I know I'm ready to tell them to take themselves and their charity and go try it on someone else, because that's not what a decent, God-fearing man wants, no it's not. You can get suspicious, like they say we are. The coal people come in here, and they're tearing up everything they can get their hands on, and maybe they'll give you the money, the wages, but sure as hell they get more out of it than all of us ever will, and then the next thing you know they've gone, and all we have for it is that they've torn up a whole mountain and what's left of the mountain is falling down on us in a landslide, and we're supposed to get out, fast. If you don't get suspicious over that, then you're not right in your head. Then you know they've been taking our timber away, by the hillful, since way back, and right in front of our eyes that's what's been happening since I guess Abraham Lincoln or someone was President. So, why shouldn't we go and tell our children to watch out when some big-smiling city slicker comes here with a dozen lawyers standing guard over him?

26   "Sure we're afraid of them all coming here; we can smell

the trouble before it gets to the first hill in Kentucky—or over in West Virginia. But if they came to us and wanted to bring in some work here, and it didn't mean tearing up the whole country, and it didn't mean eating up our lungs, then we'd be just like any American—glad to have a job, you bet your life. We'd want to sit here and be ourselves, of course. We wouldn't want to act like some of the people you see on television. We wouldn't want to dress as they do, and talk as they do, no matter how much money we made. We'd want to live as we do. But we'd be working, and that would sure be a welcome change hereabouts."

27   Many of us on the "outside" have yet to convince a man like Marie's father that we really understand what we claim is obvious to us; for he thinks we would only pity him and his kin, even as we pity the children of sharecroppers and of migrant farmers. Our pity will give very little to anyone, and it enrages the mountaineers—who know very well what kind of justice they require and what justice we in America have so far done and not done.

Questions on Content

1. What was Danny Workman's experience with the land up to age three? How was this experience acquired?
2. Why does Billy Potter maintain that his is "the best place to be in the whole world"?
3. How is Marie Lewis' situation different from that of the other children in the selection?
4. What is the main change Sally would like to make in her surroundings?
5. What kinds of relationships between parents and children predominate in these examples?
6. Summarize George Lewis' attitudes toward the world outside the mountains.

Questions on Invention, Design, and Style

1. This selection, although long, can be divided into six parts: an introduction (*paragraphs 1 and 2*); four extended illustrations, each centering on a child within a family group (*paragraphs 3–23*); and George Lewis' final remarks (*paragraphs 24–26*). Look

again at the illustrations of Danny (*paragraphs 3–8*), Billy (*paragraphs 9–12*), Marie (*paragraphs 13–19*), and Sally (*paragraphs 20–23*). What does each contribute to the essay?

2. What logic do you see in the order in which Coles presents the four stories?
   a. Why does Danny's story come first?
   b. What similarities of setting and other elements tie Danny's and Billy's stories together? Marie's and Sally's?
   c. Why does Sally's story come last?

3. Why are George Lewis' remarks more effective after Sally's story than they would have been after the story of his daughter Marie?

4. Look again at paragraph 2. How are statements there developed in the four stories that follow?

5. This selection is composed largely of direct quotations. How does allowing the mountaineers to speak for themselves add credibility to the essay? What quotations in the selection are especially effective?

6. Coles' descriptive passages, though usually brief, are effective.
   a. Reread the description of Billy (*paragraph 9*). What information does this give about him that you do not get from what he says of himself?
   b. Reread the description of Sally's home and its contents (*paragraphs 20 and 21*). What does this tell you about her life? Why is it longer than the other descriptive passages?

7. What is Coles' attitude toward the mountaineers and their way of life? How do sequence, repetition, and commentary (such as the concluding paragraph) help you decide?

Applications

1. Interview members of a group that interests you (a club, religious group, athletic team, or special-interest group), and write an article for the campus newspaper blending direct quotation, multiple illustration, and your own commentary.

2. Observe or recall details about a group of young people whose way of life is different from yours. To illustrate the way they live, write a paper focusing on three or more individuals in sequence.

Part two
Comparison and Contrast

Comparison and Contrast

Similarities and differences
Explaining the unknown in terms of the known
Comparisons and contrasts for emphasis
Appropriateness of comparisons and contrasts

Like illustrations, *comparisons* and *contrasts* clarify the writer's meaning; they are yet another way that the writer can *show* the reader what he means, instead of just *telling* him. A comparison highlights the *similarities* between two or more things; a contrast highlights the *differences*. Unlike illustrations, each of which is concentrated primarily upon one thing, comparisons and contrasts enable the writer to pair two or more things and then to show them to us in a new and revealing way.

Suppose, for example, you are trying to tell one of your friends from high school about the impressive teacher you had for your history course. You could write a series of illustrations for your friend, telling how the teacher enters the classroom, what he looks like, how he lectures. You could tell your friend how the history professor got your attention that first day of class when he slammed the classroom door, called the roll while at the same time arranging the class in alphabetical order, and then, calling upon each student by first and last names, asked everyone to describe his or her high-school history course. Finally, you could tell how impressed you were with his taking history so seriously, the thoroughness of his examinations, and how confident in your understanding of history you feel after a semester in his course.

But, even though this illustration would give your friend a clear view of your impression of the history teacher, you could accomplish the same thing more quickly and perhaps more completely by comparing and contrasting the college teacher (the *unknown* to your friend) with a teacher or teachers that both of you had in high school (the *known*).   The college teacher may look very much like one of your former teachers, have a similar sense of humor, yet have a very different approach to his subject.   Picturing the college teacher and the high-school teacher together, their similarities and differences, your friend can clearly imagine why and in what way you have been so impressed.   You have communicated your meaning by comparing and contrasting the unknown with the known.

You may also find talking about similarities and differences useful when you want to describe a course you are taking this semester.   You may remark to a classmate:

comparison   This Spanish class looks as if it's going to be just like the English class we had last year.   We spend a lot of time reviewing grammar because half the class has forgotten it.

But your classmate replies:

contrast   I think this class is going to be a lot harder than English was.   In English I can at least think out loud.   In Spanish I can hardly speak.

The conversation continues to explore similarities and differences:

contrast   Okay, maybe first-year Spanish is harder than first-year
comparison   English.   But after that they're about the same: You read literature and write papers about it.

contrast   Sure.   But I'll always find Spanish plays harder than English plays!

But comparisons and contrasts not only enable a writer to clarify his meaning quickly and completely; they also allow him at the same time to make a deep impression upon the reader.   Consider, for example, the following passage from a letter to the editor of a large city newspaper:

When is the city going to get rid of the rats in abandoned houses? The rats in one house on Cooper Street are as big as quart jars. They walk upright on two legs—like people.

Here the writer concisely establishes a correspondence between the sizes of rats and of quart jars (a familiar image to most readers of the daily newspaper) and a second correspondence between the rats' shocking mobility and the way people walk. Of course, these comparisons heighten and intensify the menacing quality of the rats. The comparisons help the writer to achieve his purpose of impressing upon the editor and the general reading public the seriousness of the rat problem and how urgent it is that the city take immediate action to solve it. And, if we look closely at the words the writer has used and the comparisons he has drawn, we see that they were carefully selected with that purpose and audience in mind.

Comparisons and contrasts, then, show us what the writer means. Even though the writer may simply want the reader to understand what it was like to ride in a boat on rough water, drawing a comparison or contrast can make that meaning clear in such a way that it will leave a lasting impression upon the reader. Consider, for instance, the following use of comparison by Stephen Crane:

> A seat in this boat was not unlike a seat upon a bucking broncho, and by the same token a broncho is not much smaller. The craft pranced and reared and plunged like an animal. As each wave came, and she rose for it, she seemed like a horse making at a fence outrageously high. The manner of her scramble over these walls of water is a mystic thing, and, moreover, at the top of them were ordinarily these problems in white water, the foam racing down from the summit of each wave requiring a new leap, and a leap from the air. Then, after scornfully bumping a crest, she would slide and race and splash down a long incline, and arrive bobbing and nodding in front of the next menace.

By speaking of the boat ride in terms of a bronco ride Crane made it possible for us to imagine more clearly how rough it was, how difficult it must have been to stay aboard, and how the boat seemed to have a will of its own.

If we could single out one reason for the effectiveness of the comparisons and contrasts that the writers in this section have used, it would no doubt be the *appropriateness* of their comparisons and contrasts. First of all, the comparisons and contrasts are appropriate to the subject—riding in a boat and riding a bucking bronco, rather than mashing a potato or making a peanut-butter sandwich.   Too, the comparisons and contrasts are appropriate for the audience—like comparing your college history teacher with the teacher you and your friend had in high school last year, rather than with your sister's ballet teacher.

As you read the essays in this section, pay close attention to the author's selection of comparisons and contrasts that fit the subject and audience and to how the author selects particular comparisons and contrasts from the many that he could have selected.   The range is a broad one, from Norman Cousins' comparison of card playing with free will and determinism to E. B. White's comparison and contrast of the lake as it is now and as it was when he was a boy and of the experience of going to the lake then for him and now for his son.

Simple Comparison and Contrast

Simple comparison and contrast as part of a larger essay
Simile
Metaphor
Analogy
Symbol

As you probably know, the color of one's eyes is assumed to be relatively constant after infancy. Yet you may have had the mildly startling experience of discovering that, wearing his new green shirt, your supposedly blue-eyed friend displays depths of green in his eyes, which you had always considered blue. Your discovery comes from seeing the eyes and the green shirt at the same instant. In simple comparison and contrast we often discover significant and unsuspected similarities and differences between two things. What we understand as a result, then, is different, and in many ways greater, from what it would be if we had observed either one individually.

Simple comparisons and contrasts rarely serve as the bases for whole essays. Generally they form striking, and vital, parts of larger works. In fact, in their most basic form, simple comparisons and contrasts are *similes* or *metaphors*. A simile is a statement that one thing is *like* another, for example,

Bill is *like* an ox.
Carol's skin is smooth *as* satin.
Reading poetry is *like* using your left hand to scratch your right ear.

A metaphor establishes a more direct relationship between the elements being compared and contrasted; in one sense, it functions as a shorthand simile, in that it frequently states that one thing *is* another, rather than simply *like* it:

> Bill *is* an ox.
> Carol's skin *is* satin.
> Reading poetry *is* using your left hand to scratch your right ear.

But metaphors are often presented more subtly, as when Bruce Catton speaks (in "Two Visions of Equal Force") of a haunting experience that "cut a hard groove" in his mind. The direct comparison in this metaphor is between Catton's experience and a knife; the experience is treated as if it *were* a knife, one that left a distinct mark on his memory.

The usefulness of both metaphor and simile to a writer can be demonstrated by an example from the work of Eldridge Cleaver. An experienced and skillful writer, in *Soul on Ice* Cleaver speaks about the image of a person he loves as "slipping away from the weak fingers of his mind" (metaphor); he tells of how he "hoards" her fading memory "like a miser gloating over a folio of blue-chip stocks" (simile).

Norman Cousins' essay in this section, for example, is based on a simile—"Free will and determinism . . . are like a game of cards"—that enables the author to draw an *analogy* between card playing and the question of free will and determinism. An *analogy* is an extended or applied simile or metaphor; in the analogy similarities are explored in detail and their implications are pursued. As a result two apparently unlike things (playing cards and the subject of free will and determinism) are shown to be alike in significant ways (playing the cards in your hand and having free will, for instance). In another selection, "Definition as Power" by Thomas Szasz, it is a metaphor—"The struggle for definition is . . . the struggle for life itself"—that makes possible the analogy between struggling for the definition of a word and struggling for a gun in a western movie.

A related form of comparison is the *symbol*—a concrete image that represents something other than or more than itself, very often a visual image standing in for a more abstract and nonmaterial concept. For instance, reading Gwendolyn Brooks' "A Song in the Front Yard," we soon come to see that the front and back yards are symbols of two contrasting approaches to life. In "Circles and Squares," John G. Neihardt compares the life of the Sioux to circles and the life of the white man to squares and then contrasts these two life styles.

These forms of simple comparison and contrast suggest innumerable possibilities for clarifying brief points within a larger work. Occasionally they can even suggest the overall design of an entire work. "Stars: Where Life Begins," for instance, is a complex essay based on a recurring analogy between the human life cycle and the processes by which stars are formed, develop through stages, and eventually "die." Similarly, Jonathan Swift uses an analogy between the raising of animals for butchering and the raising of Irish girls and boys for a similar end.

The Card Game
Norman Cousins

Editor and essayist Norman Cousins explores several contradictions in human nature, focusing on the question of free will versus determinism and resolving it with a simile that is developed into a brief analogy.

1   Ever since I was old enough to read books on philosophy I have been intrigued by the discussions on the nature of man. The philosophers have been debating for years about whether man is primarily good or primarily evil, whether he is primarily altruistic or selfish, cooperative or competitive, gregarious or self-centered, whether he enjoys free will or whether everything is predetermined.

. . .

2   I don't presume to be able to resolve the contradictions. In fact, I don't think we have to. It seems to me that the debate over good and evil in man, over free will and determinism, and over all the other contradictions—that this debate is a futile one. For man is a creature of dualism. He is both good and

evil, both altruistic and selfish.   He enjoys free will to the extent that he can make decisions in life, but he can't change his chemistry or his relatives or his physical endowments—all of which were determined for him at birth.   And rather than speculate over which side of him is dominant, he might do well to consider what the contradictions and circumstances are that tend to bring out the good or evil, that enable him to be nobler and a responsible member of the human race.   And so far as free will and determinism are concerned, something I heard in India on a recent visit to the subcontinent may be worth passing along.   Free will and determinism, I was told, are like a game of cards.   The hand that is dealt you represents determinism. The way you play your hand represents free will.

Questions on Content

1. List the five questions Cousins raises about human nature in paragraph 1.   Why does Cousins think these questions are futile ones?
2. According to Cousins, to what extent can people exercise free will?   In what areas are they not free to exercise it?
3. What is the source of Cousins' simile?
4. How is determinism like the hand of cards that is dealt?   How is free will like the playing of the hand?

Questions on Invention, Design, and Style

1. In paragraph 1 Cousins introduces his subject to the reader. How does his use of the first person help to arouse the reader's interest in this subject?   How does this use of the first person enable Cousins to make a smooth transition between the first and second paragraphs?
2. What examples does Cousins give to show that "man is a creature of dualism"?
3. What material in this selection originated in Cousins' experience? his observations?
4. In what way is the card game an appropriate analogy to free will and determinism in people's lives?   How could the analogy be extended even farther?

Applications

1. Select one or more of the following similes and develop it into a brief analogy: A girl is like an orange; a boy is like a beehive; a roommate is like adhesive tape; a history exam is like a candy machine.
2. Invent a simile and brief analogy to make a point about one or more of the following: campus food, parking on campus, new friends, old movies, conceited people.

Definition as Power
Thomas Szasz

To show us the power of words, psychiatrist Thomas Szasz draws an unusual analogy between the struggle for definition and the struggle for survival.

The struggle for definition is veritably the struggle for life itself. In the typical Western two men fight desperately for the possession of a gun that has been thrown to the ground: whoever reaches the weapon first, shoots and lives; his adversary is shot and dies. In ordinary life, the struggle is not for guns but for words: whoever first defines the situation is the victor; his adversary, the victim. For example, in the family, husband and wife, mother and child do not get along; who defines whom as troublesome or mentally sick? Or, in the apocryphal story about Emerson visiting Thoreau in jail; Emerson asks: "Henry, what are you doing over there?" Thoreau replies: "Ralph, what are you doing over there?" In short, he who first seizes the word imposes reality on the other: he who defines thus dominates and lives; and he who is defined is subjugated and may be killed.

Questions on Content

1. What is the similarity between the struggle for definition and a western gun fight? What is the difference?

2. How can this struggle for definition operate in family situations?
3. Who won the struggle between Emerson and Thoreau? How did he win it?
4. Who is the winner and who is the subjugated in a struggle for definition?

Questions on Invention, Design, and Style

1. Szasz states his main point in the first and last sentences. What then are the purposes of the sentences in between?
2. How appropriate is the analogy between a word battle and a gun battle? Are the situations essentially similar? Are the results essentially similar?
3. How do the examples of word battles in the family and the encounter between Emerson and Thoreau further develop Szasz' point?
4. How effectively does the final sentence summarize Szasz' main point and conclude the paragraph?
5. The paragraph contains some very effectively designed sentences. How are both comparison and contrast used in the three-part structure of the second sentence to develop Szasz' point? How does the design of the third sentence parallel that of the second sentence? What is the purpose of this parallel?

Applications

1. Using Szasz' metaphor—the struggle for definition as the struggle for life itself—in your topic sentence, write a paragraph developing an analogy of your own to clarify this relationship.
2. Invent an analogy to make the point that a person can either enjoy or detest college. Write a paragraph in which this analogy is developed and illustrated, as Szasz developed and illustrated his.

A Song in the Front Yard
Gwendolyn Brooks

Using the back yard and front yard to symbolize two life styles, poet Gwendolyn Brooks contrasts a young girl's own familiar life with one that seems infinitely better to her. Our understanding of these two

approaches to life results primarily from this contrast, which the author establishes early and then develops.

I've stayed in the front yard all my life.
I want a peek at the back
Where it's rough and untended and hungry weed grows.
A girl gets sick of a rose.

I want to go in the back yard now   5
And maybe down the alley,
To where the charity children play.
I want a good time today.

They do some wonderful things.
They have some wonderful fun.   10
My mother sneers, but I say it's fine
How they don't have to go in at a quarter to nine.

My mother she tells me that Johnnie Mae
Will grow up to be a bad woman.
That George'll be taken to jail soon or late.   15
(On account of last winter he sold our back gate.)

But I say it's fine. Honest I do.
And I'd like to be a bad woman too,
And wear the brave stockings of night-black lace.
And strut down the street with paint on my face.   20

Questions on Content

1. What are the characteristics of the back yard? What does the speaker find attractive about it? How much experience has she had in it?
2. What is her mother's opinion of the "charity children"?
3. What are the children in the back yard allowed to do that the speaker is not allowed to do?
4. What does being a "bad woman" mean to the speaker?

Questions on Invention, Design, and Style

1. What do the front yard and the back yard represent in the poem?
2. How do their locations and their appearances help to clarify the meanings of these two symbols?

3. What is the significance of the contrast between "a rose" (*line 4*) and "rough and untended and hungry weed" (*line 3*)?
4. As the poem progresses, the speaker's attraction to the back-yard life style becomes stronger, and her resistance to her mother's style becomes bolder. How has Brooks' five-part design emphasized this progression?

Applications

1. Write a paper in which you contrast two types of people. You may find it effective to illustrate them through two individuals— their homes, parents, friends, clothing, physical appearances, attitudes, and behavior. Reach a conclusion about the two types of people after setting up the contrast.
2. Write about a friend or acquaintance you admire and respect but have always secretly envied. In your paper, work out a contrast between your life and his or hers.
3. Consider older people who represent different versions of the person you might someday be. Write a paper in which you project two different courses your future life might take—two different people you might become. Which future would you rather have? How might you attain that future rather than the other?

Circles and Squares
John G. Neihardt

Black Elk, a holy man of the Oglala Sioux, contrasts life as the Sioux sees it with the way white people force him to live it. As recorded by John G. Neihardt early this century, Black Elk's ideas demonstrate effective use of metaphor and analogy, as well as visual contrast.

1   After the heyoka ceremony,[1] I came to live here where I am now between Wounded Knee Creek and Grass Creek. Others came too, and we made these little gray houses of logs that you see, and they are square. It is a bad way to live, for there can be no power in a square.

2   You have noticed that everything an Indian does is in a cir-

---

[1] Ceremony of sacred fools, who do everything wrong or backward.

cle, and that is because the Power of the World always works in circles, and everything tries to be round.   In the old days when we were a strong and happy people, all our power came to us from the sacred hoop of the nation, and so long as the hoop was unbroken, the people flourished.   The flowering tree was the living center of the hoop, and the circle of the four quarters nourished it.   The east gave peace and light, the south gave warmth, the west gave rain, and the north with its cold and mighty wind gave strength and endurance.   This knowledge came to us from the outer world with our religion.   Everything the Power of the World does is done in a circle.   The sky is round, and I have heard that the earth is round like a ball, and so are all the stars.   The wind, in its greatest power, whirls. Birds make their nests in circles, for theirs is the same religion as ours.   The sun comes forth and goes down again in a circle. The moon does the same, and both are round.   Even the seasons form a great circle in their changing, and always come back again to where they were.   The life of a man is a circle from childhood to childhood, and so it is in everything where power moves.   Our tepees were round like the nests of birds, and these were always set in a circle, the nation's hoop, a nest of many nests, where the Great Spirit meant for us to hatch our children.

3   But the Wasichus[2] have put us in these square boxes.   Our power is gone and we are dying, for the power is not in us any more.   You can look at our boys and see how it is with us. When we were living by the power of the circle in the way we should, boys were men at twelve or thirteen years of age.   But now it takes them very much longer to mature.

Questions on Content

1. According to Black Elk, what is the reason that "everything an Indian does is in a circle"?
2. What examples does Black Elk give to show that the world "works in circles"?
3. What was the "living center" of the "hoop of the nation"?

---

[2] White men.

4. What are the four quarters of the circle? What does each quarter give?
5. When they were living by the power of the circle, what happened to boys by the age of twelve or thirteen?

Questions on Invention, Design, and Style

1. Reread paragraphs 1 and 3, omitting paragraph 2. How much of the force of Black Elk's dislike for the "square boxes" is lost without the contrast of his love for the circle?
2. How would you express in your own words Black Elk's statement, "The Power of the World always works in circles, and everything tries to be round"? How does his series of comparisons in paragraph 2 help you to understand his meaning?
3. What is Black Elk's conception of nature? What does he think man's relationship to nature should be?
4. Make a list of as many words from the selection as you can that suggest roundness, such as "hoop." Then make another list of all the other words suggesting roundness that you can think of. Mark those that would not be appropriate to the style or subject matter of the Neihardt passage—"gyroscope," for example. Explain why each would not be appropriate.

Applications

1. Take a walk outdoors and look for round and square forms of all textures and sizes—a leaf or the curve of a hill, perhaps. What differences do you find in these forms? What similarities? Write a description of what you observe, noting both similarities and differences.
2. As you read the following passage from James Joyce's "Araby," imagine the life of a young boy or girl in Ireland during the early twentieth century.

> When the short days of winter came dusk fell before we had well eaten our dinners. When we met in the street the houses had grown somber. The space of sky above us was the colour of ever-changing violet[,] and towards it the lamps of the street lifted their feeble lanterns. The cold air stung us and we played till our bodies glowed. Our shouts echoed in the silent street. The career of our play brought us through the dark muddy lanes behind the houses . . . to the back doors of the dark dripping gardens where odours arose from ashpits, to the dark odorous stables where a coachman smoothed and combed the horse or shook music from the buckled harness. When we

returned to the street[,] light from the kitchen windows had filled the areas.

Contrast this experience with your own childhood experience. Recall the place where you played as well as the games you played.   Then write a paper that either compares or contrasts that experience with Joyce's experience.   Use similes, metaphors, even symbols and analogies where appropriate.

Extended Comparison and Contrast

Exploring differences and similarities
Inventing and designing in comparison and contrast
Subject-by-subject structuring
Part-by-part structuring

As many writers have observed, human beings are comparing creatures. The human mind delights not only in *perceiving* differences and similarities—as in simple comparison and contrast—but in *exploring* them. In extended comparison and contrast we do just that: We explore to a fuller extent exactly how two things are similar and different. By extending the investigation of similarities and differences, we discover our subject more fully; we may even be said to *invent* it. At the same time, we discover a way to order the subject—to *design* it.

For example, in a recent essay a young woman contrasted two different men whom she saw separately on many occasions. Her paper was organized around the contrast between "the Debater," who liked nothing better than to sit and talk with her, anywhere, for long hours, and "the Sportsman," who preferred that he and she enjoy a morning of tennis, followed by a quick swim, followed by a leisurely motor-bike ride, and the like. By extending her consideration of the differences, in this case, between the two men, she was able to understand the subject of the two men and to design her essay accordingly.

What happens in extended comparison and contrast, then, is that the process of discovering similarities and differences takes recognizable form in the structure of the writing. That is obvious in the student's extended contrast of the two men. And the essays in this section further clarify how a writer structures an entire essay through extended comparison and contrast.

The selections by James Thurber are of this type. Implying a comparison of the actions of animals and insects to the actions of human beings, he structures his writing in the form of a fable or extended analogy. In one fable he writes of a larger spider and a fairly intelligent fly, in the other of an old turtle that appears to be far older than it actually is. In both, though, the comparisons of these insects and animals with human beings result in narratives that expose such human characteristics as overconfidence and gullibility.

But writers often structure their writing more directly around comparison and contrast. Two common structural patterns are *subject-by-subject* and *part-by-part* comparisons and contrasts. In the subject-by-subject pattern, the writer first examines one subject fully ("the Debater," for instance). He or she then shifts to the other subject ("the Sportsman"), pointing out how it is like or unlike the first. This subject-by-subject method of structuring a comparison and contrast can be diagrammed as follows:

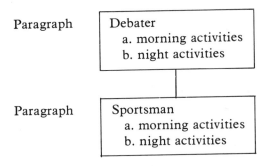

Paragraph   Debater
     a. morning activities
     b. night activities

Paragraph   Sportsman
     a. morning activities
     b. night activities

The writer has the option, however, of organizing the same material according to the part-by-part pattern. In that case, he or she would contrast specific characteristics of the two men, point by point. (Debater spends his mornings eating a late, leisurely, sociable breakfast; Sportsman eats early and lightly, then hurries off for his first game of the day. At night Debater stays up late talking; Sportsman retires early—because of exhaustion and a wish to take advantage of the first hours of daylight.) This part-by-part method of structuring the contrast can be diagrammed in the following manner:

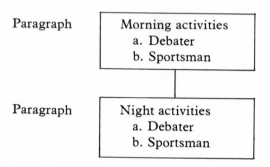

Paragraph

> Morning activities
>   a. Debater
>   b. Sportsman

Paragraph

> Night activities
>   a. Debater
>   b. Sportsman

In her essay in this section, Virginia Woolf contrasts William Shakespeare's career with that of his imaginary twin sister. By so doing, she shows us how impossible it was for a woman to have a career in the Elizabethan age—even if she were as gifted as Shakespeare himself—and how unfair conditions were.

Woolf structures her essay in a subject-by-subject pattern that emphasizes the differences between past male and female roles. After first focusing on Shakespeare, she turns her attention to his supposed sister, Judith. In a diagram, Woolf's subject-by-subject structure would appear as follows:

> William Shakespeare
>   a. schooling
>   b. boyhood activities
>   c. marriage
>   d. seeking fortune in London
>   e. career
>   f. success in theatre

Judith Shakespeare
   a. lack of schooling
   b. girlhood activities
   c. avoided marriage
   d. seeking fortune in London
   e. unfulfilled career
   f. pregnancy and death by suicide

Woolf's choice of the subject-by-subject design is clearly more appropriate than the part-by-part design would have been. She does not intend to give William and Judith equal emphasis; rather, she concentrates on the imaginary sister's frustration and fate. She has thus been free to devote less than one paragraph to William and five to Judith. In addition, she has observed the principle that the last item in a series should receive greater emphasis. The subject-by-subject arrangement has thus allowed Woolf to separate Judith's story from William's and to achieve a climax that not only makes her thesis concrete but also renders its impact more powerful.

The point to remember is that writers should make the choice between subject-by-subject and part-by-part designs consciously and intelligently. As in the choice of extended versus multiple illustration (see pp. 31–32), both alternatives may offer creative though distinctly different possibilities. But, as in this example, in some instances one alternative may be distinctly superior to the other.

As you read the other two essays in this section, by S. I. Hayakawa and Bruce Catton, try to identify the pattern each writer follows and his reasons for doing so. Note how he employs transitions (the words, phrases, sentences, and sometimes paragraphs, by which he moves from one point to another) to make it clear to the reader how one part relates to another and one subject to another. Be aware also of the way in which the writer resolves his material and generalizes about it—that is, how he achieves his conclusion.

Two Fables for Our Time
James Thurber

One of the oldest forms of humorous writing is the animal fable, a story in which animals are used to highlight human characteristics. Ranging from ancient fables like "The Tortoise and the Hare" to their modern counterparts in comic strips and cartoons, these narratives depend for their meaning upon comparisons of animals and humans. Although plots may have some intrinsic interest, they serve primarily to clarify certain human characteristics or certain morals. In this tradition, James Thurber used insects and animals as means of commenting on human behavior and beliefs.

The Fairly Intelligent Fly

1   A large spider in an old house built a beautiful web in which to catch flies. Every time a fly landed on the web and was entangled in it the spider devoured him, so that when another fly came along he would think the web was a safe and quiet place in which to rest. One day a fairly intelligent fly buzzed around above the web so long without lighting that the spider appeared and said, "Come on down." But the fly was too clever for him and said, "I never light where I don't see other flies and I don't see any other flies in your house." So he flew away until he came to a place where there were a great many other flies. He was about to settle down among them when a bee buzzed up and said, "Hold it, stupid, that's flypaper. All those flies are trapped." "Don't be silly," said the fly, "they're dancing." So he settled down and became stuck to the flypaper with all the other flies.

2   *Moral: There is no safety in numbers, or in anything else.*

Questions on Content

1. What assumption keeps the fairly intelligent fly from taking the spider's advice?
2. What assumption keeps the fairly intelligent fly from taking the bee's advice?

3. What contrasts does the fly make between the web and the paper? How do these contrasts influence his decision?
4. What mistakes does he make in his reasoning? in his perception?
5. What human likenesses can you find in the spider? in the fairly intelligent fly? in the bee?

Questions on Invention, Design, and Style

1. Is the *tone* (see "Glossary") of this fable formal or informal? Do you think sarcasm is intended here?
2. Is Thurber's attitude serious or lighthearted? How serious is Thurber about his "moral"? Is the moral justified by the fable?
3. What are the human weaknesses that are ridiculed in this fable, and how does the fable ridicule them?

The Turtle Who Conquered Time

1 A turtle appeared in a meadow one summer's day and attracted the attention of all the creatures in the grass and in the trees, because the date 44 B.C. was carved on his shell. "Our meadow is honored indeed," exclaimed a grasshopper, "for our visitor is the oldest of all living creatures."

2 "We must build a pavilion in his honor," said a frog, and the catbirds and the swallows and the other birds built a stately pleasure dome out of twigs and leaves and blossoms for the very important turtle. An orchestra of crickets played music in his honor, and a wood thrush sang. The sounds of jubilee were heard in nearby fields and woods, and as more and more creatures turned up from farther and farther away to have a look at the ancient turtle, the grasshopper decided to charge admission to the pavilion.

3 "I will be the barker," said the frog, and, with the help of the grasshopper, he composed an impressive spiel. "Yesterday and yesterday and yesterday," it began, "creeps in this carapace from day to day to the first syllable of recorded time. This great turtle was born two thousand years ago, the year the mighty Julius Caesar died. Horace was twenty-one in 44 B.C., and Cicero had but a single year to live." The bystanders did not seem very much interested in the turtle's ancient contemporaries, but they gladly paid to go in and have a look at his ancient body.

4　Inside the pavilion, the grasshopper continued the lecture. "This remarkable turtle is a direct descendant of one of the first families of Ooze," he chanted. "His great-grandfather may have been the first thing that moved in the moist and muddy margins of this cooling planet. Except for our friend's ancestors, there was nothing but coal and blobs of glob."

5　One day a red squirrel who lived in a neighboring wood dropped in to look at the turtle and to listen to the ballyhoo. "Forty-four B.C., my foot!" scoffed the squirrel, as he glared at the grasshopper. "You are full of tobacco juice, and your friend the frog is full of lightning bugs. The carving of an ancient date on the carapace of a turtle is a common childish prank. This creep was probably born no earlier than 1902."

6　As the red squirrel ranted on, the spectators who had paid to get into the pavilion began departing quietly, and there was no longer a crowd listening to the frog out front. The crickets put away their instruments and disappeared as silently as the Arabs, and the wood thrush gathered up his sheet music and flew off and did not return. The sounds of jubilee were no longer heard in the once merry meadow, and the summer seemed to languish like a dying swan.

7　"I knew all the time he wasn't two thousand years old," admitted the grasshopper, "but the legend pleased the people, young and old, and many smiled who had not smiled for years."

8　"And many laughed who had not laughed for years," said the frog, "and many eyes sparkled and many hearts were gay." The turtle shed a turtle tear at this and crawled away.

9　"The truth is not merry and bright," said the red squirrel. "The truth is cold and dark. Let's face it." And, looking smug and superior, the iconoclast scampered impudently back to his tree in the wood. From the grass of the meadow voices once carefree and gay joined in a rueful and lonely chorus, as if someone great and wonderful had died and was being buried.

10　*Moral: Oh, why should the shattermyth have to be a crumplehope and a dampenglee?*

Questions on Content

1. Why do other animals honor the turtle? In what ways do they honor him?

2. What clues does Thurber give that the turtle and bystanders are being exploited?

3. How does the red squirrel's interpretation differ from that of the others? Why is the squirrel believed?

4. How do most of the animals react to the red squirrel's speech about the turtle? How do the grasshopper and frog react? the turtle?

5. What is the mood of the animals at the end of the fable?

6. What typical human characteristics does Thurber depict in the animals' reaction to the turtle who is supposedly very old?

7. In your own words, what is the human dilemma that Thurber explores in this fable and in the moral?

Questions on Invention, Design, and Style

1. Like several of the essays in the section on extended illustration, such as "The Irish Widow" and "Salvation," this is a *narrative*, an account of a sequence of events in chronological order. Why, then, is this fable considered an example of comparison, rather than of illustration?

2. Describe the tone of the red squirrel's speech in paragraph 5. How is the squirrel's tone conveyed by such phrases as "my foot" and "full of tobacco juice"?

3. What is Thurber's attitude toward the red squirrel? How do the terms he uses to describe the squirrel's behavior—"ranted on," "looking smug and superior," "scampered impudently"—influence your opinion?

4. As you examine the moral, do you think Thurber agrees with the red squirrel's pronouncement, "The truth is not merry and bright. . . . The truth is cold and dark. Let's face it" (*paragraph 9*)? How is your answer influenced by Thurber's apparent attitude toward the red squirrel? by the way the moral is stated in paragraph 10?

5. How does Thurber heighten the effect of his stories by choosing animals to illustrate human traits, rather than merely describing the behavior of human beings?

Applications

1. Write a paper comparing and contrasting the attitudes of red squirrel in this fable and the bee in "The Fairly Intelligent Fly."

2. Using any two animals (a poodle and a wolf, for example) as main characters, write a brief fable, serious or humorous, with a moral, about the human desire to avoid rules and restrictions.

3. Think back over a conflict you have experienced, such as whether college A or college B would be better for you or whether to take psychology or sociology. Write a paper that will make your dilemma real for your reader.

Shakespeare's Sister
Virginia Woolf

To support her thesis that talented women have often met with extreme frustration in the past, novelist Virginia Woolf focused her imagination upon histories of Elizabethan social customs and biographies of William Shakespeare to invent the life of Judith—his equally gifted twin sister.

1   It would be ambitious beyond my daring, I thought, looking about the shelves for books that were not there, to suggest to the students of those famous colleges[1] that they should rewrite history, though I own that it often seems a little queer as it is, unreal, lop-sided; but why should they not add a supplement to history? Calling it, of course, by some inconspicuous name so that women might figure there without impropriety? For one often catches a glimpse of them in the lives of the great, whisking away into the background, concealing, I sometimes think, a wink, a laugh, perhaps a tear. And, after all, we have lives enough of Jane Austen; it scarcely seems necessary to consider again the influence of the tragedies of Joanna Baillie upon the poetry of Edgar Allan Poe; as for myself, I should not mind if the homes and haunts of Mary Russell Mitford were closed to the public for a century at least. But what I find deplorable, I continued, looking about the bookshelves again, is that nothing is known about women before the eighteenth century. I have no model in my mind to turn about this way and that.

2   Here am I asking why women did not write poetry in the Elizabethan age, and I am not sure how they were educated; whether they were taught to write; whether they had sitting-

---

[1] Newnham and Girton—women's colleges of Cambridge University.

rooms to themselves; how many women had children before they were twenty-one; what, in short, they did from eight in the morning till eight at night. They had no money evidently; according to Professor Trevelyan they were married whether they liked it or not before they were out of the nursery, at fifteen or sixteen very likely. It would have been extremely odd, even upon this showing, had one of them suddenly written the plays of Shakespeare, I concluded, and I thought of that old gentleman, who is dead now, but was a bishop, I think, who declared that it was impossible for any woman, past, present, or to come, to have the genius of Shakespeare. He wrote to the papers about it. He also told a lady who applied to him for information that cats do not as a matter of fact go to heaven, though they have, he added, souls of a sort. How much thinking those old gentlemen used to save one! How the borders of ignorance shrank back at their approach! Cats do not go to heaven. Women cannot write the plays of Shakespeare.

3　Be that as it may, I could not help thinking, as I looked at the works of Shakespeare on the shelf, that the bishop was right at least in this; it would have been impossible, completely and entirely, for any woman to have written the plays of Shakespeare.

4　Let me imagine, since facts are so hard to come by, what would have happened had Shakespeare had a wonderfully gifted sister, called Judith, let us say. Shakespeare himself went, very probably—his mother was an heiress—to the grammar school, where he may have learnt Latin—Ovid, Virgil and Horace—and the elements of grammar and logic. He was, it is well known, a wild boy who poached rabbits, perhaps shot a deer, and had, rather sooner than he should have done, to marry a woman in the neighbourhood, who bore him a child rather quicker than was right. That escapade sent him to seek his fortune in London. He had, it seemed, a taste for the theatre; he began by holding horses at the stage door. Very soon he got work in the theatre, became a successful actor, and lived at the hub of the universe, meeting everybody, knowing everybody, practising his art on the boards, exercising his wits in the streets, and even getting access to the palace of the queen.

5　Meanwhile his extraordinarily gifted sister, let us suppose, remained at home.   She was as adventurous, as imaginative, as agog to see the world as he was.   But she was not sent to school. She had no chance of learning grammar and logic, let alone of reading Horace and Virgil.   She picked up a book now and then, one of her brother's perhaps, and read a few pages.   But then her parents came in and told her to mend the stockings or mind the stew and not moon about with books and papers. They would have spoken sharply but kindly, for they were substantial people who knew the conditions of life for a woman and loved their daughter—indeed, more likely than not she was the apple of her father's eye.   Perhaps she scribbled some pages up in an apple loft on the sly, but was careful to hide them or set fire to them.

6   Soon, however, before she was out of her teens, she was to be betrothed to the son of a neighbouring wool-stapler.   She cried out that marriage was hateful to her, and for that she was severely beaten by her father.   Then he ceased to scold her. He begged her instead not to hurt him, not to shame him in this matter of her marriage.   He would give her a chain of beads or a fine petticoat, he said; and there were tears in his eyes.   How could she disobey him?   How could she break his heart?   The force of her own gift alone drove her to it.   She made up a small parcel of her belongings, let herself down by a rope one summer's night and took the road to London.   She was not seventeen.

7   The birds that sang in the hedge were not more musical than she was.   She had the quickest fancy, a gift like her brother's, for the tune of words.   Like him, she had a taste for the theatre.   She stood at the stage door; she wanted to act, she said.   Men laughed in her face.   The manager—a fat, loose-lipped man—guffawed.   He bellowed something about poodles dancing and women acting—no woman, he said, could possibly be an actress.   He hinted—you can imagine what.   She could get no training in her craft.   Could she even seek her dinner in a tavern or roam the streets at midnight?   Yet her genius was for fiction and lusted to feed abundantly upon the lives of men and women and the study of their ways.

8   At last—for she was very young, oddly like Shakespeare the poet in her face, with the same grey eyes and rounded brows—at

last Nick Greene the actor-manager took pity on her; she found herself with child by that gentleman and so—who shall measure the heat and violence of the poet's heart when caught and tangled in a woman's body?—killed herself one winter's night and lies buried at some cross-roads where the omnibuses now stop outside the Elephant and Castle.

9 That, more or less, is how the story would run, I think, if a woman in Shakespeare's day had had Shakespeare's genius. But for my part, I agree with the deceased bishop, if such he was —it is unthinkable that any woman in Shakespeare's day should have had Shakespeare's genius. For genius like Shakespeare's is not born among labouring, uneducated, servile people. It was not born in England among the Saxons and the Britons. It is not born today among the working classes. How, then, could it have been born among women whose work began, according to Professor Trevelyan, almost before they were out of the nursery, who were forced to it by their parents and held to it by all the power of law and custom? Yet genius of a sort must have existed among women as it must have existed among the working classes. Now and again an Emily Brontë or a Robert Burns blazes out and proves its presence. But certainly it never got itself on to paper. When, however, one reads of a witch being ducked, or a woman possessed by devils, of a wise woman selling herbs, or even of a very remarkable man who had a mother, then I think we are on the track of a lost novelist, a suppressed poet, of some mute and inglorious Jane Austen, some Emily Brontë who dashed her brains out on the moor or mopped and mowed about the highways crazed with the torture that her gift had put her to. Indeed, I would venture to guess that Anon, who wrote so many poems without signing them, was often a woman.

Questions on Content

1. In what ways are history books "unreal" and "lop-sided" on the subject of women, according to Woolf? What does she find especially deplorable as she examines the bookshelves?
2. Why does the bishop expect us to believe that no woman could have written Shakespeare's plays? In what way does Woolf agree with the bishop?

3. Summarize William Shakespeare's education and young manhood.
4. Summarize Judith Shakespeare's education and young womanhood.
5. What were Judith's experiences in London?
6. Why did Judith commit suicide?
7. Why, according to Woolf, have there been "lost" novelists and "suppressed" poets?

Questions on Invention, Design, and Style

1. In paragraphs 3–8 Woolf summarizes the lives of the real William and the hypothetical Judith Shakespeare. What comparisons does she make between the two? what contrasts? What are the advantages gained from the subject-by-subject pattern she uses? What would the passage be like if she had used the part-by-part pattern?
2. Examine the function of paragraphs 8 and 9 within the structure of the essay. How does Woolf use the death of Judith to extend the point she is making in this essay?
3. Consider the actual historical sources and the imaginative process with which Woolf has composed the life of Judith Shakespeare. How has she used what is known about Shakespeare's home, family, and career? What use has she made of Professor Trevelyan's historical evidence, referred to in paragraph 2? How much seems to grow out of her own experience as a girl, woman, and creative artist?
4. Woolf often states her own attitude toward her subject, as in "... what I find deplorable ... is that nothing is known about women before the eighteenth century" (*paragraph 1*), and "How much thinking those old gentlemen used to save one!" (*paragraph 2*). How would you characterize her tone in these statements? Locate other passages with clear expressions of the author's attitude. How does the choice of words reveal that attitude in each case?

Applications

1. Write an essay in which you draw a comparison or contrast between an historical figure and an imaginary sister or brother (between Thomas Jefferson and his imaginary sister or Joan of Arc and her imaginary brother, for example).
2. Using significant aspects of your home life and other surround-

ings, write a brief biography of an imaginary twin sister or brother of your own. Then, draw a contrast between yourself and the imaginary person.

Insoluble Problems
S. I. Hayakawa

Are problems ever insoluble? Or are we simply too fixed in our patterns of behavior to perceive available solutions? Drawing on the results of experiments with rats and humans, semanticist and educator S. I. Hayakawa suggests a comparison and a basic contrast between the potential for problem solving in the two species.

1   Professor N. R. F. Maier of the University of Michigan performed a series of interesting experiments in which "neurosis" is induced in rats. The rats are first trained to jump off the edge of a platform at one of two doors. If the rat jumps to the right, the door holds fast, and it bumps its nose and falls into a net; if it jumps to the left, the door opens, and the rat finds a dish of food. When the rats are well trained to this reaction, the situation is changed. The food is put behind the other door, so that in order to get their reward they now have to jump to the right instead of to the left. (Other changes, such as marking the two doors in different ways, may also be introduced by the experimenter.) If the rat fails to figure out the new system, so that each time it jumps it never knows whether it is going to get food or bump its nose, it finally gives up and refuses to jump at all. At this stage, Dr. Maier says, "Many rats prefer to starve rather than make a choice."

2   Next, the rats are forced to make a choice, being driven to it by blasts of air or an electric shock. "Animals which are induced to respond in the insoluble problem situation," says Dr. Maier, "settle down to a specific reaction (such as jumping *solely* at the left-hand door) which they continue to execute regardless of consequences. . . . The response chosen under these conditions becomes fixated. . . . Once the fixation appears, the animal is incapable of learning an adaptive response in this sit-

uation." When a reaction to the left-hand door is thus fixated, *the right-hand door may be left open so that the food is plainly visible.* Yet the rat, when pushed, *continues to jump to the left,* becoming more panicky each time. When the experimenter persists in forcing the rat to make choices, it may go into convulsions, racing around wildly, injuring its claws, bumping into chairs and tables, then going into a state of violent trembling, until it falls into a coma. In this passive state, it refuses to eat, refuses to take any interest in anything: it can be rolled up into a ball or suspended in the air by its legs—the rat has ceased to care what happens to it. It has had a "nervous breakdown." *

3   It is the "insolubility" of the rat's problem that leads to its nervous breakdown, and, as Dr. Maier shows in his studies of disturbed children and adults, rats and human beings seem to go through pretty much the same stages. First, they are trained to make habitually a given choice when confronted by a given problem; secondly, they get a terrible shock when they find that the conditions have changed and that the choice doesn't produce the expected results; third, whether through shock, anxiety, or frustration, they may fixate on the original choice and continue to make that choice regardless of consequences; fourth, they sullenly refuse to act at all; fifth, when by external compulsion they are forced to make a choice, they again make the one they were originally trained to make—and again get a bump on the nose; finally, even *with the goal visible in front of them,* to be attained simply by making a different choice, they go crazy out of frustration. They tear around wildly; they sulk in corners and refuse to eat; bitter, cynical, disillusioned, they cease to care what happens to them.

4   Is this an exaggerated picture? It hardly seems so. The pattern recurs throughout human life, from the small tragedies of the home to the world-shaking tragedies among nations. In order to cure her husband's faults, a wife may nag him. His faults get worse, so she nags him some more. Naturally his faults get worse still—and she nags him even more. Governed,

* Norman R. F. Maier, *Frustration: The Study of Behavior Without a Goal* (1949). See especially Chapter 2, "Experimental Evidence of Abnormal Behavior Reactions," and Chapter 6, "Comparison of Motivational and Frustration-Induced Behavior Problems in Children."

like the rat, by a fixated reaction to the problem of her husband's faults, she can meet it only in one way. The longer she continues, the worse it gets, until they are both nervous wrecks.

5   Again, white people in a northern city, deploring the illiteracy and high crime rate among Negroes, segregate them, persecute them (it is well known that the police are almost always tougher on Negro suspects than on whites), and deny them opportunities for employment and advancement. The denial of opportunity perpetuates the illiteracy and the high crime rate, which in turn perpetuate the segregation, persecution, and denial of opportunity. The search for a way to break up this vicious circle taxes the best minds among those interested in orderly social change: city councilmen, educators, urban planners, Negro organizations, as well as state governments and federal authorities.

6   To cite another example, students trying to express themselves in writing may write poorly. In order to improve their writing, says the English teacher, I must teach them the fundamentals of grammar, spelling, and punctuation. By thus placing excessive emphasis on grammar and mechanics while ignoring the students' ideas, the teacher quickly destroys student interest in writing. That interest destroyed, the students write even more poorly. Thereupon the teacher redoubles his dose of grammar and mechanics. The students become increasingly bored and rebellious. Such students fill the ranks of "remedial English" classes in high school and college.

7   Again, a nation, believing that the only way to secure peace and dignity is through armed strength, may embark on a huge armaments program. The program arouses the fears of neighboring nations, so that they too increase their armaments to match those of the first nation. Anxiety and tension increase. It is clear, the first nation declares, that we shall continue to feel anxious about our national security so long as we are not adequately prepared for all emergencies; we must therefore *double* our armaments. This naturally makes the neighboring nations even more anxious, so that they too double their armaments. Anxiety and tension increase even more. It is clear, the first nation declares, that our mistake has been to underestimate our defensive needs. This time we must be *sure* to be suf-

ficiently armed to preserve peace. We must *triple* our armaments. . . .

8 Of course these instances are oversimplified, but it is often because of vicious circles of this kind that we are unable to get at or do anything about the conditions that lead to disaster. The pattern is frequently recognizable; the goal may be in sight, attainable by a mere change in methods. Nevertheless, governed by fixated reactions, the rat "cannot" get food, the wife "cannot" cure her husband's faults, Negroes will have to wait two or three generations "until the time is ripe" for social change, and we "cannot afford" to stop devising and manufacturing weapons so deadly that they cannot be used without destroying civilization itself.

9 There is, however, an important difference between the insolubility of the rat's problems and the insolubility of human problems. Dr. Maier's rats were driven to their nervous breakdowns by problems more complicated than would naturally occur in a rat's environment. But human breakdowns are ordinarily caused by problems that human beings themselves have created: problems of religious and ethical belief; problems of money and credit and mortgages and trust funds and stock-market fluctuations; problems of man-made custom and etiquette and social organization and law.

10 Rats can hardly be blamed for not being able to solve problems set for them by Dr. Maier; there are limits to a rat's powers of abstraction. But there are no known limits to the human capacity to abstract and organize and make use of abstractions. Hence, if human beings find problems insoluble because of fixated reactions—if they are frustrated because they can respond in only one way, regardless of context or circumstances, to certain symbolically defined situations—they are functioning at less than full human capacity. They can be said, in Korzybski's suggestive phrase, to be "copying animals" in their reactions. Wendell Johnson summarized this idea aptly when he said, "To a mouse, cheese is cheese; that's why mousetraps work."

Questions on Content

1. How were the rats in the experiment first trained to jump to the left door?

2. How did the experimenter change the situation so that the rats preferred to "starve rather than make a choice"?
3. How did the experimenter force a choice between the left door and the right? Which door did the rats choose? How did they react to habitual wrong choices?
4. What significant similarities does Dr. Maier find between the behavior of rats and disturbed human beings?
5. What four examples does Hayakawa use to illustrate the behavior pattern that Dr. Maier found?
6. What difference does Hayakawa find between rat and human mental capacities?
7. What solution to "insoluble problems" does Hayakawa imply in this essay?

Questions on Invention, Design, and Style

1. Examine the structure of this essay.
   a. How do paragraphs 1 and 2 function in the total essay? How do they prepare us for what follows? How does the first sentence of paragraph 1 introduce the first two paragraphs?
   b. How is paragraph 3 related to the preceding two paragraphs? What specific points of comparison does Hayakawa make? How does paragraph 3 prepare you for those that follow?
   c. How does each example in paragraphs 4–7 illustrate the tendency of humans to continue in fixated reactions?
   d. What is the function of paragraph 8? Is it more closely related to paragraphs 4–7 or to paragraphs 9 and 10?
   e. How does the first sentence of paragraph 9 serve to introduce paragraphs 9 and 10? How does it hark back to earlier material?
2. Trace the ways in which Hayakawa extends his comparison of fixated reactions in rats and humans. What examples does he give of fixated reactions in humans? How are the comparisons between rats and people intended to influence the reader?
3. What contrast does Hayakawa establish between fixated reactions in rats and those in people? How does this contrast help to develop the thesis of the essay?
4. Examine Hayakawa's use of transitions from one paragraph to another. Consider, for example, the beginnings of each of the first four paragraphs: "Professor N. R. F. Maier of the University of Michigan..." (*paragraph 1*), "Next, the rats are forced..." (*paragraph 2*), "It is the 'insolubility' of the rat's problem..." (*paragraph 3*), and "Is this an exaggerated picture?" (*paragraph*

4). What transitions can you locate following paragraph 4? Explain how these transitions lead the reader from one idea to another. What would be lost without them?

5. Observe the ways in which Hayakawa makes use of several printed sources, particularly Dr. Maier's book *Frustration: The Study of Behavior Without a Goal.* Why does Hayakawa quote Maier at the end of paragraph 1? after the first sentence in paragraph 2? How does Hayakawa indicate in paragraph 3 that he is still citing Maier? How does Hayakawa's use of Maier's book make his own statements on rat and human behavior seem more authoritative?

6. Does the information in paragraphs 4–7 come from Maier? How can you tell? If not Maier, what are the sources of this material?

7. What is the purpose of the short quotations from Korzybski and Johnson in paragraph 10?

Applications

1. Write a paper contrasting two individuals or groups who react in opposite ways to the same problem, and draw a conclusion about these different ways of reacting.

2. Write a paper in which you contrast Hayakawa's treatment of this subject to your own (or that of someone else). You might, for instance, develop the position that set patterns of behavior and responses are essential to man's survival. You may wish to research the subject and present one or more studies as part of your discussion.

Two Visions of Equal Force
Bruce Catton

In this essay, Bruce Catton, a modern historian of the Civil War, relates a haunting experience that cut a "hard groove" in his memory. He designs his essay around comparisons and contrasts between this experience and an earlier one to express a profound truth about human life.

1   We lived then in a time of great expectations. We believed in ourselves and in the future, and we welcomed all of the

omens that were good. We were not, to be sure, altogether half-witted. It is good to know that the world is not exactly what it seems to be, but to know this is to be dimly aware that it may be worse instead of better.

2   We had an acute sense of the impermanence of the present, and a haunting understanding that we were living for a time in a strange borderland between the real and the unreal, without enough knowledge of the country to tell one from the other. Yet there was something about our north country (or maybe it was something about me) that issued disquieting warnings now and then. There was the emptiness off to the north, thousands of miles of it, with the cold tang of the Ice Age in the air; to the south was the land of the Mound Builders, whose best efforts produced nothing more than unobtrusive scars on the earth; and all about us were the bleak acres of stumps, the dying towns and the desolate farms that were being given up, discards in a game where most of the players had lost. Now and again these things demanded thought.

3   There was for instance one January morning that winter when Lewis Stoneman and I went sailing on skates. I do not know whether anyone does that nowadays, but it was quite a thing at the time and we had read about it in some magazine. You took thick strips of wood and made an oblong frame, about four feet long by three feet wide, added a couple of cross braces for stiffening and for handholds, and covered the frame with a piece of discarded bed sheet cut to size. Then you went to the ice, put on your skates, held the frame in front of you, and let the wind take charge. I talked about this with Lewis, who was a student at the academy and was for some reason known as "Yutch," and it sounded like fun. We built the frames in the basement of Father's house, talked Mother into giving us a frayed old sheet, tacked pieces of it to the wood, got our skates, and one Saturday went down to Crystal Lake to see about it.

4   Skating conditions were perfect. The sun was bright, the bare ice was like polished steel, and there was a brisk wind from the east—which was fine, because we were at the eastern end of the lake and the open ice stretched away to the west for more than eight miles. We put on our skating shoes, knotted the laces of our regular shoes together and hung them about our

necks, got out on the frozen lake, held the sails in front of us, and took off.

5   The wind was strong, blowing steadily and without gusts, and it filled our sails and took us down the lake at what seemed a fabulous speed.   We had never moved so fast on skates before —had not imagined it was possible to move so fast—and it was all completely effortless.   All we had to do was stand erect, hold on to our sails, and glide away; it was like being a hawk, soaring above the length of a ridge on an updraft of air, and it felt more like flying than anything that ever happened to me, later on in life, in an airplane.

6   For the moment it was enough to be carried by the wind. The whole world had been made for our enjoyment.   The sky was unstained blue, with white clouds dropping shadows now and then to race along with us, the hills that rimmed the lake were white with snow, gray and blue with bare tree trunks, clear gold in places where the wind had blown the snow away from sandy bluffs, the sun was a friendly weight on our shoulders, the wind was blowing harder and we were going faster than ever, and there was hardly a sound anywhere.   I do not believe I have ever felt more completely in tune with the universe than I felt that morning on Crystal Lake.   It was friendly.   All of its secrets were good.

7   Then, suddenly, came awakening.   We had ridden the wind for six miles or more, and we were within about two miles of the western end of the lake; and we realized that not far ahead of us there was a broad stretch of sparkling, dazzling blue running from shore to shore, flecked with picturesque whitecaps— open water.   It was beautiful, but it carried the threat of sudden death. The lake had not been entirely frozen, after all.   Its west end was clear, and at the rate we were going we would reach the end of ice in a short time.   The lake was a good hundred feet deep there, the water was about one degree warmer than the ice itself, and the nearest land—wholly uninhabited in the dead of winter—was a mile away.   Two boys dropped into that would never get out alive.

8   There was also a change in the ice beneath us.   It was transparent, and the water below was black as a starless mid-

night; the ice had become thin, it was flexible, sagging a little under our weight, giving out ominous creakings and crackling sounds, and only the fact that we kept moving saved us from breaking through. It was high time, in short, for us to get off of that lake.

9   Yutch saw it at the same moment I did. We both pointed, and yelled, and then we made a 90-degree turn to the left and headed for the southern shore. If we had known how to use our sails properly the wind would have taken us there, but we knew nothing about that. All we could think of was to skate for the shore with all speed, and those sails were just in the way. We dropped them incontinently, and we never saw them again, and we made a grotesque race for safety, half-skating and half-running. We came at last to the packed floe ice over the shallows, galloped clumsily across it, reached the snow-covered beach, and collapsed on a log to catch our breath and talk in awed tones about our narrow escape.

10   We got home, eventually, somewhere along toward dusk. We at first thought we would skate back, but the wind was dead against us and skating into it seemed likely to be harder than walking along the shore, and besides we had had all of the lake we wanted for that day. We put on our other shoes and plodded cross-country through the snow, three miles to Frankfort, at which place, the afternoon train having left, we got a livery-stable rig to take us to Benzonia. (I am not sure Father altogether appreciated having to pay the liveryman the required two dollars; he earned his dollars the hard way, and he never had many of them. However, he paid up without a whimper.)

11   The whole business cut a hard groove in my mind. I found after a while that I did not want to talk about it. I did not even want to think about it, but I could not help myself. What I had seen through the transparent bending ice seemed to be nothing less than the heart of darkness. It was not just my own death that had been down there; it was the ultimate horror, lying below all life, kept away by something so fragile that it could break at any moment. Everything we did or dreamed or hoped for had this just beneath it. . . . One gets knotty thoughts, sometimes, at halfway house.

12   This seemed especially hard to digest because it came so soon after another—and quite different—experience that had happened that Christmas Eve.

13   By the time I was 16, the old excitement of Christmas gifts had of course worn somewhat thin, and I was ready to admit that the intense emotion centering about the tree in the living room was primarily something for small children. Still, that year as every year, I routinely went to the Christmas Eve celebration in the village church.

14   The church was filled with people. It was imperfectly lighted, and its interior seemed immense, larger than life, dominated by the great tree that reached up to the shadows just beneath the rafters, its tiny flames all twinkling. Just to be in the place was to partake of a mystery. When the wheezy organ sounded off with "Joy to the World," and the doors opened to let us out into the winter night, it was as if we heard the sound of far-off trumpets.

15   Walking home afterward was what did it. It was cold and there was plenty of snow, which creaked under our feet as we went along the road, and the silent air seemed to be echoing with the carols we had sung; and overhead, infinitely remote, yet for all of that very near and comforting, there was the endless host of golden stars whose clear flames denied the darkness. The message was unmistakable. Life was leading us— somewhere, somehow, miraculously—to a transfiguration.

16   It stayed with me. I felt that I had had a glimpse behind the veil. I had seen the ultimate truth, and that truth was good; or so, at any rate, it seemed to me at the time. But while this remembered vision still lingered, I had gone on that wind-borne cruise along the Crystal Lake ice, and at the far end of it I had seen something altogether different. Under the ice lay a flat denial of everything I had seen beyond the stars on Christmas Eve. I had had two visions, of the horror and of the transfiguration, and they seemed equally authentic.

17   They spoke with equal force. I could not accept one and discard the other. They went together; forget both or live with both. Since they were, as I then believed, unforgettable, it seemed to me that I had to adjust myself to them.

18   The worst and the best visions are true, and the ultimate

truth that embraces both is fantastically beyond comprehension. Life is a flame burning in water, shining on a sea that has no shore, and far overhead there are other flames which we call stars.

Questions on Content

1. What were the "disquieting warnings" that interfered with Catton's general optimism?
2. Describe the sails Catton and his friend made. Tell how they were used.
3. At what time of year did Catton and Yutch go skating? What conditions of the lake at that time made it good for skating?
4. How did Catton react to those conditions? How did he feel about being on the lake?
5. What was the first indication of danger? What was the condition of the ice the boys were skating on?
6. How did the boys get to shore? How did they get home? Why did they not skate back?
7. What other experience does Catton contrast with sailing on the lake? How does he see the relationship between them?
8. What conflicting visions does Catton speak of toward the end of the essay?

Questions on Invention, Design, and Style

1. How has Catton structured his two-part essay around the two "visions"? How has the account of the experience on thin ice served as a basis for designing paragraphs 3–11? the account of the experience of church and stars for paragraphs 12–15? Why does he reverse the chronological order of these two experiences?
2. How do paragraphs 1 and 2 function as an introduction to the essay? How do paragraphs 16–18 serve as a conclusion?
3. Early in the essay Catton states: "The whole world had been made for our enjoyment." Explain how this statement captures the mood of Catton and Yutch at that moment. Trace what happens to that mood as the essay progresses. What details does the author use to illustrate the boys' mood throughout paragraphs 3–11?
4. Catton's essay is unusually rich in concise comparisons. In each of the following passages, explain the images and comparisons and their meaning within the context of the essay:
   a. ". . . the dying towns and the desolate farms that were being

given up, discards in a game where most of the players had lost" (*paragraph 2*).
   b. "... it was like being a hawk, soaring above the length of a ridge on an updraft of air ..." (*paragraph 5*).
   c. "What I had seen through the transparent bending ice seemed to be nothing less than the heart of darkness ... it was the ultimate horror, lying below all life, kept away by something so fragile that it could break at any moment" (*paragraph 11*).
   d. "When the wheezy organ sounded off ... and the doors opened to let us out into the winter night, it was as if we heard the sound of far-off trumpets" (*paragraph 14*).
   e. "Life is a flame burning in water, shining on a sea that has no shore, and far overhead there are other flames which we call stars" (*paragraph 18*).
5. In his four final paragraphs, Catton makes considerable use of visual images and metaphors to help carry his meaning. Discuss the images and metaphors he employs.

Applications

1. Write about an experience that has cut "a hard groove" in your memory and changed the way you look at life. Contrast this new view to the one you had before.
2. Recall a time when you felt that the "whole world had been made for [your] enjoyment." Write a paper in which you relate your mood to your physical surroundings, and contrast that mood to one you have had during a very different experience.

Complex Comparison and Contrast

Demanding and complex subjects
Complexity of purpose and form
Use of part-by-part structure in complex comparison and contrast

The basic differences between complex comparison and contrast and the simple and extended types introduced previously arise from the nature of the writer's subject and from his or her uses of the similarities and differences perceived. The subject is larger, has more parts, and places greater demands upon the writer; the writer, on the other hand, explores both the similarities and differences of his subject, pursues the implications of the relations farther, and transcends the formality of a subject-by-subject or part-by-part design in drawing comparisons and contrasts. A simple analogy may help to suggest how and why these differences occur. The ice-skating events at the Olympic games are divided into two parts: *compulsory* and *free-style* events. In the compulsory part, skaters are expected to demonstrate mastery of the basic forms of ice skating. In the free-style events they go beyond these basic forms to demonstrate their creativity and originality. The two kinds of ability are not mutually exclusive. Quite the opposite is true: The skater must first have mastered the compulsory skills to be capable of effective participation in the free-style event.

In a similar way, a writer who has learned to write simple and extended comparisons and contrasts is capable of moving beyond these forms when the subject and purpose require more extensive exploration of similarities and differences, as Rollo May and E. B. White have done in the essays included in this section. Complex comparison and contrast thus make it possible to probe relationships to such a depth that subjects like going home or a trip to a spot remembered from childhood take on meanings that we have probably not considered before.   Or the relations between love and death or North and South can be treated in such original ways that we are moved to new understanding.   Writers like May and White have transcended the fundamental subject-by-subject and part-by-part designs and have entered fully into the free-style process.   In doing so, they have placed greater demands on their readers, as well as on themselves; but most perceptive and intelligent readers will agree that the rewards are worth the effort expended.

A typical example of complexity of purpose and form may be seen in the following excerpt, by Richard Hauer Costa, in which the writer contrasts an old spinster's world with the world of commercial progress:

> The quiet sixty-five year old Caroline Bullock's upbringing on a farm in Upstate New York gave her little spiritual preparation for man-made marvels like the Arterial Freeway; little insulation for accepting that a great highway could knock off a piece of the street where she lived and swallow up her property—her house and, more important to a person like Miss Caroline, her Hawaiian orchids, African violets, and other brightly-flowering plants.   A man from the State just knocked on the door one day and told Miss Caroline that her land was being appropriated.
>
> "You sell it to us and your house will be moved back out of the path of the Arterial Freeway," the man said.   The Arterial went through.   The bulldozers put an end to the carefully nurtured green things, and the house was moved back out of the way of progress.[1]

Costa's purpose, though, is larger than just to contrast the world of Miss Caroline and the world of commerce.   He aims to explain the conflict between the spinster's own sense of what is important and the pressure of commercial notions of progress.   Furthermore, he uses suggestion to make the point that not all that is called "progress" is necessarily better.

Another example of complex comparison and contrast is Joan Didion's "On Going Home."   Her subject is a large one, taking

---

[1] From "Miss Caroline" by Richard Hauer Costa.

up such interrelated topics as the relationship between city and country, past and present, husband and wife, and parent and child. To do justice to this subject she explores the similarities and differences between her home in the city and her parents' home in the country, between her present life and an earlier one, between her own childhood and the one that lies before her daughter. The result is an essay that reflects the complexity of human experience itself and shows the writer's inventiveness in observing, reflecting, and ordering her subject. The design of the essay reflects its complexity. Rather than relying on any set pattern of comparison and contrast, Didion speaks of her husband's and her own lives and backgrounds quickly and then moves on to her daughter's different beginnings and possible future.

As you study the other three essays in this section, notice the demands the subject makes on each writer and his or her commitment and involvement in it. Note, too, each writer's inventiveness in discovering and exploring his or her subject and the complexity of the design that he or she has followed.

North and South
Willie Morris

After returning to the South to visit his dying grandmother, editor and essayist Willie Morris contrasts life in the North, where he and his son now live, to life in the region where he grew up. Morris suggests differences beyond those he directly states, in a series of interrelated scenes that show contrasting attitudes based on history, region, and age.

1   The last time I had been there, I had gone to see my grandmother, whom I call Mamie. She is ninety-five years old, the youngest of sixteen children and the only one of them still alive. My mother, who lives alone with her now, telephoned me in New York to say that Mamie had just had a stroke and I should come right away; it might be my last time to see her.

2   Her great-great-uncle had been the first territorial governor

of Mississippi, before it was admitted to the Union, and her people had settled the state when it was still called "the Southwest." Another uncle had been the United States senator through the 1840s, had given the dedication address at the Washington Monument, and had defeated his blood enemy Jefferson Davis for governor in 1851; all over the South before the final break, he defended "the good old Union, the fruit of the sage counsels of our immortal ancestors." Her father had been a Confederate major and a newspaper editor; an obscure and unidentified Federal captain, under direct orders from Sherman, had deposited his printing presses in a well when his troops marched through his little town, Raymond, on the way to Jackson, which was considerably larger game. She was born not long after the Federal soldiers pulled out of Mississippi. In the old family burial plot, the only recognizable grave now is her eldest brother's; she must be one of the few living people with a sibling who was born in 1851.

3   Time weaves its small eccentric ironies on us, its children. Are we really much removed from then? A great-uncle of William Styron, my Virginia friend now living in the East, was the state treasurer when my great-uncle was governor. My great-grandfather was a leader of the Mississippi legislative committee that impeached the Republican Reconstructionist governor, a proper New Englander named Adelbert Ames, the great-grandfather of my friend George Plimpton.

4   Now Mamie lies in the back room of the house where I grew up in Yazoo. She is completely blind and almost completely deaf. Some of the time she is with us here in the present, as lucid and full of good humors as she was when I was a boy and loved her more deeply than I loved anyone else; but mostly she inhabits an old woman's whirling misty shadows and premonitions, mistaking me for her brother Samuel Dawson Harper, who has been dead sixty years, talking with the spirits of her vanished sisters when they were children in Raymond, asking my grandfather Percy if he wants his chicken fried or broiled for supper in the tiny brick house across from the Jitney Jungle on North Jefferson Street in Jackson. Sometimes she thinks my son David is me.

5   I have brought David with me on this trip. I want him to

have the chance to remember her.   He is a New York City boy. He is ten years old, and he has been riding the subways alone for three years, loving the noise and speed of those subterranean phenomena which for his father are only dark and brutal monstrosities.   Occasionally he makes fun of my Southern accent, though he asks me more and more as he gets older about where his people came from.   For a present three years ago, he typed away secretly for two days on my typewriter and later came out with a framed copy of the Gettysburg Address, done with his own fine Yankee hand.   It had its share of typos, and it began, "Dear Daddy—The Gettyburg: Four score and seeven year ago . . ." and concluded, "The Ent—Love, David."   I took him to Gettysburg after that, showing him Cemetery Ridge, Big Round Top and Little Round Top, the Wheat Field, Seminary Ridge, and the rounded green valley where on the afternoon of July 3, 1863, the idea that we were to become, after all, a mass multiracial democracy may have been decided, among American boys tearing each other to death with canister, bayonets, rifle butts, and big old stones.   He wanted a present for himself, and when I took him into a store close to where Longstreet had set up his artillery, he decided, among all the modern artifacts of what happened there, on a gray infantry hat.   While I was paying the clerk, $1.75 plus three cents Pennsylvania sales tax, I noticed he was pondering the gray hat, finally putting it back in place and taking a blue one instead, which he calmly put on his head.   When we got in the car, I said nothing for a few minutes.   The road we were driving traced the line of Lee's great retreat, and the sun's late-summer glow caught the monuments and the cannon in the splendid battlefield tableau that fills every Southern boy's heart with a wonderful dread and excitement.   Finally I said, "Why did you pick the blue hat instead of the gray one?"   He replied, "Because I don't want to be nobody's slave."

6   We had driven now the forty-eight miles from Jackson in a rented car, across the hills in autumn with their dead kudzu,[1] and we reached the town after dark.   I had timed it deliberately, because we were leaving again the next morning, and for sev-

---

[1] A vine grown as food for domestic animals.

eral quite good reasons I did not want anyone to know I was home. My mother was there, and Mamie sat up in the bed and reached out to embrace us. I had forgotten my own fears as a child of sick old people, fears of their smells, of their tenacity and irascible durability, and the boy went away for a while, to look at the various mementos in my old room, the trinkets and souvenirs of my small-town pubescence. Viola was there too— the Negro woman almost as old as my grandmother, frail and very gray now but still quite healthy, who had worked for the family for more than a generation, had slept and lived in the house during its times of crisis, who had come to know us in our several disasters of the flesh, and who now sat in a chair several hours every day next to the bed. She was a sturdy physical presence in this place of decay, and even though three others of us were here in the room with her, Mamie would extend her hand every so often, stretch out her entire gnarled and skinny old arm, and cry, *"Viola! Viola! Where's Viola?"* "I'm right here, honey," Viola would say, taking her hand and stroking it, carrying on a steady torrential half-monologue all the while. This scene, my mother said to me, took place all day long. A few days later, at a fine sophisticated dinner party given by friends on the Upper East Side, I described what I had seen. A well-known New York writer said, "That's the most racist description I've ever heard." And the writer's wife added, "It's a racist description of a corrupt and racist society."

Questions on Content

1. Describe briefly Mamie's family background.
2. Describe Mamie's physical and mental condition. What is her age?
3. What examples does Morris give of David's northern orientation and attitudes? How do these attitudes differ from Morris' own?
4. Why did Morris want to arrive in Yazoo City after dark?
5. Describe in your own words the relationship between Mamie and Viola.
6. How do the New York writer and his wife react to the scene between Mamie and Viola? What is Morris' reaction to the same scene? How can you tell?

Questions on Invention, Design, and Style

1. Consider how paragraph 1 introduces the essay. How does the author gain your interest? What does he tell about Mamie that is essential to your understanding of the essay?
2. Morris uses paragraphs 2 and 3 to tell of Mamie's (and his own) ancestors, and he refers to other relatives in paragraph 4. How does he tie his ancestors and the past to the scene with Mamie and Viola in paragraph 6? How does he show similarities and shared associations between the two women?
3. In paragraph 5, what northern attitudes toward southerners are revealed in Morris' son? How do they resemble those of the New York writer and his wife in the last three sentences of paragraph 6?
4. After careful transitions between events earlier in the essay, what is the effect in paragraph 6 of the abrupt change of scene from Mamie and Viola to the New York writer and his wife? How does Morris' own experience contrast with the New York woman's comment?
5. Exactly how does Morris succeed in contrasting past and present, old and young, South and North in this essay?

Applications

1. Contrast two different neighborhoods, cities, or regions you have known on the bases of physical settings, people, and their attitudes.
2. Recall a conversation in which another person's comment indicated a basic misunderstanding of the point you were trying to make. Write an account of the conversation with yourself as the narrator, and make clear the contrast between what you meant and what the other person understood you to mean.

On Going Home
Joan Didion

In this essay contemporary novelist Joan Didion draws a contrast between her life with her parents and her life today and between her

husband's life style and associations and those of her own family. The result is a moving account of returning home.

1   I am home for my daughter's first birthday. By "home" I do not mean the house in Los Angeles where my husband and I and the baby live, but the place where my family is, in the Central Valley of California. It is a vital although troublesome distinction. My husband likes my family but is uneasy in their house, because once there I fall into their ways, which are difficult, oblique, deliberately inarticulate, not my husband's ways. We live in dusty houses ("D-U-S-T," he once wrote with his finger on surfaces all over the house, but no one noticed it) filled with mementos quite without value to him (what could the Canton dessert plates mean to him? how could he have known about the assay scales, why should he care if he did know?), and we appear to talk exclusively about people we know who have been committed to mental hospitals, about people we know who have been booked on drunk-driving charges, and about property, particularly about property, land, price per acre and C-2 zoning and assessments and freeway access. My brother does not understand my husband's inability to perceive the advantage in the rather common real-estate transaction known as "sale-leaseback," and my husband in turn does not understand why so many of the people he hears about in my father's house have recently been committed to mental hospitals or booked on drunk-driving charges. Nor does he understand that when we talk about sale-leasebacks and right-of-way condemnations we are talking in code about the things we like best, the yellow fields and the cottonwoods and the rivers rising and falling and the mountain roads closing when the heavy snow comes in. We miss each other's points, have another drink and regard the fire. My brother refers to my husband, in his presence, as "Joan's husband." Marriage is the classic betrayal.

2   Or perhaps it is not any more. Sometimes I think that those of us who are now in our thirties were born into the last generation to carry the burden of "home," to find in family life the source of all tension and drama. I had by all objective accounts a "normal" and a "happy" family situation, and yet I was almost thirty years old before I could talk to my family on the

telephone without crying after I had hung up. We did not fight. Nothing was wrong. And yet some nameless anxiety colored the emotional charges between me and the place that I came from. The question of whether or not you could go home again was a very real part of the sentimental and largely literary baggage with which we left home in the fifties; I suspect that it is irrelevant to the children born of the fragmentation after World War II. A few weeks ago in a San Francisco bar I saw a pretty young girl on crystal take off her clothes and dance for the cash prize in an "amateur-topless" contest. There was no particular sense of moment about this, none of the effect of romantic degradation, of "dark journey," for which my generation strived so assiduously. . . .

3   That I am trapped in this particular irrelevancy is never more apparent to me than when I am home. Paralyzed by the neurotic lassitude engendered by meeting one's past at every turn, around every corner, inside every cupboard, I go aimlessly from room to room. I decide to meet it head-on and clean out a drawer, and I spread the contents on the bed. A bathing suit I wore the summer I was seventeen. A letter of rejection from *The Nation,* an aerial photograph of the site for a shopping center my father did not build in 1954. Three teacups hand-painted with cabbage roses and signed "E. M.," my grandmother's initials. There is no final solution for letters of rejection from *The Nation* and teacups hand-painted in 1900. Nor is there any answer to snapshots of one's grandfather as a young man on skis, surveying around Donner Pass[1] in the year 1910. I smooth out the snapshot and look into his face, and do and do not see my own. I close the drawer, and have another cup of coffee with my mother. We get along very well, veterans of a guerrilla war we never understood.

4   Days pass. I see no one. I come to dread my husband's evening call, not only because he is full of news of what by now seems to me our remote life in Los Angeles, people he has seen, letters which require attention, but because he asks what I have

---

[1] A pass high in the Sierras of northeast California where the Donner party of settlers was caught by an early blizzard in 1846 and forced to spend the winter. Only forty-five of the seventy-nine survived.

been doing, suggests uneasily that I get out, drive to San Francisco or Berkeley. Instead I drive across the river to a family graveyard. It has been vandalized since my last visit and the monuments are broken, overturned in the dry grass. Because I once saw a rattlesnake in the grass I stay in the car and listen to a country-and-Western station. Later I drive with my father to a ranch he has in the foothills. The man who runs his cattle on it asks us to the roundup, a week from Sunday, and although I know that I will be in Los Angeles I say, in the oblique way my family talks, that I will come. Once home I mention the broken monuments in the graveyard. My mother shrugs.

5   I go to visit my great-aunts. A few of them think now that I am my cousin, or their daughter who died young. We recall an anecdote about a relative last seen in 1948, and they ask if I still like living in New York City. I have lived in Los Angeles for three years, but I say that I do. The baby is offered a horehound drop, and I am slipped a dollar bill "to buy a treat." Questions trail off, answers are abandoned, the baby plays with the dust motes in a shaft of afternoon sun.

6   It is time for the baby's birthday party: a white cake, strawberry-marshmallow ice cream, a bottle of champagne saved from another party. In the evening, after she has gone to sleep, I kneel beside the crib and touch her face, where it is pressed against the slats, with mine. She is an open and trusting child, unprepared for and unaccustomed to the ambushes of family life, and perhaps it is just as well that I can offer her little of that life. I would like to give her more. I would like to promise her that she will grow up with a sense of her cousins and of rivers and of her great-grandmother's teacups, would like to pledge her a picnic on a river with fried chicken and her hair uncombed, would like to give her *home* for her birthday, but we live differently now and I can promise her nothing like that. I give her a xylophone and a sundress from Madeira, and promise to tell her a funny story.

Questions on Content

1. Why is Didion at her parents' home? Describe her parents and their home. What are the favorite topics of conversation?

2. What things can Didion's husband and brother not understand about each other? What does the brother call her husband?
3. Why does Didion begin after several days to dread her husband's evening phone calls?
4. What is the "particular irrelevancy" Didion speaks of in paragraph 3?
5. How do her great-aunts react to her and to the baby?
6. What does she wish for her daughter? What would she most like to give her for her birthday?
7. What conclusion does Didion come to in the final paragraph? How does she resolve the dilemma between what she wants to give her daughter and what is possible to give her?

Questions on Invention, Design, and Style

1. Didion often presents a series of impressions, rather than a direct statement of an emotional state or a frame of mind.
   a. "We did not fight. Nothing was wrong. And yet some nameless anxiety colored the emotional charges between me and the place that I came from" (*paragraph 2*).
   b. "I smooth out the snapshot and look into [my grandfather's] face, and do and do not see my own. I close the drawer, and have another cup of coffee with my mother" (*paragraph 3*).
   c. "Although I know that I will be in Los Angeles I say, in the oblique way my family talks, that I will come. Once home I mention the broken monuments in the graveyard. My mother shrugs" (*paragraph 4*).
   d. "I would like to promise her that she will grow up with a sense of her cousins and of rivers and of her great-grandmother's teacups, would like to pledge her a picnic on a river with fried chicken and her hair uncombed, would like to give her *home* for her birthday, but we live differently now and I can promise her nothing like that" (*paragraph 6*).
   Analyze each of these impressions to discover why the technique is effective. How do these impressions provide a basis for the design or structure of the essay?
2. How does the first paragraph introduce the contrast between Didion's upbringing and her state of mind while visiting her family? What is achieved by the focusing upon the difference between Didion and her daughter in the final paragraph?
3. Analyze the ways in which Didion's contrasts support the impres-

sionistic quality of her essay.   Focus on specific contrasts in your explanation.

4.   Describe Joan Didion as she is revealed in this essay.   Is she an emotional person?   What does she care about?   Does she have conflicting feelings?   What questions of values concern her?

5.   Didion says *(paragraph 2):* "Sometimes I think that those of us who are now in our thirties were born into the last generation to carry the burden of 'home,' to find in family life the source of all tension and drama."   Viewing the essay as a whole, what do you think her attitude is toward this "burden of home"?   Does she resent it? accept it?   How can you tell?

Applications

1.   Write a paper based on your own experience of going home, perhaps one of the first times you returned home after being away at work or school.   Develop a contrast between the way home was in the past and the way it is now or was during the return home.

2.   Return to a once-familiar setting—a playground at school or a house or neighborhood where you used to live, for instance. Write an essay contrasting the way it is now to the way you remember it.

Love and Death
Rollo May

In this essay contemporary psychologist Rollo May explores the nature of love as a human experience by comparing and contrasting its two opposing poles, joy and death.

1   To love means to open ourselves to the negative as well as the positive—to grief, sorrow, and disappointment as well as to joy, fulfillment, and an intensity of consciousness we did not know was possible before. . . .

2   When we "fall" in love, as the expressive verb puts it, the world shakes and changes around us, not only in the way it looks but in our whole experience of what we are doing in the world.   Generally, the shaking is consciously felt in its positive aspects—as the wonderful new heaven and earth which love with its miracle and mystery has suddenly produced.   Love is

the answer, we sing. Aside from the banality of such reassur-
ances, our Western culture seems to be engaged in a romantic—
albeit desperate—conspiracy to enforce the illusion that that is
all there is to eros. The very strength of the effort to support
that illusion betrays the presence of the repressed, opposing
pole.

3   This opposing element is the consciousness of death. For
death is always in the shadow of the delight of love. In faint
adumbration there is present the dread, haunting question, Will
this new relationship destroy us? When we love, we give up the
center of ourselves. We are thrown from our previous state of
existence into a void; and though we hope to attain a new world,
a new existence, we can never be sure. Nothing looks the
same, and may well never look the same again. The world is
annihilated; how can we know whether it will ever be built up
again? We give, and give *up*, our own center; how shall we
know that we will get it back? We wake up to find the whole
world shaking: where or when will it come to rest?

4   The most excruciating joy is accompanied by the consciousness of the imminence of death—and with the same intensity. And it seems that one is not possible without the other.

5   This experience of annihilation is an inward one and, as
the myth[1] rightly puts it, is essentially what *eros* does to us.
It is not simply what the other person does to us. To love completely carries with it the threat of the annihilation of everything. This intensity of consciousness has something in common with the ecstasy of the mystic in his union with God: just
as he can never be *sure* God is there, so love carries us to that
intensity of consciousness in which we no longer have any
guarantee of security.

6   This razor's edge, this dizzy balance of anxiety and joy, has
much to do with the exciting quality of love. The dread joy is
not just the question of whether the love will be returned in
kind. Indeed, the real dialectic is within the person himself
and the anxiety is not essentially quieted if the loved one *does*

---

[1] May refers here and elsewhere in this essay to the early Greek myth of Eros,
the creator of life, delight, and passion. In the myth Eros is both creative and
destructive—capable of causing love but also of "break[ing] the limb's
strength" in gods and human beings.

respond.   Paradoxically, the lover is sometimes *more* anxious when the love is returned than when not.   For if one loves unrequitedly, which is even an aim in some love writing, or from a safe distance, like Dante and the whole Stylist movement in Italian literature, he can at least go on about his customary daily tasks, writing his *Divine Comedy* or his sonnets or novels.   It is when the love *is* realized that eros may literally "break the limb's strength," as with Antony and Cleopatra, or Paris and Helen, or Héloïse and Abelard.   Hence, human beings are afraid of love.   And, all the saccharine books to the contrary, there is reason to be afraid.

7   In common human experience, this relationship between death and love is perhaps most clear to people when they have children.   A man may have thought very little about death—and prided himself on his "bravery"—until he becomes a father.   Then he finds in his love for his child an experience of vulnerability to death: the Cruel Imposter can at any time take away the child, the object of his love.   In this sense love is an experience of greater vulnerability.

8   Love is also a reminder of our own mortality.   When a friend or member of our family dies, we are vividly impressed by the fact that life is evanescent and irretrievable.   But there is also a deeper sense of its meaningful possibilities and an impetus to risk ourselves in taking the leap.   Some—perhaps most—human beings never know deep love until they experience, at someone's death, the preciousness of friendship, devotion, loyalty.   Abraham Maslow is profoundly right when he wonders whether we could love passionately if we knew we'd never die.

9   This is one of the reasons, mythologically speaking, why the love affairs among the immortal gods on Mt. Olympus are so insipid and boring.   The loves of Zeus and Juno are completely uninteresting until they involve a mortal.   Love has the power to change the course of history only when Zeus comes down to Leda or Io and falls in love with this mortal woman who can yearn to have a child because she knows she will not live forever.   *Love is not only enriched by our sense of mortality but constituted by it.*   Love is the cross-fertilization of mortality and immortality.   This is why the daimon Eros is described as

midway between gods and men and partakes of the nature of both.

10   I have been speaking, to some degree, in ideal terms. I am fully aware that this degree of involvement will be called neurotic by many of my colleagues. This is the day of "cool" relationships—one should never become involved to a degree which prevents his moving out at any moment! But I submit that this involvement is neurotic only if "frozen," or fixated; only if the partners demand that they live always on this level. While none of us lives on the level I am describing for very long, it remains a kind of backdrop, an ideal situation which ought to be somewhere in the relation lending meaning to the drab and dull days which also come.

11   The relation between death and love has an impressive history in literature. In Italian writing, there was the frequent play upon the words *amore*, love, with *morte*, death. The connection also has its biological analogies in nature. The male bee dies after inseminating the Queen. More vivid is the case of the praying mantis: the female bites off the head of the male as he copulates, and his death throes unite with his copulatory spasms to make the thrusts stronger. Inseminated, the female proceeds to eat him to store up food for the new offspring.

12   Freud associated this threat of death with the depletion of Eros.

> This accounts for the likeness of the condition of that following complete sexual satisfaction to dying, and for the fact that death coincides with the act of copulation in lower animals. These creatures die in the act of reproduction because, after Eros has been eliminated through the process of satisfaction, the death instinct has a free hand for accomplishing its purpose.

My viewpoint is that, in human beings, it is not merely the depletion of eros which causes the fear of death—or, as I call it above, the experience of mortality—but that in all stages of human development the experiences of love and death are interwoven.

13   The relationship between death and love is surely clear in the sex act. Every kind of mythology relates the sex act itself

to dying, and every therapist comes to see the relationship ever more clearly through his patients.   A patient, whose problem was sexual frigidity and who had never experienced an orgasm in intercourse, told me of a dream which dramatically illustrates this sex and death theme.   In her dream, she experienced herself for the first time in her own identity as a woman.   Then, still in the dream, she had the strange conviction that she would have to jump into the river and drown.   The dream ended in great anxiety.   That night, in sexual intercourse, she had an orgasm for the first time.   The capacity for surrender, for giving one's self up, must exist in love-making if there is to be the spontaneity required for orgasm.

14   Something very basic had taken place in this woman's dream—the capacity to confront death, a capacity which is a prerequisite to growth, a prerequisite to self-consciousness.   I take the orgasm here as a psychophysical symbol of the capacity to abandon one's self, to give up present security in favor of the leap toward deeper experience.   It is not by accident that the orgasm often appears symbolically as death and rebirth.   The myth of going under water, of being drowned and born again has been passed down through history in different religions and different cultures as the myth of *baptism*—the being immersed in the river to be drowned, to die, in order to be born again.   This is a daring to leap into non-being with the prospect of achieving new being.

· · ·

15   What a different light this throws on the human problems in love than all our glib talk about the art of loving, about love as the answer to all our needs, love as instant self-actualization, love as contentment, or love as a mail-order technique!   No wonder we try to reduce eros to purely physiological sex or try to avoid the whole dilemma by playing it cool, by using sex to drug and vaccinate ourselves against the anxiety-creating effects of eros.

16   It is possible to have sexual intercourse without any particular anxiety.   But by doing this in casual encounters, we shut out, by definition, our eros—that is, we relinquish passion in favor of mere sensation; we shut out our participation in the imaginative, personal significance of the act.   If we can have

sex without love, we assume that we escape the daimonic anxiety known throughout the ages as an inseparable part of human love.   And if, further, we even use sexual activity itself as an escape from the commitments eros demands of us, we may hope to have thus gained an airtight defense against anxiety.   And the motive for sex, no longer being sensual pleasure or passion, becomes displaced by the artificial one of providing identity and gaining security; and sex has been reduced to an anxiety-allaying strategy.   Thus we set the stage for the development of impotence and affectlessness later on.

Questions on Content

1. How has Western culture conspired to mislead us about the meaning of love, according to May?
2. What are the opposing poles within love?   In what way is the negative "always in the shadow of the delight of love"?
3. Why might a love that is returned produce more anxiety than one that is not?
4. How might having a child enable a person to know love as "an experience of greater vulnerability"?
5. Why are the love affairs among the gods on Mt. Olympus so boring?   In what way does love consist of our sense of mortality, according to May?   What point is he making through references to Zeus and Leda or Io?
6. In what sense does May admit that the degree of involvement he speaks of could be neurotic?   How does this involvement function properly?
7. What biological examples of the relation between death and love does May cite?
8. What significance does May find in his patient's dream of having to jump into a river and drown?
9. What are the dangers, according to May, of having sex without love? of reducing sex to an "anxiety-allaying strategy"?

Questions on Invention, Design, and Style

1. Analyze the comparisons and contrasts May develops in each of the following, and tell how each supports his thesis that "love means to open ourselves to the negative as well as the positive—to grief . . . as well as to joy . . ."
   a. "This intensity of consciousness has something in common

with the ecstasy of the mystic in his union with God: just as he can never be *sure* God is there, so love carries us to that intensity of consciousness in which we no longer have any guarantee of security" (*paragraph 5*).

b. "When a friend or member of our family dies, we are vividly impressed by the fact that life is evanescent and irretrievable. But there is also a deeper sense of its meaningful possibilities and an impetus to risk ourselves in taking the leap" (*paragraph 8*).

c. "... the love affairs among the immortal gods on Mt. Olympus are ... insipid and boring ... until they involve a mortal" (*paragraph 9*).

d. "The connection also has its biological analogies in nature. The male bee dies after inseminating the Queen. More vivid is the case of the praying mantis: the female bites off the head of the male as he copulates, and his death throes unite with his copulatory spasms to make the thrusts stronger" (*paragraph 11*).

2. In what ways is the comparison May develops between the myth of Eros and mortal love essential to his thesis?

3. May draws upon a wide variety of sources, including his professional and personal experiences, for his illustrations, comparisons, and contrasts. What are these sources?

4. What is the effect of May's use of "we" and "us" in this essay, beginning with paragraphs 1–3? Why does he shift to "I" in paragraph 10?

Applications

1. Assume for the purposes of this assignment that *hate* is the opposite of *love*. With May's definition of love in paragraph 1 as a background, define hate. Then write an essay giving illustrations and drawing comparisons and contrasts to clarify your definition.

2. Observe, recall, or imagine someone whose inhibited behavior convinces you it masks something this person must keep under control. Write an essay comparing and contrasting these two sides of the person.

3. Write an essay describing a relationship you have had that involved considerable risk. Tell how you were able or unable to take that risk. Use comparison and contrast to illustrate your awareness of the dilemma you were in.

Once More to the Lake (August 1941)
E. B. White

Returning with his son to a lake he knew as a boy, essayist E. B. White experiences the illusion that time does not exist—that his son is the boy he once was and that he is now the man his father was. Through these comparisons, White heightens our understanding of the process of growing up, the relationship between parent and child, and the fact that time does not stand still.

1   One summer, along about 1904, my father rented a camp on a lake in Maine and took us all there for the month of August. We all got ringworm from some kittens and had to rub Pond's Extract on our arms and legs night and morning, and my father rolled over in a canoe with all his clothes on; but outside of that the vacation was a success and from then on none of us ever thought there was any place in the world like that lake in Maine. We returned summer after summer—always on August 1st for one month. I have since become a salt-water man, but sometimes in summer there are days when the restlessness of the tides and the fearful cold of the sea water and the incessant wind which blows across the afternoon and into the evening make me wish for the placidity of a lake in the woods. A few weeks ago this feeling got so strong I bought myself a couple of bass hooks and a spinner and returned to the lake where we used to go, for a week's fishing and to revisit old haunts.

2   I took along my son, who had never had any fresh water up his nose and who had seen lily pads only from train windows. On the journey over to the lake I began to wonder what it would be like. I wondered how time would have marred this unique, this holy spot—the coves and streams, the hills that the sun set behind, the camps and the paths behind the camps. I was sure the tarred road would have found it out and I wondered in what other ways it would be desolated. It is strange how much you can remember about places like that once you allow your mind to return into the grooves which lead back. You remember one thing, and that suddenly reminds you of another thing. I guess I remembered clearest of all the early mornings, when the lake was cool and motionless, remembered how the bedroom

smelled of the lumber it was made of and of the wet woods whose scent entered through the screen. The partitions in the camp were thin and did not extend clear to the top of the rooms, and as I was always the first up I would dress softly so as not to wake the others, and sneak out into the sweet outdoors and start out in the canoe, keeping close along the shore in the long shadows of the pines. I remembered being very careful never to rub my paddle against the gunwale for fear of disturbing the stillness of the cathedral.

3   The lake had never been what you would call a wild lake. There were cottages sprinkled around the shores, and it was in farming country although the shores of the lake were quite heavily wooded. Some of the cottages were owned by nearby farmers, and you would live at the shore and eat your meals at the farmhouse. That's what our family did. But although it wasn't wild, it was a fairly large and undisturbed lake and there were places in it which, to a child at least, seemed infinitely remote and primeval.

4   I was right about the tar: it led to within half a mile of the shore. But when I got back there, with my boy, and we settled into a camp near a farmhouse and into the kind of summertime I had known, I could tell that it was going to be pretty much the same as it had been before—I knew it, lying in bed the first morning, smelling the bedroom, and hearing the boy sneak quietly out and go off along the shore in a boat. I began to sustain the illusion that he was I, and therefore by simple transposition, that I was my father. This sensation persisted, kept cropping up all the time we were there. It was not an entirely new feeling, but in this setting it grew much stronger. I seemed to be living a dual existence. I would be in the middle of some simple act, I would be picking up a bait box or laying down a table fork, or I would be saying something, and suddenly it would be not I but my father who was saying the words or making the gesture. It gave me a creepy sensation.

5   We went fishing the first morning. I felt the same damp moss covering the worms in the bait can, and saw the dragonfly alight on the tip of my rod as it hovered a few inches from the surface of the water. It was the arrival of this fly that convinced me beyond any doubt that everything was as it always had been,

that the years were a mirage and there had been no years.   The small waves were the same, chucking the rowboat under the chin as we fished at anchor, and the boat was the same boat, the same color green and the ribs broken in the same places, and under the floor-boards the same fresh-water leavings and débris —the dead helgramite,[1] the wisps of moss, the rusty discarded fishhook, the dried blood from yesterday's catch.   We stared silently at the tips of our rods, at the dragonflies that came and went.   I lowered the tip of mine into the water, tentatively, pensively dislodging the fly, which darted two feet away, poised, darted two feet back, and came to rest again a little farther up the rod.   There had been no years between the ducking of this dragonfly and the other one—the one that was part of memory. I looked at the boy, who was silently watching his fly, and it was my hands that held his rod, my eyes watching.   I felt dizzy and didn't know which rod I was at the end of.

6   We caught two bass, hauling them in briskly as though they were mackerel, pulling them over the side of the boat in a businesslike manner without any landing net, and stunning them with a blow on the back of the head.   When we got back for a swim before lunch, the lake was exactly where we had left it, the same number of inches from the dock, and there was only the merest suggestion of a breeze.   This seemed an utterly enchanted sea, this lake you could leave to its own devices for a few hours and come back to, and find that it had not stirred, this constant and trustworthy body of water.   In the shallows, the dark, water-soaked sticks and twigs, smooth and old, were undulating in clusters on the bottom against the clean ribbed sand, and the track of the mussel was plain.   A school of minnows swam by, each minnow with its small individual shadow, doubling the attendance, so clear and sharp in the sunlight. Some of the other campers were in swimming, along the shore, one of them with a cake of soap, and the water felt thin and clear and unsubstantial.   Over the years there had been this person with the cake of soap, this cultist, and here he was.   There had been no years.

7   Up to the farmhouse to dinner through the teeming, dusty

---

[1] Insect used for bait.

field, the road under our sneakers was only a two-track road.
The middle track was missing, the one with the marks of the
hooves and the splotches of dried, flaky manure. There had always been three tracks to choose from in choosing which track
to walk in; now the choice was narrowed down to two. For a
moment I missed terribly the middle alternative. But the way
led past the tennis court, and something about the way it lay
there in the sun reassured me; the tape had loosened along the
backline, the alleys were green with plantains and other weeds,
and the net (installed in June and removed in September)
sagged in the dry noon, and the whole place steamed with mid-
day heat and hunger and emptiness. There was a choice of pie
for dessert, and one was blueberry and one was apple, and the
waitresses were the same country girls, there having been no
passage of time, only the illusion of it as in a dropped curtain—
the waitresses were still fifteen; their hair had been washed,
that was the only difference—they had been to the movies and
seen the pretty girls with the clean hair.

8   Summertime, oh summertime, pattern of life indelible, the
fade-proof lake, the woods unshatterable, the pasture with the
sweetfern and the juniper forever and ever, summer without
end; this was the background, and the life along the shore was
the design, the cottages with their innocent and tranquil design,
their tiny docks with the flagpole and the American flag floating against the white clouds in the blue sky, the little paths over
the roots of the trees leading from camp to camp and the paths
leading back to the outhouses and the can of lime for sprin-
kling, and at the souvenir counters at the store the miniature
birch-bark canoes and the post cards that showed things looking a little better than they looked. This was the American
family at play, escaping the city heat, wondering whether the
newcomers in the camp at the head of the cove were "common"
or "nice," wondering whether it was true that the people who
drove up for Sunday dinner at the farmhouse were turned away
because there wasn't enough chicken.

9   It seemed to me, as I kept remembering all this, that those
times and those summers had been infinitely precious and
worth saving. There had been jollity and peace and goodness.
The arriving (at the beginning of August) had been so big a

business in itself, at the railway station the farm wagon drawn
up, the first smell of the pine-laden air, the first glimpse of the
smiling farmer, and the great importance of the trunks and your
father's enormous authority in such matters, and the feel of the
wagon under you for the long ten-mile haul, and at the top of
the last long hill catching the first view of the lake after eleven
months of not seeing this cherished body of water. The shouts
and cries of the other campers when they saw you, and the
trunks to be unpacked, to give up their rich burden. (Arriving
was less exciting nowadays, when you sneaked up in your car
and parked it under a tree near the camp and took out the bags
and in five minutes it was all over, no fuss, no loud wonderful
fuss about trunks.)

10   Peace and goodness and jollity. The only thing that was
wrong now, really, was the sound of the place, an unfamiliar
nervous sound of the outboard motors. This was the note that
jarred, the one thing that would sometimes break the illusion
and set the years moving. In those other summertimes all motors were inboard; and when they were at a little distance, the
noise they made was a sedative, an ingredient of summer
sleep. They were one-cylinder and two-cylinder engines, and
some were make-and-break and some were jump-spark,[2] but
they all made a sleepy sound across the lake. The one-lungers
throbbed and fluttered, and the twin-cylinder ones purred and
purred, and that was a quiet sound too. But now the campers
all had outboards. In the daytime, in the hot mornings, these
motors made a petulant, irritable sound; at night, in the still
evening when the afterglow lit the water, they whined about
one's ears like mosquitoes. My boy loved our rented outboard,
and his great desire was to achieve singlehanded mastery over
it, and authority, and he soon learned the trick of choking it a
little (but not too much), and the adjustment of the needle
valve. Watching him I would remember the things you could
do with the old one-cylinder engine with the heavy flywheel,
how you could have it eating out of your hand if you got really
close to it spiritually. Motor boats in those days didn't have
clutches, and you would make a landing by shutting off the mo-

---

[2] Different ignition systems.

tor at the proper time and coasting in with a dead rudder.   But
there was a way of reversing them, if you learned the trick, by
cutting the switch and putting it on again exactly on the final
dying revolution of the flywheel, so that it would kick back
against compression and begin reversing.   Approaching a dock
in a strong following breeze, it was difficult to slow up sufficiently by the ordinary coasting method, and if a boy felt he had
complete mastery over his motor, he was tempted to keep it running beyond its time and then reverse it a few feet from the
dock.   It took a cool nerve, because if you threw the switch a
twentieth of a second too soon you would catch the flywheel
when it still had speed enough to go up past center, and the boat
would leap ahead, charging bull-fashion at the dock.

11   We had a good week at the camp.   The bass were biting
well and the sun shone endlessly, day after day.   We would be
tired at night and lie down in the accumulated heat of the little
bedrooms after the long hot day and the breeze would stir almost imperceptibly outside and the smell of the swamp drift in
through the rusty screens.   Sleep would come easily and in the
morning the red squirrel would be on the roof, tapping out his
gay routine.   I kept remembering everything, lying in bed in
the mornings—the small steamboat that had a long rounded
stern like the lip of a Ubangi, and how quietly she ran on the
moonlight sails, when the older boys played their mandolins
and the girls sang and we ate doughnuts dipped in sugar, and
how sweet the music was on the water in the shining night, and
what it had felt like to think about girls then.   After breakfast
we would go up to the store and the things were in the same
place—the minnows in a bottle, the plugs and spinners disar-
ranged and pawed over by the youngsters from the boys' camp,
the fig newtons and the Beeman's gum.   Outside, the road was
tarred and cars stood in front of the store.   Inside, all was just
as it had always been, except there was more Coca-Cola and not
so much Moxie and root beer and birch beer and sarsaparilla.
We would walk out with a bottle of pop apiece and sometimes
the pop would backfire up our noses and hurt.   We explored the
streams, quietly, where the turtles slid off the sunny logs and
dug their way into the soft bottom; and we lay on the town
wharf and fed worms to the tame bass.   Everywhere we went

I had trouble making out which was I, the one walking at my side, the one walking in my pants.

12   One afternoon while we were there at that lake a thunderstorm came up. It was like the revival of an old melodrama that I had seen long ago with childish awe. The second-act climax of the drama of the electrical disturbance over a lake in America had not changed in any important respect. This was the big scene, still the big scene. The whole thing was so familiar, the first feeling of oppression and heat and a general air around camp of not wanting to go very far away. In midafternoon (it was all the same) a curious darkening of the sky, and a lull in everything that had made life tick; and then the way the boats suddenly swung the other way at their moorings with the coming of a breeze out of the new quarter, and the premonitory rumble. Then the kettle drum, then the snare, then the bass drum and cymbals, then crackling light against the dark, and the gods grinning and licking their chops in the hills. Afterward the calm, the rain steadily rustling in the calm lake, the return of light and hope and spirits, and the campers running out in joy and relief to go swimming in the rain, their bright cries perpetuating the deathless joke about how they were getting simply drenched, and the children screaming with delight at the new sensation of bathing in the rain, and the joke about getting drenched linking the generations in a strong indestructible chain. And the comedian who waded in carrying an umbrella.

13   When the others went swimming my son said he was going in too. He pulled his dripping trunks from the line where they had hung all through the shower, and wrung them out. Languidly, and with no thought of going in, I watched him, his hard little body, skinny and bare, saw him wince slightly as he pulled up around his vitals the small, soggy, icy garment. As he buckled the swollen belt suddenly my groin felt the chill of death.

Questions on Content

1.   Why does White decide to return to the lake in Maine?
2.   What things had he remembered most clearly about the lake from his visits there as a boy?

3. When does White first begin to imagine that his son is himself as a boy and that he is now his own father? How often does this illusion come over him?

4. What convinced White that everything was the same as it had been—that "the years were a mirage and that there had been no years"?

5. What change does White notice in the road to the farmhouse? How does the change affect him?

6. What is the only difference White notices between the present-day waitresses and the ones from the past? Does this seem an important or an unimportant change to him?

7. In what ways do the boat motors of the present differ from those of the past? Which does White prefer and why?

8. What events cause White to feel "the chill of death"?

Questions on Invention, Design, and Style

1. Paragraphs 1–3 serve as the introduction to the essay. How has White used paragraph 1 to establish background information and to provide a plausible reason for revisiting the old lake? How do paragraphs 2 and 3 provide further essential information?

2. What kinds of illusions does White have during this return to the lake? Which ones recur throughout the essay? How do these illusions provide an order and a definite design for the essay?

3. What evidence is there in the essay that the present seems like the past because White *wants* it to be like the past? that life seems to be peaceful and joyful because White *wants* it to be? Show how the essay is designed, at least in part, around this wished-for similarity and a reality that contrasts sharply with it. In this light, what meaning does the final sentence in the essay have?

4. Why is White's recurring illusion that he is his father essential to an understanding of the final sentence in the essay?

5. Although White's essay is used here as an example of complex comparison and contrast, it also contains excellent examples of several kinds of illustration. For instance, how are the senses of sight, sound, touch, and smell evoked by the images in the following passage from paragraph 2?

> I guess I remembered clearest of all the early mornings, when the lake was cool and motionless, remembered how the bedroom smelled of the lumber it was made of and of the wet woods whose scent entered through the screen. The partitions in the camp were thin and did not extend clear to the top of the rooms, and as I was always the first up I would dress softly so

as not to wake the others and sneak out into the sweet outdoors and start out in the canoe, keeping close along the shore in the long shadows of the pines. I remembered being very careful never to rub my paddle against the gunwale for fear of disturbing the stillness of the cathedral.

6. Show how the sequence of images in paragraph 12 is arranged to depict the stages of a thunderstorm. What sight images are used? what sound images and metaphors? what touch images? What progression of moods is suggested in the paragraph?

Applications

1. Recall a time and a place in which you had such a pleasant experience that you wished it would continue forever. Write an essay comparing and contrasting the way you felt about the experience while it was going on and the way you felt after it ended.

2. Write a paper telling what values you would most like to pass on to your children. Show how those values are similar to or different from those you have observed in a person of importance in your life.

Part three
Analysis

Analysis

If you have studied biology, you have probably been asked to dissect some animal. If you studied its internal structure by separating out its muscles, nerves, blood vessels, organs, and skeleton, you learned about the total animal by dividing it up into its various component parts.

Something of the same sort occurs when you work a jigsaw puzzle—despite the fact that in this case you are assembling something instead of taking it apart. You fit the pieces together by trial and error until patterns of form and color and, finally, the overall design emerge. The nearer you come to finishing, the clearer your understanding of the remaining gaps. You feel a sense of accomplishment when you determine the relations among the puzzle's various parts and between the parts and the whole design.

It probably seems reasonable to you to think of your zoological dissection as a way of "analyzing." The words "analyze" and "analysis" have so often been used in this sense of dividing up that they are sometimes associated exclusively with breaking a whole down into parts. But in writing, *analysis* means considerably more: It is *the discovery of significant relationships— between parts and other parts, and between parts and wholes.* It does include the process of *division,* the breaking down of a whole into parts (as in the animal dissection), but it also in-

135

cludes the process of *synthesis,* the constructing of a whole from parts (as in putting together the jigsaw puzzle).

The point is that analysis is ultimately constructive, rather than destructive. If a whole is broken apart, it is for the purpose of solving a puzzle by understanding its component parts. When a chemist analyzes a compound, his purpose is not to destroy it but to understand it, by discovering what substances compose it and in what amounts they are present. Only when he knows this can he understand the compound's actions and reactions and thus control them. In his own way, he solves a puzzle—by taking the pieces apart to learn how they work together.

Consider another example of analysis in problem solving, one in which the final synthesis is especially important. Suppose you are an engineer who wishes to construct, through unfavorable terrain, a bridge with a larger span than any ever built: at a greater height, for the passage of larger ships, and with extra strength, for the support of heavier traffic. Because no existing bridge design meets all these requirements, you must create an entirely new concept. You draw on your knowledge of other bridges and your own design experience, but you must also use your imagination to rethink the possibilities of geometrical shapes and structural materials. You imagine and sketch many combinations, arranging and rearranging different combinations of parts, before the actual bridge can be built. The finished, or synthesized, product—the bridge—is possible only after exhaustive analysis of possible arrangements of the materials used.

Every writer faces similar problems in inventing a subject and designing the form in which it will be most functional for readers. Like the engineer, the writer employs analysis to divide the subject into its basic parts and to synthesize them in a suitable structure. Analysis preliminary to writing may also involve a process of trial and error, in which several arrangements of material are discarded before the best solution to the problem of synthesizing the material emerges. Fortunately, though, all three types of analysis suggest valuable ways of inventing and designing an essay. In some analyses writers classify, in some they examine processes, and in some they explore causes and effects.

To understand *classification analysis,* imagine yourself with a writing assignment on the subject "occupational stereotypes." In order to make this very broad topic workable, you might begin by asking:

1. What is the definition of the term?
2. How is the term used?
3. What different kinds exist?

In this way you begin your analysis—and the process of inventing your paper—by dividing the term into three different classes:

1. definition(s)
2. uses
3. kinds

But you can go farther. You might develop one of the classes more completely: *kinds* of occupational stereotypes, perhaps. You might break this class down into such subclasses as "blue-collar" and "white-collar" stereotypes. You could, of course, break each of these subclasses down further into stereotypes of specific occupations. At any level, classification analysis would offer rich possibilities for invention on the subject of "occupational stereotypes."

Instead of classifying, however, you might analyze the same subject in terms of the processes inherent in it:

1. What are the stages by which an occupation becomes stereotyped?
2. How do we apply occupational stereotypes to others?

As you worked out answers to these questions, you would be engaging in *process analysis,* studying the processes through which the stereotypes develop.

Or you might analyze on the basis of causes and effects:

1. What are the effects of stereotyping by occupation?
2. What causes occupational stereotypes?
3. What factors lead some occupations, but not others, to become stereotyped?

Exploration of such questions would be *causal analysis.*

Analysis—whether by classification, examination of process, or probing of causes and effects—provides helpful ways of thinking through an idea and giving it meaningful form. The more we can show readers about the parts of a subject and their relations to one another, the more they will understand the whole subject. Analysis—especially at the level of synthesis—is also useful in suggesting an appropriate structure for an essay and in bringing to our attention ways in which we may better clarify our subject through illustration, comparison, and contrast.

The selections in this section are arranged according to the three forms of analysis. Some deal with scientific subjects, others with the processes by which people think, listen to music, or quarrel. All suggest the precision of form and function that analytical writing can have.

Classification Analysis and Definition

Establishing relations between the whole and the parts through classification
Formal definition as classification
Use of classification to support crucial points in an essay
Use of classification as a basis for exploring a subject
Use of classification to structure an essay

Classification analysis establishes relations between a general class (the whole) and the subclasses (the parts) into which it can be divided. We have already seen how the general class of "occupational stereotypes" can be broken down into such subclasses as definition(s), uses, and kinds of occupational stereotypes. The resulting classification analysis could be diagrammed like this:

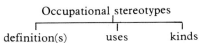

Occupational stereotypes

definition(s)　　uses　　kinds

Furthermore, we have seen that the subclass "kinds" can be subdivided into "blue-collar" and "white-collar" stereotypes and then into specific occupations:

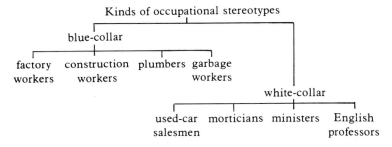

Kinds of occupational stereotypes

blue-collar

factory workers　construction workers　plumbers　garbage workers

white-collar

used-car salesmen　morticians　ministers　English professors

We can see how useful such a classification analysis is if we are to narrow a broad topic down to a manageable subject that can be treated in detail in a short paper. For instance, you could write a paper that depicts several typical stereotypes and then question their validity through illustrations of real people who do not fit the stereotypes at all.

Classification can be thought of as an extension of the process of comparison and contrast. When we divide "kinds of occupational stereotypes" into "blue-collar" and "white-collar," for instance, we do so on the basis of similarities (both are types of occupational stereotypes) and of differences (blue-collar and white-collar workers do different kinds of work). In the same way, we might divide all animals into the subclasses of vertebrates (those with backbones) and invertebrates (those without backbones) also on the basis of similarity and difference between the two subclasses.

An important type of classification is the formal definition, which clarifies the meaning of a word by identifying the general class to which it belongs and then differentiating it from other members of that class. For instance, we might define "freshman" as a college or university student (general class) who has completed fewer than thirty semester hours or forty-five quarter hours of course work (differentiation from other members of the general class). Although definitions can often be expanded and clarified through illustrations, comparisons, and contrasts, classification is almost always basic to effective ones.

Definitions and other forms of classification often provide the bases for entire essays, as in the selections in this section. Even more often, however, they serve to clarify or support specific points within a larger work. Consider, for example, how Martin Luther King, Jr., uses classification and definition to support a crucial point in his "Letter from Birmingham Jail" (which is included in the "Complex Argumentation" subsection of this book):

> Since we so diligently urge people to obey the Supreme Court's decision of 1954 outlawing segregation in the public schools, at first glance it may seem rather paradoxical for us consciously to break laws. One may well ask: "How can you advocate breaking some laws and obeying others?" The answer lies in the fact that there are

two types of laws: just and unjust.   I would be the first to advocate obeying just laws.   One has not only a legal but a moral responsibility to obey just laws.   Conversely, one has a moral responsibility to disobey unjust laws. . . .

Now, what is the difference between the two?   How does one determine whether a law is just or unjust?   A just law is a man-made code that squares with the moral law or the law of God.   An unjust law is a code that is out of harmony with the moral law.

King, in fact, uses this classification of laws into just and unjust ones, along with his definitions of the two, as the focus of a long and complex essay.

The writers represented in this subsection all use classification analysis as a basis for defining their subjects and for designing their material.   Florence Pettit classifies woods according to hardness and softness in order to tell most concisely what the advantages and disadvantages of the different species are for the carver.   Aaron Copland divides listening to music into three levels in order to pinpoint the kind that he considers the most enjoyable and makes good use of synthesis at the conclusion of his essay as well.   Warren S. Brown explains that the human brain, especially its thought processes, is divided into two distinct halves, each with its own functions.   Bernard Rudofsky, although he does not specifically mention classification, divides examples of the disfigurement of the human body according to its different parts: head, torso, and feet.   Arnold J. Mandell uses existing and widely known classifications of positions in football (offense and defense, line and backfield, and so on) to discuss different personality types among the players.   S. I. Hayakawa divides statements into reports, inferences, and judgments in an essay that also features excellent examples of formal definition supported by illustrations.

As you read the following selections, you might begin to reflect on the classifications you use to order your personal experiences and observations: types of eating places, types of courses, types of students, types of automobiles, and so on.

Woods for Carving
Florence H. Pettit

In this essay, fabric designer and metal sculptor Florence H. Pettit divides woods for carving into the classes of hard, soft, and medium, which correspond to their ease in cutting.

1   *Hard*, in terms of wood, really means *harder* to cut, but most hardwoods are also fine and even-grained. They are not apt to split, and they take polish well. For these reasons they are generally better for small wood carvings than the softwoods; most sculptors prefer to use hardwoods for large pieces, too. All the fruitwoods, like cherry, apple, pear, and orange, are hard, and so are oak, mahogany, walnut, birch, holly, and maple. Hardwoods range in color from the almost white of holly to the almost black of walnut. Oak and mahogany are the most open-grained, and therefore more apt to split. They are probably less good for small carvings than the other kinds.

2   Soft and medium woods can be used for larger carvings, because the wood shaves off more easily and in larger pieces. Not so much strength is required to use the tools. The most common softwoods are balsa, basswood, sugar pine, white pine, buckeye, poplar, and butternut. Balsa is unique because it is so soft you can dent it with your finger. It is used for model-making and for small preliminary studies for larger works, but it is not much good for anything else. The two other softest woods are basswood and sugar pine; they will not take a good polish, but are fine for things that are to be painted or do not need a high finish. The rest of the softwoods will take almost as good a finish as the hardwoods. White pine must be of what is called "clear-select" or best quality, for the hard, dark streaks and knots in the other grades would spoil the appearance of most projects and be a nuisance to the carver.

3   The medium woods—fir and redwood—are also better for larger carvings because they are open-grained and rather apt to split.

4   All of the above are domestic woods from trees that grow in various parts of the United States. Most of them can be bought from wood specialty firms. There are a number of trop-

ical and exotic foreign woods that are fine to carve, but they are not commonly available. Only seasoned wood should be used for carving, that is, wood that has been dried and aged, because green wood is apt to warp and split as it dries. The wood used by Peter Schimmel in Pennsylvania over a century ago is described as *driftwood*, which means that it was wood he picked up along rivers and streams where it had been aged by being alternately heated by the sun and wet by the waters. It is interesting, however, to note that the rule about using seasoned wood has been purposely broken by some Oriental craftsmen who *like* to have their bowls warp into odd shapes!

5   Before they are ready to be carved, logs cut from green trees require a long period of drying in a protected, ventilated place until the sap has entirely left the wood. Before you buy any wood, search your own basement and garage. You may find some nice old boards.

Questions on Content

1. What are the characteristics of hardwood? Which woods are included in this classification? What hardwoods are most open-grained and therefore most apt to split? What kinds of carvings are they less good for than other hardwoods?

2. For what kinds of carvings can soft and medium woods be used? What advantages do these woods have? What are the most common softwoods? medium woods?

3. Where can most of the woods mentioned in this selection be bought?

4. Why should seasoned woods be used for carving? What single exception does Pettit mention?

5. Under what conditions should green logs be seasoned?

Questions on Invention, Design, and Style

1. Into what two subclasses of hardwoods are the individual species divided in paragraph 1? What are the other two bases of division mentioned in this paragraph?

2. Into what two subclasses of softwoods are the individual species divided in paragraph 2?

3. Is Pettit writing for an audience of experienced woodcarvers or inexperienced ones? What, then, is her purpose in classifying woods according to their relative hardness?

Applications

1. Consider the materials used in some craft or pastime other than wood carving. Divide those materials into different kinds, and explain the nature of each class of material in such a way that a beginner can easily understand it.
2. List the ways in which you generally spend your time. Divide them into three or four main classes, and develop an essay around them.

A Psychiatrist Looks at Pro Football
Arnold J. Mandell

In response to an assignment by a professional football team, psychiatrist Arnold J. Mandell found that the personality traits of successful players correspond closely to the demands of the positions they play. The standard divisions of football players into offensive and defensive, line and backfield, and so on, become a framework for discussing various personality types among football players and people in general.

1   Two years ago, Harland Svare, then head coach of the San Diego Chargers, asked me to lunch to talk about football.   I was then, as I am now, chairman of the Department of Psychiatry at the University of California, San Diego, and I had never paid much attention to football.   The Chargers were a losing team, and at our lunch Coach Svare, an imaginative man, wondered if my training might equip me to notice things about the attitudes and the behavior of his players that could help give the team what is often called "the winning edge."   The result was that I became a sort of "psychiatrist-in-residence" for the Chargers.

2   At Svare's invitation, I began to hang around the team—in the locker room, at team lectures, at practice, on the plane to and from away games, and on the sidelines during the games. In all, I conducted over 200 hours of individual interviews with the players.   My function was to provide the coaches with a clearer understanding of these men and their positions and, more practically, to make personnel comments and recommendations.

3   When I first sat on the bench, I realized I was hearing the sounds of a Stone Age battleground.   You can't pick them up on television or from a seat in the stadium.   But on the bench you hear grunts, groans, hits—mankind's most fundamental sounds.   I quickly learned what many Sunday widows already realized—that football is not a game but a religion, a throwback of 30,000 generations of anthropological time.

4   When I was first around the team, the players thought I was spooky because I just stood there and watched.   It was to take me more than a year to break down barriers and build trust be-

tween the players and me. But, after only a few weeks, I went
to Coach Svare with my first systematic insight. "Harland," I
said, "I think I can tell whether a player is on the offensive unit
or the defensive unit just by looking at his locker. The offensive players keep their lockers clean and orderly, but the lockers
of the defensive men are a mess. In fact, the better the defensive player, the bigger the mess."

5   As I pored over scouting reports and interviewed players
and coaches from numerous NFL teams, it became clear that
offensive football players like structure and discipline. They
tend to be conservative as people, and as football players they
take comfort in repetitious practice of well-planned and well-
executed plays.

6   The defensive players, just as clearly, can't stand structure; their attitudes, their behavior and their life-styles bear
this out. They operate as though they've been put out of the
tribe and are trying to show people that tribal structure is
worthless anyway. Rules or regulations put forward by anybody, anyplace, are to be challenged. Coaches find defensive
players notably more difficult to control than their offensive
teammates, and the two types, I noticed, often had little or
nothing to do with one another.

7   I began to differentiate the personality profiles of these
men independently of any prior knowledge about the specific
requirements of their individual positions. Before long, it
became clear that in addition to athletic ability, motivation and
commitment, a suitable personality for his particular position
is the most significant and necessary component of a player's
survival in the NFL.

8   Offensive linemen, for example, are in general ambitious,
tenacious, precise. As blocking assignments become ever
more intricate, they must practice like a ballet corps to coördi-
nate their blocking patterns. They also have to stand firm and
cool when an opposing defensive line rushes their passer, no
matter what physical or verbal abuse is thrown at them. A sacrificial attitude toward the welfare of the team is integral to the
offensive lineman.

9   The center, who often has to call signals, is usually the
brightest. The guard may be more aggressive, because on

some plays he is called upon to block downfield. Stubborn tenacity is prototypical of the offensive tackle; his loyalty and
commitment to the welfare of the team know no match.

10   The wide receiver is a very special human being. He is
narcissistic and vain, and basically a loner. Essential, brilliant
and not too friendly, he's rarely a popular member of the team,
often lives by himself, and remains a bit of a mystery. Typically, too, while he is courageous and doesn't mind getting hurt
on the body, he's afraid of having his face disfigured.

11   I have found two kinds of running backs. One is like the
wide receiver: tough, treacherous, quick and lonely, like the
much-traveled Duane Thomas, now of the Washington Redskins. The other kind of offensive back—the Larry Csonka
(Miami Dolphins) kind—runs the football, and his life, straight
ahead. He's honest, tough, strong, disciplined, and if his
toughness is a touch brutal, he may be great.

12   The most difficult of the offensive players to categorize are
the quarterbacks. Given outstanding physical ability, passing
talent and intelligence, the major determinant of their success
appears to be self-confidence—a self-confidence that is akin to
super-arrogance.

13   The physical threat to a quarterback passing from the
"pocket" is intolerable. To stand there to the last millisecond,
waiting for your receiver to reach the place the ball is supposed
to go while you are being rushed by mammoth defensive linemen, takes sheer courage. How is such poise achieved? From
my observation, there appear to be at least two routes. One is
that of the naturally arrogant man who does not feel bound by
the rules governing other men—he makes his own. Such men
have run their talents and capacities to incredible self-advan-
tage with no apparent anxiety or guilt. And they win football
games—yea, even championships. Joe Namath (New York
Jets) and Sonny Jurgensen (Washington Redskins) fit well into
this category.

14   The other way to turn in successful performance under battle conditions is with assurance from On High. The Dallas
Cowboys' Roger Staubach is in this group, as is Fran Tarken-
ton, the Minnesota Vikings' renowned scrambler. We might
call them and their comrades the religious quarterbacks. They

attend church regularly, are active in such organizations as the Fellowship of Christian Athletes, and have a truly evangelical mission that they carry forward with the calm certitude of the believer. The believer quarterbacks win championships, too.

15   The defensive-team members are the renegades. The linemen, in contrast to offensive linemen, are basically angry, restless, intolerant of detail, barely under control. They take great joy in their unbridled assault on the Establishment.

16   The linebacker is a fascinating combination of control, brutality and internal conflict. He wants to look good to himself. When he fails, he can almost destroy himself in depression. Often he achieves a public image as a solid citizen; yet simultaneously he's a killer. When I asked a number of NFL scouts whom they would send behind the lines in wartime to assassinate an important enemy, they said a linebacker: his cleverness and air of legitimacy would get him into the country and let him pass as a good citizen, and his brutality would let him kill when the time came.

17   In the defensive backfield, aggression gets buried under more and more inhibition and discipline. These men are like long-distance runners; they are loners, and they experience depression and rage. They must learn zone and man-on-man pass-defense patterns that require incredible self-discipline in the furor of battle. They must not be led by their natural inclination, which is to follow receivers out of their zone before the quarterback releases the ball on a pass play. To counter running plays, however, they must move up fast and, though generally lighter and weaker than the running backs they are trying to stop, hit very hard. So they need controlled and timed brutality and anger.

18   Given roughly the same amount of athletic ability, why do some men fail and others succeed in pro football? Inevitably it is because the personality orientations of the latter better fit the tasks. In other fields as well, appropriateness of personality to one's role may be perhaps the most significant single determinant of success and happiness. De Gaulle was obviously a quarterback. Former President Nixon's stubbornly persistent and tenacious management of his crises, his attempts to be

blunt, quick and clever would have suited him to be an offensive guard.

19 Both my mother and my wife are offensive linemen; my father, a classical wide receiver. President Ford is a natural offensive lineman, which is in fact what he was at the University of Michigan. Truman Capote is a wide receiver. Kate Smith is a fullback, in more than size. Leonard Bernstein is a cross between a quarterback and a wide receiver.

20 I am often asked what I accomplished for the Chargers. The answer has to be: very little. The team's dismal record over the two-year period—6 victories in 28 games—indicates that. So does my own professional observation: that psychiatry and pro football probably don't mix. Or, if they do, the blend is best left to the brewmaster, the head coach. The shrinks should stay with the rest of the experts—in front of their television sets.

Questions on Content

1. What duties were involved in Mandell's assignment as a sort of "psychiatrist-in-residence"?
2. What was Mandell's first insight into the differing personalities of offensive and defensive players? What are his generalizations about them?
3. In addition to athletic ability, motivation, and commitment, what does Mandell judge to be the most important factor in a player's survival in professional football?
4. How do the demands placed on offensive linemen match their usual personalities?
5. What are the unusual qualities of the wide receiver?
6. What are the two basic types of running backs, according to Mandell? of quarterbacks?
7. What are the characteristics of defensive linemen? of linebackers?
8. Why are defensive-backfield players especially apt to experience "depression and rage"?

Questions on Invention, Design, and Style

1. Mandell's essay includes six paragraphs of introduction before the statement of his thesis in paragraph 7. What does Mandell accomplish in paragraphs 1–4? How do these introduce the sub-

jects of paragraphs 5 and 6? How do paragraphs 5 and 6 shift the focus of the essay from personal narrative to an objective classification analysis?

2. In paragraph 7 Mandell states his thesis: that "in addition to athletic ability, motivation and commitment, a suitable personality for his particular position is the most significant and necessary component of a player's survival in the NFL." How have paragraphs 1–6 established Mandell's credentials to make such a statement? How do paragraphs 8–17 support this statement? Why is the idea repeated in the first two sentences of paragraph 18?

3. Paragraphs 8–17 might be diagrammed as follows:

What paragraphs in the essay correspond with each element in the diagram? How have the standard classifications of positions in football determined the structure of paragraphs 8–17? Why has Mandell extended his divisions of running backs and quarterbacks to one level beyond those of the other positions?

4. Mandell's assignment took him into an unfamiliar subject area; how does he use his observation and interviews as sources in paragraphs 2 and 3? What use of his own background in psychiatry does he describe in paragraph 4? How does Mandell's back-

ground influence even the vocabulary he uses in paragraphs 9 and
10?

Applications

1. Using Mandell's classification system, classify your roommate,
   spouse, or close friend as either an offensive or a defensive
   "player." Write a paper explaining why he or she fits this classification, and extend your discussion to the subclasses and characteristics into which he or she fits.
2. Write a paper showing how three individuals you know who have
   different occupations do or do not fit the stereotypes of those
   occupations.

Left Brain, Right Brain
Warren S. Brown

**Drawing upon recent discoveries in brain research, Warren S.
Brown, professor of psychiatry at the University of California at Los
Angeles, divides mental functions into those originating in the left
brain and those originating in the right brain.**

> *What you've got here, really, are* two *realities, one of
> immediate artistic appearance and one of underlying scien-
> tific explanation.*   —Robert Pirsig
> *Zen and the Art of Motorcycle Maintenance*

1   References to a duality in the way we know and appreciate
reality are numerous in both modern and ancient writing about
human experience. Over the past two decades an increasing
amount of data has been accumulating which suggests that this
duality in thought modes is a reflection of the concentration of
different mental abilities in the right and left cerebral hemispheres of the brain.

2   The cerebral cortex of man forms the large wrinkled outer structure which sits on the lower brain structures much as a mushroom cap sits on its stalk. It is divided in half, into left and right hemispheres, by a fissure running from front to back. On the simplest levels of information processing, each hemisphere performs the same function as the other, although in a mirror-image fashion. The left hemisphere sees, feels, and hears things primarily from the world on the right side of the body, and the right hemisphere senses the left world. In the same manner, the left hemisphere controls the right hand, and the right hemisphere the left hand. This crossing of sensation and behavioral control is also a feature of the brains of other primates and lower mammals.

3   However, it is a unique aspect of the human brain that, in the case of the more complex kinds of mental processing, the right and left hemispheres appear to have quite different modes of operation. For example, 95 percent of right-handed people have language functions located in the left hemisphere, the right hemisphere having only minimal language ability, perhaps limited to habitual expressions such as "Hello," "How are you?" and a surprising vocabulary of swear words. Most left-handers (64 percent) also have language dominance in the left hemisphere, the remainder having speech located either in the right hemisphere (20 percent) or distributed between both sides (16 percent). Along with language, the left hemisphere in right-handers and most left-handers is also specialized for such mental functions as communicative gestures, the appreciation of the temporal order of events, the planning of behavioral sequences, and abstract, analytic thinking such as mathematics and logic.

4   The right hemisphere was for many years considered the "silent hemisphere" because damage to this brain area did not seem to have dramatic effects on behavior. Recent research, however, has demonstrated a set of special abilities localized on the right side which include the appreciation of spatial relationships and patterns, imagery, fantasy and dreams, music, and the recognition of facial expression and body language.

5   The difference between the functions of the two hemispheres, and the fact that either hemisphere alone is sufficient

for consciousness, personality, and thinking, has led to the theory that man has two potentially independent minds, a logical-verbal mind in the left hemisphere and a more image-oriented and intuitive mind in the right hemisphere.

6   The possible existence of a dual mind can perhaps best be illustrated by the behavior of patients who have had the large communication pathway between the hemispheres (*corpus callosum*) severed surgically as a treatment for epilepsy. Generally these patients behave quite normally. However, under controlled conditions Dr. Roger Sperry and his coworkers at the California Institute of Technology have shown that the two hemispheres of these people each have a distinct sphere of consciousness. In one of their experiments, a picture of a face, the left half of which was the face of a man and the right half the face of a gorilla, was flashed rapidly in the patient's field of view in such a way that each half of the composite face was seen by a different side of the brain. The patient was unaware of having seen anything but a normal, complete face. If asked to choose from a number of complete faces which picture was seen, the patient pointed to the man's picture when allowed to respond with the left hand and to the gorilla's picture when responding with the right hand. When asked to tell about the picture, the patient—talking, and therefore using the left hemisphere—always described the gorilla seen on the right side of the picture, denying that he had seen the picture of the man. Each hemisphere not only had a different memory of the event, but had "filled in" the rest of the picture based on the half it actually saw.

7   The human brain normally functions in a more integrated and complementary manner than this, because of the sharing of information between the hemispheres. But the degree to which the two hemispheres of a normal brain work independently, resulting in two minds in one head, is one of the exciting questions under study in brain research.

Questions on Content

1. According to recent brain research, what seems to be the basis of the artistic-scientific duality in human thought patterns?
2. Through which side of the body, primarily, does the left hemi-

sphere of the brain receive sense impressions? the right hemisphere of the brain?

3. What other mental functions are centered in the left hemisphere? in the right hemisphere?

4. How does the brain of a right-handed person function differently from that of a left-handed person? What does that difference reveal about the way the brain functions in general?

5. Why was the right hemisphere considered the "silent hemisphere"? How has recent research changed that view?

6. What are the two bases of the view that man has two brains, a left one and a right one?

7. Describe the experiment that Dr. Sperry and his coworkers conducted. What did the results of this experiment reveal about the way the brain functions?

8. Why does the human brain normally function in a more integrated way than in the patients in Dr. Sperry's experiment?

Questions on Invention, Design, and Style

1. Brown opens his essay with a quotation from Robert Pirsig's *Zen and the Art of Motorcycle Maintenance*. What important distinctions are introduced in this quotation? How does it help to support Brown's point in the first sentence of paragraph 1? How do the quotation and paragraph 1 together function as the introduction to the essay?

2. How do the first two sentences in paragraph 2 further introduce the essay and provide a basis for what follows in this paragraph?

3. The contents of paragraphs 1–5 of Brown's essay might be diagrammed as on page 155. Although this diagram shows the logical basis of the divisions in the classification analysis, it does not represent the order, or sequence, in which Brown treats them. Why does Brown take up the subject of sense perceptions for both left and right hemispheres in paragraph 2 before moving on to the more complex functions? What would have happened to the structure of the essay if he had taken up all the functions of the left hemisphere and then all the functions of the right hemisphere?

4. How does Brown's account of Dr. Sperry's experiment in paragraph 6 both illustrate and support his own thesis of "the possible existence of a dual mind"? What specific points from paragraphs 2–5 are illustrated and supported in this paragraph? What would happen to the essay if this paragraph were omitted?

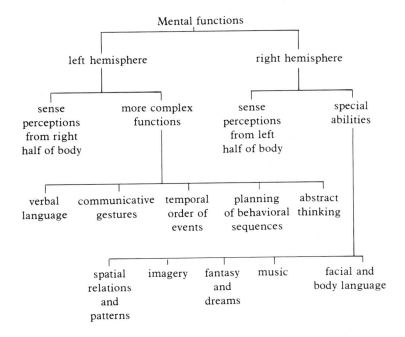

5. Paragraph 7 is Brown's conclusion. How does the first sentence serve as a transition from paragraph 6? How does the second sentence refer back to paragraph 1 in drawing the essay to a close?

Applications

1. Scan recent issues of such magazines as *Scientific American, Psychology Today,* and *Science Digest.* Read closely any articles presenting recent discoveries in human behavior that you find particularly interesting. Then write a classification analysis, dividing some aspect of human behavior into several smaller classes and discussing them; use supporting information from your reading.

2. Recall your experiences with various people—hyperactive people, cruel people, people everyone seems to love, for instance. Classify several types by the impressions they have made upon you. Then write a paper using specific illustrations to support your classification of these individuals.

Listening to Music
Aaron Copland

While explaining how we listen to music, American composer Aaron Copland also demonstrates the value of classification analysis—including both division and synthesis—as a way of understanding a subject and making it clear to readers.

1 We all listen to music according to our separate capacities. But, for the sake of analysis, the whole listening process may become clearer if we break it up into its component parts, so to speak. In a certain sense we all listen to music on three separate planes. For lack of a better terminology, one might name these: (1) the sensuous plane, (2) the expressive plane, (3) the sheerly musical plane. The only advantage to be gained from mechanically splitting up the listening process into these hypothetical planes is the clearer view to be had of the way in which we listen.

2 The simplest way of listening to music is to listen for the sheer pleasure of the musical sound itself. That is the sensuous plane. It is the plane on which we hear music without thinking, without considering it in any way. One turns on the radio while doing something else and absent-mindedly bathes in the sound. A kind of brainless but attractive state of mind is engendered by the mere sound appeal of the music.

3 You may be sitting in a room reading this book. Imagine one note struck on the piano. Immediately that one note is enough to change the atmosphere of the room—proving that the sound element in music is a powerful and mysterious agent, which it would be foolish to deride or belittle.

4 The surprising thing is that many people who consider themselves qualified music lovers abuse that plane in listening. They go to concerts in order to lose themselves. They use music as a consolation or an escape. They enter an ideal world where one doesn't have to think of the realities of everyday life. Of course they aren't thinking about the music either. Music allows them to leave it, and they go off to a place to dream, dreaming because of and apropos of the music yet never quite listening to it.

5   Yes, the sound appeal of music is a potent and primitive force, but you must not allow it to usurp a disproportionate share of your interest.   The sensuous plane is an important one in music, a very important one, but it does not constitute the whole story.

. . .

6   The second plane on which music exists is what I have called the expressive one.   Here, immediately, we tread on controversial ground.   Composers have a way of shying away from any discussion of music's expressive side.   Did not Stravinsky himself proclaim that his music was an "object," a "thing," with a life of its own, and with no other meaning than its own purely musical existence?   This intransigent attitude of Stravinsky's may be due to the fact that so many people have tried to read different meanings into so many pieces.   Heaven knows it is difficult enough to say precisely what it is that a piece of music means, to say it definitely, to say it finally so that everyone is satisfied with your explanation.   But that should not lead one to the other extreme of denying the music the right to be "expressive."

7   My own belief is that all music has an expressive power, some more and some less, but that all music has a certain meaning behind the notes and that that meaning behind the notes constitutes, after all, what the piece is saying, what the piece is about.   This whole problem can be stated quite simply by asking, "Is there a meaning to music?"   My answer to that would be, "Yes."   And "Can you state in so many words what the meaning is?"   My answer to that would be, "No."   Therein lies the difficulty.

8   Simple-minded souls will never be satisfied with the answer to the second of these questions.   They always want music to have a meaning, and the more concrete it is the better they like it.   The more the music reminds them of a train, a storm, a funeral, or any other familiar conception the more expressive it appears to be to them.   This popular idea of music's meaning—stimulated and abetted by the usual run of musical commentator—should be discouraged wherever and whenever it is met.   One timid lady once confessed to me that she sus-

pected something seriously lacking in her appreciation of music because of her inability to connect it with anything definite. That is getting the whole thing backward, of course.

9 Still, the question remains, How close should the intelligent music lover wish to come to pinning a definite meaning to any particular work? No closer than a general concept, I should say. Music expresses, at different moments, serenity or exuberance, regret or triumph, fury or delight. It expresses each of these moods, and many others, in a numberless variety of subtle shadings and differences. It may even express a state of meaning for which there exists no adequate word in any language. In that case, musicians often like to say that it has only a purely musical meaning. They sometimes go farther and say that *all* music has only a purely musical meaning. What they really mean is that no appropriate word can be found to express the music's meaning and that, even if it could, they do not feel the need of finding it.

10 But whatever the professional musician may hold, most musical novices still search for specific words with which to pin down their musical reactions. That is why they always find Tschaikovsky easier to "understand" than Beethoven. In the first place, it is easier to pin a meaning-word on a Tschaikovsky piece than on a Beethoven one. Much easier. Moreover, with the Russian composer, every time you come back to a piece of his it almost always says the same thing to you, whereas with Beethoven it is often quite difficult to put your finger right on what he is saying. And any musician will tell you that that is why Beethoven is the greater composer. Because music which always says the same thing to you will necessarily soon become dull music, but music whose meaning is slightly different with each hearing has a greater chance of remaining alive.

11 Listen, if you can, to the forty-eight fugue themes of Bach's *Well Tempered Clavichord*. Listen to each theme, one after another. You will soon realize that each theme mirrors a different world of feeling. You will also soon realize that the more beautiful a theme seems to you the harder it is to find any word that will describe it to your complete satisfaction. Yes, you will certainly know whether it is a gay theme or a sad one. You will be able, in other words, in your own mind, to draw a

frame of emotional feeling around your theme. Now study the
sad one a little closer. Try to pin down the exact quality of its
sadness. Is it pessimistically sad or resignedly sad; is it fate-
fully sad or smilingly sad?

12 Let us suppose that you are fortunate and can describe to
your own satisfaction in so many words the exact meaning of
your chosen theme. There is still no guarantee that anyone
else will be satisfied. Nor need they be. The important thing
is that each one feel for himself the specific expressive quality
of a theme or, similarly, an entire piece of music. And if it is
a great work of art, don't expect it to mean exactly the same
thing to you each time you return to it.

13 Themes or pieces need not express only one emotion, of
course. Take such a theme as the first main one of the *Ninth
Symphony*, for example. It is clearly made up of different elements. It does not say only one thing. Yet anyone hearing it
immediately gets a feeling of strength, a feeling of power. It
isn't a power that comes simply because the theme is played
loudly. It is a power inherent in the theme itself. The extraordinary strength and vigor of the theme results in the listener's
receiving an impression that a forceful statement has been
made. But one should never try to boil it down to "the fateful
hammer of life," etc. That is where the trouble begins. The
musician, in his exasperation, says it means nothing but the
notes themselves, whereas the nonprofessional is only too anxious to hang on to any explanation that gives him the illusion
of getting closer to the music's meaning.

14 Now, perhaps, the reader will know better what I mean
when I say that music does have an expressive meaning but that
we cannot say in so many words what that meaning is.

15 The third plane on which music exists is the sheerly musical plane. Besides the pleasurable sound of music and the expressive feeling that it gives off, music does exist in terms of the
notes themselves and of their manipulation. Most listeners are
not sufficiently conscious of this third plane. . . .

16 Professional musicians, on the other hand, are, if anything,
too conscious of the mere notes themselves. They often fall
into the error of becoming so engrossed with their arpeggios
and staccatos that they forget the deeper aspects of the music

they are performing. But from the layman's standpoint, it is not so much a matter of getting over bad habits on the sheerly musical plane as of increasing one's awareness of what is going on, in so far as the notes are concerned.

17 When the man in the street listens to the "notes themselves" with any degree of concentration, he is most likely to make some mention of the melody. Either he hears a pretty melody or he does not, and he generally lets it go at that. Rhythm is likely to gain his attention next, particularly if it seems exciting. But harmony and tone color are generally taken for granted, if they are thought of consciously at all. As for music's having a definite form of some kind, that idea seems never to have occurred to him.

18 It is very important for all of us to become more alive to music on its sheerly musical plane. After all, an actual musical material is being used. The intelligent listener must be prepared to increase his awareness of the musical material and what happens to it. He must hear the melodies, the rhythms, the harmonies, the tone colors in a more conscious fashion. But above all he must, in order to follow the line of the composer's thought, know something of the principles of musical form. Listening to all of these elements is listening on the sheerly musical plane.

19 Let me repeat that I have split up mechanically the three separate planes on which we listen merely for the sake of greater clarity. Actually, we never listen on one or the other of these planes. What we do is to correlate them—listening in all three ways at the same time. It takes no mental effort, for we do it instinctively.

20 Perhaps an analogy with what happens to us when we visit the theater will make this instinctive correlation clearer. In the theater, you are aware of the actors and actresses, costumes and sets, sounds and movements. All these give one the sense that the theater is a pleasant place to be in. They constitute the sensuous plane in our theatrical reactions.

21 The expressive plane in the theater would be derived from the feeling that you get from what is happening on the stage. You are moved to pity, excitement, or gayety. It is this general

feeling, generated aside from the particular words being spoken, a certain emotional something which exists on the stage, that is analogous to the expressive quality in music.

22   The plot and plot development is equivalent to our sheerly musical plane. The playwright creates and develops a character in just the same way that a composer creates and develops a theme. According to the degree of your awareness of the way in which the artist in either field handles his material will you become a more intelligent listener.

23   It is easy enough to see that the theatergoer never is conscious of any of these elements separately. He is aware of them all at the same time. The same is true of music listening. We simultaneously and without thinking listen on all three planes.

24   In a sense, the ideal listener is both inside and outside the music at the same moment, judging it and enjoying it, wishing it would go one way and watching it go another—almost like the composer at the moment he composes it; because in order to write his music, the composer must also be inside and outside his music, carried away by it and yet coldly critical of it. A subjective and objective attitude is implied in both creating and listening to music.

25   What the reader should strive for, then, is a more *active* kind of listening. Whether you listen to Mozart or Duke Ellington, you can deepen your understanding of music only by being a more conscious and aware listener—not someone who is just listening, but someone who is listening *for* something.

Questions on Content

1. Which is the simplest of the three planes into which Copland divides the process of listening to music? What criticism does Copland make of it?
2. What is controversial about the second plane? What two groups are likely to hold extreme views in this controversy?
3. What is Copland's criticism of professional musicians in regard to the third plane? nonmusicians?
4. In the theater, what is the equivalent to the sensual plane in listening to music? to the expressive plane? to the sheerly musical plane?
5. According to Copland, how should we listen to music?

Questions on Invention, Design, and Style

1. In the introduction to this essay, Copland is unusually careful to make his meaning clear to the reader. What is gained, for example, by the use of the pronoun "we"? by explaining the reason for dividing the listening process into three planes? by naming and numbering the classes into which the listening process is to be discussed? by the qualification stated in the last sentence? Find other instances late in the essay of Copland's concern that the reader fully understand the nature and purpose of his analysis.
2. What is Copland's definition of the sensuous plane of listening to music? What illustrations does he use to clarify the term and his definition?
3. Why does Copland develop his analysis of the expressive plane of listening at such great length? How does he illustrate the two extreme views concerning this term? What does he identify as a middle ground in resolving these extremes?
4. What musical values does he mention in paragraphs 17 and 18 to help clarify the sheerly musical plane of listening? How does he again establish extreme views as a preface to his adoption of a moderate position?
5. Note Copland's transitions in paragraphs 2, 6, and 15. What is gained by this enumeration and the repeated use of terms from paragraph 1?
6. In paragraphs 19–23 Copland synthesizes his discussion of the three planes of listening that he has earlier divided. What is the purpose of this synthesis? What analogy does he use to explain it? What is gained by using this analogy?
7. Although in the introduction Copland has prepared the reader for his central idea, it is not until paragraph 24 that he states it fully. What is that idea? How has the analogy of theatergoing prepared the reader for this statement? How does paragraph 23 anticipate this statement? How does paragraph 25 extend the statement and conclude the essay?

Applications

1. Analyze one of the following activities, dividing it into three or four levels: watching a movie, eating a meal, watching an athletic event. Write an essay based on this classification analysis.
2. Classify the students or instructors on your campus with reference to one particular characteristic. You might choose physical appearance or the hobbies or interests of the people involved.

Begin with an outline, and then develop it into an essay that would enable someone outside your school to understand the students or instructors better.

The Fashionable Body
Bernard Rudofsky

Senseless and sometimes dangerous practices are often taken for granted until they are pointed out to us. In this selection, Bernard Rudofsky discusses the human tendency to mutilate the body to conform to the dictates of fashion. He develops this theme by classifying the body according to its parts—head, torso, and feet—and by illustrating his points with gusto.

1   The urge to alter his body is felt by man only; animals, enjoying the advantage of healthier instincts, do not share it. Although the human shape was designed by the greatest of artists, His taste does not necessarily coincide with ours; at no time did man accept the image in which he was created as final. He decided early that there was room for improvement.

2   Neither prehistoric cave dweller nor late-industrial urban man considered the human body aesthetically satisfactory. The Aurignacians and Magdalenians[1] practiced mutilation of their hands with the same confidence that modern man brings to crippling his feet. Uneducated and oversophisticated alike seem to act on an uncontrollable impulse to rearrange their anatomy; no part of the body is spared from more or less violent interference.

3   Whatever man's reasons for wanting to change his physique, whatever the relevance of his narcissistic or autoerotic inclinations, the factor that goes farthest to account for this unholy obsession is boredom. Bored with the natural shape of his body, he delights in getting away from himself, and to judge from past and present performances, the resources at hand for

---

[1] Aurignacian: a sequence of related Upper Paleolithic cultures; Magdalenian: a European Stone Age culture of about 15,000–10,000 B.C.

making his escape are inexhaustible. Only rarely does he exercise self-restraint. To the ancient Greeks, for instance, the human body was inviolate, or almost: some plucked their pubic hair.

. . .

4   It is, of course, doubtful that a modern woman blessed with the proportions of a Greek statue would be happy. Broad hips have not been fashionable for a long time, and what modern shoe could accommodate a classical foot? . . . Changeable ideals of beauty have always been far more desirable than everlasting perfection, and with good reason.

5   Our laws permit a man to have as many wives as he pleases, provided he marries them successively. Since, however, this staggered sort of polygamy is often beyond a man's means, the way to make the monotony of marital life tolerable is to split a wife's personality. But masquerading alone won't do the trick. A new dress or a sun tan does not turn her into a new woman; the change has to be more than skin deep. Let us examine some of the alterations that she—or he—has accomplished in the pursuit of physical variety.

6   One of the boldest ways to interfere with human anatomy is to mold the skull. Among tribes who practice this art, it is part and parcel of a child's upbringing. It calls for special skills and has traditionally been a mother's duty and, we may presume, pleasure. The first provocation for a mother's pinching and kneading her baby's skull was perhaps its yielding softness. Playful handling developed into more conscious efforts to deform, and racial and aesthetic concepts were added later. Thus, broad heads were broadened, flat noses flattened closer to the face, a tapering occiput sharpened to a point—a shape mostly associated today with humanoids from outer space. These spectacular forms were achieved with the aid of contraptions no more ingenious than a common mousetrap.

7   Admiration for elongated heads has been widespread among such dissimilar peoples as the ancient Egyptians, the American Indians, and the provincial French. In some parts of France the custom of binding a child's head was observed as late as the last century. Contrary to what one would expect

from a nation known for setting ideals of elegance for much of
the world, the motives for this kind of head deformation were
eugenic rather than aesthetic.   People believed that a child's
vocation could be guided, literally, by shaping his brain.   One
nineteenth-century Jesuit priest, a Father Josset, advised mothers to work on the heads of their newborn children so that they
might one day become great orators.

8   It was a time when phrenology was the last word in head
control.   Purportedly a science, phrenology dealt with the con-
formation of the skull.   The shape of a person's head was supposed to determine his aptitudes and his moral character, and
it was thought that a direct relationship existed between the faculties of the mind and the separate portions of the brain, each
portion representing a distinct mental or moral disposition.
The number of faculties varied from twenty-seven to thirty-five,
depending on the phrenologist's persuasion.   They were classified in categories that strike us today as rather whimsical: Religion; Wit; Ideality; Cunning; Marvellousness; Mimicry;
Murder; Wonder; and so forth.
                                            . . .
9   The corset of our grandmothers was a masterpiece of functional design.   It operated on three levels—mechanical, aesthetic, and moral.   "The corset," wrote Thorstein Veblen, the
foremost portraitist of the leisure class, "is, in economic theory,
substantially a mutilation, undergone for the purpose of lowering the subject's vitality and rendering her permanently and obviously unfit for work.   It is true, the corset impairs the personal attraction of the wearer [Veblen refers of course to the
naked woman], but the loss suffered on that score is offset by
the gain in reputability which comes of her visibly increased expensiveness and infirmity."   The natural outline of the female
waist, unredeemed by art, was not savory enough for man.   It
was the *corsetière*'s business to attack the aesthetic problem at
its roots by bending women's bones into an alluring shape.
10   The whalebone corset marked an advanced technique of
disfigurement.   Although this mechanism, with its stays and
ribbons, was a comedown from the all-metal corset, the results
were complex enough.   Not only did the corset claw into the
flesh, it played havoc with the inner organs by displacing them,

eventually leading to a number of ailments. Occasionally, it caused miscarriages. On the credit side was the heightened seductiveness of the wearer, her embraceability, so to speak: the pressure applied to the waist produced the desired simultaneous inflation of the chest and buttocks, and the latter could be still further accentuated by the bustle.

. . .

11   When the harm that resulted from wearing a corset was belatedly recognized—and cavalierly dismissed—the fashion that lent an edge to men's inexhaustible appetite for swooning females was vindicated on moral grounds. People who lived in what was, from the point of view of costume history, a crustaceous age, thought of the whalebone corset as a kind of Jeanne d'Arc armor. Uncorseted women reeked of license; an unlaced waist was regarded as a vessel of sin. A heretic like Isadora Duncan, heralded by Rodin and other connoisseurs of the human physique as the embodiment of Greece, helped only to further strengthen the popular belief that the lack of a corset (or shoes) was a visible sign of depravity. Indeed, some men associate women's gradual liberation from the girdle and the garter as just another symptom of the immorality of our age.

12   Every generation has its own demented ideas on supporting some part of the human anatomy. Older people still remember a time when everybody went through life ankle-supported. Young and old wore laced boots. A shoe that did not reach well above the ankle was considered disastrous to health. What, one asks, has become of ankle support, once so warmly recommended by doctors and shoe salesmen? What keeps our ankles from breaking down in these days of low-cut shoes?

13   Ankle support has given way to arch support; millions of shoe-buying people are determined to "preserve their metatarsal arch" without so much as suspecting that it does not exist. Nevertheless, the fiction of the arch is being perpetuated to help sell "supports" and " preservers" on an impressive scale.

14   Since wearing shoes is synonymous with wearing *bad* shoes, the modern shoe inevitably becomes an instrument of deformation. The very concept of the modern shoe does not admit of an intelligent solution; it is not made to fit a human foot but to fit a wooden last whose shape is determined by the whim

of the designer. Whereas a tailor allows for a customer's un-
equal shoulders and arms, and an optometrist prescribes different lenses for the right and left eye, we buy shoes of identical
size and dimensions for our right and left foot, conveniently for-
getting—or ignoring—that, as a rule, they are not of the same
width and length. Even in countries where it is still possible
to find an artisan who is willing to make a pair of shoes to order,
chances are that he works on mass-produced lasts and comes up
with a product that, shapewise, is not much different from the
industrial one.

15   In both the manufacturer's and the customer's opinion the
shoe comes before the foot. It is less intended to protect the
foot from cold and dirt than to mold it into a fashionable
shape. Most infants' shoes are liable to dislocate the bones and
bend the foot into the shoe shape. The child does not mind the
interference; "never expect the child to complain that the shoe
is hurting him," says the podiatrist Dr. Simon Wikler, "for the
crippling process is painless." According to a ten-year study
of the Podiatry Society of the state of New York, 99 per cent of
all feet are perfect at birth, 8 per cent have developed troubles
at one year, 41 per cent at the age of five, and 80 per cent at
twenty. "We limp into adulthood," the report concludes.

16   To top it all, modern man, perhaps unknown to himself, is
afflicted with a diffuse shoe-fetishism. Inherited prejudices
derived from the Cinderella complex, practices whose origins
and reasons escape him, and traditional obtuseness combine to
make him tolerate the deformities inflicted by his shoes. In
this respect his callousness matches that of the Chinese of old.
In fact, if he ever felt a need to justify the shoes' encroachments
on his anatomy, he could cite bound feet (if he had ever heard
of them), the Chinese variety of the "correctly shaped" foot.

17   This exotic custom, which lasted nearly one thousand
years, did not extend over the whole country; the Manchus, including the imperial family, never practiced foot-binding.
Small feet are a racial characteristic of Chinese women, and the
desire to still further reduce their size in the name of beauty
seems to have been strong enough to make women tolerate ir-
revocable mutilation. As so often happens, people derive infinitely greater satisfaction from an artifact, however crude, than

from nature's product.   Besides, not only were a woman's
stunted feet highly charged with erotic symbolism, they made
her eligible for marriage.   Without them she was reduced to
spinsterhood.   Her desirability as a love object was in direct
proportion to her inability to walk.   It ought to be easy for our
women to understand the mentality of the Chinese men; every
woman knows that to wear "walking shoes"—as derogatory a
term as "sensible shoes"—puts a damper on a man's ardor.
The effect of absurdly impractical shoes, on the other hand, is
as intoxicating as a love potion.   The girl child who puts on
a pair of high-heeled shoes is magically propelled into
womanhood.

18   Modern woman is not averse to maltreating her feet for reasons similar to those of her ancient Chinese sisters, and therefore will make allowances for bunions, calluses, corns, ingrown
toenails, and hammer toes.   But she draws the line at a major
interference with her foot skeleton.   Unwilling to bother with
growing her own organic high heels, she has to get along with
artificial ones.

. . .

19   In lucid moments we look with amazement at the fraud we
perpetrate on ourselves—the bruises, mutilations, and dislo-
cated bones—but if we feel at all uncomfortable, it is not for
long.   An automatic self-defense mechanism blurs our judgment and makes right and wrong exchange places. . . .

20   Man's obsession with violating his body is not just of anthropological interest; it also helps us to understand the irrationality of dress.   The devices for interfering with human
anatomy are paralleled by a host of contraptions that simulate
deformation or are simply meant to cheat the eye: bustles, pads,
heels, wedges, codpieces, brassières, and so forth.   Once, thirty
years marked the end of a woman's desirability.   In time, this
age limit was gradually extended and pushed to a point where
it got lost altogether.   In order not only to look eternally young
but also fashionable, she had to obey ever-changing body ideals.

21   Thus a woman born at the turn of the century was a buxom
maiden in accordance with the dictates of the day.   Photographs testify to the generosity of her charms, although her
tender age ought to raise doubts about their authenticity.   In

the 1920's, when maturity and motherhood had come to her, pictures record an angular, lean, flat-chested creature. Since she did not want to renounce her attractiveness, she had to submit to an extremely unfeminine beauty ideal. Twenty years later, she was rotund again and commanded the undiminished attention of the other sex. Today, she is still in the running, ever ready to overhaul her body to prolong her youth beyond biological limits. She has inflamed three generations of men, each loyal to a different image of perfection.

22   Alas, an aged body, however arresting and deceptive the results of its updating and remodeling may be, imparts to its owner only a limited sense of youth. It serves mainly as a stylish peg for clothes. In other words, it is the clothed body that triumphs, not the naked one. As Herbert Spencer said: "The consciousness of being perfectly dressed may bestow a peace such as religion cannot give."

Questions on Content

1. How long have humans attempted to reshape their bodies? What reasons does Rudofsky give for their doing so?
2. How widespread has been the attempt to reshape the head? What reasons does Rudofsky give for this practice?
3. What is phrenology? How was it related to improving the shape of the body?
4. What three purposes did the corset serve, according to Rudofsky?
5. Why did people once wear shoes that reached well above the ankles?
6. What is the most extreme form of reshaping the human feet that Rudofsky cites?
7. How is the "irrationality of dress" related to mutilation of the body?
8. According to Rudofsky, what makes people feel most youthful and secure?

Questions on Invention, Design, and Style

1. In his first paragraph, Rudofsky conveys his attitude toward alteration of bodily shape and establishes the tone for the whole essay. What is this attitude, and what is the tone that is established? Among the sentences sustaining the tone are "Our laws permit a man to have as many wives as he pleases, provided he

marries them successively" (*paragraph 5*) and "Uncorseted women reeked of license; an unlaced waist was regarded as a vessel of sin" (*paragraph 11*). What other phrases and sentences convey Rudofsky's attitude and sustain his tone?

2. Which paragraphs make up the introduction to Rudofsky's essay? Aside from establishing the general subject matter, Rudofsky's attitude toward it, and the tone of the essay, what other functions does this introduction have? Which sentence signals to the reader that the introduction is now complete and that the main body of the essay follows?

3. Rudofsky divides his examples and illustrations of human disfigurement into three categories: disfigurations of the head, the torso, and the feet. How does he introduce each category? How does he ridicule each practice that he cites?

4. In paragraphs 9–11 Rudofsky divides the functions of the corset into three categories: "mechanical," "aesthetic," and "moral." What is the "mechanical" function? the "aesthetic" function? the "moral" function? How does Rudofsky's treatment of all three functions support his main point in the essay?

5. Paragraphs 19–22 make up the conclusion of Rudofsky's essay. Where in these paragraphs does Rudofsky pick up and develop further the idea first expressed in paragraph 5? What new perspective on body mutilation is introduced in paragraph 20? How does it prepare the reader for paragraph 22? How does the quotation from Herbert Spencer summarize this perspective and also refer back to the last two sentences of paragraph 1?

Applications

1. Observe yourself, your society, and your surroundings closely. Develop a paper on some practice that strikes you as especially ridiculous. Divide your response to the practice into at least three levels of concern.

2. Select a practice you consider extreme, unnatural, or likely to have undesirable consequences (for example, overconsumption of natural resources for industrial use). Write a paper demonstrating the soundness of your view; divide your arguments into at least three categories.

Reports, Inferences, Judgments
S. I. Hayakawa

Classifications are often most useful when they reflect small, but crucial, distinctions among similar things or ideas. S. I. Hayakawa distinguishes reports from two other kinds of statements with which we often confuse them—inferences and judgments. The result is an essay that is both valuable and informative because of its clear illustrations and definitions.

1   For the purposes of the interchange of information, the basic symbolic act is the *report* of what we have seen, heard, or felt: "There is a ditch on each side of the road." "You can get those at Smith's Hardware Store for $2.75." "There aren't any fish on that side of the lake, but there are on this side." Then there are reports of reports: "The longest waterfall in the world is Victoria Falls in Rhodesia." "The Battle of Hastings took place in 1066." "The papers say that there was a smash-up on Highway 41 near Evansville." Reports adhere to the following rules: first, they are *capable of verification;* second, they *exclude,* as far as possible, *inferences* and *judgments.* (These terms will be defined later.)

. . .

2   Reports are verifiable. We may not always be able to verify them ourselves, since we cannot track down the evidence for every piece of history we know, nor can we all go to Evansville to see the remains of the smash-up before they are cleared away. But if we are roughly agreed upon the names of things, upon what constitutes a "foot," "yard," "bushel," "kilogram," "meter," and so on, and upon how to measure time, there is relatively little danger of our misunderstanding each other. Even in a world such as we have today, in which everybody seems to be quarreling with everybody else, *we still to a surprising degree trust each other's reports.* We ask directions of total strangers when we are traveling. We follow directions on road signs without being suspicious of the people who put them up. We read books of information about science, mathematics, automotive engineering, travel, geography, the history of costume, and other such factual matters, and we usually assume that the author is doing his best to tell us as truly as he can what he

knows.   And we are safe in so assuming most of the time.
With the interest given today to the discussion of biased newspapers, propagandists, and the general untrustworthiness of
many of the communications we receive, we are likely to forget
that we still have an enormous amount of reliable information
available and that deliberate misinformation, except in warfare,
is still more the exception than the rule.   The desire for self-
preservation that compelled men to evolve means for the exchange of information also compels them to regard the giving
of false information as profoundly reprehensible.

3   At its highest development, the language of reports is the
language of science.   By "highest development" we mean
greatest general usefulness.   Presbyterian and Catholic, work-
ingman and capitalist, East German and West German *agree* on
the meanings of such symbols as *2 × 2 = 4, 100° C, HNO₃, 3:35
A.M., 1940 A.D., 1,000 kilowatts, Quercus agrifolia,* and so on.
But how, it may be asked, can there be agreement about even
this much among people who disagree about political philoso-
phies, ethical ideas, religious beliefs, and the survival of my
business versus the survival of yours?   The answer is that circumstances *compel men to agree,* whether they wish to or not.
If, for example, there were a dozen different religious sects in
the United States, each insisting on its own way of naming the
time of the day and the days of the year, the mere necessity of
having a dozen different calendars, a dozen different kinds of
watches, and a dozen sets of schedules for business hours,
trains, and television programs, to say nothing of the effort that
would be required for translating terms from one nomenclature
to another, would make life as we know it impossible.*

---

* According to information supplied by the Association of American Railroads,
"Before 1883 there were nearly 100 different time zones in the United States.   It
wasn't until November 18 of that year that . . . a system of standard time was
adopted here and in Canada.   Before then there was nothing but local or 'solar'
time. . . .   The Pennsylvania Railroad in the East used Philadelphia time,
which was five minutes slower than New York time and five minutes faster
than Baltimore time.   The Baltimore & Ohio used Baltimore time for trains
running out of Baltimore, Columbus time for Ohio, Vincennes (Indiana) time
for those going out of Cincinnati. . . .   When it was noon in Chicago, it was
12:31 in Pittsburgh, 12:24 in Cleveland, 12:17 in Toledo, 12:13 in Cincinnati,
12:09 in Louisville, 12:07 in Indianapolis, 11:50 in St. Louis, 11:48 in Dubuque, 11:39 in St. Paul, and 11:27 in Omaha.   There were 27 local time zones

4   The language of reports, then, including the more accurate reports of science, is "map" language, and because it gives us reasonably accurate representations of the "territory," it enables us to get work done. Such language may often be dull reading: one does not usually read logarithmic tables or telephone directories for entertainment. But we could not get along without it. There are numberless occasions in the talking and writing we do in everday life that *require that we state things in such a way that everybody will be able to understand and agree with our formulation.*

. . .

5   An inference, as we shall use the term, is a *statement about the unknown made on the basis of the known.* We may *infer* from the material and cut of a woman's clothes her wealth or social position; we may *infer* from the character of the ruins the origin of the fire that destroyed the building; we may *infer* from a man's calloused hands the nature of his occupation; we may *infer* from a senator's vote on an armaments bill his attitude toward Russia; we may *infer* from the structure of the land the path of a prehistoric glacier; we may *infer* from a halo on an unexposed photographic plate its past proximity to radioactive materials; we may *infer* from the sound of an engine the condition of its connecting rods. Inferences may be carefully or carelessly made. They may be made on the basis of a broad background of previous experience with the subject matter or with no experience at all. For example, the inferences a good mechanic can make about the internal condition of a motor by listening to it are often startlingly accurate, while the inferences made by an amateur (if he tries to make any) may be entirely wrong. But the common characteristic of inferences is that they are statements about matters which are not directly known, made on the basis of what has been observed.*

---

in Michigan alone. . . . A person traveling from Eastport, Maine, to San Francisco, if he wanted always to have the right railroad time and get off at the right place, had to twist the hands of his watch 20 times en route." Chicago *Daily News* (September 29, 1948).

* The behaviorist school of psychology tries to avoid inferences about what is going on in other people's minds by describing only external behavior. A famous joke about behaviorism goes: Two behaviorists meet on the street. The first says, "You're fine. How am I?"

6   The avoidance of inferences ... requires that we make no guesses as to what is going on in other people's minds. When we say, "He was angry," we are not reporting; we are making an inference from such observable facts as the following: "He pounded his fist on the table; he swore; he threw the telephone directory at his stenographer." In this particular example, the inference appears to be safe; nevertheless, it is important to remember, especially for the purposes of training oneself, that it is an inference. Such expressions as "He thought a lot of himself," "He was scared of girls," "He has an inferiority complex," made on the basis of casual observation, and "What Russia really wants to do is to establish a communist world dictatorship," made on the basis of casual reading, are highly inferential. We should keep in mind their inferential character and ... should substitute for them such statements as "He rarely spoke to subordinates in the plant," "I saw him at a party, and he never danced except when one of the girls asked him to," "He wouldn't apply for the scholarship, although I believe he could have won it easily," and "The Russian delegation to the United Nations has asked for $A, B,$ and C. Last year they voted against M and N and voted for X and Y. On the basis of facts such as these, the newspaper I read makes the inference that what Russia really wants is to establish a communist world dictatorship. I agree."

7   Even when we exercise every caution to avoid inferences and to report only what we see and experience, we all remain prone to error, since the making of inferences is a quick, almost automatic process. We may watch a car weaving as it goes down the road and say, "Look at that *drunken driver*," although what we *see* is only *the irregular motion of the car*. I once saw a man leave a dollar at a lunch counter and hurry out. Just as I was wondering why anyone should leave so generous a tip in so modest an establishment, the waitress came, picked up the dollar, put it in the cash register as she punched up ninety cents, and put a dime in her pocket. In other words, my description to myself of the event, "a dollar tip," turned out to be not a report but an inference.

8   All this is not to say that we should never make inferences. The inability to make inferences is itself a sign of men-

tal disorder. For example, the speech therapist Laura L. Lee writes, "The aphasic [brain-damaged] adult with whom I worked had great difficulty in making inferences about a picture I showed her. She could tell me what was happening at the moment in the picture, but could not tell me what might have happened just before the picture or just afterward." * Hence the question is not whether or not we make inferences; the question is whether or not we are aware of the inferences we make.

. . .

9   By judgments, we shall mean *all expressions of the writer's approval or disapproval of the occurrences, persons, or objects he is describing.* For example, a report cannot say, "It was a wonderful car," but must say something like this: "It has been driven 50,000 miles and has never required any repairs." Again, statements such as "Jack lied to us" must be suppressed in favor of the more verifiable statement, "Jack told us he didn't have the keys to his car with him. However, when he pulled a handkerchief out of his pocket a few minutes later, a bunch of car keys fell out." Also a report may not say, "The senator was stubborn, defiant, and uncooperative," or "The senator courageously stood by his principles"; it must say instead, "The senator's vote was the only one against the bill."

10   Many people regard statements such as the following as statements of "fact": "Jack *lied* to us," "Jerry is a *thief,*" "Tommy is *clever.*" As ordinarily employed, however, the word "lied" involves first an inference (that Jack knew otherwise and deliberately misstated the facts) and second a judgment (that the speaker disapproves of what he has inferred that Jack did). In the other two instances, we may substitute such expressions as, "Jerry was convicted of theft and served two years at Waupun," and "Tommy plays the violin, leads his class in school, and is captain of the debating team." After all, to say of a man that he is a "thief" is to say in effect, "He has stolen *and will steal again*"—which is more of a prediction than a report. Even to say, "He has stolen," is to make an inference

---

* "Brain Damage and the Process of Abstracting: A Problem in Language Learning," *ETC.: A Review of General Semantics,* XVI (1959), 154–62.

(and simultaneously to pass a judgment) on an act about which there may be difference of opinion among those who have examined the evidence upon which the conviction was obtained. But to say that he was "convicted of theft" is to make a statement capable of being agreed upon through verification in court and prison records.

11   Scientific verifiability rests upon the external observation of facts, not upon the heaping up of judgments. If one person says, "Peter is a deadbeat," and another says, "I think so too," the statement has not been verified. In court cases, considerable trouble is sometimes caused by witnesses who cannot distinguish their judgments from the facts upon which those judgments are based. Cross-examinations under these circumstances go something like this:

> WITNESS: That dirty double-crosser Jacobs ratted on me.
> DEFENSE ATTORNEY: Your honor, I object.
> JUDGE: Objection sustained. (Witness's remark is stricken from the record.) Now, try to tell the court exactly what happened.
> WITNESS: He double-crossed me, the dirty, lying rat!
> DEFENSE ATTORNEY: Your honor, I object!
> JUDGE: Objection sustained. (Witness's remark is again stricken from the record.) Will the witness try to stick to the facts.
> WITNESS: But I'm telling you the facts, your honor. He did double-cross me.

This can continue indefinitely unless the cross-examiner exercises some ingenuity in order to get at the facts behind the judgment. To the witness it is a "fact" that he was "double-crossed." Often patient questioning is required before the factual bases of the judgment are revealed.

12   Many words, of course, simultaneously convey a report and a judgment on the fact reported. . . . For the purposes of a report as here defined, these should be avoided. Instead of "sneaked in," one might say "entered quietly"; instead of "politician," "congressman" or "alderman" or "candidate for office"; instead of "bureaucrat," "public official"; instead of "tramp," "homeless unemployed"; instead of "dictatorial setup," "centralized authority"; instead of "crackpot," "holder of nonconformist views." A newspaper reporter, for example, is

not permitted to write, "A crowd of suckers came to listen to Senator Smith last evening in that rickety firetrap and ex-dive that disfigures the south edge of town." Instead he says, "Between 75 and 100 people heard an address last evening by Senator Smith at the Evergreen Gardens near the South Side city limits."

Questions on Content

1. What is the definition of a report, according to Hayakawa? What rules must it follow?
2. In everyday activities, how completely do we trust the reports of others? How does the desire for self-preservation shape our attitudes toward verifiability?
3. In what sense is the language of a scientific report the "highest development" of the language of reports?
4. What, according to Hayakawa, compels men to agree—whether they wish to or not? How does he illustrate this in paragraph 3?
5. Despite the fact that the language of reports often makes dull reading, it can accomplish certain things that other language cannot. What are they?
6. What is an inference, according to Hayakawa? What is the common characteristic of inferences?
7. Why is it necessary to train oneself to avoid inferences at times? Total inability to make an inference is a sign of what? How does Hayakawa illustrate this point?
8. How does Hayakawa define judgments? How are they different from reports? from inferences?
9. In a report, why is it important to avoid simultaneously making a judgment on the facts being reported? How does Hayakawa illustrate this point?

Questions on Invention, Design, and Style

1. In what ways does Hayakawa's introduction in paragraph 1 indicate to the reader that the essay's focus is on reports, rather than equally divided among reports, inferences, and judgments? What is the purpose of the illustrations of reports and "reports of reports" in this paragraph? How does the final sentence introduce the main body of the essay that follows?
2. In paragraphs 2–4 Hayakawa explores the subject of reports and their verifiability. What specific points does he make in paragraph 2? in paragraph 3? in paragraph 4? What point is illus-

trated by the footnote on pp. 172–173? Why do you think Hayakawa has put this information about time zones before 1883 in a
footnote, rather than incorporating it into his main text?

3. Paragraphs 5–8 introduce and develop the subject of inferences.
   How does paragraph 5 function as an introduction to this section
   of the essay? How does paragraph 6 help the reader to distinguish between inferences and reports? What is the main point
   of paragraph 7? How is this point illustrated by Hayakawa's story
   of the dollar and the waitress? What is his important point in paragraph 8? How does he support it?

4. Paragraphs 9–12 introduce and develop the subject of judgments. How does Hayakawa distinguish between judgments and
   reports in paragraph 9? among judgments, inferences, and reports
   in paragraph 10? between judgments and reports in paragraphs 11
   and 12?

5. Consider the last sentence of paragraph 1 as a definition that
   might be worded, "Reports are statements that are capable of verification and that exclude, as far as possible, inferences and judgments." Then examine it along with the definitions of inference
   (*paragraph 5*) and judgment (*paragraph 9*). How closely do they
   conform to the pattern of formal definition as seen in the introduction to "Classification Analysis and Definition"? How effectively do they differentiate the three key terms in the essay from
   one another? How effectively is each supported by illustrations?

6. Beginning in paragraph 1 and continuing throughout the essay,
   Hayakawa's tone is straightforward and matter of fact. How does
   this tone become apparent in the rather abrupt beginning? in the
   quotations? in the choice of words? in the punctuation and sentence length and structure? What does the first sentence in paragraph 2 contribute to this tone? How is Hayakawa able—despite
   the pronoun "we"—to maintain this tone in paragraph 2? in presenting his own personal experience in paragraph 7?

Applications

1. In a briefer essay than that of Hayakawa, follow his distinctions
   between reports, inferences, and judgments. In the main body of
   the essay, clarify the terms in your own words, and illustrate them
   by means of three versions of the same event: one that is strictly
   a report, one that is largely inference, and one that is largely
   judgment.

2. Consider the individual members of your composition class and
   the number of possible bases for dividing them into groups; for

example, you might divide them according to sex, hair color, eye color, major field of study, personality type, religious orientation, leisure activities, and so on. In an attempt to understand your own identity and your relations to other class members, consider how you fit and do not fit into some of these groups. Then write an essay, using classification analysis and presenting your findings about yourself and your relationships.

3. Consider the many different groups (for example, age, social, ethnic, religious, or interest groups) to which you belong. Then select one that you consider particularly significant, and write a paper defining what it means to be a member of that group. Use your own experience and your observations of others to formulate examples that will illustrate the qualities of this group.

Process Analysis

Directions, instructions, and the importance of process analysis
Dividing a process into its stages or steps
The process or operation as a whole
The steps or stages as the parts
Process analysis as part of a larger essay
Two basic types of process analysis: giving directions and narrating
   how a process works

If you have ever been frustrated by confusing directions on how to get somewhere you needed to be or by unclear instructions on how to bake a soufflé or install stereo speakers in your car, you already recognize the importance of clear instructions. But if you have ever tried to give directions to someone else, you know that it's not always easy to do so clearly.

Knowing the principles of analysis can help in such cases. Think of the *whole* as the entire operation to be performed and the *parts* as steps or stages in that process. *Process analysis* is the examination of these steps or stages and how they fit together to make up the whole operation or action.

If the process is to be laid out clearly for the reader, you should divide it into major stages as well as into individual steps. Here the diagram we used in the introduction to "Classification Analysis and Definition" is helpful. Consider this brief process analysis of skate sailing in Bruce Catton's "Two Visions of Equal Force," for example:

> You took thick strips of wood and made an oblong frame, about four feet long by three feet wide, added a couple of cross braces for stiffening and for handholds, and covered the frame with a piece of discarded bed sheet cut to size. Then you went to the ice, put on your skates, held the frame in front of you, and let the wind take charge.

Here Catton divides the process into the stages of building and of sailing, as we can see in his two parallel sentences separated by the word "then." The parallelism of the three individual steps in both sentences is also made clear by the fact that all six are stated as verbs with direct objects. The whole pattern can be diagrammed as follows:

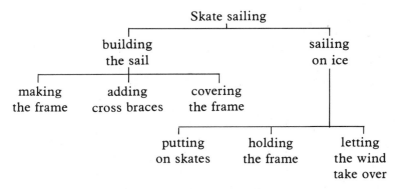

Catton's process analysis, although only two sentences long, works very well in the larger context of his essay, where it very quickly lets the reader know what a skate sail looks like and how it is used. Process analysis, then, like the other patterns described in this book, is often used to clarify a point in a few sentences within a longer work.

Another brief process analysis within a larger essay can be found in the third paragraph of S. I. Hayakawa's "Insoluble Problems," on page 94. Hayakawa carefully enumerates the six stages by which rats and humans become increasingly frustrated when their actions fail to give the results they have been conditioned to expect:

First, they are trained to make habitually a given choice when confronted by a given problem; secondly, they get a terrible shock when they find that the conditions have changed and that the choice doesn't produce the expected results; third, whether through shock, anxiety, or frustration, they may fixate on the original choice and continue to make that choice regardless of consequences; fourth, they sullenly refuse to act at all; fifth, when by external compulsion they are forced to make a choice, they again make the one they were originally trained to make—and again get a bump on the nose; finally, even *with the goal visible in front of them,* to be attained simply by making a different choice, they go crazy out of frustration.

Notice that the entire process analysis consists of one sentence divided into six independent clauses, each one numbered (*first* through *finally*). Hayakawa thus emphasizes the importance of the order, or sequence, of the steps in the process.

The same attention to clear division into major stages (as in the Catton excerpt) and to clear establishment of a sequence of steps (as in the Hayakawa excerpt) should underlie the planning and writing of any process analysis, whether it is a single sentence or many pages in length, a set of directions or the narrative of a process.

Process analyses can be divided into two basic types: those that give directions on how to perform the process and those that simply narrate how a process is or was performed.

The first type is intended to give readers the information necessary to perform the process themselves and is usually written in the second person ("Go straight ahead until you come to the second stop light and then turn right . . ."). Three of the essays in this subsection are of this "how-to" type: Peter Elbow's "Freewriting," Robert Angus' "Good Keyboard Recording," and Caroline Seebohm's "How to Change Your Point of View." We are all familiar with recipes, instruction booklets, and other forms of directions that are intended to accomplish the same kinds of things. Angus' essay provides an excellent model; it begins with a statement of what equipment is needed (recorder, microphone and stand, headphones, and tape) before it gives directions for the actual recording process. How many times have you started to follow instructions, only to find that midway in the process you needed an ingredient or tool that wasn't readily at hand?

The other type of process analysis is intended to narrate, or report, to readers about a process that they cannot perform or are unlikely to, as in the Hayakawa excerpt. In "A Delicate Operation," for example, Roy C. Selby, Jr. narrates the process of a brain operation. He tells his readers not how to perform it but how a surgeon already has performed it. In the same way, Jessica Mitford, in "To Bid the World Farewell," doesn't give directions on how to embalm a human body, but she does tell how the embalmer does so. Finally, in "Stars: Where Life Begins," the editors of *Time* narrate the process by which stars develop and disintegrate—clearly not a how-to essay. Further examples might include an account of how any machine works (as opposed to directions on how to operate it) or of how rats and humans exhibit frustration (rather than how to frustrate them).

Freewriting
Peter Elbow

In frequent freewriting sessions, composition teacher Peter Elbow has found that writers can learn to separate the producing process from the editing process and as a result can significantly improve their writing.

1   The most effective way I know to improve your writing is to do freewriting exercises regularly. At least three times a week. They are sometimes called "automatic writing," "babbling," or "jabbering" exercises. The idea is simply to write for ten minutes (later on, perhaps fifteen or twenty). Don't stop for anything. Go quickly without rushing. Never stop to look back, to cross something out, to wonder how to spell something, to wonder what word or thought to use, or to think about what you are doing. If you can't think of a word or a spelling, just use a squiggle or else write, "I can't think of it." Just put down something. The easiest thing is just to put down whatever is in your mind. If you get stuck it's fine to write "I can't think what to say, I can't think what to say" as many times as you want; or repeat the last word you wrote over and over again; or anything else. The only requirement is that you *never* stop.

2   What happens to a freewriting exercise is important. It must be a piece of writing which, even if someone reads it, doesn't send any ripples back to you. It is like writing something and putting it in a bottle in the sea. The teacherless class helps your writing by providing maximum feedback. Freewrit-

ings help you by providing no feedback at all.   When I assign one, I invite the writer to let me read it, but also tell him to keep it if he prefers.   I read it quickly and make no comments at all and I do not speak with him about it.   The main thing is that a freewriting must never be evaluated in any way; in fact there must be no discussion or comment at all.

3   Here is an example of a fairly coherent exercise (sometimes they are very incoherent, which is fine):

> I think I'll write what's on my mind, but the only thing on my mind right now is what to write for ten minutes.   I've never done this before and I'm not prepared in any way—the sky is cloudy today, how's that? now I'm afraid I won't be able to think of what to write when I get to the end of the sentence—well, here I am at the end of the sentence—here I am again, again, again, again, at least I'm still writing—Now I ask is there some reason to be happy that I'm still writing—ah yes!   Here comes the question again—What am I getting out of this?   What point is there in it?   It's almost obscene to always ask it but I seem to question everything that way and I was gonna say something else pertaining to that but I got so busy writing down the first part that I forgot what I was leading into.   This is kind of fun oh don't stop writing—cars and trucks speeding by somewhere out the window, pens clittering across peoples' papers.   The sky is still cloudy—is it symbolic that I should be mentioning it?   Huh?   I dunno.   Maybe I should try colors, blue, red, dirty words—wait a minute—no can't do that, orange, yellow, arm tired, green pink violet magenta lavender red brown black green—now that I can't think of any more colors—just about done—relief? maybe.
>
> . . .

4   Freewriting may seem crazy but actually it makes simple sense.   Think of the difference between speaking and writing. Writing has the advantage of permitting more editing.   But that's its downfall too.   Almost everybody interposes a massive and complicated series of editings between the time words start to be born into consciousness and when they finally come off the end of the pencil or typewriter onto the page.   This is partly because schooling makes us obsessed with the "mistakes" we make in writing.   Many people are constantly thinking about spelling and grammar as they try to write.   I am always thinking about the awkwardness, wordiness, and general

mushiness of my natural verbal product as I try to write down words.

5   But it's not just "mistakes" or "bad writing" we edit as we write. We also edit unacceptable thoughts and feelings, as we do in speaking. In writing there is more time to do it so the editing is heavier: when speaking, there's someone right there waiting for a reply and he'll get bored or think we're crazy if we don't come out with *something*. Most of the time in speaking, we settle for the catch-as-catch-can way in which the words tumble out. In writing, however, there's a chance to try to get them right. But the opportunity to get them right is a terrible burden: you can work for two hours trying to get a paragraph "right" and discover it's not right at all. And then give up.

6   Editing, *in itself*, is not the problem. Editing is usually necessary if we want to end up with something satisfactory. The problem is that editing goes on *at the same time* as producing. The editor is, as it were, constantly looking over the shoulder of the producer and constantly fiddling with what he's doing while he's in the middle of trying to do it. No wonder the producer gets nervous, jumpy, inhibited, and finally can't be coherent. It's an unnecessary burden to try to think of words and also worry at the same time whether they're the right words.

7   The main thing about freewriting is that it is *nonediting*. It is an exercise in bringing together the process of producing words and putting them down on the page. Practiced regularly, it undoes the ingrained habit of editing at the same time you are trying to produce. It will make writing less blocked because words will come more easily. You will use up more paper, but chew up fewer pencils.

8   Next time you write, notice how often you stop yourself from writing down something you were going to write down. Or else cross it out after it's written. "Naturally," you say, "it wasn't any good." But think for a moment about the occasions when you spoke well. Seldom was it because you first got the beginning just right. Usually it was a matter of a halting or even garbled beginning, but you kept going and your speech finally became coherent and even powerful. There is a lesson here for writing: trying to get the beginning just right is a formula for failure—and probably a secret tactic to make yourself

give up writing. Make some words, whatever they are, and then grab hold of that line and reel in as hard as you can. Afterwards you can throw away lousy beginnings and make new ones. This is the quickest way to get into good writing.

9   The habit of compulsive, premature editing doesn't just make writing hard. It also makes writing dead. Your voice is damped out by all the interruptions, changes, and hesitations between the consciousness and the page. In your natural way of producing words there is a sound, a texture, a rhythm—a voice—which is the main source of power in your writing. I don't know how it works, but this voice is the force that will make a reader listen to you, the energy that drives the meanings through his thick skull. Maybe you don't *like* your voice; maybe people have made fun of it. But it's the only voice you've got. It's your only source of power. You better get back into it, no matter what you think of it. If you keep writing in it, it may change into something you like better. But if you abandon it, you'll likely never have a voice and never be heard.

Questions on Content

1. Describe the process of "freewriting" as Elbow defines it. What is the only absolute requirement?
2. What kind of discussion and comment should a piece of freewriting receive?
3. What does Elbow think about when he does freewriting?
4. What, beside "mistakes" and "bad writing," do we edit out when we write? When should editing take place, according to Elbow?
5. In what way is the advantage of writing over speaking also a disadvantage?
6. According to Elbow, how much time should be spent beginning a piece of writing?
7. How does freewriting help to overcome the problem of editing at the wrong time?
8. How does premature and compulsive editing lead to dead writing?
9. What is the advantage of practicing freewriting regularly?
10. What is the source of power in writing, according to Elbow? What are the consequences of abandoning that source of power?
11. What, according to Elbow, should be the relation between producing and editing?

Questions on Invention, Design, and Style

1. Review Elbow's directions for the freewriting process in paragraph 1. Are they clear? Could you follow them without confusion? Why or why not? If not, what has interfered with effective communication?

2. What purpose is served by the example of a fairly coherent freewriting exercise in paragraph 3? Does it encourage or discourage you to try the same thing?

3. Consider paragraph 8 as an analysis of the larger process of writing, which includes both producing and editing. In relation to what comes before and after, does this paragraph provide sufficient detail to be clear? Does it help the reader to understand Elbow's claim about what the relation between producing and editing should be?

4. Elbow is adept at using illustrations, comparisons, and contrasts to enliven his points. Consider, for example, how the following passages help to strengthen his message:
   a. "[Freewriting] doesn't send any ripples back to you. It is like writing something and putting it in a bottle in the sea" (*paragraph 2*).
   b. "... grab hold of that line and reel in as hard as you can" (*paragraph 8*).
   What other examples of concrete imagery add life to Elbow's message?

5. How would you characterize Elbow's tone in this essay? Support your characterization with specific examples. Do you consider the tone appropriate for Elbow's purpose? Why or why not?

6. How do Elbow's examples show that he is drawing from his experience as a writer and as a teacher of writing?

7. How does paragraph 9 conclude the essay and clarify Elbow's purpose in writing it?

Applications

1. Write directions for performing a relatively simple action, using a style appropriate to your subject. Try out your instructions on a classmate who has never performed the operation that you describe.

2. Following Elbow's directions, practice freewriting for ten minutes. On the basis of this experience, decide whether or not you

would profit from repeating it three times a week, as Elbow suggests.

3. As clearly and honestly as you can, analyze the process by which you write for this course, beginning with the physical setting and including the prewriting stage. Try to identify your strengths, problem areas, and possibilities for improvement.

4. Both Ray Bradbury (pp. 34–36, *especially paragraphs 10–12*) and Peter Elbow stress the importance of viewing writing as a process with two stages: producing and editing. Make a list of the characteristics that Bradbury and Elbow assign to each of these stages. Then, using their experiences and your own as sources, develop an analysis of the writing process. Give credit to Bradbury and Elbow whenever you refer directly to their ideas or repeat their words.

How to Change Your Point of View
Caroline Seebohm

As an alternative approach to solving problems in our culture, Caroline Seebohm suggests *lateral thinking*, which involves looking at problems from different angles and working with, rather than against, them. In this essay she explains and clarifies the process through illustrations, contrasts, and various forms of comparison.

1   The famous Dr. Edward Jenner was busy trying to solve the problem of smallpox. After studying case after case, he still found no possible cure. *He had reached an impasse in his thinking.* At this point, he changed his tactics. Instead of focusing on people who had smallpox, he switched his attention to people who did *not* have smallpox. It turned out that dairymaids apparently never got the disease. From the discovery that harmless cowpox gave protection against deadly smallpox came vaccination and the end of smallpox as a scourge in the Western world.

2   We often reach an impasse in our thinking. We are looking at a problem and trying to solve it and it seems there is a deadend, an "aporia" (the technical term in logic meaning "no opening"). It is on these occasions that we become tense, we

feel pressured, overwhelmed, in a state of stress. We struggle vainly, fighting to solve the problem.

3   Dr. Jenner, however, did something about this situation. He stopped fighting the problem and simply changed his point of view—from patients to dairymaids. Picture the process going something like this: Suppose the brain is a computer. This computer has absorbed into its memory bank all your history, your experiences, your training, your information received through life, and it is programmed according to all this data. To change your point of view, you must reprogram your computer, thus freeing yourself to take in new ideas and develop new ways of looking at things. Dr. Jenner, in effect, by reprogramming his computer, erased the old way of looking at his smallpox problem and was free to receive new alternatives.

4   That's all very well, you may say, but how do we actually *do* that?

5   Doctor and philosopher Edward de Bono has come up with a technique for changing our point of view, and he calls it Lateral Thinking.

6   The normal Western approach to a problem is to *fight* it. The saying, "When the going gets tough, the tough get going," epitomizes this aggressive, combat-ready attitude toward problem-solving. No matter what the problem is, or the techniques available for solving it, the framework produced by our Western way of thinking is *fight*. Dr. de Bono calls this *vertical* thinking; the traditional, sequential, Aristotelian thinking of logic, moving firmly from one step to the next, like toy blocks being built one on top of the other. The flaw is, of course, that if at any point one of the steps is not reached, or one of the toy blocks is incorrectly placed, then the whole structure collapses. Impasse is reached, and frustration, tension, feelings of *fight* take over.

7   Lateral thinking, Dr. de Bono says, is a new technique of thinking about things—a technique that avoids this fight altogether, and solves the problem in an entirely unexpected fashion.

8   In one of Sherlock Holmes's cases, his assistant, Dr. Watson, pointed out that a certain dog was of no importance to the

case because it did not appear to have done anything. Sherlock
Holmes took the opposite point of view and maintained that the
fact the dog had done nothing was of the utmost significance,
for it should have been expected to do something, and on this
basis he solved the case. This, and the Dr. Jenner example,
come from Dr. de Bono's book, *New Think* (Basic Books).

9   Lateral thinking sounds simple. And it is. Once you
have solved a problem laterally, you wonder how you could ever
have been hung up on it. The knack is making that vital shift
in emphasis, that sidestepping of the problem, instead of grappling with it head-on. It could even be as simple as going to
a special part of the house, which is quiet and restful; buying
a special chair, an "escape" chair, where we can lose our day-to-
day preoccupations and allow our computers to reprogram
themselves and become free to take in new ideas, see things in
a different light.

10   Dr. A. A. Bridger, psychiatrist at Columbia University and
in private practice in New York, explains how lateral thinking
works with his patients. "Many people come to me wanting to
stop smoking, for instance," he says. "Most people fail when
they are trying to stop smoking because they wind up telling
themselves, 'No, I will not smoke; no, I shall not smoke; no,
I will not; no, I cannot . . .' It's a fight—and fighting makes
as much sense as telling yourself over and over again not to
think of what you want—what happens is you end up smoking
more.

11   "So instead of looking at the problem from the old way of
no, and fighting it, I show them how to reinforce a position of
yes. I give them a whole new point of view—that you are your
body's keeper, and your body is a physical plant through which
you experience life. If you stop to think about it, there's really
something helpless about your body. It can do nothing for itself. It has no choice, it is like a baby's body. You begin then
a whole new way of looking at it—'I am now going to take care
of myself, and give myself some respect and protection, by not
smoking.' So that *not* giving yourself respect and protection
becomes a deprivation.

12   "There is a Japanese parable about a jackass tied to a pole
by a rope. The rope rubs tight against his neck. The more the

jackass fights and pulls on the rope, the tighter and tighter it gets round his throat—until he winds up dead as a doornail. On the other hand, as soon as he stops fighting, he finds that the rope gets slack, he can walk around, maybe find some grass to eat. . . . That's the same principle: The more you fight something, the more anxious you become—the more you're involved in a bad pattern, the more difficult it is to escape pain.

13 "Lateral thinking," Dr. Bridger goes on, "is simply approaching a problem with what I would call an Eastern flanking maneuver. You know, when a zen archer wants to hit the target with a bow and arrow, he doesn't concentrate on the target, he concentrates rather on what he has in his hands, so when he lets the arrow go, his focus is on the end-result of the arrow, rather than the target. This is what an Eastern flanking maneuver implies—instead of approaching the target directly, you approach it from a sideways point of view—or laterally instead of vertically."

14 Dr. Bridger has made a shift away from traditional thinking in his practice. "We are finally beginning to realize that many long-term problems can be resolved in short-term ways. People for years have always felt that problems that have been around for a long time will take a very long time to solve. That just does not happen to be so. For instance, when a patient is anxious, fighting a problem, often he can be taught, in one hypnotic session, how to relax and lower his psychic tension. This creates a much more workable feeling-tone for problem-solving. While medicines can also lower tension, all medicines, after all, are poisons. Other forms of relaxation, such as transcendental meditation, take a very long period of time to get going. Hypnosis, by contrast, is a safe, quick lateral technique of lowering psychic tension and shifting gears. This increases receptivity for looking at a problem in a new way."

15 Reminding ourselves we are in a period called an *Intermediate Impossible* is another useful technique. That is, looking at our current situation in life as only an intermediate step toward something else, so that we don't get bogged down and can go on to the next step. The medical student, for instance, unless he accepted his training as an intermediate impossible,

would never get through it. Another familiar example is the
harassed mother raising young children—going through the
"Terrible Twos." She sees her life as a nightmare, "God, this
is going to be the way it is until they are grown up . . ." as opposed to seeing the "Terrible Twos" as an intermediate impossible. If only she could remind herself that the current situation is intermediate, only a phase, she might relax—if only she
could look at her situation laterally, instead of fighting it.

16   Lateral thinking, in short, is most valuable in those problem situations where vertical thinking has been unable to provide a solution. When you reach that impasse, and feel the
fight upon you, quickly reprogram your thinking.

1. Is there any other way the problem can be expressed?
2. What random ideas come to mind when you relax and think about
    it?
3. Can you turn the problem upside down?
4. Can you invent another problem to take its place?
5. Can you shift the emphasis from one part of the problem to
    another?

17   These are difficult questions, and it takes imagination to
ask and to answer them. But that is how we change our point
of view—by being imaginative enough to think up new ideas,
find new ways of looking at old problems, invent new methods
for dealing with old patterns. Think laterally instead of vertically. Take the *fight* out of our lives. Move Eastward in our
attitudes.

18   "I think the answer lies in that direction," affirms Dr.
Bridger. "Take the situation where someone is in a crisis. The
Chinese word for crisis is divided into two characters, one
meaning *danger* and the other meaning *opportunity*. We in
the Western world focus only upon the danger aspect of crisis.
Crisis in Western civilization has come to mean danger, period. And yet the word can also mean opportunity. Let us
now suggest to the person in crisis that he cease concentrating
so upon the dangers involved and the difficulties, and concentrate instead upon the opportunity—for there is always opportunity in crisis. Looking at a crisis from an opportunity point of
view is a lateral thought.

19   "It's about time we stopped fighting in order to find a solution.   Let us float along with the problem so that we can look at it from lateral points of view.   Then we can be receptive to new ideas, renew and restimulate our senses, find a new way of living."

Questions on Content

1. How did Dr. Jenner discover the solution to the problem of smallpox?   What conditions led to his discovery?
2. What is an *aporia*?   How does it affect someone who tries to solve a problem?
3. How is the brain like a computer in lateral thinking, according to Seebohm?
4. What is lateral thinking for Dr. de Bono?   What is vertical thinking?   What is the usual Western way of thinking? the Aristotelian way?
5. What approach does Dr. Bridger use to help patients stop smoking?
6. What part does imagination play in changing our point of view, according to Seebohm?
7. What characters form the Chinese word for *crisis*?   Which concept is emphasized in Western thinking?   Which is emphasized in lateral thinking?

Questions on Invention, Design, and Style

1. Seebohm describes thought processes chiefly through illustrations, parables, and analogies, such as the story of Dr. Jenner. Show other instances where she uses examples rather than direct statements.   How effective is this technique?   Is it appropriate to the general point she is making?
2. How is Seebohm's first paragraph different from many of the opening paragraphs that we have seen in other essays?   Is it an effective introduction?   Why or why not?
3. How is Seebohm's computer analogy helpful in explaining the process by which Jenner made his discovery?
4. Seebohm uses brief comparisons and contrasts to highlight advantages of lateral thought:
   a. "Instead of focusing on people who had smallpox, he switched his attention to people who did *not* have smallpox" (*paragraph 1*).

b. "The knack is making . . . that sidestepping of the problem, instead of grappling with it head-on" (*paragraph 9*).

c. "So instead of looking at the problem from the old way of *no*, and fighting it, I show them how to reinforce a position of *yes*" (*paragraph 11*).

How do these quick contrasts help to develop the author's point about changing your point of view?   Can you find other examples of contrasts or comparisons that function in this way?

5. How do the illustrations from Dr. Bridger's practice clarify the usefulness of lateral thinking?

6. What purposes do the Japanese parable of the jackass and the example of the Zen archer serve?

7. What is the function of paragraph 16?   What is its relation to the various illustrations, parables, and analogies in the preceding paragraphs?

Applications

1. Think back to the last time that you reached an impasse in trying to solve a problem.   Write a paper telling how you solved (or might have solved) the problem through the process of lateral thinking.

2. If you have read Hayakawa's "Insoluble Problems" (p. 93), review it in the light of Seebohm's essay.   Consider which of the problems mentioned by Hayakawa might be approached effectively through lateral thinking.   Write a process analysis showing how lateral thinking might supply an answer to one of them.

3. Write a paper about an athletic event you witnessed or participated in, in which alternative strategies were used (or could have been used) effectively by one side.

4. Consider your college course work and extracurricular activities from a vertical point of view.   This would probably stress a career or a major course of study.   Now adopt a lateral view—seeing also the things you enjoy most and do best, activities you want to pursue, instructors whose courses you would like to take.   In a paper set forth the alternatives in course work and extracurricular activities offered by a lateral point of view.

Good Keyboard Recording
Robert Angus

In a practical, workmanlike manner, *Music Journal* columnist Robert Angus outlines the necessary equipment for recording and divides the process of recording into clear, easily followed steps.

1   You don't have to be a recording expert to make really good keyboard recordings, but you do have to have the right equipment, you do have to know how to use it, and you do have to be willing to take the time to experiment.   Actually, that last quality overcomes a good many shortcomings in the first two.

2   For example, having the right equipment doesn't necessarily mean having a 16-channel console and completely equipped recording studio, with a battery of condenser microphones and a professional open reel tape deck operating at 15 or 30 inches per second.   You'd be surprised what really good results you can get with a good quality cassette deck, a good but not necessarily expensive microphone and the right recording tape.

3   The beauty of keyboard recording is that for optimum results you don't need dozens of mikes, miles of cable and a mixing panel.   In the case of most piano or organ recordings, a single microphone (or two, if you're recording in stereo) will be plenty.   Since there's no mixing to be done, you have only one set of controls to worry about—those on your recorder.   Setting them properly is a two-man job (one plays the piano while the other makes the necessary adjustments), and a really good recording demands some preliminary work.

4   Let's start with what you do need.   Firstly, there's the recorder.   Obviously, the better it is, the better the finished result will be.   A good open reel recorder operating at 7½ or 15 inches per second will produce the best results, but a good cassette deck is capable of making a tape good enough to cut records from.   Since both pianos and organs are capable of producing sustained tones, a recording on an inferior deck will contain audible wow—a variation in pitch.   So if you have a choice between two recorders, pick the one with lowest wow and flutter.

5   Next, you need a microphone. . . .   For solo keyboard recording in a small room where there are no external sounds, I

prefer a good omnidirectional microphone, capable of capturing some of the ambience of the auditorium as well as the direct sound of the instrument.   This is particularly true in the case of a cathedral or church pipe organ when no audience is present.

6   Where there is an audience present, or there's some other extraneous sound (a train rattling by every twenty minutes or so, or children playing outside), you'll need a good cardioid or unidirectional microphone.   Whichever type you choose, you're also going to need something to mount it on.   You may choose a floor stand, a microphone boom, or some means of suspending it from the ceiling in an auditorium.   That means having some idea in advance where you're going to locate the mike.   The exact height and distance from the instrument is a matter of trial-and-error we'll cover later on.   Whichever type of mount you select, make sure (1) that it will hold the microphone securely and (2) that it won't vibrate during recording, adding an unwanted signal of its own.   You'll also need a good pair of stereo headphones, so that you can hear what's coming into the recorder. Pick a pair which surrounds the ear and cuts out as much external sound as possible.

7   The only other thing you're going to need is tape.   How much you need depends on the length of the program you're going to record, whether you'll have a chance to do more than one take, what tape speed you're using, and the like.   The type of tape you select depends on the flexibility of your recorder, your budget and your own ear.   For example, one of the most expensive cassettes available is chromium dioxide, which offers good high frequency response and very good signal-to-noise ratio. But I find that it imparts a steely quality to piano recordings, while doing very nice things indeed for a pipe organ.   Conversely, I much prefer the warmer, bassier sound of a good ferric oxide tape for piano recording, while noting that organ recordings on it sometimes sound tubbier to me than on chromium dioxide or ferrichrome tape.   Nor are all ferric oxide tapes alike.   If you're in doubt about which one to use, you'd be well advised to buy two or three different kinds and make test recordings.   The same thing applies to ferric oxide open reel tape. Your ear and personal preference are more important here than

manufacturer's specifications or dealer recommendations. Whatever you're recording, make sure you have plenty of tape. In the case of open reel recording, that means extra reels or extra-play tape. In the case of cassettes, I'd have about twice as many C-60 or C-90 cassettes as I'd expect to need. Despite their extra playing time, I wouldn't use C-120s for recording live music because the extra-thin base makes stretching possible, because there's more danger of print-through of the recorded signal from one layer of tape to the next, and because bass frequency response usually isn't as good.

8   Where to put the microphone? In the case of a solo piano, the most common location is on a floor-mount mike stand about four to six feet off the floor and two to five feet from the bend in the piano. A common record company practice is to remove the lid of a grand piano altogether and to suspend a single microphone directly over the top of the piano some four or five feet above the strings. Still another technique is to use a boom which places the mike between the raised lid of the piano and the strings. Whichever approach you take—and my advice is to start with the first one—you'll want to shift the microphone up and down, back and forth until the sound is the best obtainable.

9   To check, put a tape on your recorder and put it in record mode with the pause button in place. Then switch to tape monitor. Plug in your headphones and listen as an assistant moves the microphone while the performer you're going to record plays the piano. You should be hearing exactly what the tape will hear when you release the pause button. If you listen carefully, you'll notice minute changes in tone color, in balance. You may even want to try an experimental recording, to make absolutely sure.

10   The same procedure applies to selecting a spot for organ recording, although in the case of organs the microphone generally is located somewhat farther away. Frequently in the case of church organs, the microphone (or microphones, if you're recording in stereo) is suspended ten or twelve feet off the floor over the first row or two of the congregation. In the case of cathedral organs, it may take you some time and a considerable amount of experimentation to locate just the right spot for the

kind of recording you have in mind. For other keyboard instruments, experimentation is the order of the day.

11   If your mike or mikes are in place and you've remembered to put tape on the machine, let's check recording levels. Ask your performer for a sample passage, preferably something with a double forte or fortissimo. The needle on your recorder's volume meter should peak at 0 VU (in the case of cassette equipment) or at +2 or +3 VU in the case of open reel (if the instruction book accompanying your recorder advises something other than these limits, follow its advice). You may need several sample passages before settling on exactly the right volume levels. Adjust each channel of a stereo setup separately. The location of one microphone might mean lower volume on one channel, or the use of two microphones not sold originally as a stereo pair might require some volume boost or reduction. Check pianissimos too, if possible, to be sure you can hear them clearly through your headphones. Once you've set your volume levels to accommodate the loudest passages you're likely to encounter, *leave the volume controls alone.* Too many recordings are marred by engineers who try to ride gain during the recording procedure. The result is a lack of dynamics in the finished recording, a tape which sounds dull and lifeless. And it's much more work to keep fiddling with those volume controls than to leave them alone. In fact, once you press the start button, most of the hard work is over.

12   Now let's push the start button. If you're recording at a live concert, there's not much you can do, except to change tapes before they run out. But if you can start and stop the performer and do repeat takes when necessary, you're likely to end up with a more professional-sounding tape. In fact, by rerecording a complete short selection or a movement of a longer work, you can eliminate any errors the performer may make, as well as any blemishes in the recording. Unless you're highly skilled at tape splicing and editing, don't try to record phrases or short passages with the idea of editing them in to cover up a defect. Instead, record complete sections or works. A bad splice or edit sounds much worse than the blemish you're trying to hide. Use a silent spot on the tape to make your splice.

13   When you've finished your recording, before everybody

goes home and you dismantle your equipment, listen to what you've recorded, from beginning to end. If there are any rough spots, you still have the chance to correct them. As long as the microphones are still in place, you can record corrections and splice them into the body of the tape without abrupt changes in the acoustics. Besides, the performer usually enjoys hearing how he sounds.

Questions on Content

1. What three things are necessary for good keyboard recordings?
2. In what way is a keyboard recording simpler than one that involves more instruments?
3. What does a person *not* need in order to make a good keyboard recording? What *does* he need?
4. What is the most important consideration in choosing a tape recorder for music?
5. What special precautions must be taken when there is an audience or some extraneous sound present during the recording?
6. What kind of tape is generally better for piano recordings? for organ recordings? Why does Angus not recommend C-120 tapes?
7. What is the most common microphone placement for recording a solo piano? How can the placement be checked?
8. How should the recording level be set for cassette recording equipment? How much should it be changed during the actual recording?
9. Why should you not plan to edit phrases or short passages of the music?

Questions on Invention, Design, and Style

1. For what type of reading audience has Angus written his analysis? How do the types of examples he uses and the detail of his analysis reveal the nature of this audience?
2. Consider paragraphs 1–3 as the introduction to this essay. What is Angus' reason for minimizing the amount of equipment needed for such a recording? By what other statements does Angus encourage the skeptical reader that he or she is capable of making a good keyboard recording?
3. In paragraphs 4–7 Angus enumerates and explains each item of equipment needed for the recording. What kinds of considerations does he take into account? Why does he concentrate on the

points he does?   How does he indicate in paragraph 7 that tape
is the last item of equipment he will discuss?

4. In paragraphs 8–13 Angus analyzes the process of actually recording.   What is the first step?   What is the relationship of paragraph 9 to paragraph 8?   of paragraph 10 to paragraph 8?   How
does Angus indicate to the reader that the second step in the process will be discussed in paragraph 11?   How does he indicate
that the third step will be discussed in paragraph 12?   How does
paragraph 13 both introduce a final step in the process and bring
the essay to a conclusion?

5. Examine Angus' writing style closely.   What purpose is served
by his use of direct address: "You don't have to . . ." (*paragraph
1*), "You'd be surprised . . ." (*paragraph 2*), "you don't need dozens of mikes . . ." (*paragraph 3*), "Let's start with what you do
need" (*paragraph 4*), and so on?   What purpose is served by his
diction in the following examples: "I prefer a good omnidirectional microphone . . ." (*paragraph 5*); "you'll need a good cardioid or unidirectional microphone . . ." (*paragraph 6*)?   Why has
Angus written in such an informal style yet used terms that are
quite technical?

Applications

1. Think of a process familiar to you that involves several items of
equipment.   Write an essay in which you first arouse your readers' interest in the subject, then explain what equipment is
needed, and, finally, give clear and practical directions for performing the process step by step with minimum danger of failure.

2. Write an essay in which you explain the best procedure to follow
in carrying out such a common task as packing a car, painting a
bookcase, or keeping a stereo in top working condition.

A Delicate Operation
Roy C. Selby, Jr.

**Neurosurgeon Roy C. Selby, Jr., bases this analysis of the process of
brain surgery on an actual operation conducted in 1973.   By means
of detailed description and skillfully handled suspense, he not only**

brings us into the operating room with the surgeon but he also makes us aware of the human concerns and anxieties that the surgeon and husband share before, during, and after the operation.

1   In the autumn of 1973 a woman in her early fifties noticed, upon closing one eye while reading, that she was unable to see clearly. Her eyesight grew slowly worse. Changing her eyeglasses did not help. She saw an ophthalmologist, who found that her vision was seriously impaired in both eyes. She then saw a neurologist, who confirmed the finding and obtained X rays of the skull and an EMI scan—a photograph of the patient's head. The latter revealed a tumor growing between the optic nerves at the base of the brain. The woman was admitted to the hospital by a neurosurgeon.

2   Further diagnosis, based on angiography, a detailed X-ray study of the circulatory system, showed the tumor to be about two inches in diameter and supplied by many small blood vessels. It rested beneath the brain, just above the pituitary gland, stretching the optic nerves to either side and intimately close to the major blood vessels supplying the brain. Removing it would pose many technical problems. Probably benign and slow-growing, it may have been present for several years. If left alone it would continue to grow and produce blindness and might become impossible to remove completely. Removing it, however, might not improve the patient's vision and could make it worse. A major blood vessel could be damaged, causing a stroke. Damage to the undersurface of the brain could cause impairment of memory and changes in mood and personality. The hypothalamus, a most important structure of the brain, could be injured, causing coma, high fever, bleeding from the stomach, and death.

3   The neurosurgeon met with the patient and her husband and discussed the various possibilities. The common decision was to operate.

4   The patient's hair was shampooed for two nights before surgery. She was given a cortisonelike drug to reduce the risk of damage to the brain during surgery. Five units of blood were cross-matched, as a contingency against hemorrhage. At 1:00 P.M. the operation began. After the patient was anesthetized her hair was completely clipped and shaved from the

scalp. Her head was prepped with an organic iodine solution for ten minutes. Drapes were placed over her, leaving exposed only the forehead and crown of the skull. All the routine instruments were brought up—the electrocautery used to coagulate areas of bleeding, bipolar coagulation forceps to arrest bleeding from individual blood vessels without damaging adjacent tissues, and small suction tubes to remove blood and cerebrospinal fluid from the head, thus giving the surgeon a better view of the tumor and surrounding areas.

5   A curved incision was made behind the hairline so it would be concealed when the hair grew back. It extended almost from ear to ear. Plastic clips were applied to the cut edges of the scalp to arrest bleeding. The scalp was folded back to the level of the eyebrows. Incisions were made in the muscle of the right temple, and three sets of holes were drilled near the temple and the top of the head because the tumor had to be approached from directly in front. The drill, powered by nitrogen, was replaced with a fluted steel blade, and the holes were connected. The incised piece of skull was pried loose and held out of the way by a large sponge.

6   Beneath the bone is a yellowish leatherlike membrane, the dura, that surrounds the brain. Down the middle of the head the dura carries a large vein, but in the area near the nose the vein is small. At that point the vein and dura were cut, and clips made of tantalum, a hard metal, were applied to arrest and prevent bleeding. Sutures were put into the dura and tied to the scalp to keep the dura open and retracted. A malleable silver retractor, resembling the blade of a butter knife, was inserted between the brain and skull. The anesthesiologist began to administer a drug to relax the brain by removing some of its water, making it easier for the surgeon to manipulate the retractor, hold the brain back, and see the tumor. The nerve tracts for smell were cut on both sides to provide additional room. The tumor was seen approximately two-and-one-half inches behind the base of the nose. It was pink in color. On touching it, it proved to be very fibrous and tough. A special retractor was attached to the skull, enabling the other retractor blades to be held automatically and freeing the surgeon's

hands.   With further displacement of the frontal lobes of the
brain, the tumor could be seen better, but no normal structures
—the carotid arteries, their branches, and the optic nerves—
were visible. The tumor obscured them.

7   A surgical microscope was placed above the wound. The
surgeon had selected the lenses and focal length prior to the operation. Looking through the microscope, he could see some
of the small vessels supplying the tumor and he coagulated
them. He incised the tumor to attempt to remove its core and
thus collapse it, but the substance of the tumor was too firm to
be removed in this fashion. He then began to slowly dissect the
tumor from the adjacent brain tissue and from where he believed the normal structures to be.

8   Using small squares of cotton, he began to separate the tumor from very loose fibrous bands connecting it to the brain and
to the right side of the part of the skull where the pituitary gland
lies. The right optic nerve and carotid artery came into view,
both displaced considerably to the right. The optic nerve had
a normal appearance. He protected these structures with cotton compresses placed between them and the tumor. He began
to raise the tumor from the skull and slowly to reach the point
of its origin and attachment—just in front of the pituitary gland
and medial to the left optic nerve, which still could not be
seen. The small blood vessels entering the tumor were cauter-
ized. The upper portion of the tumor was gradually separated
from the brain, and the branches of the carotid arteries and the
branches to the tumor were coagulated. The tumor was slowly
and gently lifted from its bed, and for the first time the left carotid artery and optic nerve could be seen. Part of the tumor ad-
hered to this nerve. The bulk of the tumor was amputated,
leaving a small bit attached to the nerve. Very slowly and carefully the tumor fragment was resected.

9   The tumor now removed, a most impressive sight came
into view—the pituitary gland and its stalk of attachment to the
hypothalamus, the hypothalamus itself, and the brainstem,
which conveys nerve impulses between the body and the brain.
As far as could be determined, no damage had been done to
these structures or other vital centers, but the left optic nerve,

from chronic pressure of the tumor, appeared gray and thin. Probably it would not completely recover its function.

10   After making certain there was no bleeding, the surgeon closed the wounds and placed wire mesh over the holes in the skull to prevent dimpling of the scalp over the points that had been drilled. A gauze dressing was applied to the patient's head. She was awakened and sent to the recovery room.

11   Even with the microscope, damage might still have occurred to the cerebral cortex and hypothalamus. It would require at least a day to be reasonably certain there was none, and about seventy-two hours to monitor for the major postoperative dangers—swelling of the brain and blood clots forming over the surface of the brain. The surgeon explained this to the patient's husband, and both of them waited anxiously. The operation had required seven hours. A glass of orange juice had given the surgeon some additional energy during the closure of the wound. Though exhausted, he could not fall asleep until after two in the morning, momentarily expecting a call from the nurse in the intensive care unit announcing deterioration of the patient's condition.

12   At 8:00 A.M. the surgeon saw the patient in the intensive care unit. She was alert, oriented, and showed no sign of additional damage to the optic nerves or the brain. She appeared to be in better shape than the surgeon or her husband.

Questions on Content

1. What symptoms led the woman to see a neurologist? What was his diagnosis?
2. What was the neurosurgeon's diagnosis? Of the possibilities that he discussed with them, what was the common decision that the patient and her husband came to?
3. How was the incision made so that it would be concealed when the hair grew back?
4. Where exactly was the tumor located? What did it look like? How did it feel to the touch?
5. What steps did the surgeon take in removing the tumor? What did he try first?
6. Once the tumor was removed, what impressive sight came into view?

7. When the tumor was removed, what procedure did the surgeon follow before sending the patient to the recovery room?
8. What dangers did the surgeon watch for in the hours after the surgery—dangers that made him and the patient's husband wait anxiously?
9. What contrast does Selby draw at the end of the essay?

Questions on Invention, Design, and Style

1. In order to explain the process of brain surgery, Selby might have been much more formal in tone and generalized in treatment. What is the effect of his concentrating on a specific (and apparently true) example of such an operation? of narrating the operation in the past tense, rather than of presenting it as a series of directions to his readers?
2. Consider paragraphs 1–3 as the introduction to the essay. How does Selby establish the importance of brain surgery here? How does he arouse interest in the subject? What elements of suspense are introduced in paragraph 2? How effective are they?
3. What stages of the process are described in paragraphs 4, 5, and 6? What is the importance of the complication mentioned in the last sentence of paragraph 6?
4. Paragraphs 7 and 8 narrate the removal of the tumor itself. How has this material been prepared for in paragraph 2? in paragraph 6? What new complication arises in paragraph 7? How does the final sentence of paragraph 7 introduce paragraph 8? Why is paragraph 8 one of the longest in the essay?
5. What stage in the process is narrated in paragraph 9? What is the importance of this stage? What stage is narrated in paragraph 10? Why is this a comparatively brief paragraph?
6. What points are of greatest importance in paragraphs 11 and 12? What points about the surgeon are developed in the last four sentences of paragraph 11 and in paragraph 12? What does this final passage suggest about the surgeon's relation to his profession and to his patient? How does paragraph 12 resolve the suspense aroused in paragraph 2 and later in the essay? What is the function of the final sentence in the essay?
7. Selby illustrates the process of brain surgery especially well, as we saw in the discussion of illustration, in which we singled out several phrases for praise (see pp. 5–6). Locate three or four other passages in Selby's essay in which elements of the process are effectively illustrated.

Applications

1. Write an essay describing the woman's brain operation from the husband's point of view.   Describe the events before, during, and after the operation as he must have experienced and understood them.
2. Write a process analysis in which you tell how you were treated by a professional person, such as a doctor or a dentist.   Introduce the essay in such a way that you effectively arouse your readers' interest in the process, divide the process itself into stages, and bring the essay to an effective conclusion.

To Bid the World Farewell
Jessica Mitford

Through skillful choice of detail, British writer Jessica Mitford describes the processes of embalming and restoration so vividly that the essay provokes strong responses in readers.

1   Embalming is indeed a most extraordinary procedure, and one must wonder at the docility of Americans who each year pay hundreds of millions of dollars for its perpetuation, blissfully ignorant of what it is all about, what is done, how it is done.   Not one in ten thousand has any idea of what actually takes place.   Books on the subject are extremely hard to come by.   They are not to be found in most libraries or bookshops.

2   In an era when huge television audiences watch surgical operations in the comfort of their living rooms, when, thanks to the animated cartoon, the geography of the digestive system has become familiar territory even to the nursery school set, in a land where the satisfaction of curiosity about almost all matters is a national pastime, the secrecy surrounding embalming can, surely, hardly be attributed to the inherent gruesomeness of the subject.   Custom in this regard has within this century suffered a complete reversal.   In the early days of American embalming, when it was performed in the home of the deceased, it was almost mandatory for some relative to stay by the em-

balmer's side and witness the procedure. Today, family members who might wish to be in attendance would certainly be dissuaded by the funeral director. All others, except apprentices, are excluded by law from the preparation room.

3   A close look at what does actually take place may explain in large measure the undertaker's intractable reticence concerning a procedure that has become his major *raison d'être*. Is it possible he fears that public information about embalming might lead patrons to wonder if they really want this service? If the funeral men are loath to discuss the subject outside the trade, the reader may, understandably, be equally loath to go on reading at this point. For those who have the stomach for it, let us part the formaldehyde curtain. . . .

4   The body is first laid out in the undertaker's morgue—or rather, Mr. Jones is reposing in the preparation room—to be readied to bid the world farewell.

5   The preparation room in any of the better funeral establishments has the tiled and sterile look of a surgery, and indeed the embalmer–restorative artist who does his chores there is beginning to adopt the term "dermasurgeon" (appropriately corrupted by some mortician–writers as "demisurgeon") to describe his calling. His equipment, consisting of scalpels, scissors, augers, forceps, clamps, needles, pumps, tubes, bowls and basins, is crudely imitative of the surgeon's as is his technique, acquired in a nine- or twelve-month post-high-school course in an embalming school. He is supplied by an advanced chemical industry with a bewildering array of fluids, sprays, pastes, oils, powders, creams, to fix or soften tissue, shrink or distend it as needed, dry it here, restore the moisture there. There are cosmetics, waxes and paints to fill and cover features, even plaster of Paris to replace entire limbs. There are ingenious aids to prop and stabilize the cadaver: a Vari-Pose Head Rest, the Edwards Arm and Hand Positioner, the Repose Block (to support the shoulders during the embalming), and the Throop Foot Positioner, which resembles an old-fashioned stocks.

6   Mr. John H. Eckels, president of the Eckels College of Mortuary Science, thus describes the first part of the embalm-

ing procedure: "In the hands of a skilled practitioner, this work may be done in a comparatively short time and without mutilating the body other than by slight incision—so slight that it scarcely would cause serious inconvenience if made upon a living person. It is necessary to remove the blood, and doing this not only helps in the disinfecting, but removes the principal cause of disfigurements due to discoloration."

7   Another textbook discusses the all-important time element: "The earlier this is done, the better, for every hour that elapses between death and embalming will add to the problems and complications encountered. . . ." Just how soon should one get going on the embalming? The author tells us, "On the basis of such scanty information made available to this profession through its rudimentary and haphazard system of technical research, we must conclude that the best results are to be obtained if the subject is embalmed before life is completely extinct—that is, before cellular death has occurred. In the average case, this would mean within an hour after somatic death." For those who feel that there is something a little rudimentary, not to say haphazard, about this advice, a comforting thought is offered by another writer. Speaking of fears entertained in early days of premature burial, he points out, "One of the effects of embalming by chemical injection, however, has been to dispel fears of live burial." How true; once the blood is removed, chances of live burial are indeed remote.

8   To return to Mr. Jones, the blood is drained out through the veins and replaced by embalming fluid pumped in through the arteries. As noted in *The Principles and Practices of Embalming*, "every operator has a favorite injection and drainage point—a fact which becomes a handicap only if he fails or refuses to forsake his favorites when conditions demand it." Typical favorites are the carotid artery, femoral artery, jugular vein, subclavian vein. There are various choices of embalming fluid. If Flextone is used, it will produce a "mild, flexible rigidity. The skin retains a velvety softness, the tissues are rubbery and pliable. Ideal for women and children." It may be blended with B. and G. Products Company's Lyf-Lyk tint, which is guaranteed to reproduce "nature's own skin texture

. . . the velvety appearance of living tissue." Suntone comes in three separate tints: Suntan; Special Cosmetic Tint, a pink shade "especially indicated for young female subjects"; and Regular Cosmetic Tint, moderately pink.

9　About three to six gallons of a dyed and perfumed solution of formaldehyde, glycerin, borax, phenol, alcohol and water is soon circulating through Mr. Jones, whose mouth has been sewn together with a "needle directed upward between the upper lip and gum and brought out through the left nostril," with the corners raised slightly "for a more pleasant expression." If he should be bucktoothed, his teeth are cleaned with Bon Ami and coated with colorless nail polish. His eyes, meanwhile, are closed with flesh-tinted eye caps and eye cement.

10　The next step is to have at Mr. Jones with a thing called a trocar. This is a long, hollow needle attached to a tube. It is jabbed into the abdomen, poked around the entrails and chest cavity, the contents of which are pumped out and replaced with "cavity fluid." This done, and the hole in the abdomen sewed up, Mr. Jones's face is heavily creamed (to protect the skin from burns which may be caused by leakage of the chemicals), and he is covered with a sheet and left unmolested for a while. But not for long—there is more, much more, in store for him. He has been embalmed, but not yet restored, and the best time to start the restorative work is eight to ten hours after embalming, when the tissues have become firm and dry.

11　The object of all this attention to the corpse, it must be remembered, is to make it presentable for viewing in an attitude of healthy repose. "Our customs require the presentation of our dead in the semblance of normality . . . unmarred by the ravages of illness, disease or mutilation," says Mr. J. Sheridan Mayer in his *Restorative Art*. This is rather a large order since few people die in the full bloom of health, unravaged by illness and unmarked by some disfigurement. The funeral industry is equal to the challenge: "In some cases the gruesome appearance of a mutilated or disease-ridden subject may be quite discouraging. The task of restoration may seem impossible and shake the confidence of the embalmer. This is the time for intestinal fortitude and determination. Once the formative work is begun and affected tissues are cleaned or removed, all doubts of success vanish.   It is surprising and gratifying to discover the results which may be obtained."

12   The embalmer, having allowed an appropriate interval to elapse, returns to the attack, but now he brings into play the skill and equipment of sculptor and cosmetician.   Is a hand missing?   Casting one in plaster of Paris is a simple matter. "For replacement purposes, only a cast of the back of the hand is necessary; this is within the ability of the average operator and is quite adequate."   If a lip or two, a nose or an ear should be missing, the embalmer has at hand a variety of restorative waxes with which to model replacements.   Pores and skin texture are simulated by stippling with a little brush, and over this cosmetics are laid on.   Head off?   Decapitation cases are rather routinely handled.   Ragged edges are trimmed, and head joined to torso with a series of splints, wires and sutures.   It is a good idea to have a little something at the neck—a scarf or high collar—when time for viewing comes.   Swollen mouth?   Cut out tissue as needed from inside the lips.   If too much is removed, the surface contour can easily be restored by padding with cotton.   Swollen necks and cheeks are reduced by removing tissue through vertical incisions made down each side of the neck. "When the deceased is casketed, the pillow will hide the suture incisions . . . as an extra precaution against leakage, the suture may be painted with liquid sealer."

13   The opposite condition is more likely to be present itself— that of emaciation.   His hypodermic syringe now loaded with massage cream, the embalmer seeks out and fills the hollowed and sunken areas by injection.   In this procedure the backs of the hands and fingers and the under-chin area should not be neglected.

14   Positioning the lips is a problem that recurrently challenges the ingenuity of the embalmer.   Closed too tightly, they tend to give a stern, even disapproving expression.   Ideally, embalmers feel, the lips should give the impression of being ever so slightly parted, the upper lip protruding slightly for a more youthful appearance.   This takes some engineering, however, as the lips tend to drift apart.   Lip drift can sometimes be remedied by pushing one or two straight pins through the inner mar-

gin of the lower lip and then inserting them between the two front upper teeth.   If Mr. Jones happens to have no teeth, the pins can just as easily be anchored in his Armstrong Face Former and Denture Replacer.   Another method to maintain lip closure is to dislocate the lower jaw, which is then held in its new position by a wire run through holes which have been drilled through the upper and lower jaws at the midline.   As the French are fond of saying, *il faut souffrir pour être belle.*[1]

15   If Mr. Jones has died of jaundice, the embalming fluid will very likely turn him green.   Does this deter the embalmer?   Not if he has intestinal fortitude.   Masking pastes and cosmetics are heavily laid on, burial garments and casket interiors are color-correlated with particular care, and Jones is displayed beneath rose-colored lights.   Friends will say, "How *well* he looks." Death by carbon monoxide, on the other hand, can be rather a good thing from the embalmer's viewpoint: "One advantage is the fact that this type of discoloration is an exaggerated form of a natural pink coloration."   This is nice because the healthy glow is already present and needs but little attention.

16   The patching and filling completed, Mr. Jones is now shaved, washed and dressed.   Cream-based cosmetic, available in pink, flesh, suntan, brunette and blond, is applied to his hands and face, his hair is shampooed and combed (and, in the case of Mrs. Jones, set), his hands manicured.   For the horny-handed son of toil special care must be taken; cream should be applied to remove ingrained grime, and the nails cleaned.   "If he were not in the habit of having them manicured in life, trimming and shaping is advised for better appearance—never questioned by kin."

17   Jones is now ready for casketing (this is the present participle of the verb "to casket").   In this operation his right shoulder should be depressed slightly "to turn the body a bit to the right and soften the appearance of lying flat on the back."   Positioning the hands is a matter of importance, and special rubber positioning blocks may be used.   The hands should be cupped slightly for a more lifelike, relaxed appearance.   Proper placement of the body requires a delicate sense of balance.   It

---

[1] "One must suffer in order to be beautiful."

should lie as high as possible in the casket, yet not so high that the lid, when lowered, will hit the nose. On the other hand, we are cautioned, placing the body too low "creates the impression that the body is in a box."

18   Jones is next wheeled into the appointed slumber room where a few last touches may be added—his favorite pipe placed in his hand or, if he was a great reader, a book propped into position. (In the case of little Master Jones a Teddy bear may be clutched.) Here he will hold open house for a few days, visiting hours 10 A.M. to 9 P.M.

Questions on Content

1. How have embalming customs been reversed during this century? Who may now legally be present during an embalming?
2. What makes undertakers afraid to inform their patrons about their work?
3. What equipment does the "embalmer-restorative artist" require?
4. What preprofessional training do "dermasurgeons" usually receive?
5. How is time important in the embalming process? What is the ideal time to begin the process?
6. What is the first step in embalming? How does it "dispel fears of live burial"?
7. What does embalming fluid do?
8. What are some of the embalmer's favorite injection and drainage points?
9. Why is the process of restoration important? What makes it difficult? Give three examples of restorative processes.

Questions on Invention, Design, and Style

1. Which paragraphs constitute the introduction? How does paragraph 1 gain the readers' attention and interest? How do paragraphs 2 and 3 further prepare readers for the explanation of the process?
2. Mitford divides the process into at least two parts: embalming and restoration, although she does not keep the parts entirely separate. In which paragraphs does she introduce the equipment used for the process? In which paragraphs does she describe the embalming stage? Into what two steps does she subdivide the embalming stage?

3. In which paragraphs does Mitford treat the restoration stage? In which paragraph does she examine the main reason for restoration? examples of replacement? examples of filling hollow areas? lip positioning? coloring? grooming?

4. Paragraph 17 might be considered either as a subdivision of the restoration stage or as a third major division—that of "casketing." In your opinion, how should it be classified, and what are the reasons for your opinion?

5. Mitford's selection abounds in vivid, concise detail, For each of the senses of sight, touch, and smell, find two or three examples of vivid images.

6. What is achieved by direct quotation (*as in paragraph 6*) as opposed to a brief summary of the same material?

7. Analyze Mitford's tone in this essay. Consider, for example, the following:

   a. "The body is first laid out in the undertaker's morgue—or rather, Mr. Jones is reposing in the preparation room . . ." (*paragraph 4*).

   b. "On the other hand, we are cautioned, placing the body too low 'creates the impression that the body is in a box' " (*paragraph 17*).

   c. The references to "Mr. Jones," "Mrs. Jones," "Little Master Jones," and "open house . . . 10 A.M. to 9 P.M." (*paragraphs 15–18*).

   Explain what these statements and terms reflect about her attitude toward the subject. Locate other passages to support your explanation.

8. What sources has Mitford drawn upon for the evidence of her essay? What does her use of these sources reveal about her attitude toward the subject? toward the audience she is addressing?

9. In paragraph 1, Mitford states her thesis: She wonders why Americans pay so much money each year to perpetuate embalming when they are so "blissfully ignorant" of what that process involves. What supporting detail follows this statement in paragraph 1? How do the paragraphs that follow—including the process analysis—support and develop this thesis?

Applications

1. Assume that you are an embalmer and have just read a glowing review of Mitford's essay. As a rebuttal to Mitford, write an analysis of the same process from a positive point of view, emphasiz-

ing its benefits. Selby's essay "A Delicate Operation" might be used as a model in which the practitioner is treated seriously and sympathetically.

2. Write a step-by-step analysis of any process, stressing the negative or positive value of the result.

3. Analyze a process related to a custom that you believe should be abolished. Write a paper describing the process, making your attitude toward the custom clear and convincing.

Stars: Where Life Begins
Time

Through an analysis of the birth, life, and death processes of stars, the writer of the following *Time* magazine article shows how the sun, earth, and even our own lives are vitally connected to this continuous cycle of star formation.

1   Stars, by living and dying, enable whole new worlds to be born. Conceived in the frigid darkness of space, stars during their lives produce the elements that make life possible and sustain it. When they die, they sow these substances like seeds across the heavens. The elements eventually become part of new stars and planets. Thus in death there is rebirth.

2   In fact, the earth and its star—the sun—are built in part from the ashes of dead stars, and human beings are literally star children. People—and all other forms of life on earth—are collections of atoms forged in stellar furnaces. "All of chemistry and therefore all of life has been formed by stars," says Astrophysicist Patrick Thaddeus of NASA's Goddard Institute for Space Studies in New York City. "With the exception of hydrogen, everything in our bodies has been produced in the thermonuclear reactions within stars."

. . .

3   In our galaxy and in galaxies yet to be discovered, stars are going through a continuous cycle of birth, life and death. Indeed, there are places where the observer who knows what to look for can practically see stars forming before his eyes. These

star wombs are great clouds of gas and dust floating in interstellar space. Like the clouds that formed in the expanding primordial fireball shortly after the big bang, they consist mostly of nature's simplest molecule, hydrogen. A star is born when some force, perhaps a shock wave, drives enough of the hydrogen molecules in a cloud sufficiently close to one another that they are held together by their mutual gravity. As a result, a huge pocket of condensed gas, trillions of miles across, is formed at the edge of the larger cloud. In a model proposed by Astronomers Bruce Elmegreen and Charles Lada of the Harvard–Smithsonian Center for Astrophysics, shock waves from the ignition of earlier massive stars help create the conditions for the birth of other stars from the same cloud.

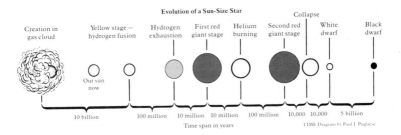

Evolution of a Sun-Size Star

4   Under the force of their own gravity, the great clouds of gas slowly begin to contract, raising the pressures and temperatures at their centers. They have become embryonic stars. The process continues for some 10 million years, during which the clouds shrink to globes more than a million miles in diameter. At this point, temperatures near the centers of the great gas balls have reached the critical level of 20 million degrees F., hot enough to cause fusion—the awesome process that occurs in a detonating hydrogen bomb.

5   Long since stripped of their electrons by the high temperatures, the nuclei of the hydrogen atoms slam together at tremendous speeds, fusing to form helium and releasing huge amounts of energy. Though the nuclear fires have been lit, the actual ignition is hidden deep within the interstellar clouds. "Nature very discreetly pulls the curtain over the act of birth," says Thaddeus. But the infant star soon makes its presence known,

shining through and illuminating the obscuring cloud. This process is occurring in the Orion Nebula, . . . the illuminated portion of a gigantic cloud of gas and dust that is giving birth to new stars. Some of the stars spawned by the nebula have been formed as recently as the time when the human species first stood upright; the newest offspring are only about 100,000 years old—mere infants by stellar standards.

6   The fusion of hydrogen to form helium marks the beginning of a long and stable period in the evolution of the star—a combination of adolescence and middle age that constitutes 99% of the lifespan of a sun-size star. During this period, the tremendous energy radiating from the star's center neutralizes its gravitational force, and the great glowing orb shrinks no further. But as it must to all stars, death eventually comes. How long a star lives depends on its mass. Generally, the more massive a star is, the shorter its life is. Stars with a mass significantly greater than that of the sun burn their fuel in a profligate manner and die young; a star ten times as massive as the sun, for example, burns 1,000 times faster and survives only 100 million years. The sun, which is some 5 billion years old, is only at the mid-point in life. Smaller stars, on the other hand, are the Methuselahs of the celestial community. A star with one-tenth the mass of the sun can burn for a trillion years.

. . .

7   The beginning of the end comes when the star has exhausted much of the hydrogen near its core and starts to burn the hydrogen in its outer layers. This process causes the star gradually to turn red and swell to 100 times its previous size, pouring out prodigious amounts of energy. Betelgeuse, in the constellation Orion, is such a "red giant," visible to the naked eye. When the sun undergoes a similar metamorphosis, it will envelop Mercury and Venus and vaporize the earth. By that time, 5 billion years from now, man's descendants may have found a new home in an outer planet or beyond.

8   A star's red-giant phase lasts until the hydrogen in the layer around the core is exhausted, perhaps as long as a billion years. The stage that follows is short-lived. Its fires banked, the star is deprived of the outward radiation pressure. It contracts violently, driving the core temperature up again, until it

reaches 200 million degrees. That is hot enough to ignite the helium, which fuses into a still heavier element: carbon. Its radiation energy restored, the star zooms back toward red-giant status 100 times faster than it took to get there the first time.

9 What happens after the helium is consumed depends on the size of the star. If a star's mass is no more than about four times that of the sun, its second red-giant stage may be its death rattle. As the star contracts again, its gravitational energy cannot produce enough heat to fuse carbon into heavier elements. But as its internal temperature rises, the outer envelope expands and cools. Held loosely by gravity, the outer layers then slough off into space in a billow of gas. All that is left behind is the core, which continues contracting into a ball a few thousand miles in diameter with a density of tons per cubic inch. The result is a "white dwarf," hotter than the surface of the sun but only about the size of the earth and ready to enter a long period of stellar senility. As the millenniums pass, the white dwarf gradually loses its heat, turning first yellow, then red; eventually, its fires burn out entirely, leaving behind a "black dwarf," a cold cinder in the graveyard of space.

10 Many large stars manage to lose much of their mass as they evolve, shedding their matter as gas and dust. If they manage to shed sufficient mass, in fact, they can die quietly as white dwarfs. But for stars with a mass greater than four times that of the sun, the end may be far more dramatic. In these giant stars, fusion does not end when all the helium has been converted into carbon. In some of the massive stars, in a catastrophic event known as a supernova, the carbon core explodes, dispersing most of the elements it has produced into space. Stars of more than eight solar masses may go through several more contracting and expanding cycles, forming elements such as magnesium, silicon, sulfur, cobalt, nickel and ultimately iron. When the star has formed an iron core, its fate is sealed. It begins to contract again, but does not have enough gravity to cause fusion of the densely packed nuclei of iron. Instead of being suspended again by the energy of a rekindled nuclear fire, the great mass of the star continues to fall toward the core, unable to resist the pull of its own gravity.

11 This event is also catastrophic. In a matter of seconds, a

star that has lived several million years caves in with a devastating crash, most of its material crushing into an incredibly dense and small sphere at the center.   Then, like a giant spring, the star rebounds from this collapse in a massive explosion.   The result is another kind of supernova, a fantastic explosion that blows the star to smithereens, dispersing into space most of the remaining elements that it has manufactured during its lifetime.   So brilliant is the light from the exploding star that it briefly outshines all of the galaxy's other billions of stars combined.   The last supernova observed in the Milky Way Galaxy was seen by Johannes Kepler in 1604.

12   What remains after this explosion again depends on the size of the star.   Its death throes may leave behind a rapidly spinning, incredibly dense sphere (about ten miles in diameter), consisting only of tightly packed neutrons.   Such an object, called a neutron star, or pulsar, has been located in the center of the Crab Nebula, a glowing cloud that is still expanding from a supernova reported by the Chinese in A.D. 1054.

13   A very massive star may have an even stranger fate. Driven by its own immense gravitation, it collapses through its neutron star stage, crushing its matter into a volume so small that it virtually ceases to exist.   The gravity of its tiny remnant is so great that nothing, not even light, can escape from it.   All external evidence of its presence disappears, and the star, like the Cheshire cat, vanishes, leaving behind only the grin of its disembodied gravity. Anything that fell into such a "black hole" would quite literally be crushed out of existence.

14   Because black holes emit no light or other radiation, their existence, predicted by the laws of relativity, cannot be confirmed by direct observation, but it can be inferred.   Astronomers have identified a powerful X-ray source in the constellation Cygnus. Some suspect the source, which has been labeled Cygnus X-1, may be just such a black hole.   It appears to be rotating with a visible star around a common center of gravity—a dead partner of a dual-star system.   Scientists believe material from the glowing star is being drawn into the black hole with such force that the material becomes hot enough to emit X rays.

15   While neutron stars and black holes can result from the death of massive stars, the explosions that precede them create

elements essential to the birth of new stars and spread through the universe the materials essential to life. "Stars have two purposes," says Stanford University Astrophysicist Robert Wagoner. "They give energy in the form of light, and they produce the heavy elements that we are made of."

16 Indeed, scientists believe hydrogen and helium were the only two elements in the primordial universe. But when stars formed in the clouds of these two gases, they began the manufacture of the other elements now found in nature. That this sequence occurred seems to be supported by spectral-line evidence in starlight. Older stars, formed when the universe was young, have only traces of the heavier elements. Stars born more recently have more of the heavy elements produced by their predecessors. Those currently forming in interstellar dust clouds can be expected to have significant proportions of the atoms produced in celestial forges. Says Thaddeus of the clouds: "We can see the lovely fertilizer, this compost heap just sitting there waiting to be consumed in star formation."

17 The great interstellar clouds also contain another kind of fertilizer. In 1963 a team of researchers from the Massachusetts Institute of Technology and the Lincoln Laboratory used a radio telescope to discover the hydroxyl radical (two-thirds of the water molecule) in space. Since then, more than three dozen molecules have been found floating in the galactic clouds, including those of methane, formaldehyde, ammonia, hydrogen cyanide, ethyl alcohol and carbon monoxide.

18 These findings were particularly exciting in light of a classic experiment carried out in 1953 by Stanley Miller and Harold Urey at the University of Chicago. They discovered that when electric sparks were sent through water vapor, ammonia and methane in a sealed container, they combined to form amino acids, the building blocks of protein found in living organisms. Says Astrophysicist Herbert Friedman of the Naval Research Laboratory in Washington: "We believe the gas in space can form complex molecules that can eventually lead to life."

19 The implications are staggering. Though the space between the stars seems hostile to the formation of life, the evidence that organic chemistry is not unique to earth makes it probable that life exists on planets elsewhere. The universe

contains billions of sunlike stars built from the remains of earlier stellar explosions. Many of them may well have planets,
which some scientists believe condense from a disc of gas and
dust that forms around a developing star.

. . .

20   Says Astrophysicist [Jesse] Greenstein [of the California Institute of Technology], "I find a certain pleasure and honor in
belonging to the universe of stars, of these events that have
created the materials of which the earth and I are made." It
is a sentiment many can echo. The final consolation has always been, as humanity looking upward measured its own fi-
niteness against the infinity of the stars, that it is better to have
been for a season, even a moment, than not to have been at all.
The stars thus are no less symbols in their newly understood
mortality than they were, seemingly eternal in their courses, in
remote times.

Questions on Content

1.   In what sense do stars produce the "elements" that make life pos-
     sible and sustain it?   In what sense are human beings "star
     children"?
2.   How are stars born?   Although nature "pulls the curtain over the
     act of birth," what happens soon after?
3.   What governs the life span of a star?   How old is our sun?   At
     what point in its total life span is our sun at the present time?
4.   What are the first signs that a star is coming to the end of its life
     span?   What will happen when the sun reaches that point?   How
     far off is that?
5.   What stages does a star pass through in dying?   What colors are
     associated with each stage?
6.   If a star manages to lose much of its mass as it evolves, then it
     can look forward to what kind of death?   In what way is the death
     of a large star a dramatic death?   How is it also catastrophic?
7.   What stranger fate may often await a very massive star?   What can
     result from the deaths of these massive stars?
8.   How do the deaths of stars create elements essential to the birth
     of new stars?   What two purposes do stars serve, according to
     Wagoner?
9.   What kinds of fertilizer are contained in interstellar clouds? What

experiments relative to these space fertilizers have been conducted and what implications do they lead scientists to draw?

Questions on Invention, Design, and Style

1. This process analysis features a continuing analogy between the "life cycle" of stars and that of living beings. In what ways is this analogy outlined in paragraph 1? What metaphors are used to develop this analogy in paragraph 3? paragraph 4? paragraph 5? paragraph 6? paragraph 9? paragraph 12? paragraph 16? What effects are achieved through this continuing analogy?
2. In addition to introducing the continuing analogy, how do paragraphs 1 and 2 serve as an introduction to the entire essay?
3. What stage of star development is the subject of paragraphs 3–5? How does the analogy to the human life cycle help explain this stage? What other devices does the writer use to explain this stage?
4. Paragraphs 6–8 depict several more stages of star development. What stage is depicted in paragraph 6? How does the writer make the point that the duration of this stage varies tremendously according to the mass of the star? How does he explain the stages by which a star twice becomes a "red giant"?
5. Paragraphs 9–14 depict alternative ends of the life cycle of stars. What is the process leading to a "black dwarf"? to a supernova in which the carbon core explodes? to the formation of further elements? to a supernova in which the iron core explodes? to a neutron star? to a "black hole"?
6. What new process (referred to in paragraphs 1 and 2) is introduced in paragraph 15? How does paragraph 16 help support this point in paragraph 15?
7. What additional new process is introduced in paragraphs 17–19? How does the evidence cited in paragraph 17 and that cited in paragraph 18 support the conclusion drawn in paragraph 19?
8. In what ways is paragraph 20 a fitting conclusion to the essay?
9. Analyze the importance of each of the following elements in designing this process analysis: direct quotation, analogy and metaphor, illustration, and sequencing?

Applications

1. Through an analogy to a process familiar to most readers, write an essay analyzing a process that, while important, is virtually unknown to your readers.

2. Observe the typical routine in any of the classes you are now taking. Who usually starts the class? How does it often end? Who
   participates, and in what way? Who interrupts whom? Is someone usually late? How much time is consumed by testing, reading, and lecturing? Organize and write your observations of a
   typical day in the class.
3. Write a process analysis in which beyond a certain point there are
   several alternative possibilities—for example, in choosing college
   courses beyond the basic requirements.

Causal Analysis

When we inquire into *why* something has happened, is happening, or will probably happen, we inquire into its *causes*. When we inquire into the *results* of a happening, we inquire into its *effects*. *Causal analysis* is the examination of relations between causes and effects. As in other forms of analysis, we are concerned with a whole (the entire cause-effect relationship) and its parts (the individual causes and effects).

Suppose you are passing all your courses except American history and you want to determine why you are having difficulties in that subject so that you can make improvements where they are most obviously needed. You would begin with the *effect*—your failure in American history—and try to analyze its causes. These might include the fact that you've never liked history, the facts that the class meets from 8:00 to 10:00 on Mondays and Fridays and that you are not a morning person, your habit of leaving your history reading until last, and your difficulty in following the lectures. You could diagram your analysis of possible causes as at the top of page 224, using an arrow (↑) to point toward the effect and away from the causes.

Once you have spelled out the causes in this way, you can probably eliminate some of them immediately. For instance, you might remember other history classes that you have enjoyed and done well in; you might recall that you are doing well in your math class, which meets from 8:00 to 10:00 A.M. on

223

Tuesdays and Thursdays, thus eliminating another cause. But how would you choose between the remaining possible causes —leaving the history reading until last and your difficulty in understanding the lectures?

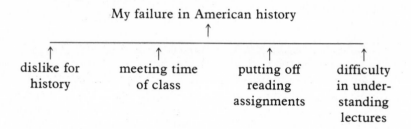

You could begin by examining both more closely. You might find that your habit of putting off the reading is caused by your eyes' being tired and that this condition is in turn caused by a need for new glasses. At this point you would be considering the possibility of a *causal chain,* a situation in which the cause of one effect is in turn the effect of another cause. Your causal analysis would now look like this:

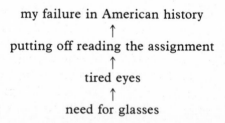

The next stage might be to have your eyes checked.

But suppose you find that your eyes (or your present glasses) are not the problem. Then you could consider the other possible cause for failure—your difficulty in understanding the lectures, from which so many of the exam questions seem to be taken. You might try another diagram, thinking of possible causes for this difficulty:

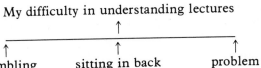

My difficulty in understanding lectures

| mumbling instructor | sitting in back of a large lecture hall | problem with my hearing |

Again, you might test the first cause and find that others in the class don't think the instructor mumbles at all and have no difficulty hearing him.   Finally, you decide that the cause may well be a combination of the other two possibilities.   The diagram of this causal chain would be as follows:

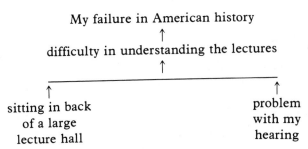

My failure in American history

difficulty in understanding the lectures

| sitting in back of a large lecture hall | problem with my hearing |

So far we have been operating in one of the two directions possible for a causal analysis—from effect to cause.   But suppose you are faced with a situation in which you must determine the possible results, or effects, of an action.   For instance, you might consider what would happen if you decided to hold yourself to a strict time limit of one hour for writing the next paper for your composition class.   You could diagram the situation like this:

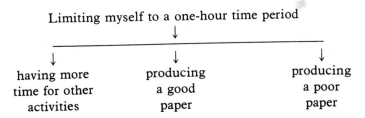

Limiting myself to a one-hour time period

| having more time for other activities | producing a good paper | producing a poor paper |

The first effect, having more time for other activities, seems fairly obvious. The real question, though, is what kind of paper you would be more likely to produce. After considering your past performance on papers in class and examinations, you may decide that a good paper is at least a real possibility and worth trying the experiment for. If the experiment works, the diagram would look like this:

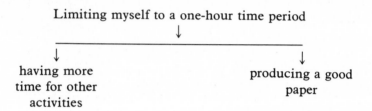

Limiting myself to a one-hour time period

↓

having more
time for other
activities

producing a good
paper

In any causal analysis two questions should be raised if mistakes are to be avoided.

First, am I considering all the possible causes or effects? Omissions can be crucial. If you considered the instructor's apparent mumbling as the only cause of your difficulty with the history lectures, for example, you would be ignoring the real causes and thus the steps you could take to improve your performance. And, if you considered only a poor paper as the effect of setting a one-hour limit for writing it, you would shut out the possibility that the limit could produce real benefits.

Second, am I assuming a cause-effect relation when in fact there is none? Raising this question provides a further check, for it leads to testing the relation. For instance, you tested whether or not the cause of your difficulty in hearing the history lecture was actually the instructor's apparent mumbling and found that other members of the class didn't have the same experience. You therefore decided that there was no cause-effect relation. In a similar way, you decided to test whether a good paper or a poor one would be the effect of holding yourself to a one-hour limit in writing your next paper.

The main points in causal analysis are to consider as many

reasonable possibilities as you can and to test the analysis whenever possible.

So far we have considered causal analysis as a thought process often aided by diagrams. The points made are intended to help with the "invention stage" of writing—the time of struggle to develop and refine the subject through considering, testing, and selecting different points and emphases.

If you are writing a causal analysis, dealing with the two questions raised here is essential as you think about the causes of student apathy at your school or what the effects of a new policy on grades are likely to be. But causal analysis is essential to the invention of *any* paper, as the writer asks him- or herself, what will be the effects of including or excluding a particular illustration, comparison, or the like.

In designing the causal analysis, the fundamental question is whether the arrangement of materials should be from cause to effect or from effect to cause. You should consider several factors before making a final decision:

First, an effective causal analysis often begins with the statement of a puzzle to be solved: a known condition whose causes or effects are unknown. X. J. Kennedy, in "Who Killed King Kong?" provides an excellent example of how this device can win reader interest, by asking why a B-grade motion picture of 1933 still draws large audiences decades later—the effect. Then the essay goes on to enumerate various causes for this continuing popularity. But an effective analysis could also begin with a known cause and then work toward a resolution of possible effects, as we have seen.

Second, arranging materials in a climactic order, saving the most important point for last, is always a good rule to follow. Again, Kennedy's "Who Killed King Kong?" provides an excellent model, for the causes of the movie's popularity are laid out clearly, and the last one is the most important.

Finally, if the subject matter or the cause-effect relation is particularly complex, a cause-to-effect arrangement will be the safer choice, for it follows the normal chronological sequence and is thus the one readers are most likely to expect. J. Bronowski's "Human Sexuality," for instance, might be diagrammed (with some oversimplification) this way:

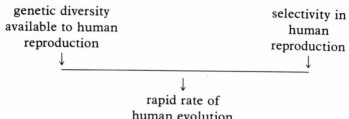

genetic diversity
available to human
reproduction
↓

selectivity in
human
reproduction
↓

↓
rapid rate of
human evolution

In like manner, Erich Fromm's "The Worker as Creator or Machine," a particularly complex causal analysis featuring a causal chain, moves steadily from cause to effect. Although both essays perhaps lose some suspense through not stating a problem or puzzle at the beginning, both have the virtue of treating complex and significant issues—love and work—with depth and power.

As you read and analyze the essays in this section, try to determine why the writers made the choices that they did in designing their materials and how their analyses of the causes and effects enlarge the reader's understanding of the subjects treated.

Who Killed King Kong?
X. J. Kennedy

In this lively essay, which first appeared in 1960, poet and essayist X. J. Kennedy accounts for the continuing popularity of the 1933 movie *King Kong*. While examining several causes for this popularity, he also makes some incisive comments on American urban life.

1   The ordeal and spectacular death of King Kong, the giant ape, undoubtedly have been witnessed by more Americans than have ever seen a performance of *Hamlet, Iphigenia at Aulis,* or even *Tobacco Road*. Since RKO-Radio Pictures first released *King Kong*, a quarter-century has gone by; yet year after year, from prints that grow more rain-beaten, from sound tracks that grow more tinny, ticket-buyers by thousands still pursue Kong's luckless fight against the forces of technology, tabloid

journalism, and the DAR. They see him chloroformed to sleep, see him whisked from his jungle isle to New York and placed on show, see him burst his chains to roam the city (lugging a frightened blonde), at last to plunge from the spire of the Empire State Building, machine-gunned by model airplanes.

2 Though Kong may die, one begins to think his legend unkillable. No clearer proof of his hold upon the popular imagination may be seen than what emerged one catastrophic week in March 1955, when New York WOR-TV programmed *Kong* for seven evenings in a row (a total of sixteen showings). Many a rival network vice-president must have scowled when surveys showed that *Kong*—the 1933 B-picture—had lured away fat segments of the viewing populace from such powerful competitors as Ed Sullivan, Groucho Marx and Bishop Sheen.

3 But even television has failed to run *King Kong* into oblivion. Coffee-in-the-lobby cinemas still show the old hunk of hokum, with the apology that in its use of composite shots and animated models the film remains technically interesting. And no other monster in movie history has won so devoted a popular audience. None of the plodding mummies, the stultified draculas, the white-coated Lugosis[1] with their shiny pinball-machine laboratories, none of the invisible stranglers, berserk robots, or menaces from Mars has ever enjoyed so many resurrections.

4 Why does the American public refuse to let King Kong rest in peace? It is true, I'll admit, that *Kong* outdid every monster movie before or since in sheer carnage. Producers Cooper and Schoedsack crammed into it dinosaurs, headhunters, riots, aerial battles, bullets, bombs, bloodletting. Heroine Fay Wray, whose function is mainly to scream, shuts her mouth for hardly one uninterrupted minute from first reel to last. It is also true that *Kong* is larded with good healthy sadism, for those whose joy it is to see the frantic girl dangled from cliffs and harried by pterodactyls. But it seems to me that the abiding appeal of the giant ape rests on other foundations.

5 Kong has, first of all, the attraction of being manlike. His

---

[1] A reference to Bela Lugosi, a popular actor in horror movies during the 1930s and 1940s.

simian nature gives him one huge advantage over giant ants and walking vegetables in that an audience may conceivably identify with him. Kong's appeal has the quality that established the Tarzan series as American myth—for what man doesn't secretly image himself a huge hairy howler against whom no other monster has a chance? If Tarzan recalls the ape in us, then Kong may well appeal to that great-granddaddy primordial brute from whose tribe we have all deteriorated.

6 Intentionally or not, the producers of *King Kong* encourage this identification by etching the character of Kong with keen sympathy. For the ape is a figure in a tradition familiar to moviegoers: the tradition of the pitiable monster. We think of Lon Chaney in the role of Quasimodo, of Karloff in the original *Frankenstein*. As we watch the Frankenstein monster's fumbling and disastrous attempts to befriend a flower-picking child, our sympathies are enlisted with the monster in his impenetrable loneliness. And so with Kong. As he roars in his chains, while barkers sell tickets to boobs who gape at him, we perhaps feel something more deep than pathos. We begin to sense something of the problem that engaged Eugene O'Neill in *The Hairy Ape*: the dilemma of a displaced animal spirit forced to live in a jungle built by machines.

7 *King Kong*, it is true, had special relevance in 1933. Landscapes of the depression are glimpsed early in the film when an impresario, seeking some desperate pretty girl to play the lead in a jungle movie, visits souplines and a Woman's Home Mission. In Fay Wray—who's been caught snitching an apple from a fruitstand—his search is ended. When he gives her a big feed and a movie contract, the girl is magic-carpeted out of the world of the National Recovery Act. And when, in the film's climax, Kong smashes that very Third Avenue landscape in which Fay had wandered hungry, audiences of 1933 may well have felt a personal satisfaction.

8 What is curious is that audiences of 1960 remain hooked. For in the heart of urban man, one suspects, lurks the impulse to fling a bomb. Though machines speed him to the scene of his daily grind, though IBM comptometers ("freeing the human mind from drudgery") enable him to drudge more efficiently once he arrives, there comes a moment when he wishes to turn

upon his machines and kick hell out of them. He wants to hurl his combination radio-alarmclock out the bedroom window and listen to its smash. What subway commuter wouldn't love— just for once—to see the downtown express smack head-on into the uptown local? Such a wish is gratified in that memorable scene in *Kong* that opens with a wide-angle shot: interior of a railway car on the Third Avenue El. Straphangers are nodding, the literate refold their newspapers. Unknown to them, Kong has torn away a section of trestle toward which the train now speeds. The motorman spies Kong up ahead, jams on the brakes. Passengers hurtle together like so many peas in a pail. In a window of the car appear Kong's bloodshot eyes. Women shriek. Kong picks up the railway car as if it were a rat, flips it to the street and ties knots in it, or something. To any commuter the scene must appear one of the most satisfactory pieces of celluloid ever exposed.

9   Yet however violent his acts, Kong remains a gentleman. Remarkable is his sense of chivalry. Whenever a fresh boa constrictor threatens Fay, Kong first sees that the lady is safely parked, then manfully thrashes her attacker. (And she, the ingrate, runs away every time his back is turned.) Atop the Empire State Building, ignoring his pursuers, Kong places Fay on a ledge as tenderly as if she were a dozen eggs. He fondles her, then turns to face the Army Air Force. And Kong is perhaps the most disinterested lover since Cyrano: his attentions to the lady are utterly without hope of reward. After all, between a five-foot blonde and a fifty-foot ape, love can hardly be more than an intellectual flirtation. In his simian way King Kong is the hopelessly yearning lover of Petrarchan convention. His forced exit from his jungle, in chains, results directly from his single-minded pursuit of Fay. He smashes a Broadway theater when the notion enters his dull brain that the flashbulbs of photographers somehow endanger the lady. His perilous shinnying up a skyscraper to pluck Fay from her boudoir is an act of the kindliest of hearts. He's impossible to discourage even though the love of his life can't lay eyes on him without shrieking murder.

10   The tragedy of King Kong then, is to be the beast who at the end of the fable fails to turn into the handsome prince.

This is the conviction that the scriptwriters would leave with us in the film's closing line. As Kong's corpse lies blocking traffic in the street, the entrepreneur who brought Kong to New York turns to the assembled reporters and proclaims: "That's your story, boys—it was Beauty killed the Beast!" But greater forces than those of the screaming Lady have combined to lay Kong low, if you ask me. Kong lives for a time as one of those persecuted near-animal souls bewildered in the middle of an industrial order, whose simple desires are thwarted at every turn. He climbs the Empire State Building because in all New York it's the closest thing he can find to the clifftop of his jungle isle. He dies, a pitiful dolt, and the army brass and publicity-men cackle over him. His death is the only possible outcome to as neat a tragic dilemma as you can ask for. The machine-guns do him in, while the manicured human hero (a nice clean Dartmouth boy) carries away Kong's sweetheart to the altar. O, the misery of it all. There's far more truth about upper-middle-class American life in *King Kong* than in the last seven dozen novels of John P. Marquand.

. . .

11 Every day in the week on a screen somewhere in the world, King Kong relives his agony. Again and again he expires on the Empire State Building, as audiences of the devout assist his sacrifice. We watch him die, and by extension kill the ape within our bones, but these little deaths of ours occur in prosaic surroundings. We do not die on a tower, New York before our feet, nor do we give our lives to smash a few flying machines. It is not for us to bring to a momentary standstill the civilization in which we move. King Kong does this for us. And so we kill him again and again, in much-spliced celluloid, while the ape in us expires from day to day, obscure, in desperation.

Questions on Content

1. When was *King Kong* first released? Briefly summarize the plot.
2. What evidence that the Kong legend is virtually unkillable does Kennedy offer?
3. What reasons have been offered for King Kong's appeal—reasons that Kennedy does not consider the basic ones?

4. What is the first important reason Kennedy gives for *King Kong*'s popularity? In what ways do audiences identify with Kong?
5. How do the 1933 and 1960 audiences differ in the ways they relate to *King Kong*?
6. What conviction would the *King Kong* scriptwriters leave audiences with at the end of the movie?
7. What truth about upper-middle-class life does Kennedy see in *King Kong*?
8. What final reason for the appeal of *King Kong* does Kennedy come to at the end of his essay?

Questions on Invention, Design, and Style

1. Characterize the predominant tone of Kennedy's essay. How do such phrases as "lugging a frightened blonde" (*paragraph 1*), "old hunk of hokum" (*paragraph 3*), "larded with good healthy sadism" (*paragraph 4*), "great-granddaddy primordial brute from whose tribe we have all deteriorated" (*paragraph 5*), "the most disinterested lover since Cyrano" (*paragraph 9*), and "He dies, a pitiful dolt, and the army brass and publicity-men cackle over him" (*paragraph 10*) contribute to this tone? Why does the tone shift in paragraph 10? What is the tone of that paragraph?
2. Consider the beginning paragraphs, through the first sentence of paragraph 4, as the introduction to this essay. How does it set the tone for what follows? What elements attest to the continuing popularity of *King Kong*? What elements make the continuing popularity of the movie difficult to explain and thus arouse the readers' interest? Which sentence serves as a transition from the introduction to the body of the essay?
3. What is the function of paragraph 4 after the first sentence? How does it arouse further reader interest and also further define Kennedy's subject?
4. If the causal analysis in this essay can be diagrammed as at the top of page 234, what does the diagram suggest about Kennedy's ordering of causes for the continuing popularity of *King Kong*?
5. Comment on the effectiveness of Kennedy's illustrations, comparisons, and contrasts in clarifying his points. Give an especially effective example or two of each.
6. How effective is paragraph 11 in stating Kennedy's final cause and bringing the essay to a conclusion? What earlier elements in the essay have prepared readers for the seriousness of this paragraph?

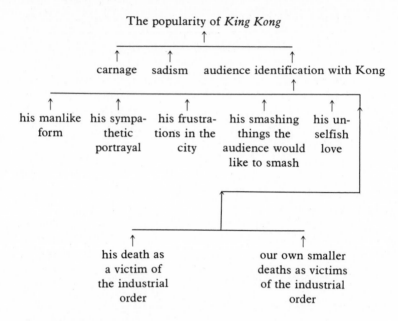

Applications

1. Select a popular movie, song, or custom, and write an essay analyzing the causes for its popularity.
2. If you have seen the 1976 version of *King Kong*, analyze the causes for its appeal to the audience of the 1970s. Then write an essay developing this analysis for your reader.
3. If you have seen both the 1933 and 1976 versions of *King Kong*, write an essay analyzing the causes of the superiority of one over the other.

Why the Sky Looks Blue
Sir James Jeans

When we see the sky as blue we are not likely to wonder why, yet the reasons for this sensory perception are surprisingly complex. Curiosity led British astrophysicist Sir James Jeans to analyze the causes of our perception of sky color; he clarifies his analysis by means of an analogy to an imaginary experience by the sea.

1   Imagine that we stand on an ordinary seaside pier, and watch the waves rolling in and striking against the iron columns of the pier. Large waves pay very little attention to the columns—they divide right and left and reunite after passing each column, much as a regiment of soldiers would if a tree stood in their road; it is almost as though the columns had not been there. But the short waves and ripples find the columns of the pier a much more formidable obstacle. When the short waves impinge on the columns, they are reflected back and spread as new ripples in all directions. To use the technical term, they are "scattered." The obstacle provided by the iron columns hardly affects the long waves at all, but scatters the short ripples.

2   We have been watching a sort of working model of the way in which sunlight struggles through the earth's atmosphere. Between us on earth and outer space the atmosphere interposes innumerable obstacles in the form of molecules of air, tiny droplets of water, and small particles of dust. These are represented by the columns of the pier.

3   The waves of the sea represent the sunlight. We know that sunlight is a blend of many colors—as we can prove for ourselves by passing it through a prism, or even through a jug of water, or as nature demonstrates to us when she passes it through the raindrops of a summer shower and produces a rainbow. We also know that light consists of waves, and that the different colors of light are produced by waves of different lengths, red light by long waves and blue light by short waves. The mixture of waves which constitutes sunlight has to struggle past the columns of the pier. And these obstacles treat the light waves much as the columns of the pier treat the sea-waves. The long waves which constitute red light are hardly affected but the short waves which constitute blue light are scattered in all directions.

4   Thus the different constituents of sunlight are treated in different ways as they struggle through the earth's atmosphere. A wave of blue light may be scattered by a dust particle, and turned out of its course. After a time a second dust particle again turns it out of its course, and so on, until finally it enters our eyes by a path as zigzag as that of a flash of lightning.

Consequently the blue waves of the sunlight enter our eyes from all directions.   And that is why the sky looks blue.

Questions on Content

1. What similarities exist between waves working their way into shore and sunlight struggling through the earth's atmosphere?
2. What color are long light waves? short light waves?
3. How do dust particles affect short light waves?
4. Why do blue light waves enter our eyes from all directions?

Questions on Invention, Design, and Style

1. How do Jeans' illustrations and comparisons in paragraph 1 help us imagine standing on a seaside pier and watching waves roll in?
2. What illustrations does Jeans provide in support of his statement, "We know that sunlight is a blend of many colors"?
3. Evaluate this selection as a causal analysis.   Does it communicate clearly the reasons why the sky appears blue?   If so, what techniques contribute to its clarity?
4. Diagram the causal relations in this essay according to the models in the introduction to "Causal Analysis" (pp. 223–228) and in Question 4 on p. 233.

Applications

1. Write an essay explaining why you enjoyed a movie you have seen, a book you have read, or a sports event you have attended.
2. What is the most important (not necessarily the most valuable) thing you own?   Write a paper analyzing why you came to regard it so highly and why its loss or destruction would distress you.
3. Write an essay showing why you experience a particular sensation every time you attend a certain class, meet a particular person, hear a certain song, or react to some other familiar stimulus.

The Iks
Lewis Thomas

Through examination of the thesis of a book he has recently read, physician and medical researcher Lewis Thomas arrives at an alter-

native explanation of the bizarre behavior of the Iks, based on a radically different view of basic human nature.

1   The small tribe of Iks, formerly nomadic hunters and gatherers in the mountain valleys of northern Uganda, have become celebrities, literary symbols for the ultimate fate of disheartened, heartless mankind at large. Two disastrously conclusive things happened to them: the government decided to have a national park, so they were compelled by law to give up hunting in the valleys and become farmers on poor hillside soil, and then they were visited for two years by an anthropologist who detested them and wrote a book[1] about them.

2   The message of the book is that the Iks have transformed themselves into an irreversibly disagreeable collection of unattached, brutish creatures, totally selfish and loveless, in response to the dismantling of their traditional culture. Moreover, this is what the rest of us are like in our inner selves, and we will all turn into Iks when the structure of our society comes all unhinged.

3   The argument rests, of course, on certain assumptions about the core of human beings, and is necessarily speculative. You have to agree in advance that man is fundamentally a bad lot, out for himself alone, displaying such graces as affection and compassion only as learned habits. If you take this view, the story of the Iks can be used to confirm it. These people seem to be living together, clustered in small, dense villages, but they are really solitary, unrelated individuals with no evident use for each other. They talk, but only to make ill-tempered demands and cold refusals. They share nothing. They never sing. They turn the children out to forage as soon as they can walk, and desert the elders to starve whenever they can, and the foraging children snatch food from the mouths of the helpless elders. It is a mean society.

4   They breed without love or even casual regard. They defecate on each other's doorsteps. They watch their neighbors for signs of misfortune, and only then do they laugh. In the book they do a lot of laughing, having so much bad luck. Several

---

[1] C. M. Turnbull, *The Mountain People*. New York: Simon and Schuster, 1972.

times they even laughed at the anthropologist, who found this especially repellent (one senses, between the lines, that the scholar is not himself the world's luckiest man). Worse, they took him into the family, snatched his food, defecated on his doorstep, and hooted dislike at him. They gave him two bad years.

5   It is a depressing book. If, as he suggests, there is only Ikness at the center of each of us, our sole hope for hanging on to the name of humanity will be in endlessly mending the structure of our society, and it is changing so quickly and completely that we may never find the threads in time. Meanwhile, left to ourselves alone, solitary, we will become the same joyless, zestless, untouching lone animals.

6   But this may be too narrow a view. For one thing, the Iks are extraordinary. They are absolutely astonishing, in fact. The anthropologist has never seen people like them anywhere, nor have I. You'd think, if they were simply examples of the common essence of mankind, they'd seem more recognizable. Instead, they are bizarre, anomalous. I have known my share of peculiar, difficult, nervous, grabby people, but I've never encountered any genuinely, consistently detestable human beings in all my life. The Iks sound more like abnormalities, maladies.

7   I cannot accept it. I do not believe that the Iks are representative of isolated, revealed man, unobscured by social habits. I believe their behavior is something extra, something laid on. This unremitting, compulsive repellence is a kind of complicated ritual. They must have learned to act this way; they copied it, somehow.

8   I have a theory, then. The Iks have gone crazy.

9   The solitary Ik, isolated in the ruins of an exploded culture, has built a new defense for himself. If you live in an unworkable society you can make up one of your own, and this is what the Iks have done. Each Ik has become a group, a one-man tribe on its own, a constituency.

10   Now everything falls into place. This is why they do seem, after all, vaguely familiar to all of us. We've seen them before. This is precisely the way groups of one size or another, ranging from committees to nations, behave. It is, of course,

this aspect of humanity that has lagged behind the rest of evolution, and this is why the Ik seems so primitive. In his absolute selfishness, his incapacity to give anything away, no matter what, he is a successful committee. When he stands at the door of his hut, shouting insults at his neighbors in a loud harangue, he is city addressing another city.

11   Cities have all the Ik characteristics. They defecate on doorsteps, in rivers and lakes, their own or anyone else's. They leave rubbish. They detest all neighboring cities, give nothing away. They even build institutions for deserting elders out of sight.

12   Nations are the most Iklike of all. No wonder the Iks seem familiar. For total greed, rapacity, heartlessness, and irresponsibility there is nothing to match a nation. Nations, by law, are solitary, self-centered, withdrawn into themselves. There is no such thing as affection between nations, and certainly no nation ever loved another. They bawl insults from their doorsteps, defecate into whole oceans, snatch all the food, survive by detestation, take joy in the bad luck of others, celebrate the death of others, live for the death of others.

13   That's it, and I shall stop worrying about the book. It does not signify that man is a sparse, inhuman thing at his center. He's all right. It only says what we've always known and never had enough time to worry about, that we haven't yet learned how to stay human when assembled in masses. The Ik, in his despair, is acting out this failure, and perhaps we should pay closer attention. Nations have themselves become too frightening to think about, but we might learn some things by watching these people.

Questions on Content

1. What two "disastrously conclusive" things happened to the small tribe of Iks?
2. What was the message of Turnbull's book about the Iks?
3. How did they treat him? What kind of person does Thomas think Turnbull is?
4. How does Turnbull believe Ik behavior will compare with that of other human beings whose society breaks down?
5. Why does Thomas not believe that the Iks are representative of

man in isolation?   What is the basis for his theory about the Iks?
6. Based on this theory about the behavior of the Iks, what observation does Thomas make about human behavior generally?   How are cities and nations Iklike?
7. What, according to Thomas, might we learn by watching the Iks?

Questions on Invention, Design, and Style

1. Paragraph 1 identifies the Iks and includes a brief causal analysis of why they have become "celebrities, literary symbols for the ultimate fate of . . . mankind at large."   Diagram this causal analysis according to the models in the introduction to "Causal Analysis" (pp. 223–228).
2. Paragraph 2 summarizes Turnbull's book.   What are the two basic parts of this summary?   In what places does Thomas develop the first part of this summary in greater detail?   How does he imply that he agrees with this aspect of the book?   In what places does he develop the second part of the summary?   In what ways does he make known his disagreement with this aspect of the book?
3. Diagram Thomas' account of Turnbull's causal analysis of why the Iks behave as they do.
4. Diagram Thomas' own causal analysis of why the Iks behave as they do.
5. Consider how Thomas tends to prejudice the reader against Turnbull and his analysis.   How do the following contribute to this effect: "an anthropologist who detested them" (*paragraph 1*), "irreversibly disagreeable . . . creatures" (*paragraph 2*), "this is what the rest of us are like" (*paragraph 2*), "You have to agree . . . that man is fundamentally a bad lot" (*paragraph 3*), "one senses . . . the scholar is not himself the world's luckiest man" (*paragraph 4*), "they . . . defecated on his doorstep" (*paragraph 4*), "It is a depressing book" (*paragraph 5*)?   Locate instances in which Thomas depicts himself as having more in common with the reader than Turnbull does.
6. Evaluate the soundness of Thomas' analogies between Ik behavior and that of committees, cities, and nations.   How sound are these analogies as support for his thesis?

Applications

1. Taking either Turnbull's or Thomas' assessment of human behavior, write an essay exploring the effects of such behavior as seen in several different social situations.

2. Observe or recall examples of human behavior that are especially unusual. Write an essay analyzing the causes for such behavior.
3. Read the accounts given in newspapers and magazines of the behavior of a person on trial for a serious crime. Write an essay analyzing the causes for that behavior, and draw a conclusion about how the defendant should be punished or rehabilitated.

Why We Make Excuses
C. S. Lewis

In a carefully designed essay, British professor and scholar C. S. Lewis analyzes the causes of the common human practices of quarreling and making excuses.

1 Every one has heard people quarrelling. Sometimes it sounds funny and sometimes it sounds merely unpleasant; but however it sounds, I believe we can learn something very important from listening to the kinds of things they say. They say things like this: "How'd you like it if anyone did the same to you?"—"That's my seat, I was there first"—"Leave him alone, he isn't doing you any harm"—"Why should you shove in first?"—"Give me a bit of your orange, I gave you a bit of mine"—"Come on, you promised." People say things like that every day, educated people as well as uneducated, and children as well as grown-ups.

2 Now what interests me about all these remarks is that the man who makes them is not merely saying that the other man's behaviour does not happen to please him. He is appealing to some kind of standard of behaviour which he expects the other man to know about. And the other man very seldom replies: "To hell with your standard." Nearly always he tries to make out that what he has been doing does not really go against the standard, or that if it does there is some special excuse. He pretends there is some special reason in this particular case why the person who took the seat first should not keep it, or that things were quite different when he was given the bit of orange, or that something has turned up which lets him off keeping his

promise.   It looks, in fact, very much as if both parties had in mind some kind of Law or Rule of fair play or decent behaviour or morality or whatever you like to call it, about which they really agreed.   And they have.   If they had not, they might, of course, fight like animals, but they could not *quarrel* in the human sense of the word.   Quarrelling means trying to show that the other man is in the wrong.   And there would be no sense in trying to do that unless you and he had some sort of agreement as to what Right and Wrong are; just as there would be no sense in saying that a footballer had committed a foul unless there was some agreement about the rules of football.

3   Now this Law or Rule about Right and Wrong used to be called the Law of Nature.   Nowadays, when we talk of the "laws of nature" we usually mean things like gravitation, or heredity, or the laws of chemistry.   But when the older thinkers called the Law of Right and Wrong "the Law of Nature," they really meant the Law of *Human* Nature.   The idea was that, just as all bodies are governed by the law of gravitation and organisms by biological laws, so the creature called man also had *his* law—with this great difference, that a body could not choose whether it obeyed the law of gravitation or not, but a man could choose either to obey the Law of Human Nature or to disobey it.

4   We may put this in another way.   Each man is at every moment subjected to several sets of law but there is only one of these which he is free to disobey.   As a body, he is subjected to gravitation and cannot disobey it; if you leave him unsupported in mid-air, he has no more choice about falling than a stone has.   As an organism, he is subjected to various biological laws which he cannot disobey any more than an animal can. That is, he cannot disobey those laws which he shares with other things; but the law which is peculiar to his human nature, the law he does not share with animals or vegetables or inorganic things, is the one he can disobey if he chooses.

5   This law was called the Law of Nature because people thought that every one knew it by nature and did not need to be taught it.   They did not mean, of course, that you might not find an odd individual here and there who did not know it, just as you find a few people who are colour-blind or have no ear

for a tune. But taking the race as a whole, they thought that the human idea of decent behaviour was obvious to every one. And I believe they were right. If they were not, then all the things we said about the war were nonsense. What was the sense in saying the enemy were in the wrong unless Right is a real thing which the Nazis at bottom knew as well as we did and ought to have practiced? If they had no notion of what we mean by right, then, though we might still have had to fight them, we could no more have blamed them for that than for the colour of their hair.

6 I know that some people say the idea of a Law of Nature or decent behaviour known to all men is unsound, because different civilisations and different ages have had quite different moralities.

7 But this is not true. There have been differences between their moralities, but these have never amounted to anything like a total difference. If anyone will take the trouble to compare the moral teaching of, say, the ancient Egyptians, Babylonians, Hindus, Chinese, Greeks and Romans, what will really strike him will be how very like they are to each other and to our own. Some of the evidence for this I have put together in the appendix of another book called *The Abolition of Man*; but for our present purpose I need only ask the reader to think what a totally different morality would mean. Think of a country where people were admired for running away in battle, or where a man felt proud of doublecrossing all the people who had been kindest to him. You might just as well try to imagine a country where two and two made five. Men have differed as regards what people you ought to be unselfish to—whether it was only your own family, or your fellow countrymen, or everyone. But they have always agreed that you ought not to put yourself first. Selfishness has never been admired. Men have differed as to whether you should have one wife or four. But they have always agreed that you must not simply have any woman you liked.

8 But the most remarkable thing is this. Whenever you find a man who says he does not believe in a real Right and Wrong, you will find the same man going back on this a moment later. He may break his promise to you, but if you try breaking one

to him he will be complaining "It's not fair" before you can say Jack Robinson. A nation may say treaties do not matter; but then, next minute, they spoil their case by saying that the particular treaty they want to break was an unfair one. But if treaties do not matter, and if there is no such thing as Right and Wrong —in other words, if there is no Law of Nature—what is the difference between a fair treaty and an unfair one? Have they not let the cat out of the bag and shown that, whatever they say, they really know the Law of Nature just like anyone else?

9   It seems, then, we are forced to believe in a real Right and Wrong. People may be sometimes mistaken about them, just as people sometimes get their sums wrong; but they are not a matter of mere taste and opinion any more than the multiplication table. Now if we are agreed about that, I go on to my next point, which is this. None of us are really keeping the Law of Nature. If there are any exceptions among you, I apologize to them. They had much better read some other work, for nothing I am going to say concerns them. And now, turning to the ordinary human beings who are left:

10   I hope you will not misunderstand what I am going to say. I am not preaching, and Heaven knows I do not pretend to be better than anyone else. I am only trying to call attention to a fact; the fact that this year, or this month, or, more likely, this very day, we have failed to practice ourselves the kind of behaviour we expect from other people. There may be all sorts of excuses for us. That time you were so unfair to the children was when you were very tired. That slightly shady business about the money—the one you have almost forgotten—came when you were very hard up. And what you promised to do for old So-and-so and have never done—well, you never would have promised if you had known how frightfully busy you were going to be. And as for your behaviour to your wife (or husband) or sister (or brother) if I knew how irritating they could be, I would not wonder at it—and who the dickens am I, anyway? I am just the same. That is to say, I do not succeed in keeping the Law of Nature very well, and the moment anyone tells me I am not keeping it, there starts up in my mind a string of excuses as long as your arm. The question at the moment is not whether they are good excuses. The point is that they are one more proof

of how deeply, whether we like it or not, we believe in the Law of Nature. If we do not believe in decent behaviour, why should we be so anxious to make excuses for not having behaved decently? The truth is, we believe in decency so much— we feel the Rule of Law pressing on us so—that we cannot bear to face the fact that we are breaking it, and consequently we try to shift the responsibility. For you notice that it is only for our bad behaviour that we find all these explanations. It is only our bad temper that we put down to being tired or worried or hungry; we put our good temper down to ourselves.

11 These, then, are the two points I wanted to make. First, that human beings, all over the earth, have this curious idea that they ought to behave in a certain way, and cannot really get rid of it. Secondly, that they do not in fact behave in that way. They know the Law of Nature; they break it. These two facts are the foundation of all clear thinking about ourselves and the universe we live in.

Questions on Content

1. What, according to Lewis, can we learn from the kinds of things people say when they quarrel?
2. If man did not have some kind of law or rule of fair play, what would he do instead of quarrel?
3. How does Lewis define quarreling?
4. What analogy does Lewis draw between the rules of decent behavior and the rules of football?
5. How does Lewis define the law of nature? How does this definition differ from the more modern use of the term? What is the distinction between the law of nature and man's law?
6. Which law can man disobey if he wishes? Why?
7. How does Lewis refute the opposing argument that the idea of a law of nature is unsound because different civilizations and different ages have had different moralities?
8. What, according to Lewis, is the most remarkable thing about a man who does not believe in a real right and wrong?
9. What examples does Lewis give of humans who do not conform to the law of nature? What typical excuses does he give for each?
10. What do we do when someone accuses us of not keeping the law of nature? How does this reaction reveal the strength of our belief in it?

11. What two points does Lewis offer at the end of the essay to sum
     up what he has said?

Questions on Invention, Design, and Style

1. According to Lewis, what is the *cause* of human quarreling (*par-
    agraph 2*)? What is the *cause* of excuse making about behavior?
    Using the model from the introduction to "Causal Analysis" (pp.
    223–228) and question number 4 on p. 233, diagram these two
    causal analyses.
2. Consider paragraphs 1 and 2 as the introduction to this essay.
    By what distinct stages does this introduction lead into Lewis'
    first point: that people generally have a set of standards of right
    and wrong behavior?
3. Paragraphs 3–8 develop this point at some length. In what ways
    does Lewis define "law of nature"? How does he differentiate it
    from some other kinds of laws? How does he illustrate the term?
4. In paragraph 6 Lewis concedes that not all people will agree with
    him about the law of nature. What is the function, then, of para-
    graphs 7 and 8? What methods does Lewis use here to achieve
    this function?
5. Paragraph 9 reiterates Lewis' first point and also states his sec-
    ond. In what earlier paragraphs has Lewis prepared the reader
    for this second point? Why is his development of this second
    point (*in paragraph 10*) so much shorter than that of his first
    point?
6. Lewis' conclusion in paragraph 11 reiterates his two main points.
    What is his purpose in this reiteration?
7. In paragraph 10 Lewis assumes a much more personal relation
    to his individual readers. Cite several devices, such as use of the
    pronoun *you*, by which he achieves this more personal stance.
    Why does Lewis do so at this particular stage in his essay?

Applications

1. Pick a common behavior pattern of people who live around you,
    and analyze the causes for this behavior.
2. Using as a basis Lewis' point that "we believe in decency so
    much . . . that we cannot bear to face the fact" that we violate its
    principles, write a causal analysis developing one or more effects
    of that cause in detail.
3. Consider the Iks as described in Lewis Thomas' essay (p. 236)
    in the light of C. S. Lewis' concept of the law of nature. Write
    a causal analysis of Ik behavior, explaining why it does or does

not contradict Lewis' claim that people "have always agreed that you ought not to put yourself first"—that "selfishness has never been admired."

Human Sexuality
J. Bronowski

In a thoughtful essay that gains emphasis by contrasting human sexuality both with asexual reproduction and with sexuality in lower animals, mathematician and biologist J. Bronowski seeks the causes for the remarkably rapid rate of human evolution.

1   Every cell in the body carries the complete potential to make the whole animal, except only the sperm and egg cells. The sperm and the egg are incomplete, and essentially they are half cells: they carry half the total number of genes.   Then when the egg is fertilised by the sperm, the genes from each come together in pairs . . . and the total of instructions is assembled again.   The fertilised egg is then a complete cell, and it is the model of every cell in the body.   For every cell is formed by division of the fertilised egg, and is therefore identical with it in its genetic make-up.   Like a chick embryo, the animal has the legacy of the fertilised egg all through life.

. . .

2   The baby is an individual from birth.   The coupling of genes from both parents stirred the pool of diversity.   The child inherits gifts from both parents, and chance has now combined these gifts in a new and original arrangement.   The child is not a prisoner of its inheritance; it holds its inheritance as a new creation which its future actions will unfold.

3   The child is an individual.   The bee is not, because the drone bee is one of a series of identical replicas.   In any hive the queen is the only fertile female.   When she mates with a drone in mid-air, she goes on hoarding his sperms; the drone dies.   If the queen now releases a sperm with an egg she lays, she makes a worker bee, a female.   If she lays an egg but releases no sperm with it, a drone bee is made, a male, in a sort

of virgin birth.   It is a totalitarian paradise, for ever loyal, for ever fixed, because it has shut itself off from the adventure of diversity that drives and changes the higher animals and man.
4   A world as rigid as the bee's could be created among higher animals, even among men, by cloning: that is, by growing a colony or clone of identical animals from cells of a single parent. Begin with a mixed population of an amphibian, the axolotl. Suppose we decided to fix on one type, the speckled axolotl. We take some eggs from a speckled female and grow an embryo which is destined to be speckled.   Now we tease out from the embryo a number of cells.   Wherever in the embryo we take them from, they are identical in their genetic make-up, and each cell is capable of growing into a complete animal—our procedure will prove that.
5   We are going to grow identical animals, one from each cell. We need a carrier in which to grow the cells: any axolotl carrier will do—she can be white.   We take unfertilised eggs from the carrier and destroy the nucleus in each egg.   And into it we insert one of the single identical cells of the speckled parent of the clone.   These eggs will now grow into speckled axolotls.
6   The clone of identical eggs made in this way are all grown at the same time.   Each egg divides at the same moment—divides once, divides twice, and goes on dividing.   All that is normal, exactly as in any egg.   At the next stage, single cell divisions are no longer visible.   Each egg has turned into a kind of tennis ball, and begins to turn itself inside out—or it would be more literal to say, outside in.   Still all the eggs are in step. Each egg folds over to form the animal, always in step: a regimented world in which the units obey every command identically at the identical moment. . . .   And finally we have the clone of individual axolotls, each of them an identical copy of the parent, and each of them a virgin birth like the drone bee.
7   Should we make clones of human beings—copies of a beautiful mother, perhaps, or of a clever father?   Of course not. My view is that diversity is the breath of life, and we must not abandon that for any single form which happens to catch our fancy—even our genetic fancy.   Cloning is the stabilisation of one form, and that runs against the whole current of creation— of human creation above all.   Evolution is founded in variety

and creates diversity; and of all animals, man is most creative because he carries and expresses the largest store of variety. Every attempt to make us uniform, biologically, emotionally, or intellectually, is a betrayal of the evolutionary thrust that has made man its apex.

. . .

8   Happily we are not frozen into identical copies. In the human species sex is highly developed. The female is receptive at all times, she has permanent breasts, she takes an active part in sexual selection. Eve's apple, as it were, fertilises mankind; or at least spurs it to its ageless preoccupation.

9   It is obvious that sex has a very special character for human beings. It has a special biological character. Let us take one simple, down-to-earth criterion for that: we are the only species in which the female has orgasms. That is remarkable, but it is so. It is a mark of the fact that in general there is much less difference between men and women (in the biological sense and in sexual behaviour) than there is in other species. That may seem a strange thing to say. But to the gorilla and the chimpanzee, where there are enormous differences between male and female, it would be obvious. In the language of biology, sexual dimorphism is small in the human species.

10   So much for biology. But there is a point on the borderline between biology and culture which really marks the symmetry in sexual behaviour, I think, very strikingly. It is an obvious one. We are the only species that copulates face to face, and this is universal in all cultures. To my mind, it is an expression of a general equality which has been important in the evolution of man, I think, right back to the time of *Australopithecus* [1] and the first tool-makers.

11   Why do I say that? Well, we have something to explain. We have to explain the speed of human evolution over a matter of one, three, let us say five million years at most. That is terribly fast. Natural selection simply does not act as fast as that on animal species. We, the hominids, must have supplied a form of selection of our own; and the obvious choice is sexual selection. There is evidence now that women marry men who

[1] An early manlike primate.

are intellectually like them, and men marry women who are intellectually like them. And if that preference really goes back over some million of years, then it means that selection for skills has always been important on the part of both sexes.

12   I believe that as soon as the forerunners of man began to be nimble with their hands in making tools and clever with their brains in planning them, the nimble and clever enjoyed a selective advantage. They were able to get more mates and to beget and feed more children than the rest. If my speculation about this is right, it explains how the nimble-fingered and quick-witted were able to dominate the biological evolution of man, and take it ahead so fast. And it shows that even in his biological evolution, man has been nudged and driven by a cultural talent, the ability to make tools and communal plans. I think that is still expressed in the care that kindred and community take in all cultures, and only in human cultures, to arrange what is revealingly called a good match.

13   Yet if that had been the only selective factor then, of course, we should be much more homogeneous than we are. What keeps alive the variety among human beings? That is a cultural point. In every culture there are also special safeguards to make for variety. The most striking of them is the universal prohibition of incest (for the man in the street—it does not always apply to royal families). The prohibition of incest only has a meaning if it is designed to prevent older males dominating a group of females, as they do in (let us say) ape groups.

14   The preoccupation with the choice of a mate both by male and female I regard as a continuing echo of the major selective force by which we have evolved. All that tenderness, the postponement of marriage, the preparations and preliminaries that are found in all cultures, are an expression of the weight that we give to the hidden qualities in a mate. Universals that stretch across all cultures are rare and tell-tale. Ours is a cultural species, and I believe that our unique attention to sexual choice has helped to mould it.

15   Most of the world's literature, most of the world's art, is preoccupied with the theme of boy meets girl. We tend to think of this as being a sexual preoccupation that needs no explana-

tion. But I think that is a mistake. On the contrary, it expresses the deeper fact that we are uncommonly careful in the choice, not of whom we take to bed, but by whom we are to beget children. Sex was invented as a biological instrument by (say) the green algae. But as an instrument in the ascent of man which is basic to his cultural evolution, it was invented by man himself.

Questions on Content

1. What parallel does Bronowski draw between the animal and chick embryos?
2. In what sense is a child not a prisoner of its inheritance?
3. What contrast does Bronowski draw between a child and a bee? What makes the bee's world rigid?
4. How could man's world be made as rigid as that of the bee? What examples does Bronowski give of rigidity in animals higher than the bee? How do they illustrate this step-by-step, regimented world?
5. Why, according to Bronowski, should we not make clones of human beings? In what way does it run "against the whole current of creation" to do so?
6. What rescues humans from being "frozen into identical copies"?
7. How is the human sexual experience different from those of other species? How does the difference between male and female in humans contrast with the difference between male and female in many other species?
8. What is the point on the borderline between biology and culture that marks "symmetry in sexual behaviour"? What does this mean to Bronowski?
9. What form of selection has helped man to evolve? Upon what basis is this selection made?
10. How is diversity kept alive in every culture?
11. What evidence does Bronowski offer for the concern that humans show for the "hidden qualities in a mate"?
12. What is the meaning of sex "as an instrument in the ascent of man"?

Questions on Invention, Design, and Style

1. Consider paragraphs 1 and 2 as the introduction to this essay. What is the causal relationship between the statements that "the

child inherits gifts from both parents, and chance has now combined these gifts in a new and original arrangement" and that "the child is not a prisoner of its inheritance; it holds its inheritance as a new creation which its future actions will unfold"?

2. How is the concept of a being that *is* "a prisoner of its inheritance" developed in paragraphs 3–6? How important are process analysis and contrast in these paragraphs?

3. What is the importance of paragraph 7 in Bronowski's essay? How is the principle of contrast used here?

4. Paragraphs 8–15 focus on human sexuality in contrast to cloning and to sexuality in lower animals. What are the biological factors that distinguish human sexuality (*paragraphs 7 and 9*)? What are the cultural factors in human sexuality (*paragraphs 10–14*)? How may both groups of factors be viewed as causes for the "terribly fast" rate of human evolution?

5. How effective are paragraphs 14 and 15 in drawing the essay to a close? Do these paragraphs tend to make readers consider the subject a closed one or to stimulate further thought about it?

6. Consider Bronowski's apparent attitudes toward human beings and human sexuality. How can they be discovered from his choice of words and phrases, his illustrations, and his general tone? Do they add to or detract from the effectiveness of the essay?

Applications

1. Consider paragraph 7 in Bronowski's essay again, and write an essay in which you analyze the possible effects on society of the cloning of human beings.

2. Consider paragraph 14 in Bronowski's essay again, and write a causal analysis of why various cultures encourage "the postponement of marriage" and elaborate "preparations and preliminaries" for it and what the effects of these practices are.

3. Write an essay in which you analyze the causes of some aspect of human behavior, emphasizing its contrast with a parallel aspect of animal behavior.

The Worker as Creator or Machine
Erich Fromm

In a historical survey of attitudes toward work and his own analysis based on that survey, psychologist Erich Fromm considers why modern men and women relate as they do to their work.

1   Unless man exploits others, he has to work in order to live. However primitive and simple his method of work may be, by the very fact of production, he has risen above the animal kingdom; rightly has he been defined as "the animal that produces." But work is not only an inescapable necessity for man. Work is also his liberator from nature, his creator as a social and independent being. *In the process of work, that is, the molding and changing of nature outside of himself, man molds and changes himself.* He emerges from nature by mastering her; he develops his powers of co-operation, of reason, his sense of beauty. He separates himself from nature, from the original unity with her, but at the same time unites himself with her again as her master and builder. The more his work develops, the more his individuality develops. In molding nature and re-creating her, he learns to make use of his powers, increasing his skill and creativeness. Whether we think of the beautiful paintings in the caves of Southern France, the ornaments on weapons among primitive people, the statues and temples of Greece, the cathedrals of the Middle Ages, the chairs and tables made by skilled craftsmen, or the cultivation of flowers, trees or corn by peasants—all are expressions of the creative transformation of nature by man's reason and skill.

2   In Western history, craftsmanship, especially as it developed in the thirteenth and fourteenth centuries, constitutes one of the peaks in the evolution of creative work. Work was not only a useful activity, but one which carried with it a profound satisfaction. The main features of craftsmanship have been very lucidly expressed by C. W. Mills. "There is no ulterior motive in work other than the product being made and the processes of its creation. The details of daily work are meaningful because they are not detached in the worker's mind from the product of the work. The worker is free to control his own

working action. The craftsman is thus able to learn from his work; and to use and develop his capacities and skills in its prosecution. There is no split of work and play, or work and culture. The craftsman's way of livelihood determines and infuses his entire mode of living." *

3   With the collapse of the medieval structure, and the beginning of the modern mode of production, the meaning and function of work changed fundamentally, especially in the Protestant countries. Man, being afraid of his newly won freedom, was obsessed by the need to subdue his doubts and fears by developing a feverish activity. The outcome of this activity, success or failure, decided his salvation, indicating whether he was among the saved or the lost souls. *Work, instead of being an activity satisfying in itself and pleasurable, became a duty and an obsession.* The more it was possible to gain riches by work, the more it became a pure means to the aim of wealth and success. Work became, in Max Weber's terms, the chief factor in a system of "inner-worldly asceticism," an answer to man's sense of aloneness and isolation.

4   However, work in this sense existed only for the upper and middle classes, those who could amass some capital and employ the work of others. For the vast majority of those who had only their physical energy to sell, work became nothing but forced labor. The worker in the eighteenth or nineteenth century who had to work sixteen hours if he did not want to starve was not doing it because he served the Lord in this way, nor because his success would show that he was among the "chosen" ones, but because he was forced to sell his energy to those who had the means of exploiting it. The first centuries of the modern era find the meaning of work divided into that of *duty* among the middle class, and that of *forced labor* among those without property.

5   The religious attitude toward work as a duty, which was still so prevalent in the nineteenth century, has been changing considerably in the last decades. Modern man does not know what to do with himself, how to spend his lifetime meaningfully, and he is driven to work in order to avoid an unbearable

---

* C. W. Mills, *White Collar*, Oxford University Press, New York, 1951, p. 220.

boredom. But work has ceased to be a moral and religious obligation in the sense of the middle-class attitude of the eighteenth and nineteenth centuries. Something new has emerged. Ever-increasing production, the drive to make bigger and better things, have become aims in themselves, new ideals. Work has become alienated from the working person.

6   What happens to the industrial worker? He spends his best energy for seven or eight hours a day in producing "something." He needs his work in order to make a living, but his role is essentially a passive one. He fulfills a small isolated function in a complicated and highly organized process of production, and is never confronted with "his" product as a whole, at least not as a producer, but only as a consumer, provided he has the money to buy "his" product in a store. He is concerned neither with the whole product in its physical aspects nor with its wider economic and social aspects. He is put in a certain place, has to carry out a certain task, but does not participate in the organization or management of the work. He is not interested nor does he know why one produces this, instead of another commodity—what relation it has to the needs of society as a whole. The shoes, the cars, the electric bulbs, are produced by "the enterprise," using the machines. He is a part of the machine, rather than its master as an active agent. The machine, instead of being in his service to do work for him which once had to be performed by sheer physical energy, has become his master. Instead of the machine being the substitute for human energy, man has become a substitute for the machine. *His work can be defined as the performance of acts which cannot yet be performed by machines.*

7   Work is a means of getting money, not in itself a meaningful human activity. P. Drucker, observing workers in the automobile industry, expresses this idea very succinctly: "For the great majority of automobile workers, the only meaning of the job is in the pay check, not in anything connected with the work or the product. Work appears as something unnatural, a disagreeable, meaningless and stultifying condition of getting the pay check, devoid of dignity as well as of importance. No wonder that this puts a premium on slovenly work, on slowdowns, and on other tricks to get the same pay check with less

work.   No wonder that this results in an unhappy and discontented worker—because a pay check is not enough to base one's self-respect on." *

8   This relationship of the worker to his work is an outcome of the whole social organization of which he is a part.   Being "employed," he is not an active agent, has no responsibility except the proper performance of the isolated piece of work he is doing, and has little interest except the one of bringing home enough money to support himself and his family.   Nothing more is expected of him, or wanted from him.   He is part of the equipment hired by capital, and his role and function are determined by this quality of being a piece of equipment.   In recent decades, increasing attention has been paid to the psychology of the worker, and to his attitude toward his work, to the "human problem of industry"; but this very formulation is indicative of the underlying attitude; there is a human being spending most of his lifetime at work, and what should be discussed is the *"industrial problem of human beings," rather than "the human problem of industry."*

9   Most investigations in the field of industrial psychology are concerned with the question of how the productivity of the individual worker can be increased, and how he can be made to work with less friction; psychology has lent its services to "human engineering," an attempt to treat the worker and employee like a machine which runs better when it is well oiled.   While Taylor was primarily concerned with a better organization of the technical use of the worker's physical powers, most industrial psychologists are mainly concerned with the manipulation of the worker's psyche.   The underlying idea can be formulated like this: if he works better when he is happy, then let us make him happy, secure, satisfied, or anything else, provided it raises his output and diminishes friction.   In the name of "human relations," the worker is treated with all devices which suit a completely alienated person; even happiness and human values are recommended in the interest of better relations with the public.   Thus, for instance, according to *Time* magazine, one of the

---

* Peter F. Drucker, *Concept of the Corporation*, The John Day Company, New York, 1946, p. 179.

best-known American psychiatrists said to a group of fifteen hundred Supermarket executives: "It's going to be an increased satisfaction to our customers if we are happy. . . . It is going to pay off in cold dollars and cents to management, if we could put some of these general principles of values, human relationships, really into practice." One speaks of "human relations" and one means the most in-human relations, those between alienated automatons; one speaks of happiness and means the perfect routinization which has driven out the last doubt and all spontaneity.

10 The alienated and profoundly unsatisfactory character of work results in two reactions: one, the ideal of complete *laziness*; the other a deep-seated, though often unconscious *hostility* toward work and everything and everybody connected with it.

11 It is not difficult to recognize the widespread longing for the state of complete laziness and passivity. Our advertising appeals to it even more than to sex. There are, of course, many useful and labor saving gadgets. But this usefulness often serves only as a rationalization for the appeal to complete passivity and receptivity. A package of breakfast cereal is being advertised as *"new—easier to eat."* An electric toaster is advertised with these words: ". . . the most distinctly different toaster in the world! Everything is done *for* you with this new toaster. You need not even bother to lower the bread. Power-action, through a unique electric motor, *gently takes the bread right out of your fingers!"* How many courses in languages, or other subjects, are announced with the slogan "effortless learning, no more of the old drudgery." Everybody knows the picture of the elderly couple in the advertisement of a life-insurance company, who have retired at the age of sixty, and spend their life in the complete bliss of having nothing to do except just travel.

12 Radio and television exhibit another element of this yearning for laziness: the idea of "push-button power"; by pushing a button, or turning a knob on my machine, I have the power to produce music, speeches, ball games, and on the television set, to command events of the world to appear before my eyes. The pleasure of driving cars certainly rests partly upon this same satisfaction of the wish for push-button power. By the ef-

fortless pushing of a button, a powerful machine is set in motion; little skill and effort [are] needed to make the driver feel that he is the ruler of space.

13   But there is far more serious and deep-seated reaction to the meaninglessness and boredom of work.   It is a hostility toward work which is much less conscious than our craving for laziness and inactivity.   Many a businessman feels himself the prisoner of his business and the commodities he sells; he has a feeling of fraudulency about his product and a secret contempt for it.   He hates his customers, who force him to put up a show in order to sell.   He hates his competitors because they are a threat; his employees as well as his superiors, because he is in a constant competitive fight with them.   Most important of all, he hates himself, because he sees his life passing by, without making any sense beyond the momentary intoxication of success.   Of course, this hate and contempt for others and for oneself, and for the very things one produces, is mainly unconscious, and only occasionally comes up to awareness in a fleeting thought, which is sufficiently disturbing to be set aside as quickly as possible.

Questions on Content

1.   What interactions occur between workers and their work, according to Fromm?   What relationship with nature can people have as a result of work?

2.   How did the meaning of work change after the collapse of the medieval social structure?   How did people's sense of insecurity influence their work?   What part did religion play?

3.   What two views of work were common during the first centuries of the modern era?   How did different classes view work differently?   How, according to Fromm, did these views emerge?

4.   What does Fromm cite as the chief reason, other than financial, that people work today?

5.   How has the industrial worker's role changed?   What is his relation to the machine?

6.   What, according to Peter Drucker, is the meaning of a job in the automobile industry?   Why is this meaning inadequate for the worker?

7.   What has most concerned researchers in industrial psychology?   How has the comparison of the worker to a machine influenced these investigations?

8. The alienated nature of work today has resulted in what two reactions, according to Fromm?

Questions on Invention, Design, and Style

1. Look closely at Fromm's first paragraph. What positive values of work are mentioned? What illustrations of man's "creative transformation of nature by . . . reason and skill" are given? How do these ideas prepare for paragraph 2?
2. How does paragraph 2 provide the definition of an ideal kind of work?
3. How does the quotation from C. W. Mills support the point Fromm is making in paragraph 2? What is the effect of a direct quotation, rather than a paraphrase?
4. How do the first two paragraphs provide a contrast to work as it is described in the rest of the essay?
5. In paragraph 7, Fromm states: "Work is a means of getting money, not in itself a meaningful human activity." Explain how the quotation from Drucker supports and develops Fromm's point. Why is a quotation more effective than a summary?
6. Why are industrial psychologists concerned with "human relations," according to Fromm? What are their objectives? What is their model of the human being? What are Fromm's reactions to their endeavors? How does he make his reactions clear to his readers?
7. Review the ways in which Fromm demonstrates that work "has become alienated" from people. When did this alienation begin? What caused it? What have been its effects?
8. Explain how Fromm's survey of the history of people's attitudes toward work is essential to the development of his causal analysis.

Applications

1. Consider people you know who enjoy their work. What do you believe explains that enjoyment? Write a paper analyzing the causes of their enjoyment of work.
2. Think back to a job you had that you disliked. Write a paper describing your dissatisfaction and analyzing its causes.
3. In Shakespeare's *King Henry IV*, Part I, Prince Hal says to the idle Falstaff, "If all the year were playing holidays, to sport would be as tedious as to work." Write an essay based on this quotation by defining *work*, analyzing recent changes in attitudes toward work, and predicting further changes resulting from increased leisure time.

Part four
Argument

Cremation isn't for Everyone.

appeal — statements
reason — (logic, facts, figures) out
emotion —
writers trustworthiness

Argument

Persuasive and argumentative writing
Appeals to emotion and reason
Principles of inventing and designing a sound argument
Sensitivity to audience

rebuttal - opp view pt.

Argument is a form of writing that deliberately sets out to convince readers that the writer's thesis is valid and, in some cases, should be acted on. Although it often informs and explains as well, argument is aimed primarily at convincing readers to accept the writer's views, even in place of their own convictions. To do so effectively, such writing must be based upon both a logical and rational analysis of the subject (considerations of the argumentative mode) and an appeal to the emotions (considerations of the persuasive mode). This type of writing is argumentative in that it convinces readers to accept the validity and even superiority of its solution to a problem; it is persuasive in that it convinces readers to act on the proposed solution.

Of course, writers who can influence their audiences in this way command great respect. These writers are successful because they can determine the degree to which they should appeal to their audience's sense of what is *reasonable* and the degree to which they should appeal to its more *emotional* nature. In addition, the most successful writing of this type, such as that of Martin Luther King, Jr., in this section, leaves the reader with the impression that *the writer himself* is a reasonable and fair person, one who can be safely trusted. Briefly stated, then, effective argument combines solid factual information and effective use of logic with an appropriate appeal to the emotions; as a result, readers develop a sense of trust in the soundness of the argument and fairness of the writer.

Attempting to persuade or influence others is quite common. We do it every day. For instance, even on relatively minor matters, such as convincing someone to go to the movies with us instead of studying for the chemistry final exam that everyone is dreading, we instinctively employ these characteristics of a persuasive argument: appeal to *reason*, appeal to *emotion*, appeal to our own *trustworthiness*. With one person we may appeal predominantly to reason: "You and I did well on every quiz in this course. We've already studied longer than anybody else. And our psychology text says that it's better to study in shorter, more frequent sessions than in one long one." But our listener, though admitting that what we have said seems reasonable, may point out certain fallacies in our logic. Or, speaking from his emotional side, to which our argument does not appeal, he may confess that he's just too frightened to stop studying.

At this point we may seek out another companion, this time using a greater appeal to the emotions of our audience: "I've been worrying about this final test for four days and nights and I'm about at the breaking point. You've simply got to help me get away from here for a while! Come on, let's go to the movies." Our friend, ordinarily a sympathetic person, recognizes that this is not a very authentic *emotional* appeal because we are not nearly as upset as we say we are. But, above all, our argument does not take into account our friend's very reasonable awareness that, as a chemistry major, he must do well on this examination.

In writing an essay that urges readers to accept your belief or to take a particular action, you cannot, of course, adjust the appeals of your argument as quickly as the individual in the above example of oral argument. But in writing, as in oral communication, one must follow the same principles of inventing and designing a sound argument. To understand these principles better, think of the whole process of inventing and designing an argument as having five basic stages:

1. Formulating your belief or position and discovering supporting reasons,
2. Introducing your belief or position and establishing common ground with your readers,
3. Presenting evidence that is appropriate to your belief or position, to the subject or issue, and to your readers,

4. Clarifying how the evidence leads to and justifies the belief, and
5. Appealing to the emotion and reason of your readers.

The processes of formulating beliefs or positions for the purpose of argument and then discovering supporting reasons offer the writer a chance to understand and test his or her beliefs more fully than ever before.   Jonathan Swift and Thomas Jefferson, writers in this section, both have formulated their beliefs on similar subjects: the British oppression of the Irish in the one case and of the American colonists in the other.   The ways in which they formulate their beliefs through classification, definition, process and causal analysis, illustration, and comparison and contrast offer models of inventing and designing an argument.   In its final form Swift's essay uses irony and satire in having an imaginary speaker propose a deliberately ridiculous solution to the Irish problem.   Jefferson speaks out directly for declaring independence in order to solve the problem of British oppression.   In both cases, the writers have clearly formulated their beliefs and arrived at reasons for these beliefs.

Second, in the actual writing of an argument, the writer makes clear to the reader exactly what his belief or position is and then establishes a point of agreement with him.   What C. S. Lewis stated about "quarrelling" in his essay "Why We Make Excuses" (pp. 241–245) could well be said about argument at this point.

[It] means trying to show that the other man is in the wrong.   And there would be no sense in trying to do that unless you and he had some sort of agreement as to what Right and Wrong are; just as there would be no sense in saying that a footballer had committed a foul unless there was some agreement about the rules of football.

By establishing this point of agreement, you not only increase your credibility with your readers but you can also demonstrate for them the logical connection between what you and they agree upon and the evidence of your argument.   It is possible at that point for you to demonstrate how logically the conclusion follows from the evidence of your argument.   John Robinson clearly states his belief that the sentimental treatment of deer resulting from the movie *Bambi* has led to conditions that are ridiculous and also dangerous to both man and animal. The point of agreement he establishes is that none of us want the balance of nature so disturbed that crops are destroyed and deer starved to death. He demonstrates how logically and reasonably his belief follows from the evidence he presents.

Third, the evidence must be appropriate to the writer's belief, to his subject, and to his audience. Thomas Henry Huxley's "Everyone Is a Scientist" certainly follows this characteristic of sound argument. He believes that the principles of science are nothing more than the normal working of the human mind. The examples he offers—the similar measuring scales of the butcher and baker and those of the chemist, the experiment leading to the conclusion that green and hard apples are sour, the hypothesis to explain how a teapot was stolen, and so on—support this belief that scientific discovery is a refinement of everyday thinking and is appropriate to a general, nonspecialized audience.

Fourth, how the evidence *leads to* and *justifies* your belief or position must be made clear if your argument is to be convincing. Consider the argument of Jefferson and others that the English government had become so destructive of the rights of the people that the colonies must separate from England. The wrongs of the king are clearly enumerated—he has forbidden his governors from passing laws, made judges dependent on his will, "plundered our seas, ravaged our Coasts, burnt our towns, and destroyed the lives of our people," and so on. These examples of injustices, the writers then make clear, lead to and support the conclusion that the colonies should be free and independent and absolved from all allegiance to England.

Finally, a persuasive argument must strike an effective *balance between reason and emotion*; the writer appeals to the whole person—to both emotional and rational sides of the reader. The writers of the essays in the subsection on "Emotion in Argument," for example, make clear and deliberate use of the appeal to emotion. But while appealing to emotion, they present evidence for the reasonableness of their conclusions. In "Little Brother of the Wolf," for instance, Cleveland Amory appeals to our sense of pity for the coyote in the light of his mistreatment.   But at the same time, he presents evidence that this animal is more clever and more determined than he has been assumed to be by his tormentors and that he is so vital to the balance of nature that the reader is tempted to agree with the author.   The reader not only pities and admires the poor coyote, but he begins to believe that it is completely *reasonable* that the coyote should not be so mistreated.

In this particular argument, Amory has drawn his evidence from a variety of sources—his personal experiences, his conversations and observations, and his readings.   Obviously, he has made a careful selection from the many possible pieces of evidence, and he has obviously made this selection upon the basis of what evidence would be most effective for the general audience he is addressing.   You can easily imagine how he might have chosen different evidence if he were addressing a group of coyote sympathizers, a group of small children, a group of hunters, or a group of ranchers.

Sensitivity to audience is perhaps even more important in argument than in other forms of writing.   The writer needs to consider any possible *rebuttal*, a systematic answer or counterproof, his audience might make in response.   Although his own convictions—sometimes his most deeply held beliefs—are an important part of his argument, the writer must also consider the convictions of his readers.   He will not convince them by ranting and scolding.   Indeed, he must realize that, the closer he comes to challenging their fundamental convictions, the more resistance he will arouse.   The writer can overcome this resistance only by dealing sensitively and effectively with his audience's assumptions, attitudes, and beliefs.   If he is to gain the audience's trust and establish his credibility, he must care not only about his subject, but about how his subject will be received.

But regardless of the audience, the writer wishes to present the persona of a fair, knowledgeable, honest, and intelligent person—one the reader can trust.   No matter how thoroughly the writer has thought through his argument, gathered his information, and arranged his presentation of it, he will not reach his audience if he is perceived as biased, uncertain, or seeking only his selfish interests.

Readings in this section show the range of purposes argument can serve. Some of the authors address profound questions with deep conviction, attempting to influence not only our thinking but our beliefs and even our actions, as Martin Luther King does in his extraordinary "Letter from Birmingham Jail." Others provide calmly reasoned discussions in which they hope to shape our thinking about their subjects. Always, though, argument aims to lead the reader to perceive the subject as the author perceives it.

Reason in Argument

Choosing a subject for argument
Collecting information
Logical Connections
Deduction
Induction
Hypothesis

If an argument is to be more than an appeal to its readers' prejudices and feelings (however worthwhile and noble those prejudices and sentiments *may* be), it must contain strong elements of *reason* built into both its invention and its design. In other words, the argument that is marked by soundness and validity has these qualities because the writer has incorporated them from the thinking process that precedes the writing, through the writing process, and into the finished product of the essay itself. Such an argument has benefited from the writer's search for and use of the most reliable information available, the use of reason and logic in drawing conclusions from that information, and skill in designing the clearest possible structure for the finished essay. Reasoned argument should not only *seem* reasonable and logical, it should *be* as reasonable and as logical as the writer can make it.

To begin with, the subject for the argument must be carefully chosen. It should be one in which you have a strong interest and about which you have strong convictions. The essential point is that you want to get to the truth of the matter as far as possible and will not let your convictions and beliefs blind you to the directions in which evidence and reason might take you. Marchette Chute states an important principle briefly and well when she says, "You will never succeed in getting at the truth if you think you know, ahead of time, what the truth ought to

269

be." [1]   If you have qualms about your openness to other views on a subject—whether nuclear power represents a viable solution to the energy problem, for instance—pick another in which you also have an interest and commitment but more objectivity.

After choosing a subject, the next stage is collecting as much reliable information as possible within practical considerations. Make the best use you can of the library resources available to you—periodical indexes, abstracts, card catalogs, and human resources as well, such as instructors, librarians, and specialists in the area of your subject.   In fact, as you get into the process of finding information on your subject you are more likely to find that there is more available to you than you can possibly read or use, rather than not enough.   Thus, you will more likely be faced with the problem of how to select what is most worthwhile out of the mass of data and opinion available.

Two main points should help in making such selections:

1. The materials should be drawn from a broad range that includes different opinions and attitudes toward the subject.
2. The materials should go deeply enough into the subject that you have access to concrete, factual evidence, so that you are not limited to a superficial outlook that includes generalities, inferences, and judgments to the exclusion of factual reports.

The first point may seem fairly obvious, but it is often overlooked by those writers who decide too quickly what the "correct" opinion is.   Such writers thus miss out on the stage of examining a range of opinion that forces them to consider alternate views seriously in order to formulate their own.   Also, writers who do not take the opposing side seriously run the very serious risk of failing to speak effectively to the proponents of that side because they ignore the evidence the opposition can muster.   Two essays that gain effectiveness by showing their authors' awareness of the opposing point of view and speaking directly to it are Dorothy Z. Seymour's "Understanding Language Differences," in which she acknowledges the objections of those who do not take Black English seriously as a distinct dialect of the language, and Martin Luther King, Jr.'s, "Letter

---

[1] "Getting at the Truth," *Saturday Review*, September 19, 1953, p. 44.

from Birmingham Jail," in which he considers point by point the objections a group of clergymen have made to his civil rights activities.

The second point is no less important. Any argument that commands the respect of an intelligent audience must show that the writer has done his homework by digging out the relevant facts of the matter accurately. But the raw materials gathered must also be arranged in sequences that make their logical connections clear. As Douglas Ehninger puts the matter, argument "confronts the understanding of the reader or listener directly, laying out for his inspection and analysis the facts and reasons."[2]

These logical connections—the clear and sound relations between facts, reasons, and conclusions—can be divided into two basic types: *deduction* and *induction*.

Deductive reasoning begins with at least one accepted generalization and, through certain rules of logic, yields a conclusion that follows necessarily and inevitably from the reasons, or *premises*. This process often takes the form of a *syllogism*, a formal argument consisting of a major premise, a minor premise, and a conclusion. In "Everyone Is a Scientist," Thomas Henry Huxley cites the following syllogism as an example of deduction:

All hard and green apples are sour;	major premise
This apple is hard and green;	minor premise
Therefore this apple is sour.	conclusion

Note that the conclusion follows necessarily from the two premises; if both premises are true, the conclusion must also be true.

Another useful deductive form is the conditional argument, an argument based on at least one conditional premise ("If . . . , then . . ."). It is the basis for the arguments of two selections in this section: Andrew Marvell's appeal "To His Coy Mistress" and the Declaration of Independence. Conditional

---

[2] Douglas Ehninger, *Influence, Belief, and Argument: An Introduction to Responsible Persuasion* (Glenview, Ill.: Scott, Foresman, 1974), p. 4.

arguments are closely related to syllogisms, and Huxley's example can easily be converted into the following conditional argument:

If this is a hard and green apple, then it is a
   sour apple;   first premise
This is a hard and green apple;   second premise
Therefore this is a sour apple.   conclusion

Such deductive patterns, as already pointed out, can serve as the bases for entire selections; more often they are used as parts of larger arguments in support of conclusions.

Induction, the opposite process of reasoning, ordinarily produces the generalizations that serve as premises in deductive reasoning. The major premise in the example drawn from Huxley's essay was arrived at through the process of induction. Huxley describes this process briefly:

You go into a fruiterer's shop, wanting an apple,—you take up one, and, on biting it, you find it is sour; you look at it, and see that it is hard and green. You take up another one, and that too is hard, green, and sour. The shopman offers you a third; but, before biting it, you examine it, and find that it is hard and green, and you immediately say that you will not have it, as it must be sour, like those that you have already tried.

In induction we examine enough representative parts of the whole to satisfy ourselves and our audience that our generalization, or inductive leap, is warranted. In the case of the green apples, we can generalize that "all hard and green apples are sour," which, as we have seen, can easily become the premise for a deductive argument.

The importance of inductive reasoning will become clear as you study the essays in this section. The Declaration of Independence, for instance, contains inductive support for one of its premises Dorothy Z. Seymour's "Understanding Language Differences" is primarily inductive in its reasoning. To support her conclusion that Black English is a distinct dialect rather than a form of substandard English, the author cites instances of consistency in Black English. George Bernard

Shaw, too, reasons inductively when he cites individual instances to support his generalization that "law is indispensable."

Both inductive and deductive kinds of reasoning are put to important uses in the forming of an *hypothesis*, a conclusion of the probable cause for a particular effect based upon available evidence. If, for instance, you find upon returning to your room or apartment that the door is standing wide open, and, upon further inspection, you find that the contents of your desk drawer have been dumped in the middle of the floor and that your guitar and most of your records are missing, then you are in a position to form an hypothesis. Such an hypothesis would take into account past conclusions that you formed inductively about the ways in which a person's possessions show up missing. These conclusions then become *deductive* premises for analyzing the present situation. Your most probable hypothesis, although several others are no doubt possible, is that "Someone has come into my room and stolen my guitar and records."

The essays in this section establish logical connections that effectively appeal to the reader's sense of what is reasonable. Pay close attention, as you read them, to the authors' use of inductive and deductive reasoning in persuading you of the truth of their arguments.

Everyone Is a Scientist
Thomas Henry Huxley

Building his essay on two extended illustrations, British biologist and educator Thomas Henry Huxley argues that scientific investigation is much like ordinary problem solving.

1   The method of scientific investigation is nothing but the expression of the necessary mode of working of the human mind. It is simply the mode at which all phenomena are reasoned about, rendered precise and exact. There is no more difference, but there is just the same kind of difference, between

the mental operations of a man of science and those of an ordinary person, as there is between the operations and methods of a baker or of a butcher weighing out his goods in common scales, and the operations of a chemist in performing a difficult and complex analysis by means of his balance and finely-graduated weights. It is not that the action of the scales in the one case, and the balance in the other, differ in the principles of their construction or manner of working; but the beam of one is set on an infinitely finer axis than the other, and of course turns by the addition of a much smaller weight.

2   You will understand this better, perhaps, if I give you some familiar example. You have all heard it repeated, I dare say, that men of science work by means of induction and deduction, and that by the help of these operations, they, in a sort of sense, wring from Nature certain other things, which are called natural laws, and causes, and that out of these, by some cunning skill of their own, they build up hypotheses and theories. And it is imagined by many, that the operations of the common mind can be by no means compared with these processes, and that they have to be acquired by a sort of special apprenticeship to the craft. To hear all these large words, you would think that the mind of a man of science must be constituted differently from that of his fellow men; but if you will not be frightened by terms, you will discover that you are quite wrong, and that all these terrible apparatus are being used by yourselves every day and every hour of your lives.

3   There is a well-known incident in one of Molière's plays, where the author makes the hero express unbounded delight on being told that he had been talking prose during the whole of his life. In the same way, I trust, that you will take comfort, and be delighted with yourselves, on the discovery that you have been acting on the principles of inductive and deductive philosophy during the same period. Probably there is not one who has not in the course of the day had occasion to set in motion a complex train of reasoning, of the very same kind, though differing of course in degree, as that which a scientific man goes through in tracing the causes of natural phenomena.

4   A very trivial circumstance will serve to exemplify this. Suppose you go into a fruiterer's shop, wanting an apple,—you

take up one, and, on biting it, you find it is sour; you look at it, and see that it is hard and green. You take up another one, and that too is hard, green, and sour. The shopman offers you a third; but, before biting it, you examine it, and find that it is hard and green, and you immediately say that you will not have it, as it must be sour, like those that you have already tried.

5 Nothing can be more simple than that, you think; but if you will take the trouble to analyze and trace out into its logical elements what has been done by the mind, you will be greatly surprised. In the first place, you have performed the operation of induction. You found that, in two experiences, hardness and greenness in apples went together with sourness. It was so in the first case, and it was confirmed by the second. True, it is a very small basis, but still it is enough to make an induction from; you generalize the facts, and you expect to find sourness in apples where you get hardness and greenness. You found upon that a general law, that all hard and green apples are sour; and that, so far as it goes, is a perfect induction. Well, having got your natural law in this way, when you are offered another apple which you find is hard and green, you say, "All hard and green apples are sour; this apple is hard and green, therefore the apple is sour." That train of reasoning is what logicians call a syllogism, and has all its various parts and terms—its major premiss, its minor premiss, and its conclusion. And, by the help of further reasoning, which, if drawn out, would have to be exhibited in two or three other syllogisms, you arrive at your final determination, "I will not have that apple." So that, you see, you have, in the first place, established a law by induction, and upon that you have founded a deduction, and reasoned out the special conclusion of the particular case.

6 Well now, suppose, having got your law, that at some time afterwards, you are discussing the qualities of apples with a friend: you will say to him, "It is a very curious thing,—but I find that all hard and green apples are sour!" Your friend says to you, "But how do you know that?" You at once reply, "Oh, because I have tried them over and over again, and have always found them to be so." Well, if we were talking science instead of common sense, we should call that an experimental verification. And, if still opposed, you go further, and say, "I have

heard from the people of Somersetshire and Devonshire, where a large number of apples are grown, that they have observed the same thing. It is also found to be the case in Normandy, and in North America. In short, I find it to be the universal experience of mankind wherever attention has been directed to the subject." Whereupon, your friend, unless he is a very unreasonable man, agrees with you, and is convinced that you are quite right in the conclusion you have drawn. He believes, although perhaps he does not know he believes it, that the more extensive verifications are,—that the more frequently experiments have been made, and results of the same kind arrived at, —that the more varied the conditions under which the same results are attained, the more certain is the ultimate conclusion, and he disputes the question no further. He sees that the experiment has been tried under all sorts of conditions, as to time, place, and people, with the same result; and he says with you, therefore, that the law you have laid down must be a good one, and he must believe it.

7   In science we do the same thing;—the philosopher exercises precisely the same faculties, though in a much more delicate manner. In scientific inquiry it becomes a matter of duty to expose a supposed law to every possible kind of verification, and to take care, moreover, that this is done intentionally, and not left to a mere accident, as in the case of the apples. And in science, as in common life, our confidence in a law is in exact proportion to the absence of variation in the result of our experimental verifications. For instance, if you let go your grasp of an article you may have in your hand, it will immediately fall to the ground. That is a very common verification of one of the best established laws of nature—that of gravitation. The method by which men of science establish the existence of that law is exactly the same as that by which we have established the trivial proposition about the sourness of hard and green apples. But we believe it in such an extensive, thorough, and unhesitating manner because the universal experience of mankind verifies it, and we can verify it ourselves at any time; and that is the strongest possible foundation on which any natural law can rest.

8   So much, then, by way of proof that the method of estab-

lishing laws in science is exactly the same as that pursued in common life. Let us now turn to another matter (though really it is but another phase of the same question), and that is, the method by which, from the relations of certain phenomena, we prove that some stand in the position of causes towards the others.

9 I want to put the case clearly before you, and I will therefore show you what I mean by another familiar example. I will suppose that one of you, on coming down in the morning to the parlour of your house, finds that a tea-pot and some spoons which had been left in the room on the previous evening are gone,—the window is open, and you observe the mark of a dirty hand on the window-frame, and perhaps, in addition to that, you notice the impress of a hob-nailed shoe on the gravel outside. All these phenomena have struck your attention instantly, and before two seconds have passed you say, "Oh, somebody has broken open the window, entered the room, and run off with the spoons and the tea-pot!" That speech is out of your mouth in a moment. And you will probably add, "I know there has; I am quite sure of it!" You mean to say exactly what you know; but in reality you are giving expression to what is, in all essential particulars, an hypothesis. You do not *know* it at all; it is nothing but an hypothesis rapidly framed in your mind. And it is an hypothesis founded on a long train of inductions and deductions.

10 What are those inductions and deductions, and how have you got at this hypothesis? You have observed, in the first place, that the window is open; but by a train of reasoning involving many inductions and deductions, you have probably arrived long before at the general law—and a very good one it is—that windows do not open of themselves; and you therefore conclude that something has opened the window. A second general law that you have arrived at in the same way is, that tea-pots and spoons do not go out of a window spontaneously, and you are satisfied that, as they are not now where you left them, they have been removed. In the third place, you look at the marks on the window-sill, and the shoe-marks outside, and you say that in all previous experience the former kind of mark has never been produced by anything else but the hand of a human

being; and the same experience shows that no other animal but man at present wear shoes with hob-nails in them such as would produce the marks in the gravel.   I do not know, even if we could discover any of those "missing links" that are talked about, that they would help us to any other conclusion!   At any rate the law which states our present experience is strong enough for my present purpose.   You next reach the conclusion, that as these kinds of marks have not been left by any other animals than men, or are liable to be formed in any other way than by a man's hand and shoe, the marks in question have been formed by a man in that way.   You have, further, a general law, founded on observation and experience, and that, too, is, I am sorry to say, a very universal and unimpeachable one,—that some men are thieves; and you assume at once from all these premisses—and that is what constitutes your hypothesis—that the man who made the marks outside and on the window-sill, opened the window, got into the room, and stole your tea-pot and spoons.   You have now arrived at a *vera-causa*;—you have assumed a cause which, it is plain, is competent to produce all the phenomena you have observed.   You can explain all these phenomena only by the hypothesis of a thief.   But that is a hypothetical conclusion, of the justice of which you have no absolute proof at all; it is only rendered highly probable by a series of inductive and deductive reasonings.

11   I suppose your first action, assuming that you are a man of ordinary common sense, and that you have established this hypothesis to your own satisfaction, will very likely be to go for the police, and set them on the track of the burglar, with the view to the recovery of your property.   But just as you are starting with this object, some person comes in, and on learning what you are about, says, "My good friend, you are going on a great deal too fast.   How do you know that the man who really made the marks took the spoons?   It might have been a monkey that took them, and the man may have merely looked in afterward."   You would probably reply, "Well, that is all very well, but you see it is contrary to all experience of the way tea-pots and spoons are abstracted; so that, at any rate, your hypothesis is less probable than mine."   While you are talking the thing over in this way, another friend arrives.   And he might say,

"Oh, my dear sir, you are certainly going on a great deal too fast. You are most presumptuous. You admit that all these occurrences took place when you were fast asleep, at a time when you could not possibly have known anything about what was taking place. How do you know that the laws of nature are not suspended during the night? It may be that there has been some kind of supernatural interference in this case." In point of fact, he declares that your hypothesis is one of which you cannot at all demonstrate the truth and that you are by no means sure that the laws of nature are the same when you are asleep as when you are awake.

12 Well, now, you cannot at the moment answer that kind of reasoning. You feel that your worthy friend has you somewhat at a disadvantage. You will feel perfectly convinced in your own mind, however, that you are quite right, and you say to him, "My good friend, I can only be guided by the natural probabilities of the case, and if you will be kind enough to stand aside and permit me to pass, I will go and fetch the police." Well, we will suppose that your journey is successful, and that by good luck you meet with a policeman; that eventually the burglar is found with your property on his person, and the marks correspond to his hand and to his boots. Probably any jury would consider those facts a very good experimental verification of your hypothesis, touching the cause of the abnormal phenomena observed in your parlour, and would act accordingly.

13 Now, in this suppositious case, I have taken phenomena of a very common kind, in order that you might see what are the different steps in an ordinary process of reasoning, if you will only take the trouble to analyze it carefully. All the operations I have described, you will see, are involved in the mind of any man of sense in leading him to a conclusion as to the course he should take in order to make good a robbery and punish the offender. I say that you are led, in that case, to your conclusion by exactly the same train of reasoning as that which a man of science pursues when he is endeavouring to discover the origin and laws of the most occult phenomena. The process is, and always must be, the same; and precisely the same mode of reasoning was employed by Newton and Laplace in their endeav-

ours to discover and define the causes of the movements of the heavenly bodies, as you, with your own common sense, would employ to detect a burglar.

Questions on Content

1. What similarities and differences between the chemist and the butcher does Huxley point out?
2. Briefly define the following steps in logic: *induction, deduction, hypothesis,* and *verification.*
3. By which type of reasoning do we arrive at the general law that hard and green apples are sour?
4. How are laws in science exposed to verification?
5. What hypotheses can be formulated in the teapot theft that Huxley describes? Which is the most probable?

Questions on Invention, Design, and Style

1. Huxley's essay is built around two extended illustrations, which he uses to clarify complex reasoning processes. What is the first extended illustration, and how does it illustrate induction? What is the second, and how does it illustrate hypothesis? How do the two extended illustrations clarify Huxley's thesis? What is the relation between induction and deduction?
2. Consider Huxley's structure. What is the thesis he states in paragraph 1? How is it clarified in the analogy of the scales and balances? What transition does the author provide to move smoothly from the first extended illustration to the second?
3. In attempting to instruct by starting with what the reader already knows, Huxley uses illustration, comparison, and contrast, as in "... the author makes the hero express unbounded delight on being told that he had been talking prose during the whole of his life. In the same way, I trust, that you will ... be delighted ... that you have been acting on the principles of inductive and deductive philosophy...." (*paragraph 3*). Find other passages relying on illustration, comparison, and contrast to clarify a point.
4. Who is Huxley's audience? What evidence can you find of his sensitivity to that audience? Consider, for example, the use of "I" and "you" throughout the essay—how do this and other techniques reveal Huxley as meeting his audience on common ground?
5. Huxley also uses classification, process, and causal analysis in this essay. What is the classification analysis in paragraph 5?

How is paragraph 5 also a process analysis? How is the process of verification analyzed in paragraph 6? What is the causal analysis in paragraphs 9–12? How is this also a process analysis?

Applications

1. Remember a problem you have had (such as a car that wouldn't start or an appliance that wouldn't work) and that you solved by acting on your hypothesis of what was wrong. Analyze the process by which you formulated your hypothesis and solved the problem. Then write a paper arguing for the use of that procedure in solving similar problems.
2. Write an argument in which you attempt to win support for your position on a controversial issue by beginning with an analysis of something your audience already knows and accepts. Be sure to establish a convincing connection between what is familiar and what you are trying to prove.

To His Coy Mistress
Andrew Marvell

In a witty, formal argument, the speaker in Andrew Marvell's poem seeks to persuade his lady that life is too short for coyness. Marvell's language is from an earlier period, but his argument is timeless.

> Had we but world enough, and time,
> This coyness, Lady, were no crime.
> We would sit down and think which way
> To walk and pass our long love's day.
> Thou by the Indian Ganges' side   5
> Shouldst rubies find; I by the tide
> Of Humber[1] would complain. I would
> Love you ten years before the Flood,

---

[1] The river flowing by the town of Hull, where Marvell lived.

And you should, if you please, refuse
Till the conversion of the Jews.   10
My vegetable love should grow
Vaster than empires, and more slow;
An hundred years should go to praise
Thine eyes and on thy forehead gaze;
Two hundred to adore each breast,   15
But thirty thousand to the rest;
An age at least to every part,
And the last age should show your heart.
For, Lady, you deserve this state,
Nor would I love at lower rate.   20
　　But at my back I always hear
Time's wingéd chariot hurrying near;
And yonder all before us lie
Deserts of vast eternity.
Thy beauty shall no more be found,   25
Nor, in thy marble vault, shall sound
My echoing song; then worms shall try
That long preserved virginity,
And your quaint honor turn to dust,
And into ashes all my lust: 30
The grave's a fine and private place,
But none, I think, do there embrace.
　　Now therefore, while the youthful hue
Sits on thy skin like morning dew,
And while thy willing soul transpires   35
At every pore with instant fires,
Now let us sport us while we may,
And now, like amorous birds of prey,
Rather at once our time devour
Than languish in his slow-chapped[2] power.   40
Let us roll all our strength and all
Our sweetness up into one ball,
And tear our pleasures with rough strife
Thorough[3] the iron gateṣ of life:
Thus, though we cannot make our sun   45
Stand still, yet we will make him run.

---

[2] Slow-jawed, slowly devouring.
[3] Through

Questions on Content

1. In what sense is the speaker's mistress coy?
2. Why is her coyness a crime, according to the speaker?
3. If time permitted, how long would the speaker praise and adore his mistress?
4. What prevents the speaker from praising and adoring her for as long as she deserves?
5. What effects does the speaker foresee if they take unlimited time?
6. How will the action he proposes change these effects?

Questions on Invention, Design, and Style

1. The argument the speaker advances in this poem is based upon conditional reasoning ("If this is true, then that will follow") and upon reasoning from a basic premise. What basic assumptions are stated in lines 1 and 2? What important shifts take place at lines 21 and 33? How would you restate simply the author's line of reasoning? How does the poem's structure reflect this reasoning?
2. Marvell expresses himself metaphorically, as in:

   But at my back I always hear
   Time's wingéd chariot hurrying near (*lines 21 and 22*)

   What comparison is Marvell making in these lines, and what does the metaphor contribute to the poem? Find other metaphors that clarify Marvell's points and advance his argument.
3. Consider the speaker's tone, his attitude, and his appeals to his mistress. Is the speaker serious? formal? playful? At what level and in what sense is he sincere? To what qualities and attitudes in his mistress does he appeal?

Applications

1. Imagine yourself misunderstood or falsely accused by someone— friend, classmate, teacher, parent, employer—and realizing that an outburst of anger will not settle the matter. Write a response to that person, setting out the situation clearly and justifying your actions in a logical, orderly way that will appeal to the other person's reason.
2. Decide on a subject you can write about convincingly because of your own experience with it. Write a paper in which you use deductive reasoning as a basis for your argument.

Declaration of Independence
Thomas Jefferson and Others

Thomas Jefferson and other members of the Second Continental Congress used a simple and clearly designed deductive structure, supported by basic assumptions and a list of grievances, in developing an impressive argument for American independence.

IN CONGRESS, JULY 4, 1776
THE UNANIMOUS DECLARATION OF THE
THIRTEEN UNITED STATES OF AMERICA

1   When in the Course of human events it becomes necessary for one people to dissolve the political bands which have connected them with another, and to assume among the powers of the earth, the separate and equal station to which the Laws of Nature and of Nature's God entitle them, a decent respect to the opinions of mankind requires that they should declare the causes which impel them to the separation.

2   We hold these truths to be self-evident, that all men are created equal, that they are endowed by their Creator with certain unalienable Rights, that among these are Life, Liberty and the pursuit of Happiness. That to secure these rights, Governments are instituted among Men, deriving their just powers from the consent of the governed, That whenever any Form of Government becomes destructive of these ends, it is the Right of the People to alter or to abolish it, and to institute new Government, laying its foundation on such principles and organizing its powers in such form, as to them shall seem most likely to affect their Safety and Happiness. Prudence, indeed, will dictate that Governments long established should not be changed for light and transient causes; and accordingly all experience hath shewn that mankind are more disposed to suffer, while evils are sufferable, than to right themselves by abolishing the forms to which they are accustomed. But when a long train of abuses and usurpations, pursuing invariably the same Object evinces a design to reduce them under absolute Despotism, it is their right, it is their duty, to throw off such

Government, and to provide new Guards for their future security. Such has been the patient sufferance of these Colonies; and such is now the necessity which constrains them to alter their former Systems of Government. The history of the present King of Great Britain is a history of repeated injuries and usurpations, all having in direct object the establishment of an absolute Tyranny over these States. To prove this, let Facts be submitted to a candid world.

3   He has refused his Assent to Laws, the most wholesome and necessary for the public good.

4   He has forbidden his Governors to pass laws of immediate and pressing importance, unless suspended in their operation till his Assent should be obtained; and when so suspended, he has utterly neglected to attend to them.

5   He has refused to pass other Laws for the accommodation of large districts of people, unless those people would relinquish the right of Representation in the Legislature, a right inestimable to them and formidable to tyrants only.

6   He has called together legislative bodies at places unusual, uncomfortable, and distant from the depository of their Public Records, for the sole purpose of fatiguing them into compliance with his measures.

7   He has dissolved Representative Houses repeatedly, for opposing with manly firmness his invasions on the rights of the people.

8   He has refused for a long time, after such dissolutions, to cause others to be elected; whereby the Legislative Powers, incapable of Annihilation, have returned to the People at large for their exercise; the State remaining in the mean time exposed to all the dangers of invasion from without, and convulsions within.

9   He has endeavored to prevent the population of these States; for that purpose obstructing the Laws for Naturalization of Foreigners; refusing to pass others to encourage their migration hither, and raising the conditions of new Appropriations of Lands.

10   He has obstructed the Administration of Justice, by refusing his Assent to Laws for establishing Judiciary Powers.

11   He has made Judges dependent on his Will alone, for the

tenure of their offices, and the amount and payment of their salaries.

12 He has erected a multitude of New Offices, and sent hither swarms of Officers to harass our people, and eat out their substance.

13 He has kept among us, in times of peace, Standing Armies without the Consent of our legislatures.

14 He has affected to render the Military independent of and superior to the Civil Power.

15 He has combined with others to subject us to a jurisdiction foreign to our constitution, and unacknowledged by our laws; giving his Assent to their Acts of pretended Legislation: For quartering large bodies of armed troops among us: For protecting them, by a mock Trial, from punishment for any Murders which they should commit on the Inhabitants of these States: For cutting off our Trade with all parts of the world: For imposing Taxes on us without our Consent: For depriving us in many cases, of the benefits of Trial by Jury: For transporting us beyond Seas to be tried for pretended offenses: For abolishing the free System of English Laws in a neighboring Province, establishing therein an Arbitrary government, and enlarging its Boundaries so as to render it at once an example and fit instrument for introducing the same absolute rule into these Colonies: For taking away our Charters, abolishing our most valuable Laws and altering fundamentally the Forms of our Governments: For suspending our own Legislatures, and declaring themselves invested with power to legislate for us in all cases whatsoever.

16 He has abdicated Government here, by declaring us out of his Protection and waging War against us.

17 He has plundered our seas, ravaged our Coasts, burnt our towns, and destroyed the lives of our people.

18 He is at this time transporting large Armies of foreign Mercenaries to complete the works of death, desolation and tyranny, already begun with circumstances of Cruelty & Perfidy scarcely paralleled in the most barbarous ages, and totally unworthy the Head of a civilized nation.

19 He has constrained our fellow Citizens taken Captive on the high Seas to bear Arms against their Country, to become the

executioners of their friends and Brethren, or to fall themselves by their Hands.

20 He has excited domestic insurrections amongst us, and has endeavored to bring on the inhabitants of our frontiers, the merciless Indian Savages, whose known rule of warfare, is an undistinguished destruction of all ages, sexes, and conditions.

21 In every stage of these Oppressions We have Petitioned for Redress in the most humble terms: Our repeated Petitions have been answered only by repeated injury. A Prince, whose character is thus marked by every act which may define a Tyrant, is unfit to be the ruler of a free people.

22 Nor have We been wanting in attention to our British brethren. We have warned them from time to time of attempts by their legislature to extend an unwarrantable jurisdiction over us. We have reminded them of the circumstances of our emigration and settlement here. We have appealed to their native justice and magnanimity, and we have conjured them by the ties of our common kindred to disavow these usurpations, which would inevitably interrupt our connections and correspondence. They too have been deaf to the voice of justice and of consanguinity. We must, therefore, acquiesce in the necessity, which denounces our Separation, and hold them, as we hold the rest of mankind, Enemies in War, in Peace Friends.

23 We, THEREFORE, the Representatives of the UNITED STATES OF AMERICA, in General Congress, Assembled, appealing to the Supreme Judge of the world for the rectitude of our intentions, do, in the Name, and by Authority of the good People of these Colonies, solemnly publish and declare, That these United Colonies are, and of Right ought to be FREE AND INDEPENDENT STATES; that they are Absolved from all Allegiance to the British Crown, and that all political connection between them and the State of Great Britain, is and ought to be totally dissolved; and that as Free and Independent States, they have full Power to levy War, conclude Peace, contract Alliances, establish Commerce, and to do all other Acts and Things which Independent States may of right do. And for the support of this Declaration, with a firm reliance on the protection of Divine Providence, we mutually pledge to each other our Lives, our Fortunes, and our sacred Honor.

Questions on Content

1. Why, according to the document, should people who separate from their government give causes for that separation?
2. What truths do the framers of the Declaration consider "self-evident"?
3. Why are governments formed? Why do they continue?
4. When do the people have the right to alter or abolish an old government and institute a new one?
5. Summarize the list of grievances against the King of Great Britain.
6. Give an example of each grievance you listed under question 5.
7. How have the colonists previously made their grievances known to the King and the British public? What were the responses to those grievances?
8. What do the framers "publish and declare" at the conclusion of the document?

Questions on Invention, Design, and Style

1. The basic reasoning underlying the Declaration of Independence can be stated as a simple conditional argument, using the "If . . . , then. . . ." construction:

    (stated as a consequence of a self-evident truth) — If a government is despotic, then it should be replaced and a new one established.

    (supported by a list of grievances) — This government is despotic.

    (valid conclusion) — This government should be replaced and a new one established.

   a. How does paragraph 1 of the document prepare for the argument that follows?
   b. What premises of the argument are advanced in paragraph 2?
   c. What are the functions of paragraphs 3–20? In what way do they furnish a causal analysis?
   d. Show how paragraphs 21 and 22 advance the argument.
   e. What conclusion to the argument is stated in paragraph 23?
2. What purpose is served by the enumeration of injuries and usurpations suffered by the American colonies? In what way do these appeal to the readers' reason? to their sense of what is right? to their sense of justice?

3. In order for the acts enumerated in paragraphs 3–20 to be accepted as "injuries" and "usurpations," what basic assumptions must be made concerning the nature of an acceptable government and the relationship between that government and its people? Where are these assumptions stated by the framers, and what are the assumptions?
4. How would you characterize the tone of this document, as you read it today? What language and ideas convey that tone? How might the tone have struck you if you had been King George III? if you had been an American colonist in 1776?

Applications

1. Find one of the "self-evident" truths in paragraph 2 of the Declaration of Independence that particularly interests you. Write a paper arguing for or against its self-evident nature on the basis of evidence and reasoning.
2. Consider the governing bodies, major or minor, with which you are familiar. What purposes do they serve? What needs do they fulfill, and how effective are they? Using a simple deductive structure, write a declaration of purposes for one such governing body, including the reasons for its existence and the function it serves. Choose any governing body—from the officers of your dormitory to the U.N. Security Council—of which you have knowledge.

Understanding Language Differences
Dorothy Z. Seymour

Linguist Dorothy Z. Seymour argues that Black English is a separate dialect of American English and that schools must keep this in mind as they teach Standard English. Although she acknowledges that people can be quick to judge others on the basis of their speech, she restricts most of her essay to an analysis of Black English and withholds her own attitude until the end.

1   "Cmon, man, les git goin'!" called the boy to his companion. "Dat bell ringin'. It say, 'Git in rat now!' " He dashed into the school yard.

2   "Aw, f'get you," replied the other. "Whe' Richuh? Whe' da' muvvuh? He be goin' to schoo'."

3   "He in de' now, man!" was the answer as they went through the door.

4   In the classroom they made for their desks and opened their books. The name of the story they tried to read was "Come." It went:

> Come, Bill, come.
> Come with me.
> Come and see this.
> See what is here.

The first boy poked the second. "Wha' da' wor'?"

5   "Da' wor' *is*, you dope."

6   "*Is?* Ain't no wor' *is*. You jivin' me? Wha' da' wor' mean?"

7   "Ah dunno. Jus' *is*."

8   To a speaker of Standard English, this exchange is only vaguely comprehensible. But it's normal speech for thousands of American children. In addition it demonstrates one of our biggest educational problems: children whose speech style is so different from the writing style of their books that they have difficulty learning to read. These children speak Black English, a dialect characteristic of many inner-city Negroes. Their books are, of course, written in Standard English. To complicate matters, the speech they use is also socially stigmatized. Middle-class whites and Negroes alike scorn it as low-class poor people's talk.

9   Teachers sometimes make the situation worse with their attitudes toward Black English. Typically, they view the children's speech as "bad English" characterized by "lazy pronunciation," "poor grammar," and "short, jagged words." One result of this attitude is poor mental health on the part of the pupils. A child is quick to grasp the feeling that while school speech is "good," his own speech is "bad," and that by extension he himself is somehow inadequate and without value. Some children react to this feeling by withdrawing; they stop talking entirely. Others develop the attitude of "F'get you, honky." In either case, the psychological results are devastating and lead straight to the dropout route.

10 It is hard for most teachers and middle-class Negro parents to accept the idea that Black English is not just "sloppy talk" but a dialect with a form and structure of its own. Even some eminent black educators think of it as "bad English grammar" with "slurred consonants" (Professor Nick Aaron Ford of Morgan State College in Baltimore) and "ghettoese" (Dr. Kenneth B. Clark, the prominent educational psychologist).

11 Parents of Negro schoolchildren generally agree. Two researchers at Columbia University report that the adults they worked with in Harlem almost unanimously preferred that their children be taught Standard English in school.

12 But there is another point of view, one held in common by black militants and some white liberals. They urge that middle-class Negroes stop thinking of the inner-city dialect as something to be ashamed of and repudiated. Black author Claude Brown, for example, pushes this point of view.

13 Some modern linguists take a similar stance. They begin with the premise that no dialect is intrinsically "bad" or "good," and that a nonstandard speech style is not defective speech but different speech. More important, they have been able to show that Black English is far from being a careless way of speaking the Standard; instead, it is a rather rigidly constructed set of speech patterns, with the same sort of specialization in sounds, structure and vocabulary as any other dialect.

14 Middle-class listeners who hear black inner-city speakers say "dis" and "tin" for "this" and "thin" assume that the black speakers are just being careless. Not at all; these differences are characteristic aspects of the dialect. The original cause of such substitutions is generally the carry-over from one's original language or that of his immigrant parents. The interference from that carry-over probably caused the substitution of /d/ for the voiced *th* sound in *this*, and /t/ for the unvoiced *th* sound in *thin*. (Linguists represent language sounds by putting letters within slashes or brackets.) Most speakers of English don't realize that the two *th* sounds of English are lacking in many other languages and are difficult for most foreigners trying to learn English. Germans who study English, for example, are surprised and confused about these sounds because the only Germans who use them are the ones who lisp. These two

sounds are almost nonexistent in the West African languages which most black immigrants brought with them to America.

15   Similar substitutions used in Black English are /f/, a sound similar to the unvoiced *th*, in medial word-position, as in *birfday* for *birthday*, and in final word-position, as in *roof* for *Ruth*, as well as /v/ for the voiced *th* in medial position, as in *bruvver* for *brother*. These sound substitutions are also typical of Gullah, the language of black speakers in the Carolina Sea Islands. Some of them are also heard in Caribbean Creole. Another characteristic is the lack of /l/ at the end of words, sometimes replaced by the sound /w/. This makes a word like *tool* sound like *too*.

16   One difference that is startling to middle-class speakers is the fact that Black English words appear to leave off some consonant sounds at the end of words. Like Italian, Japanese and West African words, they are more likely to end in vowel sounds. Standard English *boot* is pronounced *boo* in Black English. *What* is *wha*. *Sure* is *sho*. *Your* is *yo*. This kind of difference can make for confusion in the classroom. Dr. Kenneth Goodman, a psycholinguist, tells of a black child whose white teacher asked him to use *so* in a sentence—not "sew a dress" but "the other *so*." The sentence the child used was "I got a *so* on my leg."

17   A related feature of Black English is the tendency in many cases not to use sequences of more than just one final consonant sound. For example, *just* is pronounced *jus'*, *past* is *pass*, *mend* sounds like *men* and *hold* sounds like *hole*. *Six* and *box* are pronounced *sick* and *bock*. Why should this be? Perhaps because West African languages, like Japanese, have almost no clusters of consonants in their speech. The Japanese, when importing a foreign word, handle a similar problem by inserting vowel sounds between every consonant, making *baseball* sound like *besuboru*. West Africans probably make a simpler change, merely cutting a series of two consonant sounds down to one. Speakers of Gullah, according to one linguist, have made the same kind of adaptation of Standard English.

18   Teachers of black children seldom understand the reason for these differences in final sounds. They are apt to think that careless speech is the cause. Actually, black speakers aren't

"leaving off" any sounds; how can you leave off something you never had in the first place?

19 Differences in vowel sounds are also characteristic of the nonstandard language. Dr. Goodman reports that a black child asked his teacher how to spell rat. "R-a-t," she replied. But the boy responded, "No ma'am, I don't mean rat mouse, I mean rat now." In Black English *right* sounds like *rat*. A likely reason is that in West African languages, there are very few vowel sounds of the type heard in the word *right*. This type is common in English. It is called a glided or diphthong-ized vowel sound. A glided vowel sound is actually a close combination of two vowels; in the word *right* the two parts of the sound "eye" are really "ah-ee." West African languages have no such long, two-part, changing vowel sounds; their vowels are generally shorter and more stable. This may be why in Black English, *time* sounds like *Tom*, *oil* like *all*, and *my* like *ma*.

20 Black English differs from Standard English not only in its sounds but also in its structure. The way the words are put together does not always fit the description in English grammar books. The method of expressing time, or tense, for example, differs in significant ways.

21 The verb *to be* is an important one in Standard English. It's used as an auxiliary verb to indicate different tenses. But Black English speakers use it quite differently. Sometimes an inner-city Negro says "He coming"; other times he says "He be coming." These two sentences mean different things. To understand why, let's look at the tenses of West African languages; they correspond with those of Black English.

22 Many West African languages have a tense which is called the habitual. This tense is used to express action that is always occurring, and it is formed with a verb that is translated as *be*. "He be coming" means something like "He's always coming," "He usually comes," or "He's been coming."

23 In Standard English there is no regular grammatical construction for such a tense. Black English speakers, in order to form the habitual tense in English, use the word *be* as an auxiliary: *He be doing it. My Momma be working. He be running.* The habitual tense is not the same as the present tense, which

is constructed in Black English without any form of the verb *to be*: *He do it. My Momma working. He running.* (This means the action is occurring right now.)

24   There are other tense differences between Black English and Standard English. For example, the nonstandard speech does not use changes in grammar to indicate the past tense. A white person will ask, "What did your brother say?" and the black person will answer, "He say he coming." "How did you get here?" "I walk." This style of talking about the past is paralleled in the Yoruba, Fante, Hausa, and Ewe languages of West Africa.

25   Expression of plurality is another difference. The way a black child will talk of "them boy" or "two dog" makes some white listeners think Negroes don't know how to turn a singular word into a plural word. As a matter of fact, it isn't necessary to use an *s* to express plurality. For example, in Chinese it's correct to say "There are three book on the table." This sentence already has two signals of the plural, *three* and *are*; why require a third? This same logic is the basis of plurals in most West African languages, where nouns are often identical in the plural and the singular. For example, in Ibo, one correctly says *those man*, and in both Ewe and Yoruba one says *they house*. American speakers of Gullah retain this style; they say *five dog*.

26   Gender is another aspect of language structure where differences can be found. Speakers of Standard English are often confused to find that the nonstandard vernacular often uses just one gender of pronoun, the masculine, and refers to women as well as men as *he* or *him*. "He a nice girl" and even "Him a nice girl" are common. This usage probably stems from West African origins too, as does the use of multiple negatives such as "Nobody don't know it."

27   Vocabulary is the third aspect of a person's native speech that could affect his learning of a new language. The strikingly different vocabulary often used in Negro Nonstandard English is probably the most obvious aspect of it to a casual white observer. But its vocabulary differences don't obscure its meaning the way different sounds and different structure often do.

28 Recently there has been much interest in the African origins of words like *goober* (peanut), *cooter* (turtle), and *tote* (carry), as well as others that are less certainly African, such as *to dig* (possibly from the Wolof *degan*, "to understand"). Such expressions seem colorful rather than low class to many whites; they become assimilated faster than their black originators do. English professors now use *dig* in their scholarly articles, and current advertising has enthusiastically adopted *rap*.

29 Is it really possible for old differences in sound, structure and vocabulary to persist from the West African languages of slave days into present-day inner-city Black English? Easily. Nothing else really explains such regularity of language habits, most of which persist among black people in various parts of the Western Hemisphere. For a long time scholars believed that certain speech forms used by Negroes were merely leftovers from archaic English preserved in the speech of early English settlers in America and copied by their slaves. But this theory has been greatly weakened, largely as the result of the work of a black linguist, Dr. Lorenzo Dow Turner of the University of Chicago. Dr. Turner studied the speech of Gullah Negroes in the Sea Islands off the Carolina coast and found so many traces of West African languages that he thoroughly discredited the archaic-English theory.

30 When anyone learns a new language, it's usual to try to speak the new language with the sounds and structure of the old. If a person's first language does not happen to have a particular sound needed in the language he is learning, he will tend to substitute a similar or related sound from his native language and use it to speak the new one. When Frenchman Charles Boyer said "Zees ees my heart," and when Latin American Carmen Miranda sang "Souse American way," they were simply using sounds from their native languages in trying to pronounce sounds of English. West Africans must have done the same thing when they first attempted English words. The tendency to retain the structure of the native language is a strong one, too. That's why a German learning English is likely to put his verb at the end: "May I a glass of beer have?" The vocabulary of one's original language may also furnish some holdovers. Jewish immigrants did not stop using the

word *bagel* when they came to America; nor did Germans stop saying *sauerkraut*.

31   Social and geographical isolation reinforces the tendency to retain old language habits. When one group is considered inferior, the other group avoids it. For many years it was illegal to give any sort of instruction to Negroes, and for slaves to try to speak like their masters would have been unthinkable. Conflict of value systems doubtless retards changes, too. As Frantz Fanon observed in *Black Skin, White Masks*, those who take on white speech habits are suspect in the ghetto, because others believe they are trying to "act white."   Dr. Kenneth Johnson, a black linguist, put it this way: "As long as disadvantaged black children live in segregated communities and most of their relationships are confined to those within their own subculture, they will not replace their functional nonstandard dialect with the nonfunctional standard dialect."

32   Linguists have made it clear that language systems that are different are not necessarily deficient.   A judgment of deficiency can be made only in comparison with another language system.   Let's turn the tables on Standard English for a moment and look at it from the West African point of view.   From this angle, Standard English (1) is lacking in certain language sounds; (2) has a couple of unnecessary language sounds for which others may serve as good substitutes; (3) doubles and drawls some of its vowel sounds in sequences that are unusual and difficult to imitate; (4) lacks a method of forming an important tense; (5) requires an unnecessary number of ways to indicate tense, plurality and gender; and (6) doesn't mark negatives sufficiently for the result to be a good strong negative statement.

33   Now whose language is deficient?

34   How would the adoption of this point of view help us?   Say we accepted the evidence that Black English is not just a sloppy Standard but an organized language style which probably has developed many of its features on the basis of its West African heritage. What would we gain?

35   The psychological climate of the classroom might improve if teachers understood why many black students speak as they do. But we still have not reached a solution of the main prob-

lem.   Does the discovery that Black English has pattern and structure mean that it should not be tampered with?   Should children who speak Black English be excused from learning the Standard in school?   Should they perhaps be given books in Black English to learn from?

36   Any such accommodation would surely result in a hardening of the new separatism being urged by some black militants. It would probably be applauded by such people as Roy Innis, Director of C.O.R.E., who is currently recommending dual autonomous education systems for white and black.   And it might facilitate learning to read, since some experiments have indicated that materials written in Black English syntax aid problem readers from the inner city.

37   But determined resistance to the introduction of such printed materials into schools can be expected.   To those who view inner-city speech as bad English, the appearance in print of sentences like "My mama, he work" can be as shocking and repellent as a four-letter word.   Middle-class Negro parents would probably mobilize against the move.   Any stratagem that does not take into account such practicalities of the matter is probably doomed to failure.   And besides, where would such a permissive policy on language get these children in the larger society, and in the long run? If they want to enter an integrated America they must be able to deal with it on its own terms. Even Professor Toni Cade of Rutgers, who doesn't want "ghetto accents" tampered with, advocates mastery of Standard English because, as she puts it, "If you want to get ahead in this country, you must master the language of the ruling class." This has always been true, wherever there has been a minority group.

38   The problem then appears to be one of giving these children the ability to speak (and read) Standard English without denigrating the vernacular and those who use it, or even affecting the ability to use it.   The only way to do this is to officially espouse bidialectism.   The result would be the ability to use either dialect equally well—as Dr. Martin Luther King did— depending on the time, place, and circumstances.   Pupils would have to learn enough about Standard English to use it when necessary, and teachers would have to learn enough about

the inner-city dialect to understand and accept it for what it is—not just a "careless" version of Standard English but a different form of English that's appropriate at certain times and places.

39 Can we accomplish this? If we can't, the result will be the continued alienation of a large section of the population, continued dropout trouble with consequent loss of earning power and economic contribution to the nation, but most of all, loss of faith in America as a place where a minority people can at times continue to use those habits that remind them of their link with each other and with their past.

Questions on Content

1. What type of English instruction do parents in Harlem want their children to receive, according to a study Seymour cites?
2. What point of view on Black English is shared by black militants, some white liberals, and some modern linguists, according to the author?
3. How do most middle-class listeners react when they hear Black English, according to Seymour?
4. Why does Seymour say it is unreasonable to believe that black children are "leaving off" the final sounds in words?
5. What is the "habitual" tense? What are the differences in the ways Black English and Standard English indicate past tense, plurality, and gender?
6. How is it possible, according to Seymour, for sound, structure, and vocabulary to carry over from West African languages into present-day Black English?
7. In what ways does Seymour believe Standard English is deficient when viewed from the West African point of view?
8. What will a bidialectal program require of teachers and students, according to Seymour?

Questions on Invention, Design, and Style

1. Seymour has structured this argument inductively; that is, she states a problem, examines evidence and causes, and draws a logical conclusion based on her analysis. Trace the arrangement of the material in groups of paragraphs and the transition from one part to the next. Review the solution Seymour proposes in paragraph 38, and determine why it has been withheld until the end of the essay.

2. Consider paragraphs 14–28 as a classification analysis of Black English.
   a. What three basic language components are common to Standard and nonstandard English? What is the effect of the author's drawing distinctions between Standard and nonstandard dialects?
   b. What basic component is investigated in paragraphs 20–26?
   c. What subcomponent is investigated in paragraphs 21–23? in paragraph 24? in paragraph 25? in paragraph 26?
   d. What basic component is discussed in paragraphs 27 and 28?
3. After studying the classification analysis in paragraphs 14–28, look at the dialogue between the two boys in paragraphs 1–7. Explain the characteristics of Black English it illustrates, and rewrite the dialogue in Standard English.
4. Consider paragraphs 29–31 as a causal analysis of Black English. How has this causal analysis been prepared for in earlier paragraphs? What hypothesis about the origins of Black English does Seymour discard and why? What causes does she cite for the differences between Black English and Standard English?
5. Questions writers use to produce effects instead of to elicit replies are called *rhetorical questions*. What rhetorical questions does Seymour use in paragraphs 33–35? What examples can you find elsewhere in the essay?
6. What are the sources of Seymour's evidence? What is drawn from her personal experience? from her study? her observations? from her own thought and imagination?
7. Characterize the tone of this essay. Is it subjective? objective? ironic? Is it consistent? Explain why you think so.
8. Explain how the personality Seymour projects in the essay, the tone she establishes, and the sources from which she draws her evidence all contribute to the effectiveness of her argument.

Applications

1. How many dialects or regional variants of English do you speak? How many languages other than English do you speak? Would you like any children you may have to speak as many dialects as you do? more? fewer? Write a paper in which you build a case, through logical reasoning, for your position. Use illustrations from the dialects and languages you speak.
2. In the past century, there has been a movement for the adoption of Esperanto, a universal language derived from existing language structures and vocabulary. Write an argumentative essay,

appealing to reason, in which you support or oppose the concept
of a universal language.

3. If you have read Coles' "A Domain (Of Sorts)" (pp. 51–61), Morris' "North and South" (pp. 107–110), or Didion's "On Going
Home" (pp. 111–114), review one or more of them in the light of
Seymour's essay. Write a paper on the advantages of group identity, analyzing the needs that it serves and arguing for ways in
which it can best be achieved.

Law Is Indispensable
George Bernard Shaw

**In this concise, carefully ordered essay, British dramatist and social
critic George Bernard Shaw argues for the truth of the paradox that
law is both necessary and dangerous.**

1   The truth is, laws, religions, creeds, and systems of ethics,
instead of making society better than its best unit, make it worse
than its average unit, because they are never up to date. You
will ask me: "Why have them at all?" I will tell you. They
are made necessary, though we all secretly detest them, by the
fact that the number of people who can think out a line of conduct for themselves even on one point is very small, and the
number who can afford the time for it still smaller. Nobody
can afford the time to do it on all points. The professional
thinker may on occasion make his own morality and philosophy
as the cobbler may make his own boots; but the ordinary man
of business must buy at the shop, so to speak, and put up with
what he finds on sale there, whether it exactly suits him or not,
because he can neither make a morality for himself nor do without one. This typewriter with which I am writing is the best
I can get; but it is by no means a perfect instrument; and I have
not the smallest doubt that in fifty years' time authors will
wonder how men could have put up with so clumsy a contriv-
ance. When a better one is invented, I shall buy it: until then,
not being myself an inventor, I must make the best of it, just
as my Protestant and Roman Catholic and Agnostic friends
make the best of their imperfect creeds and systems. . . .

2   Besides, what have deep thinking and moralizing to do with the most necessary and least questionable side of law? Just consider how much we need law in matters which have absolutely no moral bearing at all. Is there anything more aggravating than to be told, when you are socially promoted, and are not quite sure how to behave yourself in the circles you enter for the first time, that good manners are merely a matter of good sense . . . ? Imagine taking the field with an army which knew nothing, except that the soldier's duty is to defend his country bravely, and think, not of his own safety, nor of home and beauty, but of ENGLAND! Or of leaving the traffic of Piccadilly or Broadway[1] to proceed on the understanding that every driver should keep to that side of the road which seemed to him to promote the greatest happiness of the greatest number! Or of stage-managing Hamlet by assuring the Ghost that whether he enter from the right or the left could make no difference to the greatness of Shakespeare's play, and that all he need concern himself about was holding the mirror up to nature!

3   Law is never so necessary as when it has no ethical significance whatever, and is pure law for the sake of law. The law that compels me to keep to the left when driving along Oxford Street[2] is ethically senseless, as is shown by the fact that keeping to the right answers equally well in Paris; and it certainly destroys my freedom to choose my side; but by enabling me to count on everyone else keeping to the left also, thus making traffic possible and safe, it enlarges my life and sets my mind free for nobler issues. Most laws, in short, are not the expression of the ethical verdicts of the community, but pure etiquet and nothing else.

4   What they do express is the fact that over most of the field of social life there are wide limits within which it does not matter what people do, though it matters enormously whether under given circumstances you depend on their all doing the same thing. The wasp, who can be depended on absolutely to sting you if you squeeze him, is less of a nuisance than the man who tries to do business with you not according to the customs

---

[1] Extremely congested traffic arteries in London and New York City.

[2] An important business street in London.

of business, but according to the Sermon on the Mount. . . .
Even your man of genius accepts a hundred rules for every one
he challenges; and you may lodge in the same house with an
Anarchist for ten years without noticing anything exceptional
about him.   Martin Luther, the priest, horrified the greater half
of Christendom by marrying a nun, yet was a submissive con-
formist in countless ways, living orderly as a husband and
father, wearing what his bootmaker and tailor made for him,
and dwelling in what the builder built for him, although he
would have died rather than take his Church from the Pope.
And when he got a Church made by himself to his liking, generations of men calling themselves Lutherans took that Church
from him just as unquestioningly as he took the fashion of his
clothes from his tailor.

5   As the race evolves, many a convention which recommends
itself by its obvious utility to everyone passes into an automatic
habit, like breathing.   Doubtless also an improvement in our
nerves and judgment may enlarge the list of emergencies which
individuals may be trusted to deal with on the spur of the moment without reference to regulations; but a ready-made code
of conduct for general use will always be needed as a matter of
overwhelming convenience by all members of communities.

6   The continual danger to liberty created by law arises, not
from the encroachments of Governments, which are always regarded with suspicion, but from the immense utility and consequent popularity of law, and the terrifying danger and obvious
inconvenience of anarchy; so that even pirates appoint and obey
a captain.   Law soon acquires such a good character that people will believe no evil of it; and at this point it becomes possible for priests and rulers to commit the most pernicious crimes
in the name of law and order.   Creeds and laws come to be regarded as applications to human conduct of eternal and immut-
able principles of good and evil; and breakers of the law are ab-
horred as sacrilegious scoundrels to whom nothing is sacred.
Now this, I need not tell you, is a very serious error.

7   No law is so independent of circumstances that the time
never comes for breaking it, changing it, scrapping it as obsolete, and even making its observance a crime.   In a developing
civilization nothing can make laws tolerable unless their

changes and modifications are kept as closely as possible on the heels of the changes and modifications in social conditions which development involves. Also there is a bad side to the very convenience of law. It deadens the conscience of individuals by relieving them of the ethical responsibility of their own actions. When this relief is made as complete as possible, it reduces a man to a condition in which his very virtues are contemptible. Military discipline, for example, aims at destroying the individuality and initiative of the soldier whilst increasing his mechanical efficiency, until he is simply a weapon with the power of hearing and obeying orders. In him you have legality, duty, obedience, self-denial, submission to external authority, carried as far as it can be carried; and the result is that in England, where military service is voluntary, the common soldier is less respected than any other serviceable worker in the community. The police constable, who is a civilian and has to use his own judgment and act on his own responsibility in innumerable petty emergencies, is by comparison a popular and esteemed citizen. . . .

8   The moral evolution of the social individual is from submission and obedience as economizers of effort and responsibility, and safeguards against panic and incontinence, to wilfulness and self-assertion made safe by reason and self-control, just as plainly as his physical growth leads from the perambulator and the nurse's apron-string to the power of walking alone, and from the tutelage of the boy to the responsibility of the man. But it is useless for impatient spirits . . . to call on people to walk before you can stand. Without high gifts of reason and self-control: that is, without strong common-sense, no man dares yet trust himself out of the school of authority. What he does is to claim gradual relaxations of the discipline, so as to have as much liberty as he thinks is good for him, and as much government as he thinks he needs to keep him straight. If he goes too fast he soon finds himself asking helplessly "What ought I to do?" and so, after running to the doctor, the lawyer, the expert, the old friend, and all the other quacks for advice, he runs back to the law again to save him from all these and from himself. The law may be wrong; but anyhow it spares him the responsibility of choosing, and will either punish those

who make him look ridiculous by exposing its folly, or, when
the constitution is too democratic for this, at least guarantee
that the majority is on his side.

Questions on Content

1. According to Shaw, what makes laws necessary?
2. Why does Shaw consider most laws nothing more than etiquette?
3. How do laws become convenient and habitual?
4. What is the negative aspect of law, according to Shaw? In what
   way do virtues become contemptible when law's negative aspects
   dominate?
5. How much liberty and how much government should man have,
   according to Shaw?
6. How are laws both necessary and dangerous?

Questions on Invention, Design, and Style

1. Shaw builds this essay around a *paradox*—a statement that seems
   to contradict itself but may nevertheless be true. What is this
   paradox? How do the title and the first sentence of the essay introduce it? How is the paradox developed in the essay and ultimately resolved in paragraph 8? Shaw also uses paradox in less
   important ways throughout the essay. Find examples, and explain how they clarify the point under discussion.
2. Shaw introduces his essay with a rhetorical question to prepare
   the reader for his own answer. What answer does Shaw give to
   his first rhetorical question? What answer does he give to the
   rhetorical question that begins paragraph 2?
3. What audience is Shaw addressing? How does he convey his
   analyses and insights to that audience? Consider the statement
   "Law is never so necessary as when it has no ethical significance
   whatever, and is pure law for the sake of law" (*paragraph 3*).
   What qualifies Shaw to make declarations of this nature?
4. Throughout the essay, Shaw supports his statements with illustrations. Some are *hypothetical* ("Imagine taking the field with
   an army which knew nothing . . .") and some *factual*. Find examples of both. How do Shaw's illustrations appeal to the
   reader's sense of reason? What other appeals to reason do you
   find in this essay?
5. Study Shaw's tone in this example: "The wasp, who can be depended on absolutely to sting you if you squeeze him, is less of
   a nuisance than the man who tries to do business with you not

according to the customs of business, but according to the Sermon on the Mount" (*paragraph 4*). What does the tone of the essay reveal about Shaw's own attitude toward the subject? How is this tone important to the persuasiveness of his argument?

Applications

1. Select one of the following statements from Shaw's essay with which you strongly agree or disagree. Write a thoughtful, well-developed essay arguing either for or against that statement.
   a. "... laws, religions, creeds, and systems of ethics, instead of making society better than its best unit, make it worse than its average unit, because they are never up to date" (*paragraph 1*).
   b. "[Laws] are made necessary ... by the fact that the number of people who can think out a line of conduct for themselves even on one point is very small, and the number who can afford the time for it still smaller" (*paragraph 1*).
   c. "No law is so independent of circumstances that the time never comes for breaking it, changing it, scrapping it as obsolete, and even making its observance a crime" (*paragraph 7*).
2. Consider a paradox—such as "Freedom is possible only within a system of rules" or "Teachers are helpful but critical and judgmental"—or some puzzling situation you have observed, thought about, or experienced. Analyze it thoroughly, and write an argument based upon your analysis.
3. New attitudes can sometimes make legislation necessary in an area where there previously was none. Such questions have been raised with regard to the rights of children, prisoners, homosexuals, military personnel, and women. Write an essay arguing for a new view of some group or situation and the kind of new legislation that might be required by this view.

Emotion in Argument

The place of emotional appeals in argument
Adapting emotional appeals to a particular audience
Emotional appeals leading readers to act
Excessive appeals to emotion

Appeal to emotion is potentially so effective—as is clear, for example, from its widespread use in marketing and advertisement—that writers cannot afford to ignore the emotional side of their readers. In fact, many of our decisions, market researchers have repeatedly found, are made in response to appeals to our emotions. James L. Kinneavy and others in a recent publication even state, "Most of us, if we are willing to admit it, are more interested in things which touch us emotionally or imaginatively than we are in statistics or in elaborate logic." [1]

As a reader of the essays in this book, you have no doubt become aware of the fact that the writers were appealing to our compassion, admiration, outrage, fear, anger, and love. But, although in this subsection we are considering uses of emotional appeal in writing, we must remind ourselves again that effective arguments are written by writers who can determine how much to appeal to the emotions and how much to appeal to the reason of their particular audiences; they do not rely on one to the exclusion of the other. Indeed, appealing to the readers' emotions actually makes it possible for a writer to gain effective responses from his readers, responses such as "exciting," "inspiring," "compelling," "persuasive."

How a writer appeals to emotion in his readers we can ob-

---

[1] James L. Kinneavy, John Q. Cope, and J. W. Campbell, *Aims and Audiences in Writing* (Dubuque: Kendall/Hunt Publishing Company, 1976), p. 31.

serve in John Robinson's "The Bambi Syndrome" and Cleveland Amory's "Little Brother of the Wolf." Robinson plays on our sense of the ridiculous by pointing out the disastrous consequences of the tendency to humanize deer, the tendency to have sympathy for all deer in the same way that we, as children, did for Bambi. Furthermore, he appeals to our sense of outrage at the extent to which deer have overpopulated some areas, the destruction caused by deer, and so on.

Cleveland Amory, in contrast to Robinson, appeals to our emotions to develop a position favorable to an animal, the coyote. He appeals to our sense of pity for this mistreated and persecuted animal and to our sense of admiration for the coyote's cleverness, courage, and character under such unfavorable circumstances. And, by attributing human characteristics to the animal, he helps us to identify with the coyote and actually to fear for this poor and allegedly noble creature. Furthermore, many of the words Amory selects have emotional overtones—"varmint," "man, the rational animal, the pinnacle of evolution, the great humanitarian," "coyote family," "mother coyote did not betray her family," "coyote's charm and loyalty," and so on.

Excessive use of appeals to emotion, though, can mislead the reader and distort the subject. In fact, excessive emotional appeal is the favorite device used by the propagandist to cover up the lack of a solid factual basis for his position or the lack of sound reasoning behind the belief that he is urging the reader to accept.

Among the most common of these propaganda devices that distort the subject and mislead the reader are: *namecalling* (avoiding the issue by resorting to emotionally slanted words: "The scoundrel we have for a governor would do anything short of murder"); *stereotyping* (avoiding the issue by putting all into one group: "We know that cooks are invariably drunks"); *bandwagon* (avoiding the issue by suggesting that the reader will be left out if he doesn't hurry and join in: "Everyone is switching to Sudsy soap"); *cardstacking* (avoiding the issue by omitting evidence that does not support the writer's position: "Only good has come from the new experimental course in criminology");

and *hasty generalizing* (avoiding the issue by generalizing on the basis of an inadequate sample: "As these two students clearly show, the university student of today is only interested in leisure activities"). In all these fallacies common to highly emotional arguments, the writer has failed to deal with the subject on any basis but a highly emotional one.

The critically sensitive reader will, of course, detect this imbalance. He will see that effective argument combines solid factual information and effective use of logic with an appropriate appeal to the emotions. In this way an argument gains the reader's trust in the soundness of the argument and the fairness of the writer.

As you read the essays by Anne Roiphe, Mark Twain, and Jonathan Swift—as well as those by Robinson and Amory—pay close attention to how an appropriate and effective appeal to readers' emotions is absolutely essential if the writer is to achieve his or her purpose. Note too the broad range of emotions that these writers tap—humor and fair play in Roiphe's essay, and ridicule and humor in Twain's and Swift's essays, for instance.

The Bambi Syndrome
John Robinson

John Robinson, a writer of many travel books, attacks both seriously and humorously the notion that deer are shy, defenseless creatures at the mercy of sadistic, inhumane hunters.

1   In the 1930s I was visiting my hometown and talking to a girl with whom I had gone to school. She was entranced by a Disney movie she had just seen—*Bambi*. I remember she sketched in the plot for me with something like: "And they got married and had this beautiful baby."

2   Unbelievable as it may seem today, such coy anthropomorphism was typical of the cultural level of the town at that time, which must have been a major factor in my decision to leave. But, more important, the remark has historical significance as an early manifestation of the new and peculiar attitude Ameri-

cans were to adopt toward deer after the appearance of that particular movie.

3   I call it the "Bambi syndrome." Elk and antelope are as beautiful as deer, and more interesting. Mountain goats and sheep are fascinating and rare. Conservationists are slowly bringing back the bison. Yet nobody gets choked up over these other native American ruminants.

4   Moose are also interesting, although admittedly it is difficult to make a case for their beauty. The fascination they hold for us is more like that of an old steam locomotive. They are more formidable than deer, although a deer can tear you up pretty badly with its front hooves if you get too close. This happens infrequently; deer mostly concentrate on maintaining their public image as shy, defenseless creatures.

5   The truth is, deer are a long way from being an endangered species. They survive in a man-dominated environment almost as well as the Norway rat, partly because man obligingly kills off the deer's predators. In a classic experiment some years ago in the Kaibab Forest in Arizona, local hunters prevailed on government rangers to eliminate the entire cougar population so that man would be the only deer predators. Man turned out to be less efficient than the cougar. In a few years the forest was populated by thousands of bony deer starving to death; all vegetation within their reach had been gnawed down to bare wood. At great expense, the government had to trap cougars elsewhere and bring them into the Kaibab.

6   Hunters kill about 750,000 deer in the U.S. every year. Automobiles decimate another 150,000 to 200,000. People afflicted with the Bambi syndrome raise their hands in horror at all this butchering, but wildlife officials look upon the annual kill as reaping a harvest—which it is if you consider that deer dress out at 75 to 100 pounds of tasty meat.

7   Despite the kill figures, deer are more abundant in America today than when Columbus arrived. If nobody shot them, all of us in the countryside might need eight-foot fences around our property. And the poor farmers!

8   Like many others who have achieved their dream of moving to the country, my wife and I have learned that the good life is not all beer and skittles. One of the major drawbacks is deer.

They regard just about everything planted by man preferable to the native plants and shrubs the books say they should want. If you are at all inclined toward gardening, deer become your *bête noire*. They always select the choicest shrubs and flowers to chew down to the ground. Flower buds of all kinds are their hors d'oeuvres. So are all young fruit trees. They will fight their way through a dense jungle of toothsome shrubs to get at roses. And vegetables are delicacies of the highest order, except squash, which for some reason they disdain.

9   Several of our neighbors, however, are so thoroughly saturated in the Bambi tradition that they feed the deer to encourage them to hang around. One lady even allowed her garage to be used as a delivery room for twin fawns. Such people plant only oleanders and conifers, which deer pass up. They run from their homes shrieking at you if you attempt to discourage one of the beasts with a slingshot.

10   My own attitude is closer to that of a national park ranger I once met. A young deer was standing near us looking for a handout, and when I commented, the ranger exploded. "We call them goats!" he said with measurable disgust. "They get used to being fed by summer visitors, then when winter comes they starve to death." The ones around my home never starve. They just eat more of our valuable shrubs.

11   I find that a surprising number of people feel as I do about deer, especially if one reason they are living in the country is to raise their own food. But we comprise a secret fellowship, afraid of public criticism, like men who don't believe in women's lib but are reluctant to say so. In the land of the Bambi syndrome, our feelings about deer are best left in the closet next to our hunting jackets.

Questions on Content

1. What does Robinson mean by "coy anthropomorphism"? How does his hometown experience illustrate his meaning?
2. How did Americans' attitude toward deer change after the movie *Bambi*? What is the definition of "Bambi syndrome"? What contrasts are made between deer and elk, antelope, and moose?
3. What is the truth, according to Robinson, of the claim that deer

are an endangered species? What happened in Arizona when the deer's predators were killed?

4. How do wildlife officials and people afflicted with the "Bambi syndrome" differ in the way they view the annual deer-kill figures? How does the deer population today compare with that in the time of Columbus?

5. What would be the consequence of not shooting any deer? How are deer threatening to gardeners?

6. When deer get used to being fed in national parks, what happens to them during the winter? What happens to those around Robinson's house?

7. Why is the fellowship of people *not* afflicted by the "Bambi syndrome" a *secret* fellowship?

Questions on Invention, Design, and Style

1. Consider paragraphs 1–4 as the introduction to Robinson's essay. What is accomplished by the illustration in paragraph 1? What is the relation of this paragraph to paragraph 2? of these paragraphs to the first sentence of paragraph 3?

2. How do the contrasts developed in paragraphs 3 and 4 contribute to Robinson's purpose in the essay? What is the purpose of the statements about deer in the last two sentences of paragraph 4?

3. In paragraphs 5–7 Robinson develops the point made in the first sentence of paragraph 5. What support does Robinson provide for this statement? How does paragraph 7 bring this section of the essay to a conclusion?

4. Paragraphs 8–10 develop the related points that deer are destructive and that the "Bambi syndrome" results in destructiveness both to property and to the deer themselves. How has Robinson prepared for this stage of the essay in paragraphs 1 and 4? How does he support these points further in paragraphs 8–10?

5. In paragraph 11 Robinson acknowledges that many who feel as he does about deer are silent because of fear of criticism. What kind of criticism does he refer to? How is the word choice as well as content in paragraph 8 intended to show that Robinson is not a crude or brutal person? What other instances do you find in the essay where Robinson attempts to shatter stereotypes about people who agree with him about deer?

6. What persuasive devices, as distinct from evidence, has Robinson used to weigh the case against deer and perpetuators of the "Bambi syndrome"? Locate several examples and explain their purposes in the essay.

Applications

1. Select instances in which individuals have gone to such extremes in their treatment of pets that they treat the pets almost as people. Using Robinson's essay as a model, write an argument for more reasonable treatment of pets.
2. Presenting yourself as a humane, fair-minded person and subjecting your opposition to gentle, good-natured ridicule, write a persuasive essay on a controversial issue on which you take a minority position.

Little Brother of the Wolf
Cleveland Amory

Appealing to strong emotions in his readers, social observer Cleveland Amory argues for new attitudes and behavior toward the coyote, the "little brother of the wolf."

1   "Next to God," goes the Mexican saying, "the coyote is the smartest person on earth." Even if this is exaggerated, the fact remains that the coyote, if not the most intelligent of all animals, is certainly the cleverest. He would have to be.

2   Man has made his very name suspect. The second definition for the word "coyote" in the new *American Heritage Dictionary* is "contemptible sneak." For two hundred years, the coyote has faced a steadily increasing campaign to eradicate him from the face of the earth. Many animals have faced such campaigns, but against no other animal has the campaign reached such heights of cruelty.

3   In the old days, the coyote was hunted for his pelt. When pelts dropped in price, he was hunted because he was supposed to be a cattle killer. When it was proven he wasn't a cattle killer—he lives almost exclusively on mice, moles, rabbits, insects, snakes and even eats fruit for dessert—he was hunted because he was supposed to be a sheep killer. Finally, when it was proven he wasn't a sheep killer, he was hunted because—well, he was supposed to hunt what man wanted to hunt. The coyote is classed, simply, as a "varmint."

4   As such, there is no season for hunting coyote. For him, it is always open season. He is hunted by land and by air. He has learned that the air can be dangerous; when he hears or sees a plane he takes cover, and like a trained guerilla fighter, camouflages himself. The coyote is regularly jack-hunted by light at night, something forbidden by law for most animals. "Most hunters," says one hunting magazine, "clamp a powerful light directly to their guns and keep it on at all times."

5   In the winter, snowmobiles hunt the coyote down, with the hunters signaling to each other by walkie-talkies. In the summer, trained hunting dogs run him down in relays. Often, the coyote is chased by dogs riding in automobiles. When he begins to tire, the automobiles are stopped and the dogs are released.

6   In such situations, the coyote's only hope lies in his cleverness. And stories of coyotes outwitting hunters are legion. Coyotes will work in teams, alternately resting and running to escape dogs set upon them. They have even been known to jump on automobiles and flat cars to escape dogs. And they have also successfully resisted bombing. Lewis Nordyke reports that once when a favorite coyote haunt in Texas became a practice range for bombing, the coyotes left—temporarily. Soon they were back to investigate and found that the bombing kept people out. They decided to stay. Meanwhile, they learned the bombing schedule and avoided bombs.

7   Many a coyote has gotten along with its lower jaw shot off. Joe Van Wormer reports a coyote in Idaho whose mouth had been cruelly wired shut. It was able to open it only half an inch, but nonetheless had been able to survive. A coyote in Montana also had her jaw wired shut—she was used by a hunter to "train" his dogs. And a female coyote killed in Tule Lake in northern California was found to have four healthy pups in her den. She had managed to fend for them although she herself had been shot in both eyes with a shotgun and was totally blind.

8   From some hunts, of course, there is no escape. John Farrar, in his *Autobiography of a Hunter*, writes of an all too typical hunt in the sandhill region of Nebraska. It was, he writes, "a well-planned military maneuver," with a plane overhead to spot

the coyotes and, below, hundreds of hunters. "They came in pickups," he says, "armed with shortwave radios, powerful engines, clinging snow tires . . . each nervously fingering a high-powered rifle with telescopic sight."

> At the next section line 12 men awaited [the coyote's] approach. At 100 yards head-on, it began. His faltering speed spared him as bullets churned the snow ahead. As he reached the ditch he sank shoulder deep and floundered desperately. Astonished, ashamed or angry, no one fired. As he struggled across the road and into the next section, he seemed to crawl. As if he were shielded, 30 or more rounds left him untouched. In a weedy draw he could run no further. In cover no more than 12 inches high, he disappeared.
> The plane circled and then the men closed in afoot. Talk of letting this one go passed idly. Twenty-five armed men closed in on one terrified, exhausted animal. The enclosed area dwindled to the size of a football field and less. Still no coyote.
> Then he appeared, staggering, worn, mouth agape. He weaved pitifully up the hill among the hunters, as if defying death, or seeking it.
> Then man, the rational animal, the pinnacle of evolution, the great humanitarian, gunned him down.
> There was little laughing or joking, little back slapping. Just a sickening, nauseating silence. The day ended. With it ended my coyote hunting.

9   When the coyote is not hunted, he is trapped. For the coyote, there are especially horrible traps—to match his ingenuity. So-called "passion bait" is soaked in a piece of wool and put under a pan. When the coyote investigates, the slightest pressure releases the deadly steel leghold.

10   Once the coyote is caught, he has been known to chew off his own leg rather than remain in the trap. Literally thousands of coyotes have existed for life on three legs. Also, amazingly, there are thousands of two-legged coyotes. One female coyote in Michigan had only stubs for front legs—she ran like a kangaroo—and yet, when killed, was bearing five unborn pups. A coyote in Colorado existed for more than a year missing two feet—the left front and right hind. In New Mexico, a coyote got along somehow with both feet missing from his right

side, and still managed to raise a family. Trapper Art Cooper once caught a coyote in two traps at once. One trap caught him by a front foot, one by a hind. The two-trap set was fastened to an iron drag, and when Cooper and a companion came upon the coyote he was trying to cross a plowed field. Seeing the man, the coyote grabbed the drag in his mouth and took off.

11 Marguerite Smelser tells an even more remarkable coyote trapping story. Two government trappers spent weeks tracking down and trying to kill a whole coyote family. First the nursing mother was trapped, then released after the trappers had fastened a collar and tire chain to her. By the trail of the dragging chain, the trappers expected to follow her to her den where they could then wipe out the pups.

12 But for two weeks the mother coyote did not betray her family. Her mate brought food to her at night and kept the pups fed. And so, after days of frustration, convinced the mother would never endanger her young, the trappers tracked her down and killed her.

13 Later, however, they did get a chance at the pups. The trappers came upon them playing at the far side of the dam. At this juncture, however, the father coyote suddenly appeared and, acting as a decoy, managed to divert the trappers' attention until he was shot. His young had safely disappeared into the brush.

14 I have on my desk something called a "Humane Coyote-Getter," which is advertised as the "Marvel of the 20th Century." Humane? It is literally a whole trap gun. A bait is soaked in urine and covered with a jacket, then placed over a bullet cartridge, the whole being set in the ground. When the coyote investigates, the bullet is set off by a spring and shoots the coyote in the mouth with sodium cyanide. This in turn, on contact with the moisture in the coyote's mouth, or eyes, or wherever it hits him, releases gas and the coyote gases himself to death.

15 This Coyote-Getter is, by coyote-getting standards, actually humane—at least compared to the more general way of killing coyotes. That is, plainly and simply, by poisoning them. One state, for example, put out in one year 300,000 strychnine tablets—tablets which are slipped into an inch-

square of suet made out of sheep fat. But even strychnine is as nothing compared to the dread Compound 1080 or sodium fluoroacetate. This is a poison so lethal that there is no known antidote. It is chain-reacting. Thus, when a meadow mouse eats it and is in turn eaten by a larger animal, who is in turn eaten by a coyote, who is in turn eaten by a mountain lion, 1080 will have poisoned them all.

16 Perhaps the most horrible thing about Compound 1080 is that it is administered in small doses. Not because it is expensive—unfortunately it isn't, it is cheap. But it is administered in small doses so that the coyote will get as far away from the bait as possible before he dies and thus his body will not be able to warn other possible victims. Coyotes have been known to travel over twenty miles to die—in agony.

17 The United States government has poisoned more than a million coyotes. The real irony, though, is not that poisoning is done by the government, it is that it is done on public land. After the findings of the Leopold Report, the government's "Predator and Rodent Control Board" had to change its name to "Wildlife Services." But still, the sheep men graze their sheep on public land, which they do for a nominal fee, and then have the government poison coyotes merely on the suspicion that they kill their sheep. And this despite the Leopold Report's warning, "For every person whose sheep may be molested by a coyote, there are perhaps a thousand others who would thrill to hear a coyote chorus in the night."

18 Texas rancher Arthur Lytton, who for forty years has run a 20,000-acre spread, said, "I would never allow a predator to be killed on my land. They are necessary for the balance of nature. Kill them and you're in for nothing but trouble from rabbits and rodents and everything."

19 In 1971, the coyote poisoning program cost the public over $8 million. And, of course, the program didn't just poison coyotes. In a typical year, the wildlife "body count" was as follows: 89,653 coyotes, 24,273 foxes, 20,780 bobcats, 19,052 skunks, 10,078 raccoons, 7,615 opossums, 6,941 badgers, 6,685 porcupines, 2,771 red wolves, 1,170 beavers and 842 bears.

20 Finally, after years of effort by the Defenders of Wildlife,

Audubon, the Fund for Animals and other societies, President Nixon issued his now-historic Executive Order 11643, in February, 1972, banning the use of most predator poisons on public lands.   The order continues to be opposed by the National Wool Growers Association and others.   Coyote hunters, meanwhile, seemed to be redoubling their efforts.   One hunt in particular, out of Karval, Colorado, which boasted nine pickup trucks with specially bred "coyote dogs" (mixes of greyhounds with Irish and Russian wolfhounds) penned in quick-release cages in the back, was billed as "The Biggest Coyote Hunt in Colorado History."   Scores of hunters and dozens of dogs hunted all day.   Their total kill—five coyotes.

21   Such hunts—this latter hunt even included an official "observer" from the Department of the Interior—have outraged coyote friends.   The Fund for Animals announced a reward of $500 for prior information which led to the stopping of any such hunt, and also announced that it would back any group engaged in breaking up such hunts by any means short of actual violence.   One such group, The Defenders of the Coyote, already includes more than a hundred college and high school students as well as businessmen and housewives.

22   In the long run, some coyote friends believe the only answer is to make a pet out of him—and there has been signal success in this regard, the coyote's charm and loyalty overcoming all difficulties.   Others believe that the answer is to meet the coyote literally halfway.   Have him, in other words, as he is, half pet and half wild.   One who believes this is Los Angeles' Gerald Coward, a man who, on a lonely walk up a canyon a few years ago, managed to make a lasting friend of a coyote. Coward, a photographer and writer, gave up his job and from that day on, every day for two and a half years, he walked up his canyon.   And every day, for two and a half years, his coyote faithfully met him.   All day they played, romped and explored together, learning about each other—and then, at the end of each day, they said goodbye.   When the coyote mated, he even brought his companion to Coward at the same rendezvous.   It was a remarkable idyll that existed until the terrible Los Angeles fire—when Mr. Coward saw his coyote no more.   "The coyote," he said, "is the greatest animal there is."

Questions on Content

1. What does *coyote* mean as a description of humans?
2. Why were coyotes hunted in the old days? Why were they classed as "varmints"?
3. How are coyotes hunted today? How have they learned to adapt to these conditions?
4. What is the coyote's only hope when hunted in winter?
5. What was remarkable about the blind coyote in California that Amory describes?
6. Summarize Amory's illustration from John Farrar's *Autobiography of a Hunter*. Why were the hunters embarrassed after killing the coyote?
7. Why do sheepherders request that the government poison coyotes?
8. What was the recent historic executive order concerning coyotes? Whose effort lay behind this action?

Questions on Invention, Design, and Style

1. What reasons for man's relentless extermination of coyotes does Amory examine? Why is each unsatisfactory as a cause? How does Amory's causal analysis strengthen his argument?
2. How do Amory's examples of coyote resistance to man's hunting and trapping campaigns (*paragraphs 6–13*) win his readers' sympathy for the animal?
3. Review Amory's illustration of two trappers tracking down and trying to kill a family of coyotes (*paragraphs 11–13*). What is Amory appealing to in his audience through this illustration?
4. Consider Amory's use in paragraph 8 of the long quotation from *Autobiography of a Hunter*. Why does he quote directly, rather than summarizing? What does the quotation add to the essay? How are Farrar's language, tone, and attitude related to those of Amory?
5. Review and evaluate this essay as an argument. What evidence shows that the coyote is a beneficial animal that should not be exterminated? In what forms is this evidence given? How convincing is it to you? Why is evidence about the extensive poisoning of coyotes presented so late in the essay? What solutions to the coyote problem does Amory suggest? How persuasive is his argument? What parts are most persuasive?
6. How does Amory establish his authority to write about coyotes?

Consider his knowledge of the subject, his use of sources, his selection of examples, his objectivity, and his language.

Applications

1. Far down on the list of the recent movements is one that is coming to be known as "animal liberation," stimulated partly by proof of superior dolphin intelligence and exposés of the brutal clubbing to death of seals, both babies and pregnant females. Write an argument exploring and taking a position on animal liberation.
2. Select an animal other than the coyote that you believe is misunderstood or mistreated. Try to persuade your readers to adopt new attitudes and behavior toward that animal by writing an argument supported by facts and appealing to your readers' admiration, sympathy, and sense of fair play.
3. Assume you are a reporter for the campus newspaper. Write an exposé of some practice or state of affairs you believe will displease readers when they learn of it. You might investigate rents being charged to students living off campus or the condition and maintenance of dormitory laundry facilities. After gathering information, take a position backed by evidence and interviews with those affected by the problem. Write an article attempting to persuade your readers to support corrective action.

Confessions of a Female Chauvinist Sow
Anne Roiphe

Basing her argument on a witty analysis of a male stereotype held by some women, novelist Anne Roiphe offers some conclusions about both sexes.

1   I once married a man I thought was totally unlike my father and I imagined a whole new world of freedom emerging. Five years later it was clear even to me—floating face down in a wash of despair—that I had simply chosen a replica of my handsome daddy-true. The updated version spoke English like an angel

but—good God!—underneath he was my father exactly: wonderful, but not the right man for me.

2 Most people I know have at one time or another been fouled up by their childhood experiences. Patterns tend to sink into the unconscious only to reappear, disguised, unseen, like marionette strings, pulling us this way or that. Whatever ails people—keeps them up at night, tossing and turning—also ails movements no matter how historically huge or politically important. The women's movement cannot remake consciousness, or reshape the future, without acknowledging and shedding all the unnecessary and ugly baggage of the past. It's easy enough now to see where men have kept us out of clubs, baseball games, graduate schools; it's easy enough to recognize the hidden directions that limit Sis to cake-baking and Junior to bridge-building; it's now possible for even Miss America herself to identify what *they* have done to us, and, of course, *they* have and *they* did and *they* are. . . . But along the way we also developed our own hidden prejudices, class assumptions and an anti-male humor and collection of expectations that gave us, like all oppressed groups, a secret sense of superiority (co-existing with a poor self-image—it's not news that people can believe two contradictory things at once.)

3 Listen to any group that suffers materially and socially. They have a lexicon with which they tease the enemy: ofay, goy, honky, gringo. "Poor pale devils," said Malcolm X loud enough for us to hear, although blacks had joked about that to each other for years. Behind some of the women's liberation thinking lurk the rumors, the prejudices, the defense systems of generations of oppressed women whispering in the kitchen together, presenting one face to their menfolk and another to their card clubs, their mothers and sisters. All this is natural enough but potentially dangerous in a revolutionary situation in which you hope to create a future that does not mirror the past. The hidden anti-male feelings, a result of the old system, will foul us up if they are allowed to persist.

4 During my teen years I never left the house on my Saturday night dates without my mother slipping me a few extra dollars —mad money, it was called. I'll explain what it was for the benefit of the new generation in which people just sleep with

each other: the fellow was supposed to bring me home, lead me safely through the asphalt jungle, protect me from slithering snakes, rapists and the like.   But my mother and I knew young men were apt to drink too much, to slosh down so many rye-and-gingers that some hero might well lead me in front of an oncoming bus, smash his daddy's car into Tiffany's window or, less gallantly, throw up on my new dress.   Mad money was for getting home on your own, no matter what form of insanity your date happened to evidence.   Mad money was also a wallflower's rope ladder; if the guy you came with suddenly fancied someone else, well, you didn't have to stay there and suffer, you could go home.   Boys were fickle and likely to be unkind; my mother and I knew that, as surely as we knew they tried to make you do things in the dark they wouldn't respect you for afterwards, and in fact would spread the word and spoil your rep.   Boys liked to be flattered; if you made them feel important they would eat out of your hand.   So talk to them about their interests, don't alarm them with displays of intelligence—we all knew that, we groups of girls talking into the wee hours of the night in a kind of easy companionship we thought impossible with boys.   Boys were prone to have a good time, get you pregnant, and then pretend they didn't know your name when you came knocking on their door for finances or comfort.   In short, we believed boys were less moral than we were.   They appeared to be hypocritical, self-seeking, exploitative, untrustworthy and very likely to be showing off their precious masculinity.   I never had a girl friend I thought would be unkind or embarrass me in public.   I never expected a girl to lie to me about her marks or sports skill or how good she was in bed.   Altogether—without anyone's directly coming out and saying so—I gathered that men were sexy, powerful, very interesting, but not very nice, not very moral, humane and tender, like us.   Girls played fairly while men, unfortunately, reserved their honor for the battlefield.

5   Why are there laws insisting on alimony and child support?   Well, everyone knows that men don't have an instinct to protect their young and, given half a chance, with the moon in the right phase, they will run off and disappear.   Everyone assumes a mother will not let her child starve, yet it is necessary

to legislate that a father must not do so. We are taught to accept the idea that men are less than decent; their charms may be manifold but their characters are riddled with faults. To this day I never blink if I hear that a man has gone to find his fortune in South America, having left his pregnant wife, his blind mother and taken the family car. I still gasp in horror when I hear of a woman leaving her asthmatic infant for a rock group in Taos because I can't seem to avoid the assumption that men are naturally heels and women the ordained carriers of what little is moral in our dubious civilization.

6   My mother never gave me mad money thinking I would ditch a fellow for some other guy or that I would pass out drunk on the floor. She knew I would be considerate of my companion because, after all, I was more mature than the boys that gathered about. Why was I more mature? Women just are people-oriented; they learn to be empathetic at an early age. Most English students (students interested in humanity, not artifacts) are women. Men and boys—so the myth goes—conceal their feelings and lose interest in anybody else's. Everyone knows that even little boys can tell the difference between one kind of a car and another—proof that their souls are mechanical, their attention directed to the non-human.

7   I remember shivering in the cold vestibule of a famous men's athletic club. Women and girls are not permitted inside the club's door. What are they doing in there, I asked? They're naked, said my mother, they're sweating, jumping up and down a lot, telling each other dirty jokes and bragging about their stock market exploits. Why can't we go in? I asked. Well, my mother told me, they're afraid we'd laugh at them.

8   The prejudices of childhood are hard to outgrow. I confess that every time my business takes me past that club, I shudder. Images of large bellies resting on massage tables and flaccid penises rising and falling with the Dow Jones average flash through my head. There it is, chauvinism waving its cancerous tentacles from the depths of my psyche.

9   Minorities automatically feel superior to the oppressor because, after all, they are not hurting anybody. In fact, they feel they are morally better. The old canard that women need love,

men need sex—believed for too long by both sexes—attributes moral and spiritual superiority to women and makes of men beasts whose urges send them prowling into the night. This false division of good and bad, placing deforming pressures on everyone, doesn't have to contaminate the future. We know that the assumptions we make about each other become a part of the cultural air we breathe and, in fact, become social truths. Women who want equality must be prepared to give it and to believe in it, and in order to do that it is not enough to state that you are as good as any man, but also it must be stated that he is as good as you and both will be humans together. If we want men to share in the care of the family in a new way, we must assume them as capable of consistent loving tenderness as we.

10 I rummage about and find in my thinking all kinds of anti-male prejudices. Some are just jokes and others I will have a hard time abandoning. First, I share an emotional conviction with many sisters that women given power would not create wars. Intellectually I know that's ridiculous; great queens have waged war before; the likes of Lurleen Wallace, Pat Nixon and Mrs. General Lavelle can be depended upon in the future to guiltlessly condemn to death other people's children in the name of some ideal of their own. Little girls, of course, don't take toy guns out of their hip pockets and say "Pow, pow" to all their neighbors and friends like the average well-adjusted little boy. However, if we gave little girls the six-shooters, we would soon have double the pretend body count.

11 Aggression is not, as I secretly think, a male-sex-linked characteristic: brutality is masculine only by virtue of opportunity. True, there are 1,000 Jack the Rippers for every Lizzie Borden, but that surely is the result of social forms. Women as a group are indeed more masochistic than men. The practical result of this division is that women seem nicer and kinder, but when the world changes, women will have a fuller opportunity to be just as rotten as men and there will be fewer claims of female moral superiority.

12 Now that I am entering early middle age, I hear many women complaining of husbands and ex-husbands who are attracted to younger females. This strikes the older woman as

unfair, of course. But I remember a time when I thought all boys around my age and grade were creeps and bores. I wanted to go out with an older man: a senior or, miraculously, a college man. I had a certain contempt for my coevals, not realizing that the freshman in college I thought so desirable, was some older girl's creep. Some women never lose that contempt for men of their own age. That isn't fair either and may be one reason why some sensible men of middle years find solace in young women.

13 I remember coming home from school one day to find my mother's card game dissolved in hysterical laughter. The cards were floating in black rivers of running mascara. What was so funny? A woman named Helen was lying on a couch pretending to be her husband with a cold. She was issuing demands for orange juice, aspirin, suggesting a call to a specialist, complaining of neglect, of fate's cruel finger, of heat, of cold, of sharp pains on the bridge of the nose that might indicate brain involvement. What was so funny? The ladies explained to me that all men behave just like that with colds, they are reduced to temper tantrums by simple nasal congestion, men cannot stand any little physical discomfort—on and on the laughter went.

14 The point of this vignette is the nature of the laughter—us laughing at them, us feeling superior to them, us ridiculing them behind their backs. If they were doing it to us we'd call it male chauvinist pigness; if we do it to them, it is inescapably female chauvinist sowness and, whatever its roots, it leads to the same isolation. Boys are messy, boys are mean, boys are rough, boys are stupid and have sloppy handwriting. A cacophony of childhood memories rushes through my head, balanced, of course, by all the well-documented feelings of inferiority and envy. But the important thing, the hard thing, is to wipe the slate clean, to start again without the meanness of the past. That's why it's so important that the women's movement not become anti-male and allow its most prejudiced spokesmen total leadership. The much-chewed-over abortion issue illustrates this. The women's-liberation position, insisting on a woman's right to determine her own body's destiny, leads in fanatical extreme to a kind of emotional immaculate conception

in which the father is not judged even half-responsible—he has no rights, and no consideration is to be given to his concern for either the woman or the fetus.

15 Woman, who once was abandoned and disgraced by an unwanted pregnancy, has recently arrived at a new pride of ownership or disposal. She has traveled in a straight line that still excludes her sexual partner from an equal share in the wanted or unwanted pregnancy. A better style of life may develop from an assumption that men are as human as we. Why not ask the child's father if he would like to bring up the child? Why not share decisions, when possible, with the male? If we cut them out, assuming an old-style indifference on their part, we perpetuate the ugly divisiveness that has characterized relations between the sexes so far.

16 Hard as it is for many of us to believe, women are not really superior to men in intelligence or humanity—they are only equal.

Questions on Content

1. What is the "unnecessary and ugly baggage of the past" that the women's movement must acknowledge and shed, according to Roiphe?
2. How have women simultaneously developed a sense of superiority and a poor self-image?
3. Briefly describe the male stereotype Roiphe had built up in her mind.
4. Briefly describe the female stereotype Roiphe contrasts with the male stereotype.
5. How do alimony laws support the stereotype many women hold?
6. Why is Roiphe not shocked when men leave their families but very much alarmed when women do so?
7. Why does she still shudder when passing the athletic club? What images go through her mind? How is she chauvinistic?
8. According to Roiphe, why do minorities feel superior to their oppressors?
9. What distinction does she draw between her emotional and her intellectual convictions on whether or not women would create wars if they had the power?
10. How does the position of the women's movement on abortion illustrate "female chauvinist sowness," according to Roiphe?

Questions on Invention, Design, and Style

1. What is Roiphe's thesis? Find the first statement of it in the essay. What evidence supports and develops it in the paragraphs that follow? How is it related to the final paragraph?
2. Who is Roiphe's intended audience for this essay? men? women? To what qualities and attitudes is she appealing? Find support for your answer.
3. What comparison does Roiphe draw between women and "any group that suffers materially and socially"? Explain how this comparison supports her thesis and makes it more convincing.
4. According to Roiphe, why did the women at her mother's card game laugh at the husband-with-a-cold act? How does this illustration strengthen her analysis of and argument against the stereotyping of men?
5. In what way is Roiphe's account of the way she developed a stereotype of men a process analysis? a causal analysis? How does the account contribute to the persuasiveness of the essay?
6. Roiphe's descriptive details lend vividness and clarity to the essay. Consider, for example, "wash of despair" (*paragraph 1*) and "black rivers of running mascara" (*paragraph 13*). Find other examples of such descriptive detail. What does each add to the point she is making?
7. What contribution to Roiphe's argument is made by her statement that early experiences and learned attitudes submerge but reappear "like marionette strings, pulling us this way or that"? Trace the development of this point throughout the essay. What is its relation to her thesis?
8. Examine Roiphe's tone in phrases like "daddy-true" (*paragraph 1*), "throw up on my new dress" (*paragraph 4*), and "a kind of emotional immaculate conception in which the father is not judged even half-responsible" (*paragraph 14*). In what ways is it humorous? sarcastic? serious? informal? How is the tone important to the persuasiveness of her argument?

Applications

1. Write an essay agreeing or disagreeing with one of the following passages from Roiphe's essay. Support your argument, and make it as persuasive as you can.
   a. "Minorities automatically feel superior to the oppressor because, after all, they are not hurting anybody" (*paragraph 9*).
   b. "If we want men to share in the care of the family in a new

way, we must assume them as capable of consistent loving
tenderness as we" (*paragraph 9*).

c. "The women's movement cannot remake consciousness, or
   reshape the future, without acknowledging and shedding all
   the unnecessary and ugly baggage of the past" (*paragraph 2*).
d. "The prejudices of childhood are hard to outgrow" (*paragraph 8*).
e. "I rummage about and find in my thinking all kinds of anti-
   male prejudices" (*paragraph 10*).
f. ". . . when the world changes, women will have a fuller opportunity to be just as rotten as men . . ." (*paragraph 11*).

2. Recall an individual or group you tended to stereotype until you
   became better acquainted. Write an essay from your own experience, arguing against such stereotyping.
3. If you have read Nora Ephron's "Truth and Consequences" (pp.
   38–41 or Virginia Woolf's "Shakespeare's Sister" (pp. 88–91), review it in light of Roiphe's essay. Write a paper arguing for more
   enlightened sexual roles and calling for action in creating these
   new roles.

The War Prayer
Mark Twain

**Through a detailed narrative filled with strong emotional appeals,
American novelist, humorist, and social critic Mark Twain makes a
powerful statement about group behavior and the realities of war.**

1 It was a time of great and exalting excitement. The country was up in arms, the war was on, in every breast burned the
holy fire of patriotism: the drums were beating, the bands playing, the toy pistols popping, the bunched firecrackers hissing
and spluttering; on every hand and far down the receding and
fading spread of roofs and balconies a fluttering wilderness of
flags flashed in the sun; daily the young volunteers marched
down the wide avenue gay and fine in their new uniforms, the
proud fathers and mothers and sisters and sweethearts cheering
them with voices choked with happy emotion as they swung by;
nightly the packed mass meetings listened, panting, to patriot

oratory which stirred the deepest deeps of their hearts and which they interrupted at briefest intervals with cyclones of applause, the tears running down their cheeks the while; in the churches the pastors preached devotion to flag and country and invoked the God of Battles, beseeching His aid in our good cause in out-pouring of fervid eloquence which moved every listener. It was indeed a glad and gracious time, and the half-dozen rash spirits that ventured to disapprove of the war and cast a doubt upon its righteousness straightway got such a stern and angry warning that for their personal safety's sake they quickly shrank out of sight and offended no more in that way.

2   Sunday morning came—next day the battalions would leave for the front: the church was filled; the volunteers were there, their young faces alight with martial dreams—visions of the stern advance, the gathering momentum, the rushing charge, the flashing sabers, the flight of the foe, the tumult, the enveloping smoke, the fierce pursuit, the surrender!—then home from the war, bronzed heroes, welcomed, adored, submerged in golden seas of glory! With the volunteers sat their dear ones, proud, happy, and envied by the neighbors and friends who had no sons and brothers to send forth to the field of honor, there to win for the flag or, failing, die the noblest of noble deaths. The service proceeded; a war chapter from the Old Testament was read; the first prayer was said; it was followed by an organ burst that shook the building, and with one impulse the house rose, with glowing invocation—

> "God the all-terrible! Thou who ordainest,
> Thunder thy clarion and lightning thy sword!"

Then came the "long" prayer. None could remember the like of it for passionate pleading and moving and beautiful language. The burden of its supplication was that an ever-merciful and benignant Father of us all would watch over our noble young soldiers and aid, comfort, and encourage them in their patriotic work; bless them, shield them in the day of battle and the hour of peril, bear them in His mighty hand, make them strong and confident, invincible in the bloody onset; help them to crush the foe, grant to them and to their flag and country imperishable honor and glory—

3 An aged stranger entered and moved with slow and noiseless step up the main aisle, his eyes fixed upon the minister, his long body clothed in a robe that reached to his feet, his head bare, his white hair descending in a frothy cataract to his shoulders, his seamy face unnaturally pale, pale even to ghastliness. With all eyes following him and wondering, he made his silent way; without pausing, he ascended to the preacher's side and stood there, waiting. With shut lids the preacher, unconscious of his presence, continued his moving prayer, and at last finished it with the words, uttered in fervent appeal, "Bless our arms, grant us the victory, O Lord our God, Father and Protector of our land and flag!"

4 The stranger touched his arm, motioned him to step aside —which the startled minister did—and took his place. During some moments he surveyed the spellbound audience with solemn eyes in which burned an uncanny light; then in a deep voice he said:

5 "I come from the Throne—bearing a message from Almighty God!" The words smote the house with a shock; if the stranger perceived it he gave no attention. "He has heard the prayer of His servant your shepherd and will grant it if such shall be your desire after I, His messenger, shall have explained to you its import—that is to say, its full import. For it is like unto many of the prayers of men, in that it asks for more than he who utters it is aware of—except he pause and think.

6 "God's servant and yours has prayed his prayer. Has he paused and taken thought? Is it one prayer? No, it is two— one uttered, the other not. Both have reached the ear of Him Who heareth all supplications, the spoken and the unspoken. Ponder this—keep it in mind. If you would beseech a blessing upon yourself, beware! lest without intent you invoke a curse upon a neighbor at the same time. If you pray for the blessing of rain upon your crop which needs it, by that act you are possibly praying for a curse upon some neighbor's crop which may not need rain and can be injured by it.

7 "You have heard your servant's prayer—the uttered part of

it. I am commissioned of God to put into words the other part of it—that part which the pastor, and also you in your hearts, fervently prayed silently. And ignorantly and unthinkingly? God grant that it was so! You heard these words: 'Grant us the victory, O Lord our God!' That is sufficient. The *whole* of the uttered prayer is compact into those pregnant words. Elaborations were not necessary. When you have prayed for victory you have prayed for many unmentioned results which follow victory—*must* follow it, cannot help but follow it. Upon the listening spirit of God the Father fell also the unspoken part of the prayer. He commandeth me to put it into words. Listen!

8 "O Lord our Father, our young patriots, idols of our hearts, go forth to battle—be Thou near them! With them, in spirit, we also go forth from the sweet peace of our beloved firesides to smite the foe. O Lord our God, help us to tear their soldiers to bloody shreds with our shells; help us to cover their smiling fields with the pale forms of their patriot dead; help us to drown the thunder of guns with the shrieks of their wounded, writhing in pain; help us to lay waste their humble homes with a hurricane of fire; help us to wring the hearts of their unoffending widows with unavailing grief; help us to turn them out roofless with their little children to wander unfriended the wastes of their desolated land in rags and hunger and thirst, sports of the sun flames of summer and the icy winds of winter, broken in spirit, worn with travail, imploring Thee for the refuge of the grave and denied it—for our sakes who adore Thee, Lord, blast their hopes, blight their lives, protract their bitter pilgrimage, make heavy their steps, water their way with their tears, stain the white snow with the blood of their wounded feet! We ask it, in the spirit of love, of Him Who is the Source of Love, and Who is the ever-faithful refuge and friend of all that are sore beset and seek His aid with humble and contrite hearts. Amen.

9 (*After a pause*) "Ye have prayed it; if ye still desire it, speak! The messenger of the Most High waits."

10 It was believed afterward that the man was a lunatic, because there was no sense in what he said.

Questions on Content

1. What is the prevailing mood in the country as this selection opens?
2. What happened to those who voiced disapproval of the war?
3. What is asked for in the spoken prayer?
4. Describe the appearance of the "aged stranger."
5. In what sense is the congregation's prayer actually two prayers, according to the stranger?
6. How does the stranger illustrate the danger of asking a blessing only for oneself?
7. What is the unspoken part of the minister's prayer?
8. What is the final reaction to the stranger?

Questions on Invention, Design, and Style

1. Twain develops his argument through an extended illustration that implies his thesis, instead of directly stating it. How does the illustration clarify his thesis and make his argument convincing?
2. Who is the narrator of this selection? Why did Twain choose to use this narrative form? In paragraph 1 how closely does the narrator identify with the majority who are in a state of excitement about the war? How do you know? Is Twain's own attitude closer to that of the narrator or of the aged stranger?
3. How does the descriptive detail in paragraph 1 help to reflect the "time of great and exalting excitement"? What sight and sound images are used? What appeals are made to the readers' emotions? Find specific details in this paragraph that add concreteness and credibility to the narrative.
4. Tone and attitude are major forces in this selection. Review Twain's language to see how he establishes his tone in the first two paragraphs. Trace the ways in which this tone is sustained and developed in the rest of the essay.
5. Contrast the "long" prayer (*paragraph 2 and the end of paragraph 3*) with the "unspoken" prayer (*paragraph 8*). Which is paraphrased, and which is quoted directly? Which is more detailed and specific? Which more directly affects the emotions of the reader? What emotions are involved? What is the tone of the long prayer? of the unspoken prayer? How is this contrast important in revealing Twain's implied thesis?
6. Evaluate this selection as an argument. What appeals does it

make to the reader, and how effective are they?   Does it strike you
as a truthful portrayal of human behavior?   Is there truth in the
unspoken prayer?   How convincing is the selection as a whole?

Applications

1. As a sequel to "The War Prayer," write a narrative in which the
    aged stranger reports his version of the story to the Most High and
    argues for some action on His part.
2. Write an argument in which you make your point not by direct
    statement but by telling a story that lets your readers draw their
    own conclusions.

A Modest Proposal

*For Preventing the Children of Poor People in Ireland from
Being a Burden to Their Parents or Country, and for Making
them Beneficial to the Public*

Jonathan Swift

**With piercing irony, eighteenth-century essayist and satirist Jonathan
Swift argues against the British oppression of the Irish people by inventing a speaker who is practical, unsentimental, and economical.
The proposal this speaker makes is as reasonable as it is absurd.   The
essay was first published in 1729, yet modern readers find the proposal itself and the argument placed in the mouth of Swift's speaker
as unforgettable as Swift's own contemporaries did.**

1   It is a melancholy object to those who walk through this
great town[1] or travel in the country, when they see the streets,
the roads, and cabin doors, crowded with beggars of the female-
sex, followed by three, four, or six children, all in rags and im-
portuning every passenger for an alms.   These mothers, instead
of being able to work for their honest livelihood, are forced to
employ all their time in strolling to beg sustenance for their
helpless infants, who, as they grow up, either turn thieves for

---

[1] Dublin, Ireland.

want of work, or leave their dear native country to fight for the Pretender[2] in Spain, or sell themselves to the Barbadoes.[3]

2   I think it is agreed by all parties that this prodigious number of children in the arms, or on the backs, or at the heels of their mothers, and frequently of their fathers, is in the present deplorable state of the kingdom a very great additional grievance; and therefore whoever could find out a fair, cheap, and easy method of making these children sound, useful members of the commonwealth would deserve so well of the public as to have his statue set up for a preserver of the nation.

3   But my intention is very far from being confined to provide only for the children of professed beggars; it is of a much greater extent, and shall take in the whole number of infants at a certain age who are born of parents in effect as little able to support them as those who demand our charity in the streets.

4   As to my own part, having turned my thoughts for many years upon this important subject, and maturely weighed the several schemes of other projectors,[4] I have always found them grossly mistaken in their computation.   It is true, a child just dropped from its dam may be supported by her milk for a solar year, with little other nourishment; at most not above the value of two shillings, which the mother may certainly get, or the value in scraps, by her lawful occupation of begging; and it is exactly at one year old that I propose to provide for them in such a manner as instead of being a charge upon their parents or the parish, or wanting food and raiment for the rest of their lives, they shall on the contrary contribute to the feeding, and partly to the clothing, of many thousands.

5   There is likewise another great advantage in my scheme, that it will prevent those voluntary abortions, and that horrid practice of women murdering their bastard children, alas, too frequent among us, sacrificing the poor innocent babes, I

---

[2] The pretender, or claimant, to the throne of Great Britain, James Francis Edward Stuart.   Many Irish Catholics supported his claim and fought on his behalf.

[3] That is, "sell" themselves into servitude for a period of time to pay for transportation to the West Indies.

[4] Promoters.

doubt, more to avoid the expense than the shame, which would move tears and pity in the most savage and inhuman breast.

6   The number of souls in this kingdom being usually reckoned one million and a half, of these I calculate there may be about two hundred thousand couple whose wives are breeders; from which number I subtract thirty thousand couple who are able to maintain their own children, although I apprehend there cannot be so many under the present distresses of the kingdom; but this being granted, there will remain an hundred and seventy thousand breeders.   I again subtract fifty thousand for those women who miscarry, or whose children die by accident or disease within the year.   There only remain an hundred and twenty thousand children of poor parents annually born.   The question therefore is, how this number shall be reared and provided for, which, as I have already said, under the present situation of affairs, is utterly impossible by all the methods hitherto proposed.   For we can neither employ them in handicraft or agriculture; we neither build houses (I mean in the country) nor cultivate land.   They can very seldom pick up a livelihood by stealing till they arrive at six years old, except where they are of towardly parts; although I confess they learn the rudiments much earlier, during which time they can however be looked upon only as probationers, as I have been informed by a principal gentleman in the county of Cavan,[5] who protested to me that he never knew above one or two instances under the age of six, even in a part of the kingdom so renowned for the quickest proficiency in that art.

7   I am assured by our merchants that a boy or a girl before twelve years old is no salable commodity; and even when they come to this age they will not yield above three pounds, or three pounds and half a crown at most on the Exchange; which cannot turn to account either to the parents or the kingdom, the charge of nutriment and rags having been at least four times that value.

8   I shall now therefore humbly propose my own thoughts, which I hope will not be liable to the least objection.

9   I have been assured by a very knowing American of my ac-

---

[5] In northeastern Ireland.

quaintance in London, that a young healthy child well nursed is at a year old a most delicious, nourishing and wholesome food, whether stewed, roasted, baked, or boiled; and I make no doubt that it will equally serve in a fricassee[6] or a ragout.[7]

10   I do therefore humbly offer it to public consideration that of the hundred and twenty thousand children, already computed, twenty thousand may be reserved for breed, whereof only one fourth part to be males, which is more than we allow to sheep, black cattle, or swine; and my reason is that these children are seldom the fruits of marriage, a circumstance not much regarded by our savages, therefore one male will be sufficient to serve four females.   That the remaining hundred thousand may at a year old be offered in sale to the persons of quality and fortune through the kingdom, always advising the mother to let them suck plentifully in the last month, so as to render them plump and fat for a good table.   A child will make two dishes at an entertainment for friends; and when the family dines alone, the fore or hind quarter will make a reasonable dish, and seasoned with a little pepper or salt will be very good boiled on the fourth day, especially in winter.

11   I have reckoned upon a medium[8] that a child just born will weigh twelve pounds, and in a solar year if tolerably nursed increaseth to twenty-eight pounds.

12   I grant this food will be somewhat dear, and therefore very proper for landlords, who, as they have already devoured most of the parents, seem to have the best title to the children.

13   Infant's flesh will be in season throughout the year, but more plentiful in March, and a little before and after.   For we are told by a grave author, an eminent French physician,[9] that fish being a prolific diet, there are more children born in Roman Catholic countries about nine months after Lent than at any other season; therefore, reckoning a year after Lent, the markets will be more glutted than usual, because the number

---

[6] Finely cut and stewed meat served with a thick gravy.

[7] A stew of meat and vegetables.

[8] On an average.

[9] François Rabelais—a French physician, hardly "grave," but, like Swift, a skillful satirist.

of popish infants is at least three to one in this kingdom; and therefore it will have one other collateral advantage, by lessening the number of Papists among us.

14   I have already computed the charge of nursing a beggar's child (in which list I reckon all cottagers, laborers, and four fifths of the farmers) to be about two shillings per annum, rags included; and I believe no gentleman would repine to give ten shillings for the carcass of a good fat child, which, as I have said, will make four dishes of excellent nutritive meat, when he hath only some particular friend or his own family to dine with him.   Thus the squire will learn to be a good landlord, and grow popular among the tenants; the mother will have eight shillings net profit, and be fit for work till she produces another child.

15   Those who are more thrifty (as I must confess the times require) may flay the carcass; the skin of which artificially dressed will make admirable gloves for ladies, and summer boots for fine gentlemen.

16   As to our city of Dublin, shambles may be appointed for this purpose in the most convenient parts of it, and butchers we may be assured will not be wanting; although I rather recommend buying the children alive, and dressing them hot from the knife as we do roasting pigs.

17   A very worthy person, a true lover of his country, and whose virtues I highly esteem, was lately pleased in discoursing on this matter to offer a refinement upon my scheme.   He said that many gentlemen of this kingdom, having of late destroyed their deer, he conceived that the want of venison might be well supplied by the bodies of young lads and maidens, not exceeding fourteen years of age nor under twelve, so great a number of both sexes in every county being now ready to starve for want of work and service; and these to be disposed of by their parents, if alive, or otherwise by their nearest relations.   But with due deference to so excellent a friend and so deserving a patriot, I cannot be altogether in his sentiments; for as to the males, my American acquaintance assured me from frequent experience that their flesh was generally tough and lean, like that of our schoolboys, by continual exercise, and their taste disagreeable; and to fatten them would not answer the charge.   Then as to

the females, it would, I think with humble submission, be a loss to the public, because they soon would become breeders themselves: and besides, it is not improbable that some scrupulous people might be apt to censure such a practice (although indeed very unjustly) as a little bordering upon cruelty; which, I confess, hath always been with me the strongest objection against any project, how well soever intended.

18 But in order to justify my friend, he confessed that this expedient was put into his head by the famous Psalmanazar,[10] a native of the island Formosa, who came from thence to London above twenty years ago, and in conversation told my friend that in his country when any young person happened to be put to death, the executioner sold the carcass to persons of quality as a prime dainty; and that in his time the body of a plump girl of fifteen, who was crucified for an attempt to poison the emperor, was sold to his Imperial Majesty's prime minister of state, and other great mandarins of the court, in joints from the gibbet, at four hundred crowns. Neither indeed can I deny that if the same use were made of several plump young girls in this town, who without one single groat to their fortunes cannot stir abroad without a chair,[11] and appear at the playhouse and assemblies in foreign fineries which they never will pay for, the kingdom would not be the worse.

19 Some persons of a desponding spirit are in great concern about that vast number of poor people who are aged, diseased, or maimed, and I have been desired to employ my thoughts what course may be taken to ease the nation of so grievous an encumbrance. But I am not in the least pain upon that matter, because it is very well known that they are every day dying and rotting by cold and famine, and filth and vermin, as fast as can be reasonably expected. And as to the younger laborers, they are now in almost as hopeful a condition. They cannot get work, and consequently pine away for want of nourishment to a degree that if at any time they are accidentally hired to common labor, they have not strength to perform it; and thus the

---

[10] A French imposter who claimed to be a Formosan and wrote *Description of Formosa* (1704).

[11] Sedan chair.

country and themselves are happily delivered from the evils to come.

20 I have too long digressed, and therefore shall return to my subject. I think the advantages by the proposal which I have made are obvious and many, as well as of the highest importance.

21 For first, as I have already observed, it would greatly lessen the number of Papists, with whom we are yearly overrun, being the principal breeders of the nation as well as our most dangerous enemies; and who stay at home on purpose to deliver the kingdom to the Pretender, hoping to take their advantage by the absence of so many good Protestants, who have chosen rather to leave their country than to stay at home and pay tithes against their conscience to an Episcopal curate.

22 Secondly, the poorer tenants will have something valuable of their own, which by law may be made liable to distress,[12] and help to pay their landlord's rent, their corn and cattle being already seized and money a thing unknown.

23 Thirdly, whereas the maintenance of an hundred thousand children, from two years old and upwards, cannot be computed as less than ten shillings a piece per annum, the nation's stock will be thereby increased fifty thousand pounds per annum, besides the profit of a new dish introduced to the tables of all gentlemen of fortune in the kingdom who have any refinement in taste. And the money will circulate among ourselves, the goods being entirely of our own growth and manufacture.

24 Fourthly, the constant breeders, besides the gain of eight shillings sterling per annum by the sale of their children, will be rid of the charge of maintaining them after the first year.

25 Fifthly, this food would likewise bring great custom to taverns, where the vintners will certainly be so prudent as to procure the best receipts for dressing it to perfection, and consequently have their houses frequented by all the fine gentlemen, who justly value themselves upon their knowledge in good eating; and a skillful cook, who understands how to oblige his guests, will contrive to make it as expensive as they please.

26 Sixthly, this would be a great inducement to marriage,

---

[12] Seizure.

which all wise nations have either encouraged by rewards or enforced by laws and penalties. It would increase the care and tenderness of mothers toward their children, when they were sure of a settlement for life to the poor babes, provided in some sort by the public, to their annual profit instead of expense. We should see an honest emulation among the married women, which of them could bring the fattest child to the market. Men would become as fond of their wives during the time of their pregnancy as they are now of their mares in foal, their cows in calf, or sows when they are ready to farrow; nor offer to beat or kick them (as is too frequent a practice) for fear of a miscarriage.

27 Many other advantages might be enumerated. For instance, the addition of some thousand carcasses in our exportation of barreled beef, the propagation of swine's flesh, and improvement in the art of making good bacon, so much wanted among us by the great destruction of pigs, too frequent at our tables, which are no way comparable in taste or magnificence to a well-grown, fat, yearling child, which roasted whole will make a considerable figure at a lord mayor's feast or any other public entertainment. But this and many others I omit, being studious of brevity.

28 Supposing that one thousand families in this city would be constant customers for infants' flesh, besides others who might have it at merry meetings, particularly weddings and christenings, I compute that Dublin would take off annually about twenty thousand carcasses, and the rest of the kingdom (where probably they will be sold somewhat cheaper) the remaining eighty thousand.

29 I can think of no one objection that will possibly be raised against this proposal, unless it should be urged that the number of people will be thereby much lessened in the kingdom. This I freely own, and it was indeed one principal design in offering it to the world. I desire the reader will observe, that I calculate my remedy for this one individual kingdom of Ireland and for no other that ever was, is, or I think ever can be upon earth. Therefore let no man talk to me of other expedients: of taxing our absentees at five shillings a pound: of using neither clothes nor household furniture except what is of our own growth and manufacture: of utterly rejecting the materials and instruments

that promote foreign luxury: of curing the expensiveness of pride, vanity, idleness, and gaming in our women: of introducing a vein of parsimony, prudence, and temperance: of learning to love our country, in the want of which we differ even from Laplanders and the inhabitants of Topinamboo: of quitting our animosities and factions, nor acting any longer like the Jews, who were murdering one another at the very moment their city was taken: of being a little cautious not to sell our country and conscience for nothing: of teaching landlords to have at least one degree of mercy toward their tenants: lastly, of putting a spirit of honesty, industry, and skill into our shopkeepers; who, if a resolution could now be taken to buy only our native goods, would immediately unite to cheat and exact upon us in the price, the measure, and the goodness, nor could ever yet be brought to make one fair proposal of just dealing, though often and earnestly invited to it.[13]

30   Therefore, I repeat, let no man talk to me of these and the like expedients, till he hath at least some glimpse of hope that there will ever be some hearty and sincere attempt to put them in practice.

31   But as to myself, having been wearied out for many years with offering vain, idle, visionary thoughts, and at length utterly despairing of success, I fortunately fell upon this proposal, which, as it is wholly new, so it hath something solid and real, of no expense and little trouble, full in our own power, and whereby we can incur no danger in disobliging England. For this kind of commodity will not bear exportation, the flesh being of too tender a consistence to admit a long continuance in salt, although perhaps I could name a country which would be glad to eat up our whole nation without it.

32   After all, I am not so violently bent upon my own opinion as to reject any offer proposed by wise men, which shall be found equally innocent, cheap, easy, and effectual. But before something of that kind shall be advanced in contradiction to my scheme, and offering a better, I desire the author or authors will be pleased maturely to consider two points. First, as things

---

[13] Swift himself had favored all the proposals listed here—without significant results.

now stand, how they will be able to find food and raiment for an hundred thousand useless mouths and backs. And secondly, there being a round million of creatures in human figure throughout this kingdom, whose sole subsistence put into a common stock would leave them in debt two millions of pounds sterling, adding those who are beggars by profession to the bulk of farmers, cottagers, and laborers, with their wives and children who are beggars in effect; I desire those politicians who dislike my overture, and may perhaps be so bold to attempt an answer, that they will first ask the parents of these mortals whether they would not at this day think it a great happiness to have been sold for food at a year old in the manner I prescribe, and thereby have avoided such a perpetual scene of misfortunes as they have since gone through by the oppression of landlords, the impossibility of paying rent without money or trade, the want of common sustenance, with neither house nor clothes to cover them from the inclemencies of the weather, and the most inevitable prospect of entailing the like or greater miseries upon their breed forever.

33 I profess, in the sincerity of my heart, that I have not the least personal interest in endeavoring to promote this necessary work, having no other motive than the public good of my country, by advancing our trade, providing for infants, relieving the poor, and giving some pleasure to the rich. I have no children by which I can propose to get a single penny; the youngest being nine years old, and my wife past childbearing.

Questions on Content

1. What problem in Ireland does the speaker, the persona, of the essay find particularly disturbing? If someone could solve this problem, what would he deserve?
2. At what age will children be provided for in the speaker's proposal? What will his scheme prevent? Why is it impossible to feed all the children born annually?
3. What does the speaker propose as a method of providing for these children? How many would be involved each year? How many would be kept as breeders?
4. What did his patriotic friend tell him about the shortage of deer and the potential market for Irish girls and boys (*paragraph 17*)? What is the ideal age for butchering them?

5. What six beneficial effects will result if his proposal is implemented? What other effects could he have enumerated?

6. The speaker would be willing not to reject any proposal other than his own, provided that it met what requirements? What two points does he wish anyone to consider who is advancing any other scheme?

Questions on Invention, Design, and Style

1. Consider paragraphs 1–10 as an extended introduction to the essay. How does the speaker introduce the problems of overpopulation, poverty, and unproductive human beings who demand charity? How does paragraph 3 broaden the scope of the essay beyond what it seems at first to include? How does paragraph 4 help to prepare for the thesis (the "modest proposal") of the essay?

2. Why do paragraphs 4–7 devote so much space to statistics and to the beneficial effects of the proposal before it is actually stated in paragraphs 9 and 10? Why does paragraph 10 so quickly return to an enumeration of advantages of the proposal? Why does the speaker rely on statistics so much in his argument (*see paragraphs 11, 13, 14, and 23*)?

3. A listing (or several lists) of beneficial effects takes up much of the essay (*see paragraphs 4–6, 10–16, and 20–28*). Classify these effects under several headings, such as economic, political, religious, aesthetic, gourmetic, and the like. What concerns seem most important to the speaker? What obvious ones are lacking? How do the speaker's concerns differ from Swift's own?

4. Paragraphs 17–19 are made up of several digressions. What points are made in these digressions? How do they relate to the "modest proposal"?

5. Examine paragraphs 29 and 30 more carefully. Why does the speaker mention these alternative proposals? What is Swift's purpose, as distinct from the speaker's purpose, in expressing them in a negative manner?

6. What is Swift's purpose in paragraph 32? How is it related to his purpose in other passages like paragraphs 1, 3, 5–7, 19, 26, and 29?

7. Swift's illustrations often provoke strong emotional responses in readers. What responses are provoked, for example, by such images as "a young healthy child well nursed . . . at a year old . . . stewed, roasted, baked, or boiled . . . [or] served in a fricassee or a ragout" (*paragraph 9*), "the fore or hind quarter will make a reasonable dish and seasoned with a little pepper or salt will be very

good boiled on the fourth day" (*paragraph 10*), "the skin [of the child] artificially dressed will make admirable gloves for ladies, and summer boots for fine gentlemen" (*paragraph 15*), and "a well-grown, fat, yearling child, which roasted whole will make a considerable figure at a lord mayor's feast" (*paragraph 27*)? Locate some other images that provoke strong responses.

8. Trace the analogy that the speaker draws between raising animals —pigs, cattle, and the like—for butchering and the bringing up of Irish girls and boys for the same purpose. Consider, for example, "a child just dropped from its dam" (*paragraph 4*), "which is more than we allow to sheep, black cattle, or swine" (*paragraph 10*). How does this analogy govern the language that the speaker uses? Consider, for example, "buying the children alive, and dressing them hot from the knife as we do roasting pigs" (*paragraph 16*). What reactions is Swift trying to provoke from his readers? How does this analogy help to make the essay more persuasive?

9. Like Mark Twain in "The War Prayer" (pp. 327–330), Swift uses the device of a speaker who is not fully aware of the implications of what he is saying and who is blind to his own stupidity. Why does Swift use this device in "A Modest Proposal"? How different would the essay be if he had not used this device?

Applications

1. Write a mock argument in which a self-congratulating, but stupid, speaker argues for a position that is opposite to your own and to the point that you wish to make to your readers.

2. Rewrite, on a larger scale, Thomas Carlyle's "The Irish Widow" (pp. 16–17) as it might be stated by a speaker like the one in Swift's essay, who argues that poor people should not be such a burden on others and proposes what—to him—is an appropriate solution.

Complex Argument

Appropriate balance of reason and emotion
Sensitive emotional subjects
Respect for readers' beliefs and convictions
Emphasis upon persuasive evidence

Audiences may have negative reactions to what they interpret as overemphasis on emotion in an argument. Or they may react so unfavorably to an elaborate appeal to reason that the argument never gets through to them. Perhaps most audiences resemble the speaker in Walt Whitman's poem:

> When I heard the learn'd astronomer,
> When the proofs, the figures, were ranged in columns before me,
> When I was shown the charts and the diagrams, to add, divide, and measure them,
> When I sitting heard the astronomer where he lectured with much applause in the lecture-room,
> How soon unaccountable I became tired and sick,
> Till rising and gliding out I wander'd off by myself,
> In the mystical moist night-air, and from time to time,
> Look'd up in perfect silence at the stars.

On the one hand, Whitman is saying that rationalization can become stultifying, the astronomer too concerned with data and method. On the other hand, the poem seems to affirm the average person's wish to know more about the very stars that the "learn'd astronomer" studies.

Complex arguments are arguments that make fuller use and more sensitive balance of the appeals to the readers' emotion and reason and put a clearly heavier emphasis upon evidence and reason; they also are required by subjects that are more profound and far reaching in their importance. Joseph Fletcher, for example, focuses in his argument upon the complex and controversial subject of whether or not human beings ought to have some control over death. Martin Luther King, Jr., focuses his attention upon the difficult subject of what responsibilities one human being has to and for another.

The writers of complex argument also come nearer to appealing to their readers as complete individuals—individuals who are both rational and emotional beings. Consider, for example, how fully King makes use of an appeal to his readers' emotions in the following reply, a one-sentence response to the segregationist's insistence that Blacks should continue to "wait":

> But when you have seen vicious mobs lynch your mothers and fathers at will and drown your sisters and brothers at whim; when you have seen hate-filled policemen curse, kick, and even kill your black brothers and sisters; when you see the vast majority of your twenty million Negro brothers smothering in an airtight cage of poverty in the midst of an affluent society; when you suddenly find your tongue twisted and your speech stammering as you seek to explain to your six-year-old daughter why she can't go to the public amusement park that has just been advertised on television, and see tears welling up in her eyes when she is told that Funtown is closed to colored children, and see ominous clouds of inferiority beginning to form in her little mental sky, and see her beginning to distort her personality by developing an unconscious bitterness toward white people; when you have to concoct an answer for a five-year-old son who is asking, "Daddy, why do white people treat colored people so mean?"; when you take a cross-country drive and find it necessary to sleep night after night in the uncomfortable corners of your automobile because no motel will accept you; when you are humiliated day in and day out by nagging signs reading "white" and "colored"; when your first name becomes "nigger," your middle name becomes "boy" (however old you are) and your last name becomes "John," and your wife and mother are never given the respected title "Mrs."; when you are harried by day and haunted by night by the fact that you are a Negro, living constantly at tiptoe stance, never quite knowing what to expect next, and are plagued with inner fears and outer resentments; when you are forever fighting a degenerating sense of "nobodiness" —then you will understand why we find it difficult to wait.

Here King has appealed to our emotions to such an extent that we find ourselves, with him, concluding: "No! *Wait* is what we cannot do *anymore!*" It's as if the experiences described are our own. All of us feel what Blacks feel.

But King does not continue at this emotional level for long; he balances his appeal to emotion with an appropriate appeal to reason. In the following passage, note how King appeals to the readers' sense of what is reasonable through classification analysis, which we have already seen (pp. 142–143).

A just law is a man-made code that squares with the moral law or the law of God. An unjust law is a code that is out of harmony with the moral law. To put it in the terms of St. Thomas Aquinas: An unjust law is a human law that is not rooted in eternal law and natural law. Any law that uplifts human personality is just. Any law that degrades human personality is unjust.

Your own writing can make a similar full and effective use of the appeal to reason and emotion and can confront readers with persuasive evidence if you follow the principles of complex argumentation. One such important principle, in addition to those already discussed, is that the writer does not assume the reader to be in agreement with his or her position on a subject and is therefore respectful of the reader's opinions, beliefs, and convictions. Little can be accomplished by showing disgust or disrespect for the position you oppose in your argument; many arguments, in fact, fail because through such disrespect they make the reader mad at the writer and eliminate any possibility of agreement.

Such sensitive and implicitly emotional subjects as abortion, gun-control laws, euthanasia, or penalties for drug offenders require your understanding of and respect for the beliefs of your audience. In a rough draft of an argument, for example, one student set out an emotional condemnation of the administration's recent disciplining of students who had broken an established school policy. More of a diatribe against the opposing position than a reasoned, persuasive argument, the paper managed only to anger, alienate, or bore readers who held positions other than that of the writer. Before rewriting the final draft of her argument, though, the student was able to put herself in the position of the college administrators and to imagine how a reasonable person could hold their attention.   Only then was she able to write an argument that was respectful of the opposing position and that persuasively demonstrated, through a careful use of evidence, how the writer's own position was more feasible than that of the administration.

Both of the essays in this subsection, by Fletcher and King, are directed against opposing points of view.   Appealing to both reason and emotion, both essays show respect for opposing positions and at the same time demonstrate, through appropriate evidence, that their positions are worthy of serious consideration.   These two essays are thus useful models to follow in learning to write complex arguments.

The Control of Death
Joseph Fletcher

Joseph Fletcher argues for more realistic and sensitive treatment of the dying, which would allow terminally ill patients the freedom to choose when to die.   Fletcher, a clergyman and professor of social ethics, bases his argument on both moral and logical considerations.

1   It is harder morally to justify letting somebody die a slow and ugly death, dehumanized, than it is to justify helping him to escape from such misery.   This is the case at least in any code of ethics that is humanistic or personalistic, i.e., in any code of ethics that puts humanness and personal integrity above biological life and function.

2   What follows is a moral defense of euthanasia.   Primarily, I mean active or positive euthanasia, which helps the patient to die; not merely the passive or negative form of euthanasia, which "lets the patient go" by simply withholding life-preserving treatments.   The plain fact is that negative euthanasia is already a *fait accompli*[1] in modern medicine.   Every day in a hundred hospitals across the land decisions are made clinically that

---

[1] An accomplished, and apparently irreversible, fact.

the line has been crossed from prolonging genuinely human life to prolonging only subhuman dying. When that judgment is made, respirators are turned off, life-perpetuating intravenous infusions stopped, proposed surgery canceled and drugs countermanded. "Code 90" stickers are put on many record jackets, indicating "Give no intensive care or resuscitation." Arguing pro and con about negative euthanasia is therefore irrelevant. Ethically, the issue of whether to let the patient go is already settled.

3   Given modern medicine's capabilities, always to do what is technically possible to prolong life would be morally indefensible on any ground other than a vitalistic outlook; that is, that biological survival is the first-order value and that all other considerations, such as personality, dignity, well-being and self-possession, necessarily take second place. Vestigial last-ditch provitalists still mumble threateningly about "what the Nazis did," but, in fact, the Nazis never engaged in euthanasia or mercy killing; what they did was merciless killing, either genocidal or for ruthless experimental purposes.

4   The traditional ethics based on the sanctity of life—which was the classic doctrine of medical idealism in its prescientific phases—must give way to a code of ethics based on the quality of life. This new ethics comes about for humane reasons. It is a result of modern medicine's successes, not failures. New occasions teach new duties; time makes ancient good uncouth, as Whittier said.

5   Many of us look upon living and dying as we do upon health and medical care—as person centered. This is not solely or basically a biological understanding of what it means to be "alive" and to be "dead." It asserts that a so-called vegetable, a brain-damaged victim of an auto accident or a microencephalic[2] newborn or a case of massive neurologic deficit and lost cerebral capacity, is no longer a human being, no longer a person, no longer really alive. It is *personal* function that counts, not biological function. Humanness is understood as primarily rational, not physiological. This doctrine of man

---

[2] Having an abnormally small brain, a condition with extremely severe mental retardation.

puts man and reason before life. It holds that being human is more "valuable" than being alive.

6   Most of our major moral problems are posed by scientific discoveries and by the subsequent technical know-how we gain in the control of health, life and death. Ethical questions jump out at us from every laboratory and clinic. Every advance in medical capabilities is an increase in our moral responsibility, a widening of the range of our decision-making obligations.

7   Genetics, molecular biology, fetology and obstetrics have developed to a point where we now have effective control over the start of human life's continuum. What has taken place in birth control is equally imperative in death control. The whole armory of resuscitation and prolongation of life forces us to be responsible decision makers about death as well as about birth; there must be as much quality control in the terminating of life as in its initiating. It is ridiculous to give ethical approval to the positive ending of subhuman life in utero,[3] as we do in therapeutic abortions for reasons of mercy and compassion, but to refuse approval of positively ending a subhuman life *in extremis*.

8   A careful typology of elective death will distinguish at least four forms—ways of dying that are not willy-nilly matters of blind chance but of choice, purpose and responsible freedom.

9   (1) Euthanasia, or a "good death," can be *voluntary and direct*, i.e., chosen and carried out by the patient. The most familiar way is the overdose left near at hand for the patient. It is a simple matter of request and of personal liberty. To hold that euthanasia in this category is justifiable entails a rejection of the simplistic canard that all suicide victims are mentally disordered.

10   Voluntary euthanasia is, of course, a form of suicide. Presumably a related issue arises around the conventional notion of consent in medical ethics. The codes (American Medical Association, Helsinki, World Medical Association, Nuremberg) all contend that valid consent to surgery or any kind of medical treatment requires a reasonable prospect of benefit to the patient. What, then, is benefit? Could death in some situ-

---

[3] In the womb.

ations be a benefit? My own answer is in the affirmative.

11   (2) Euthanasia can be *voluntary but indirect*. The choice might be made either *in situ* or long in advance of a terminal illness, e.g., by exacting a promise that if and when the "bare bodkin" [4] or potion cannot be self-administered, somebody will do it for the patient. In this case, the patient gives to others— physicians, lawyers, family, friends—the discretion to end it all as and when the situation requires, if the patient becomes comatose or too dysfunctional to make the decision.

12   (3) Euthanasia may be *direct but involuntary*. This is the form in which a simple mercy killing is done on a patient's behalf without his present or past request. Instances would be giving an idiot a fatal dose; speeding up the death of a child in the worst stages of Tay-Sachs disease; [5] shooting a man trapped inextricably in a blazing fire to end his suffering; or ordering a "shutdown" on a patient deep in an irreversible mindless condition, perhaps due to an injury or an infection or some biological breakdown. It is in this form, direct but involuntary, that the problem has reached the courts in legal charges and indictments.

13   To my knowledge, Uruguay is the only country that allows this type of euthanasia. Article 37 of the *Codiga Penal* specifically states that although it is a "crime," the courts are authorized to forgo any penalty. In time the world will follow suit. Laws in Colombia and in the Soviet Union are similar to those of Uruguay, but in their codes freedom from punishment is the exception rather than the norm. In Italy, Germany and Switzerland the law provides for a reduction of penalties when euthanasia is done upon the patient's request.

14   (4)Finally, euthanasia might be *both indirect and involuntary*. This is the "letting-the-patient-go" tactic that is taking place every day in our hospitals. Nothing is done positively for the patient to release him from his tragic condition (other than "trying to make him comfortable"), and what is done negatively is decided *for* him rather than in response to his request.

---

[4] Dagger. The allusion is to *Hamlet*, Act III, Scene 1, line 76.

[5] A congenital disease of the central nervous system, resulting in blindness, paralysis, and death.

15 But ethically regarded, this indirect and involuntary form of euthanasia is manifestly superficial, morally timid and evasive of the real issue. I repeat it: it is harder morally to justify letting somebody die a slow and ugly death, dehumanized, than it is to justify helping him to avoid it.

16 What, then, is the real issue? Briefly, it is whether we can morally justify taking it into our own hands to hasten death for ourselves (suicide) or for others (mercy killing) out of reasons of compassion. The answer to this in my view is clearly yes on both sides of it. Indeed, to justify either one, suicide or mercy killing, is to justify the other.

17 The heart of the matter analytically is the question of whether the end justifies the means. If the end sought is the patient's death as a release from pointless misery and dehumanization, then the requisite or appropriate means is justified. Immanuel Kant said that if we will the end we will the means. The old maxim of some moral theologians was *finis sanctificat media*.[6] The point is that no act is anything but random and meaningless unless it is purposefully related to some end or object. To be moral, an act must be seeking an end.

18 The really searching question of conscience is, therefore, whether we are right in believing that the well-being of persons is the highest good. If so, then it follows that either suicide or mercy killing could be the right thing to do in some exigent and tragic circumstances.

19 Another way of putting this is to say that the crucial question is not whether the end justifies the means (what else could?) but *what justifies the end?* And my answer is, plainly and confidently, that human happiness and well-being are the highest good, and, therefore, any ends or purposes validated by that standard or ideal are just, right, good. This reasoning is what humanistic medicine is all about; it is what the concepts of loving concern and social justice are built upon.

20 The plain hard logic of it is that the end, or purpose, of both negative and positive euthanasia is exactly the same: to bring about the patient's death. Acts of deliberate omission are morally not different from acts of commission.

---

[6] The end sanctifies the means.

21   Careful study of the basic texts of the Hippocratic Oath shows that it says nothing at all about preserving life as such. It says that "so far as power and discernment shall be mine, I will carry out regimens for the benefit of the sick and will keep them from harm and wrong." The case for euthanasia depends upon how we understand "benefit of the sick" and "harm" and "wrong." If we regard preserving dehumanized and merely biological life as sometimes being really harmful and not beneficial, to refuse to welcome or even introduce death would be quite wrong morally.

22   In most states in this country people can and do carry cards, legally established by the Anatomical Gift Acts, explaining that when the carrier dies he wishes his organs and tissue to be used for transplant when needed by the living. The day will come when people will also be able to carry a card, notarized and legally executed, explaining that they do not want to be kept alive beyond the *humanum* point and authorizing the ending of their biological processes by any method of euthanasia that seems appropriate. Suicide may or may not be the ultimate problem of philosophy, as Albert Camus thought, but in any case it is the ultimate problem of medical ethics.

Questions on Content

1. What distinction does Fletcher make between active and passive euthanasia? Which is he concerned with in this essay? Why?
2. Rather than euthanasia, what type of killing did the Nazis do?
3. What is the difference between traditional and new ethics in medicine, according to Fletcher?
4. What distinction does Fletcher make between *personal* function and *biological* function?
5. Why, according to Fletcher, should we be as responsible about death as we are about birth? What ethical connection does he draw between the two?
6. What are Fletcher's four proposed forms of elective death?
7. In what form has the issue of euthanasia reached the courts? Explain.
8. In what way is indirect and involuntary euthanasia "mostly timid and evasive," according to Fletcher?
9. How are acts of deliberate omission not different morally from acts of commission, according to the author?

10. What is the relation of the Hippocratic Oath to euthanasia? What is the relevant section of the oath?
11. What are the cards established by the Anatomical Gift Acts?

Questions on Invention, Design, and Style

1. What type of audience is Fletcher addressing? How do you know this from his language? his tone? his illustrations? his treatment of the subject?
2. Examine the way Fletcher has structured his argument. Why is the thesis, stated in paragraph 1, repeated in paragraph 15? What is the effect of his statement, at the beginning of paragraph 2, that he will defend the practice of euthanasia? What relation is established between ethics and medicine? How does it advance his argument? In what order does he present the four forms in the typology of death in paragraphs 8–15? How is the order of presentation significant? Fletcher steps up the pace of his argument in paragraphs 16–20. How does he restate the basic issue? In what way is this section a preparation for the essay's resolution? How does Fletcher conclude his argument in paragraphs 20–22?
3. Examine the evidence Fletcher presents. What are his sources? What types of evidence does he use (facts, testimony, or his own observation and analysis)?
4. How does Fletcher appeal to his readers' emotions? to their reason?
5. Authors gain credibility through their language, the cogency of their arguments, and their knowledge of the subject. Evaluate the manner in which Fletcher establishes his credibility in this essay.

Applications

1. Write an argumentative essay developing your own position on euthanasia. Include a definition of death (and of life) based on your own observation, analysis, and study.
2. Write an argument on an emotionally charged controversial subject. In a carefully reasoned approach, try to win your readers to your position. Present yourself as an interested, reasonable person whom readers can trust.

Letter from Birmingham Jail ★
Martin Luther King, Jr.

From a Birmingham, Alabama, jail cell, Martin Luther King, Jr., replies to a letter published by eight clergymen urging him to be more moderate in demonstrations he was leading in Birmingham. King's response is a defense of his activities and an admonition to those clergymen and others. It is a model of effective persuasive writing, a precisely written and carefully controlled argument on a complex subject about which the writer has deep convictions.

My Dear Fellow Clergymen:

1   While confined here in the Birmingham city jail, I came across your recent statement calling my present activities "unwise and untimely."   Seldom do I pause to answer criticism of my work and ideas.   If I sought to answer all the criticisms that cross my desk, my secretaries would have little time for anything other than such correspondence in the course of the day, and I would have no time for constructive work.   But since I feel that you are men of genuine good will and that your criticisms are sincerely set forth, I want to try to answer your statement in what I hope will be patient and reasonable terms.

2   I think I should indicate why I am here in Birmingham, since you have been influenced by the view which argues against "outsiders coming in."   I have the honor of serving as president of the Southern Christian Leadership Conference, an organization operating in every southern state, with headquar-

---

★ This response to a published statement by eight fellow clergymen from Alabama (Bishop C. C. J. Carpenter, Bishop Joseph A. Durick, Rabbi Hilton L. Grafman, Bishop Paul Hardin, Bishop Holan B. Harmon, the Reverend George M. Murray, the Reverend Edward V. Ramage and the Reverend Earl Stallings) was composed under somewhat constricting circumstances.   Begun on the margins of the newspaper in which the statement appeared while I was in jail, the letter was continued on scraps of writing paper supplied by a friendly Negro trusty, and concluded on a pad my attorneys were eventually permitted to leave me.   Although the text remains in substance unaltered, I have indulged in the author's prerogative of polishing it for publication.

ters in Atlanta, Georgia. We have some eighty-five affiliated organizations across the South, and one of them is the Alabama Christian Movement for Human Rights. Frequently we share staff, educational, and financial resources with our affiliates. Several months ago the affiliate here in Birmingham asked us to be on call to engage in a nonviolent direct-action program if such were deemed necessary. We readily consented, and when the hour came we lived up to our promise. So I, along with several members of my staff, am here because I was invited here. I am here because I have organizational ties here.

3   But more basically, I am in Birmingham because injustice is here. Just as the prophets of the eighth century B.C. left their villages and carried their "thus saith the Lord" far beyond the boundaries of their home towns, and just as the Apostle Paul left his village of Tarsus and carried the gospel of Jesus Christ to the far corners of the Greco-Roman world, so am I compelled to carry the gospel of freedom beyond my own home town. Like Paul, I must constantly respond to the Macedonian call for aid.

4   Moreover, I am cognizant of the interrelatedness of all communities and states. I cannot sit idly by in Atlanta and not be concerned about what happens in Birmingham. Injustice anywhere is a threat to justice everywhere. We are caught in an inescapable network of mutuality, tied in a single garment of destiny. Whatever affects one directly, affects all indirectly. Never again can we afford to live with the narrow, provincial, "outside agitator" idea. Anyone who lives inside the United States can never be considered an outsider anywhere within its bounds.

5   You deplore the demonstrations taking place in Birmingham. But your statement, I am sorry to say, fails to express a similar concern for the conditions that brought about the demonstrations. I am sure that none of you would want to rest content with the superficial kind of social analysis that deals merely with effects and does not grapple with underlying causes. It is unfortunate that demonstrations are taking place in Birmingham, but it is even more unfortunate that the city's white power structure left the Negro community with no alternative.

6 In any nonviolent campaign there are four basic steps: collection of the facts to determine whether injustices exist; negotiation; self-purification; and direct action. We have gone through all these steps in Birmingham. There can be no gainsaying the fact that racial injustice engulfs this community. Birmingham is probably the most thoroughly segregated city in the United States. Its ugly record of brutality is widely known. Negroes have experienced grossly unjust treatment in courts. There have been more unsolved bombings of Negro homes and churches in Birmingham than in any other city in the nation. These are the hard, brutal facts of the case. On the basis of these conditions, Negro leaders sought to negotiate with the city fathers. But the latter consistently refused to engage in good-faith negotiation.

7 Then, last September, came the opportunity to talk with leaders of Birmingham's economic community. In the course of the negotiations, certain promises were made by the merchants—for example, to remove the stores' humiliating racial signs. On the basis of these promises, the Reverend Fred Shuttlesworth and the leaders of the Alabama Christian Movement for Human Rights agreed to a moratorium on all demonstrations. As the weeks and months went by, we realized that we were the victims of a broken promise. A few signs, briefly removed, returned; the others remained.

8 As in so many past experiences, our hopes had been blasted, and the shadow of deep disappointment settled upon us. We had no alternative except to prepare for direct action, whereby we would present our very bodies as means of laying our case before the conscience of the local and the national community. Mindful of the difficulties involved, we decided to undertake a process of self-purification. We began a series of workshops on nonviolence, and we repeatedly asked ourselves: "Are you able to accept blows without retaliating?" "Are you able to endure the ordeal of jail?" We decided to schedule our direct-action program for the Easter season, realizing that except for Christmas, this is the main shopping period of the year. Knowing that a strong economic-withdrawal program would be the by-product of direct action, we felt that this would

be the best time to bring pressure to bear on the merchants for the needed change.

9   Then it occurred to us that Birmingham's mayoral election was coming up in March, and we speedily decided to postpone action until after election day. When we discovered that the Commissioner of Public Safety, Eugene "Bull" Connor, had piled up enough votes to be in the run-off, we decided again to postpone action until the day after the run-off so that the demonstrations could not be used to cloud the issues. Like many others, we waited to see Mr. Connor defeated, and to this end we endured postponement after postponement. Having aided in this community need, we felt that our direct-action program could be delayed no longer.

10   You may well ask, "Why direct action? Why sit-ins, marches, and so forth? Isn't negotiation a better path?" You are quite right in calling for negotiation. Indeed, this is the very purpose of direct action. Nonviolent direct action seeks to create such a crisis and foster such a tension that a community which has constantly refused to negotiate is forced to confront the issue. It seeks so to dramatize the issue that it can no longer be ignored. My citing the creation of tension as part of the work of the nonviolent-resister may sound rather shocking. But I must confess that I am not afraid of the word "tension." I have earnestly opposed violent tension, but there is a type of constructive, nonviolent tension which is necessary for growth. Just as Socrates felt that it was necessary to create a tension in the mind so that individuals could rise from the bondage of myths and half-truths to the unfettered realm of creative analysis and objective appraisal, so must we see the need for nonviolent gadflies to create the kind of tension in society that will help men rise from the dark depths of prejudice and racism to the majestic heights of understanding and brotherhood.

11   The purpose of our direct-action program is to create a situation so crisis-packed that it will inevitably open the door to negotiation. I therefore concur with you in your call for negotiation. Too long has our beloved Southland been bogged down in a tragic effort to live in monologue rather than dialogue.

12   One of the basic points in your statement is that the action that I and my associates have taken in Birmingham is untimely.   Some have asked: "Why didn't you give the new city administration time to act?"   The only answer that I can give to this query is that the new Birmingham administration must be prodded about as much as the outgoing one, before it will act.   We are sadly mistaken if we feel that the election of Albert Boutwell as mayor will bring the millennium to Birmingham. While Mr. Boutwell is a much more gentle person than Mr. Connor, they are both segregationists, dedicated to maintenance of the status quo.   I have hoped that Mr. Boutwell will be reasonable enough to see the futility of massive resistance to desegregation.   But he will not see this without pressure from devotees of civil rights.   My friends, I must say to you that we have not made a single gain in civil rights without determined legal and nonviolent pressure.   Lamentably, it is an historical fact that privileged groups seldom give up their privileges voluntarily.   Individuals may see the moral light and voluntarily give up their unjust posture; but, as Reinhold Niebuhr has reminded us, groups tend to be more immoral than individuals.

13   We know through painful experience that freedom is never voluntarily given by the oppressor; it must be demanded by the oppressed.   Frankly, I have yet to engage in a direct-action campaign that was "well timed" in the view of those who have not suffered unduly from the disease of segregation.   For years now I have heard the word "Wait!"   It rings in the ear of every Negro with piercing familiarity.   This "Wait" has almost always meant "Never."   We must come to see, with one of our distinguished jurists, that "justice too long delayed is justice denied."

14   We have waited for more than 340 years for our constitutional and God-given rights.   The nations of Asia and Africa are moving with jetlike speed toward gaining political independence, but we still creep at horse-and-buggy pace toward gaining a cup of coffee at a lunch counter.   Perhaps it is easy for those who have never felt the stinging darts of segregation to say, "Wait."   But when you have seen vicious mobs lynch your mothers and fathers at will and drown your sisters and brothers

at whim; when you have seen hate-filled policemen curse, kick, and even kill your black brothers and sisters; when you see the vast majority of your twenty million Negro brothers smothering in an airtight cage of poverty in the midst of an affluent society; when you suddenly find your tongue twisted and your speech stammering as you seek to explain to your six-year-old daughter why she can't go to the public amusement park that has just been advertised on television, and see tears welling up in her eyes when she is told that Funtown is closed to colored children, and see ominous clouds of inferiority beginning to form in her little mental sky, and see her beginning to distort her personality by developing an unconscious bitterness toward white people; when you have to concoct an answer for a five-year-old son who is asking, "Daddy, why do white people treat colored people so mean?"; when you take a cross-country drive and find it necessary to sleep night after night in the uncomfortable corners of your automobile because no motel will accept you; when you are humiliated day in and day out by nagging signs reading "white" and "colored"; when your first name becomes "nigger," your middle name becomes "boy" (however old you are) and your last name becomes "John," and your wife and mother are never given the respected title "Mrs."; when you are harried by day and haunted by night by the fact that you are a Negro, living constantly at tiptoe stance, never quite knowing what to expect next, and are plagued with inner fears and outer resentments; when you are forever fighting a degenerating sense of "nobodiness"—then you will understand why we find it difficult to wait.   There comes a time when the cup of endurance runs over, and men are no longer willing to be plunged into the abyss of despair.   I hope, sirs, you can understand our legitimate and unavoidable impatience.

15   You express a great deal of anxiety over our willingness to break laws.   This is certainly a legitimate concern.   Since we so diligently urge people to obey the Supreme Court's decision of 1954 outlawing segregation in the public schools, at first glance it may seem rather paradoxical for us consciously to break laws.   One may well ask: "How can you advocate breaking some laws and obeying others?"   The answer lies in the fact that there are two types of laws: just and unjust.   I would

be the first to advocate obeying just laws.   One has not only a
legal but a moral responsibility to obey just laws.   Conversely,
one has a moral responsibility to disobey unjust laws.   I would
agree with St. Augustine that "an unjust law is no law at all."
16   Now, what is the difference between the two?   How does
one determine whether a law is just or unjust?   A just law is
a man-made code that squares with the moral law or the law of
God.   An unjust law is a code that is out of harmony with the
moral law.   To put it in the terms of St. Thomas Aquinas: An
unjust law is a human law that is not rooted in eternal law and
natural law.   Any law that uplifts human personality is just.
Any law that degrades human personality is unjust.   All segregation statutes are unjust because segregation distorts the soul
and damages the personality.   It gives the segregator a false
sense of superiority and the segregated a false sense of inferiority.   Segregation, to use the terminology of the Jewish philosopher Martin Buber, substitutes an "I-it" relationship for an
"I-thou" relationship and ends up relegating persons to the
status of things.   Hence segregation is not only politically,
economically, and sociologically unsound, it is morally wrong
and sinful.   Paul Tillich has said that sin is separation.   Is not
segregation an existential expression of man's tragic separation, his awful estrangement, his terrible sinfulness?   Thus it
is that I can urge men to obey the 1954 decision of the Supreme
Court, for it is morally right; and I can urge them to disobey
segregation ordinances, for they are morally wrong.
17   Let us consider a more concrete example of just and unjust
laws.   An unjust law is a code that a numerical or power majority group compels a minority group to obey but does not make
binding on itself.   This is *difference* made legal.   By the same
token, a just law is a code that a majority compels a minority
to follow and that it is willing to follow itself.   This is *sameness*
made legal.
18   Let me give another explanation.   A law is unjust if it is
inflicted on a minority that, as a result of being denied the right
to vote, had no part in enacting or devising the law.   Who can
say that the legislature of Alabama which set up that state's segregation laws was democratically elected?   Throughout Alabama all sorts of devious methods are used to prevent Negroes

from becoming registered voters, and there are some counties in which, even though Negroes constitute a majority of the population, not a single Negro is registered.   Can any law enacted under such circumstances be considered democratically structured?

19   Sometimes a law is just on its face and unjust in its application.   For instance, I have been arrested on a charge of parading without a permit.   Now, there is nothing wrong in having an ordinance which requires a permit for a parade.   But such an ordinance becomes unjust when it is used to maintain segregation and to deny citizens the First-Amendment privilege of peaceful assembly and protest.

20   I hope you are able to see the distinction I am trying to point out.   In no sense do I advocate evading or defying the law, as would the rabid segregationist.   That would lead to anarchy.   One who breaks an unjust law must do so openly, lovingly, and with a willingness to accept the penalty.   I submit that an individual who breaks a law that conscience tells him is unjust, and who willingly accepts the penalty of imprisonment in order to arouse the conscience of the community over its injustice, is in reality expressing the highest respect for law.

21   Of course, there is nothing new about this kind of civil disobedience.   It was evidenced sublimely in the refusal of Shadrach, Meshach, and Abednego to obey the laws of Nebuchadnezzar, on the ground that a higher moral law was at stake.   It was practiced superbly by the early Christians, who were willing to face hungry lions and the excruciating pain of chopping blocks rather than submit to certain unjust laws of the Roman Empire.   To a degree, academic freedom is a reality today because Socrates practiced civil disobedience.   In our own nation, the Boston Tea Party represented a massive act of civil disobedience.

22   We should never forget that everything Adolf Hitler did in Germany was "legal" and everything the Hungarian freedom fighters did in Hungary was "illegal."   It was "illegal" to aid and comfort a Jew in Hitler's Germany.   Even so, I am sure that, had I lived in Germany at the time, I would have aided and comforted my Jewish brothers.   If today I lived in a Communist country where certain principles dear to the Christian faith are

suppressed, I would openly advocate disobeying that country's anti-religious laws.

23   I must make two honest confessions to you, my Christian and Jewish brothers.   First, I must confess that over the past few years I have been gravely disappointed with the white moderate.   I have almost reached the regrettable conclusion that the Negro's great stumbling block in his stride toward freedom is not the White Citizen's Counciler or the Ku Klux Klanner, but the white moderate, who is more devoted to "order" than to justice; who prefers a negative peace which is the absence of tension to a positive peace which is the presence of justice; who constantly says, "I agree with you in the goal you seek, but I cannot agree with your methods of direct action"; who paternalistically believes he can set the timetable for another man's freedom; who lives by a mythical concept of time and who constantly advises the Negro to wait for a "more convenient season."   Shallow understanding from people of good will is more frustrating than absolute misunderstanding from people of ill will.   Lukewarm acceptance is much more bewildering than outright rejection.

24   I had hoped that the white moderate would understand that law and order exist for the purpose of establishing justice and that when they fail in this purpose they become the dangerously structured dams that block the flow of social progress.   I had hoped that the white moderate would understand that the present tension in the South is a necessary phase of the transition from an obnoxious negative peace, in which the Negro passively accepted his unjust plight, to a substantive and positive peace, in which all men will respect the dignity and worth of human personality.   Actually, we who engage in nonviolent direct action are not the creators of tension.   We merely bring to the surface the hidden tension that is already alive.   We bring it out in the open, where it can be seen and dealt with.   Like a boil that can never be cured so long as it is covered up but must be opened with all its ugliness to the natural medicines of air and light, injustice must be exposed, with all the tension its exposure creates, to the light of human conscience and the air of national opinion, before it can be cured.

25   In your statement you assert that our actions, even though peaceful, must be condemned because they precipitate vio-

lence. But is this a logical assertion? Isn't this like condemning a robbed man because his possession of money precipitated the evil act of robbery? Isn't this like condemning Socrates because his unswerving commitment to truth and his philosophical inquiries precipitated the act by the misguided populace in which they made him drink hemlock? Isn't this like condemning Jesus because his unique God-consciousness and never-ceasing devotion to God's will precipitated the evil act of crucifixion? We must come to see that, as the federal courts have consistently affirmed, it is wrong to urge an individual to cease his efforts to gain his basic constitutional rights because the quest may precipitate violence. Society must protect the robbed and punish the robber.

26   I had also hoped that the white moderate would reject the myth concerning time in relation to the struggle for freedom. I have just received a letter from a white brother in Texas. He writes: "All Christians know that the colored people will receive equal rights eventually, but it is possible that you are in too great a religious hurry. It has taken Christianity almost two thousand years to accomplish what it has. The teachings of Christ take time to come to earth." Such an attitude stems from a tragic misconception of time, from the strangely irrational notion that there is something in the very flow of time that will inevitably cure all ills. Actually, time itself is neutral; it can be used either destructively or constructively. More and more I feel that the people of ill will have used time much more effectively than have the people of good will. We will have to repent in this generation not merely for the hateful words and actions of the bad people, but for the appalling silence of the good people. Human progress never rolls in on wheels of inevitability; it comes through the tireless efforts of men willing to be co-workers with God, and without this hard work, time itself becomes an ally of the forces of social stagnation. We must use time creatively, in the knowledge that the time is always ripe to do right. Now is the time to make real the promise of democracy and transform our pending national elegy into a creative psalm of brotherhood. Now is the time to lift our national policy from the quicksand of racial injustice to the solid rock of human dignity.

27   You speak of our activity in Birmingham as extreme. At

first I was rather disappointed that fellow clergymen would see my nonviolent efforts as those of an extremist. I began thinking about the fact that I stand in the middle of two opposing forces in the Negro community. One is a force of complacency, made up in part of Negroes who, as a result of long years of oppression, are so drained of self-respect and a sense of "somebodiness" that they have adjusted to segregation; and in part of a few middle-class Negroes who, because of a degree of academic and economic security and because in some ways they profit by segregation, have become insensitive to the problems of the masses. The other force is one of bitterness and hatred, and it comes perilously close to advocating violence. It is expressed in the various black nationalist groups that are springing up across the nation, the largest and best-known being Elijah Muhammad's Muslim movement. Nourished by the Negro's frustration over the continued existence of racial discrimination, this movement is made up of people who have lost faith in America, who have absolutely repudiated Christianity, and who have concluded that the white man is an incorrigible "devil."

28   I have tried to stand between these two forces, saying that we need emulate neither the "do-nothingism" of the complacent nor the hatred and despair of the black nationalist. For there is the more excellent way of love and nonviolent protest. I am grateful to God that, through the influence of the Negro church, the way of nonviolence became an integral part of our struggle.

29   If this philosophy had not emerged, by now many streets of the South would, I am convinced, be flowing with blood. And I am further convinced that if our white brothers dismiss as "rabble-rousers" and "outside agitators" those of us who employ nonviolent direct action, and if they refuse to support our nonviolent efforts, millions of Negroes will, out of frustration and despair, seek solace and security in black-nationalist ideologies—a development that would inevitably lead to a frightening racial nightmare.

30   Oppressed people cannot remain oppressed forever. The yearning for freedom eventually manifests itself, and that is what has happened to the American Negro. Something within

has reminded him of his birthright of freedom, and something without has reminded him that it can be gained. Consciously or unconsciously, he has been caught up by the *Zeitgeist,* and with his black brothers of Africa and his brown and yellow brothers of Asia, South America, and the Caribbean, the United States Negro is moving with a sense of great urgency toward the promised land of racial justice. If one recognizes this vital urge that has engulfed the Negro community, one should readily understand why public demonstrations are taking place. The Negro has many pent-up resentments and latent frustrations, and he must release them. So let him march; let him make prayer pilgrimages to the city hall; let him go on freedom rides—and try to understand why he must do so. If his repressed emotions are not released in nonviolent ways, they will seek expression through violence; this is not a threat but a fact of history. So I have not said to my people, "Get rid of your discontent." Rather, I have tried to say that this normal and healthy discontent can be channeled into the creative outlet of nonviolent direct action. And now this approach is being termed extremist.

31 But though I was initially disappointed at being categorized as an extremist, as I continued to think about the matter I gradually gained a measure of satisfaction from the label. Was not Jesus an extremist for love: "Love your enemies, bless them that curse you, do good to them that hate you, and pray for them which despitefully use you, and persecute you." Was not Amos an extremist for justice: "Let justice roll down like waters and righteousness like an ever-flowing stream." Was not Paul an extremist for the Christian gospel: "I bear in my body the marks of the Lord Jesus." Was not Martin Luther an extremist: "Here I stand; I cannot do otherwise, so help me God." And John Bunyan: "I will stay in jail to the end of my days before I make a butchery of my conscience." And Abraham Lincoln: "This nation cannot survive half slave and half free." And Thomas Jefferson: "We hold these truths to be self-evident, that all men are created equal. . . ." So the question is not whether we will be extremists, but what kind of extremists we will be. Will we be extremists for hate or for love? Will we be extremists for the preservation of injustice or for the ex-

tension of justice?   In that dramatic scene on Calvary's hill three men were crucified.   We must never forget that all three were crucified for the same crime—the crime of extremism. Two were extremists for immorality, and thus fell below their environment.   The other, Jesus Christ, was an extremist for love, truth, and goodness, and thereby rose above his environment.   Perhaps the South, the nation, and the world are in dire need of creative extremists.

32   I had hoped that the white moderate would see this need. Perhaps I was too optimistic; perhaps I expected too much.   I suppose I should have realized that few members of the oppressor race can understand the deep groans and passionate yearnings of the oppressed race, and still fewer have the vision to see that injustice must be rooted out by strong, persistent, and determined action.   I am thankful, however, that some of our white brothers in the South have grasped the meaning of this social revolution and committed themselves to it.   They are still all too few in quantity, but they are big in quality.   Some— such as Ralph McGill, Lillian Smith, Harry Golden, James McBride Dabbs, Ann Braden, and Sarah Patton Boyle—have written about our struggle in eloquent and prophetic terms. Others have marched with us down nameless streets of the South.   They have languished in filthy, roach-infested jails, suffering the abuse and brutality of policemen who view them as "dirty nigger-lovers."   Unlike so many of their moderate brothers and sisters, they have recognized the urgency of the moment and sensed the need for powerful "action" antidotes to combat the disease of segregation.

33   Let me take note of my other major disappointment.   I have been so greatly disappointed with the white church and its leadership.   Of course, there are some notable exceptions.   I am not unmindful of the fact that each of you has taken some significant stands on this issue.   I commend you, Reverend Stallings, for your Christian stand on this past Sunday, in welcoming Negroes to your worship service on a nonsegregated basis.   I commend the Catholic leaders of this state for integrating Spring Hill College several years ago.

34   But despite these notable exceptions, I must honestly reiterate that I have been disappointed with the church.   I do

not say this as one of those negative critics who can always find something wrong with the church.   I say this as a minister of the gospel, who loves the church; who was nurtured in its bosom; who has been sustained by its spiritual blessings and who will remain true to it as long as the cord of life shall lengthen.

35   When I was suddenly catapulted into the leadership of the bus protest in Montgomery, Alabama, a few years ago, I felt we would be supported by the white church.   I felt that the white ministers, priests, and rabbis of the South would be among our strongest allies.   Instead, some have been outright opponents, refusing to understand the freedom movement and misrepresenting its leaders; all too many others have been more cautious than courageous and have remained silent behind the anesthetizing security of stained-glass windows.

36   In spite of my shattered dreams, I came to Birmingham with the hope that the white religious leadership of this community would see the justice of our cause and, with deep moral concern, would serve as the channel through which our just grievances could reach the power structure.   I had hoped that each of you would understand.   But again I have been disappointed.

. . .

37   There was a time when the church was very powerful—in the time when the early Christians rejoiced at being deemed worthy to suffer for what they believed.   In those days the church was not merely a thermometer that recorded the ideas and principles of popular opinion; it was a thermostat that transformed the mores of society.   Whenever the early Christians entered a town, the people in power became disturbed and immediately sought to convict the Christians for being "disturbers of the peace" and "outside agitators."   But the Christians pressed on, in the conviction that they were "a colony of heaven," called to obey God rather than man.   Small in number, they were big in commitment.   They were too God-intoxicated to be "astronomically intimidated."   By their effort and example they brought an end to such ancient evils as infanticide and gladiatorial contests.

38   Things are different now.   So often the contemporary church is a weak, ineffectual voice with an uncertain sound.

So often it is an archdefender of the status quo. Far from being disturbed by the presence of the church, the power structure of the average community is consoled by the church's silent—and often even vocal—sanction of things as they are.

39   But the judgment of God is upon the church as never before. If today's church does not recapture the sacrificial spirit of the early church, it will lose its authenticity, forfeit the loyalty of millions, and be dismissed as an irrelevant social club with no meaning for the twentieth century. Every day I meet young people whose disappointment with the church has turned into outright disgust.

40   Perhaps I have once again been too optimistic. Is organized religion too inextricably bound to the status quo to save our nation and the world? Perhaps I must turn my faith to the inner spiritual church, the church within the church, as the true *ekklesia* and the hope of the world. But again I am thankful to God that some noble souls from the ranks of organized religion have broken loose from the paralyzing chains of conformity and joined us as active partners in the struggle for freedom. They have left their secure congregations and walked the streets of Albany, Georgia, with us. They have gone down the highways of the South on torturous rides for freedom. Yes, they have gone to jail with us. Some have been dismissed from their churches, have lost the support of their bishops and fellow ministers. But they have acted in the faith that right defeated is stronger than evil triumphant. Their witness has been the spiritual salt that has preserved the true meaning of the gospel in these troubled times. They have carved a tunnel of hope through the dark mountain of disappointment.

41   I hope the church as a whole will meet the challenge of this decisive hour. But even if the church does not come to the aid of justice, I have no despair about the future. I have no fear about the outcome of our struggle in Birmingham, even if our motives are at present misunderstood. We will reach the goal of freedom in Birmingham and all over the nation, because the goal of America is freedom. Abused and scorned though we may be, our destiny is tied up with America's destiny. Before the pilgrims landed at Plymouth, we were here. Before the pen of Jefferson etched the majestic words of the Declaration of

Independence across the pages of history, we were here.   For
more than two centuries our forebears labored in this country
without wages; they made cotton king; they built the homes of
their masters while suffering gross injustice and shameful hu-
miliation—and yet out of a bottomless vitality they continued
to thrive and develop.   If the inexpressible cruelties of slavery
could not stop us, the opposition we now face will surely fail.
We will win our freedom because the sacred heritage of our nation and the eternal will of God are embodied in our echoing
demands.

42   Before closing I feel impelled to mention one other point
in your statement that has troubled me profoundly.   You
warmly commended the Birmingham police force for keeping
"order" and "preventing violence."   I doubt that you would have
so warmly commended the police force if you had seen its dogs
sinking their teeth into unarmed, nonviolent Negroes.   I doubt
that you would so quickly commend the policemen if you were
to observe their ugly and inhumane treatment of Negroes here
in the city jail; if you were to watch them push and curse old
Negro women and young Negro girls; if you were to see them
slap and kick old Negro men and young boys; if you were to observe them, as they did on two occasions, refuse to give us food
because we wanted to sing our grace together.   I cannot join
you in your praise of the Birmingham police department.

43   It is true that the police have exercised a degree of discipline in handling the demonstrators.   In this sense they have
conducted themselves rather "nonviolently" in public.   But for
what purpose?   To preserve the evil system of segregation.
Over the past few years I have consistently preached that nonviolence demands that the means we use must be as pure as the
ends we seek.   I have tried to make clear that it is wrong to use
immoral means to attain moral ends.   But now I must affirm
that it is just as wrong, or perhaps even more so, to use moral
means to preserve immoral ends.   Perhaps Mr. Connor and his
policemen have been rather nonviolent in public, as was Chief
Pritchett in Albany, Georgia, but they have used the moral
means of nonviolence to maintain the immoral end of racial injustice.   As T. S. Eliot has said, "The last temptation is the
greatest treason: To do the right deed for the wrong reason."

44   I wish you had commended the Negro sit-inners and demonstrators of Birmingham for their sublime courage, their willingness to suffer, and their amazing discipline in the midst of great provocation. One day the South will recognize its real heroes. They will be the James Merediths, with the noble sense of purpose that enables them to face jeering and hostile mobs, and with the agonizing loneliness that characterizes the life of the pioneer. They will be old, oppressed, battered Negro women, symbolized in a seventy-two-year-old woman in Montgomery, Alabama, who rose up with a sense of dignity and with her people decided not to ride segregated buses, and who responded with ungrammatical profundity to one who inquired about her weariness: "My feets is tired, but my soul is at rest." They will be the young high school and college students, the young ministers of the gospel and a host of their elders, courageously and nonviolently sitting in at lunch counters and willingly going to jail for conscience' sake. One day the South will know that when these disinherited children of God sat down at lunch counters, they were in reality standing up for what is best in the American dream and for the most sacred values in our Judaeo-Christian heritage, thereby bringing our nation back to those great wells of democracy which were dug deep by the founding fathers in their formulation of the Constitution and the Declaration of Independence.

45   Never before have I written so long a letter. I'm afraid it is much too long to take your precious time. I can assure you that it would have been much shorter if I had been writing from a comfortable desk, but what else can one do when he is alone in a narrow jail cell, other than write long letters, think long thoughts, and pray long prayers?

46   If I have said anything in this letter that overstates the truth and indicates an unreasonable impatience, I beg you to forgive me. If I have said anything that understates the truth and indicates my having a patience that allows me to settle for anything less than brotherhood, I beg God to forgive me.

47   I hope this letter finds you strong in the faith. I also hope that circumstances will soon make it possible for me to meet each of you, not as an integrationist or a civil-rights leader but as a fellow clergyman and a Christian brother. Let us all hope

that the dark clouds of racial prejudice will soon pass away and the deep fog of misunderstanding will be lifted from our fear-drenched communities, and in some not too distant tomorrow the radiant stars of love and brotherhood will shine over our great nation with all their scintillating beauty.

Yours for the cause of Peace and Brotherhood,
MARTIN LUTHER KING, JR.

Questions on Content

1. Why does King normally not answer criticism?
2. What are the "hard facts" of the Birmingham situation? How does Birmingham compare with other cities in its treatment of the Negro community, according to King?
3. What is lacking in the clergymen's concern over the demonstrations in Birmingham?
4. What are the four basic steps in a nonviolent campaign?
5. Why did the Alabama Christian Movement at first postpone direct action until after the run-off election?
6. What is the goal of "nonviolent direct action," according to King? What is the "constructive, nonviolent tension" King favors?
7. What has "wait" come to mean to every Negro, according to King?
8. What two types of laws are there, according to King? What is his attitude toward each?
9. What two confessions does King make to his Jewish and Christian brothers?
10. What two opposing forces exist in the Negro community? How has King tried to stand between them?
11. What advice has King given his people about their discontent?
12. How has King been disappointed by white moderates? by the white church?
13. If the church does not recapture its early sacrificial spirit, what will become of it, according to King? Why will King not despair even if the church does not come to his people's aid?

Questions on Invention, Design, and Style

1. How does King establish, in the salutation and the first paragraph of the letter, his reasons for writing, the setting in which he writes, his intended audience, and a sensitive and reasonable

tone?   Why is King in Birmingham (*paragraphs 2–4*)?   What is
his first reason?   What is his second reason?   Why are this reason
and the comparison he makes appropriate for his audience?
What is his third reason?

2.   In paragraphs 5–9, King explains why he has been leading demonstrations.   How does he turn the clergymen's criticism back
on them?   Paragraphs 6–9 include a process analysis of direct-action programs.   What is its purpose, and what steps does it contain?   Note how the last step of the process analysis is combined
with a causal analysis of direct action (*paragraphs 10 and 11*).
How does King reestablish common ground with his audience at
the beginning of this section?   What are the purposes of his classifications "violent tension" and "nonviolent tension"?   How
does he return to the subject of negotiation in paragraph 11?   In
what ways does he find common ground with his audience again
here?

3.   King defends himself in paragraphs 12–14 from the charge that
his actions are untimely.   How has paragraph 9 prepared for this
defense?   What reasons does King give for not waiting?   What
evidence does he give?   Paragraph 14 is one of the letter's emotional peaks.   What is its tone?   How do King's illustrations add
vividness and contribute to that tone?   To what emotions is he
appealing?   How does the tone shift toward the end of the paragraph?

4.   King explains in paragraphs 15–22 why he is willing to break
some laws.   How does King establish common ground with his
audience early in paragraph 15?   What is the paradoxical nature
of law King refers to?   How does it clarify King's thinking and
explain his actions?   Why does he cite Aquinas, the Catholic
theologian; Buber, the Jewish philosopher; and Tillich, the Protestant theologian in paragraph 16?   What similarities link the
three?   In what way is paragraph 20 a summary of this section?
What contrast does King set up here?   From what sources does
King draw the examples in paragraph 21?   Do these sources provide especially effective examples in this context?   How does paragraph 22 serve as an effective conclusion to this section on obedience to law?

5.   After defending his actions against the criticisms made by the
clergymen, King takes the offensive in paragraphs 23–44.   How
do the first two sentences in paragraph 23 signal this change?
How has paragraph 22 prepared for it?   King deals first with
white moderates.   What is the meaning and purpose of the boil

analogy in paragraph 24?   What is the function of the analogies that follow in paragraph 25?   What is the significance of the sources from which he draws his analogies?   How does King make use of the letter from "a white brother from Texas" in paragraph 26?   How does King use classification in defending himself against charges of extremism by moderates in paragraphs 27–32?   How does he use causal analysis? classification? rhetorical questions? contrast?

6.   Turning from white moderates to the white church in paragraphs 33–44, King explains his attitude.   Trace the development of King's view of the white church.   What possible effect of the present direction of the church does King cite in paragraph 39?   What causes for hope does he refer to in paragraphs 40 and 41?   What further criticism of the clergymen is developed in paragraphs 42–44?

7.   In his conclusion to the letter (*paragraphs 45–47*), King reestablishes his setting, his attitude toward the audience, and his tone.   Characterize each of these as they emerge at the end of the letter.

8.   King's letter ostensibly replies to that of the eight clergymen.   Find passages in which he addresses them, and analyze the voice he uses.   In what relation to the eight clergymen does King see himself?   He also has a secondary audience.   Who are its members?   Locate passages that seem especially directed to the secondary audience.   In what relation to this audience does King see himself?

9.   Which parts of King's argument appeal chiefly to reason?   Which parts aim primarily for an emotional response?   How are the two types of appeals interrelated in this letter?

Applications

1.   What is your firmest belief—one based on a deep emotional commitment and one that you also regard as rational?   Write an argument, appealing to both emotion and reason, presenting that belief in a form your readers will respect, if not necessarily accept.

2.   Read the "Letters to the Editor" in your local newspaper for three or four days in a row.   Choose a letter you strongly agree with or disagree with, and write your own letter to the editor, presenting your argument pro or con.   Remember to consider the audience who will read your letter.

3.   Recall an instance in which a position or belief that you held was not shared by most other members of your group, as a result of

which you were unfairly treated.   Using King's letter as a model, write your own letter to the members of this group arguing for your position and for a more understanding treatment of those who hold unpopular positions in the group.

Glossary of Terms

Allusion is a reference to a subject without the actual naming of it. Annie Dillard's allusion to the Biblical account of the parting of the Red Sea in "Learning to See," paragraph 6, page 48, is an effective example of this type of reference.

Analogy is the extension or application of a simile or metaphor. Two unlike things (struggling for the definition of a word and struggling for a gun in a western movie, for instance) are said to be similar or identical in order to make a point more clearly or powerfully. An excellent example in which two analogies are contrasted can be found in paragraph 37 of Martin Luther King, Jr.'s, "Letter from Birmingham Jail": "the church was not merely a thermometer that recorded the ideas and principles of popular opinion; it was a thermostat that transformed the mores of society," p. 367. See the introduction to "Simple Comparison and Contrast," p. 70.

Analysis is the examination and discovery of significant relationships between parts and other parts and between parts and wholes. It can involve either the process of *division* or of *synthesis* or a combination of the two. Its purpose is to provide fuller understanding of such relationships so that they and the whole and the parts being examined can be more fully understood and applied. It can be immensely useful as a principle either of invention or of design. See the introduction to "Analysis," pp. 135–138.

Appeal is the way in which writers deliberately attempt to arouse within their readers a desired response—a sense of anger, fear, humor, disgust, joy, enthusiasm—a sense of the reasonableness of a position or belief. Note the appeal to emotion in "Little Brother of the Wolf," pp. 312–317, and the appeal to reason in "Everyone Is a Scientist," pp. 273–280.

Argument is a form of writing that deliberately sets out to convince readers that the writer's thesis is valid and, in some cases, should be acted on. Although it often informs and explains as well, argument is aimed primarily at convincing readers to accept the writer's views, even in place of their own convictions. See the introduction to "Argument," pp. 263–268.

Attitude is the revealed feeling of writers toward their subject and their audience. This distinctive attitude of the writer is known also as the *tone* of a piece of writing—serious, as in "Everyone Is a Scientist," pp. 273–280; playful and ironic, as in "To His Coy Mistress," pp. 281–282; satiric, as in "A Modest Proposal," pp. 332–341, etc.

Audience is the readers for whom a writer is writing a particular piece. The purpose the writer has is directly related to that audience: to ex-

i

plain an idea *to them*, to inform *them* of a process, to convince *them* of the validity of a thesis.

Bandwagon is a propaganda device in which the writer avoids the issue at hand by suggesting that the reader will be left out if he doesn't hurry and join in: "Everyone is switching to Sudsy soap."

Cardstacking is a propaganda device in which the writer avoids the issue at hand by omitting evidence that does not support his or her position: "Only good has come from the new experimental course in criminology."

Causal Analysis as a principle of invention is the examination and discovery of relationships between causes and effects. As in other forms of analysis, we are concerned with a whole (the entire cause-effect relationship) and its parts. Such analysis can proceed from *cause to effect* or *effect to cause* and may involve a *causal chain* in either sequence. Important considerations in any causal analysis include the questions of whether all possible causes and effects are being considered and whether a cause-effect relationship in fact exists. As a principle of design, causal analysis can provide a range of sequences of material from which the writer can choose. See the introduction to "Causal Analysis," pp. 223–228.

Causal Chain is a series of at least three items in a cause/effect relationship in which at least one cause is also the effect of another cause. An example is found on p. 224 of the introduction to "Causal Analysis":

My failure in American history

↑

putting off reading the assignment

↑

tired eyes

↑

need for glasses.

Cause is anything that brings about a resulting action or state (the *effect*). For instance, the cause of a forest fire might be lightning striking dry timber. See the introduction to "Causal Analysis," pp. 223–228.

Cause to Effect as a principle of invention is the consideration first of the *cause* (such as failure to read the assignment) and second of the *effect* (such as poor performance on an exam) in order to discover what the causal relationship is. As a principle of design, *cause to effect* is the sequence in which the two are introduced in the finished writing, as determined by the complexity of the subject and the point the writer wishes to emphasize. See the introduction to "Causal Analysis," pp. 223–228.

Chronological Order is the arrangement of events into the order in which they occurred in time. See the introduction to "Extended Illustration," p.14.

Classification Analysis as a principle of invention is the examination and discovery of relationships between a general class (such as "students") and its subclasses (such as "freshmen," "sophomores," "juniors," and "seniors"). As a principle of design, classification analysis is useful in separating main topics from secondary ones. See the introduction to "Classification Analysis and Definition," pp. 139–141.

Comparison is a pointing out of the similarities between two or more things. Through comparison, writers not only clarify their meaning quickly and completely, but are also able to make a lasting impression upon the reader. See the introduction to "Comparison and Contrast," pp. 65–68.

Complex Argument is a form of writing that is deliberately intended to persuade readers that the writer's thesis is valid and, in some cases, should be acted on. Its complexity is evident in the full use of appeals to both the emotions and reason of the readers; in its heavy emphasis upon evidence; and in the treatment of subjects that are profound and far reaching in their importance. See "The Control of Death," by Joseph Fletcher, pp. 347–352, and "Letter from Birmingham Jail," by Martin Luther King, Jr.

Complex Comparison and Contrast is distinguished from the other types, *simple* and *extended*, by the nature of the writer's subject and his or her use of the similarities and differences perceived. The subject is larger, has more parts, places greater demands upon the writer; the writer, on the other hand, explores both the similarities and differences of the subject, pursues the implications of the relation further, and transcends the formality of a subject-by-subject and part-by-part design in drawing comparisons and contrasts. See the introduction to "Complex Comparison and Contrast," pp. 105–107.

Conclusion is the ending of a piece of writing, in which writers restate their thesis and sum up the main points in light of all that has been presented. See "An Introduction to Writing," pp. xxvii–xxxiv.

Conditional Argument is an argument based upon at least one conditional premise ("If . . . , then . . ."). Two selections in this book make effective use of this type of argument: Andrew Marvell's "To His Coy Mistress," pp. 281–282, and the "Declaration of Independence," pp. 284–287.

Contrast is a pointing-out of the differences between two or more things. Through contrast, writers not only clarify their meaning quickly and completely but are also able to make a lasting impression upon the reader. See the introduction to "Comparison and Contrast," pp. 65–68.

Deduction is a method of reasoning that begins with at least one accepted *generalization* and, through rules of logic, yields a conclusion that follows necessarily and inevitably from the reasons, or *premises.* (See also *syllogism.*) See the introduction to "Reason in Argument," pp. 269–273.

Definition is the clarification of the meaning of a word by identifying the formal class to which it belongs and then differentiating it from other members of that class. For instance, we might define "freshman" as a college or university student (general class) who has completed fewer than thirty semester hours or forty-five quarter hours of course work (differentiation from other members of the same general class). While definition can serve as the design principle of an entire essay, it most often serves to clarify or support specific points within a larger work. See the introduction to "Classification Analysis and Definition," pp. 139–141.

Description is an illustration extended in space to provide a word picture of an object, place, or person. A series of images is arranged in spatial order—that is, in a sequence that progresses from one point in space to another—to give them coherence. In the descriptive paragraph on p. 4, for instance, the spatial movement begins outside the boardinghouse, progresses inside and up the stairs, pauses at the door to the room, and then continues into the room. See the introduction to "Extended Illustration," pp. 14–16.

Design is the process by which writers give form and order, through selection and arrangement, to the ideas they have invented on a particular subject. The aim of effective design is to produce a finished piece of writing that presents the subject clearly to the intended audience, with the emphasis where the writer wants it to be. See "An Introduction to Writing," pp. xxvii–xxxiv.

Division is the separation of a whole thing into its component parts. It is an important element in *analysis.* See the introduction to "Analysis," pp. 135–138.

Effect is any result brought about by an antecedent, or *cause.* For instance, the effect of lightning striking dry timber might be a forest fire. See the introduction to "Causal Analysis," pp. 223–228.

Effect to Cause as a principle of invention is the consideration first of the *effect* (such as poor performance on an exam) and second of the *cause* (such as failure to read the assignment) in order to discover what the causal relationship is. As a principle of design, *effect to cause* is the sequence in which the two are introduced in the finished writing, as determined by the complexity of the subject and the point the writer wishes to emphasize. See the introduction to "Causal Analysis," pp. 223–228.

Emotional Appeal is the way in which writers of argument arouse in their readers feelings or emotions appropriate for the purpose and subject of a piece of writing. Appealing to such emotions as compassion, admiration, outrage, fear, anger, love, etc., writers can effectively convince readers not only to accept the validity of their thesis, but in some cases to act upon their views. See the introduction to "Emotion in Argument," pp. 306–308.

Example is an instance that makes a more general idea understandable. Robert Coles, for example, makes clear the general idea that Appalachian children often exhibit a mixture of sickness and health in his example of Billy Potter, quoted on p. 5.

Extended Comparison and Contrast is a form of writing that explores to a fuller extent than simple comparison and contrast exactly how two things are similar and different. This form of writing typically serves as the basis for the whole essay; the structure of the writing is typically of two types: *subject-by-subject* and *part-by-part*. See the introduction to "Reason in Argument," pp. 269–273.

Extended Illustration is an illustration that is developed by means of a series of images arranged into a *narrative* or *description* or, as is ordinarily the case, into a combination of the two. See the introduction to "Extended Illustration," pp. 14–16.

Generalization is an inference or conclusion about the whole group based upon an examination of parts of that group. The greater the number of those parts and the more representative those parts are of the whole group, the sounder the generalization will be. See the introduction to "Reason in Argument," pp. 269–273.

Hasty Generalizing is a propaganda device in which the writer avoids the issue at hand by generalizing on the basis of an inadequate sample: "As the example of these two students clearly shows, the university student of today is only interested in leisure activities."

Hypothesis is a conclusion of the probable cause for a particular effect based upon available evidence. If, for instance, you find, upon returning to your room or apartment, that the door is standing wide open, and upon further inspection you find that the contents of your desk drawer have been dumped in the middle of the floor and that your guitar and most of your records are missing, then you are in a position to form a hypothesis. The most probable hypothesis, although several others are no doubt possible, is that "Someone has come into my room and stolen my guitar and records." See the introduction to "Reason in Argument," pp. 269–273.

Illustration is a unit of language—a word, phrase, sentence, paragraph, or an even longer unit—that stimulates the reader to imagine a sight, sound, touch sensation, smell, or taste. Illustration provides a way for the writer to *show* readers what he is talking about—not simply to *tell* them in general terms. See the introduction to "Illustration," pp. 3–7.

Image is a word or phrase that causes a reader to imagine a simple sight, sound, touch sensation, smell, or taste. It is a basic component in any illustration—whether simple, extended, or multiple.   See the introduction to "Simple Illustration," pp. 8–9.

Imagination is the forming of a mental *image* in a person's consciousness.   The purpose of *illustration* is to stimulate the reader's mind to form such an image or series of images.   See the introductions to "Illustration" and to "Simple Illustration," pp. 3–7 and 8–9.

Induction is one of the two basic types of logical connection that writers make in argument.   It is a reasoning process of examining the parts of a whole group in sufficient number to make an "inductive leap," or to generalize, about the nature of that whole group.   See the introduction to "Reason in Argument," pp. 269–273.

Introduction is the beginning of a piece of writing, in which writers present their subject and themselves (the *persona*) and establish the *tone* of the essay.

Invention is the complex process of originating and discovering ideas, illustrations, comparisons, contrasts, and various forms of analysis through the working of reason and imagination upon the writer's accumulated knowledge—including personal experience, perception, reading, and education.   See "An Introduction to Writing," pp. xxvii–xxxiv.

Irony is a way of using language so as to imply something quite different, even the opposite, of what is actually stated in a piece of writing. "The War Prayer," pp. 327–330, by Mark Twain and "A Modest Proposal," pp. 332–341, by Jonathan Swift are examples of effective uses of irony.

Logical Connections are the clear and sound relations between facts, reasons, and conclusions that writers establish in an argument.   Typically these logical connections are divided into two basic types: deduction and induction.   See the introduction to "Reason in Argument," pp. 269–273.

Metaphor is a statement that one thing *is* another; it is a condensed or shorthand simile: e.g., "Bill is an ox."

Multiple Illustration is the use of two or more illustrations to make the same point or a series of closely related ones.   An important choice the writer must make is how many illustrations will most effectively develop a point.   See the introduction to "Multiple Illustration," pp. 31–33.

Namecalling is a propaganda device in which the writer avoids the issue at hand by resorting to emotionally slanted words: "The scoundrel we have for a governor would do anything short of murder."

Narrative is an illustration extended in time to provide a wordpicture of an event or series of events.   A series of images is arranged in chronological order—that is, in a sequence that progresses from one point in time to another—to give them coherence. In the first two sentences of Thomas Carlyle's "The Irish Widow," p. 16, for instance, the writer begins with one event (the death of the woman's husband) and recounts a series of events in chronological order, ending with the death of "seventeen other persons." See the introduction to "Extended Illustration," pp. 14–16.

Paradox is a statement that seems to contradict itself but may nevertheless be true. For instance, in "Law Is Indispensable," pp. 300–304, Shaw develops an important truth in the paradox that although laws and systems of ethics are never up to date and consequently make society worse than its average unit, laws and systems of ethics are nevertheless necessary and indispensable.

Part-by-Part Structuring is one of the two common structural patterns of comparison and contrast writing. In this pattern, the writer compares or contrasts specific characteristics point by point. For instance, in a paper contrasting two people, a writer could contrast the personal traits of each at the same time, then the leisurely activities of each, and so on. See the introduction to "Extended Comparison and Contrast," pp. 80–83.

Persona is the personality of the writer that is communicated to the reader through a piece of writing. A persona that is appropriate for the writer's purpose, for the subject, and for the audience makes writing more effective. For instance, in "Letter From Birmingham Jail," pp. 354–371, Martin Luther King, Jr., leaves the reader with the distinct impression that he himself is a reasonable and fair person, one who can be trusted.

Persuasive Evidence is evidence that leads readers to act on the writer's idea or solution. See Cleveland Amory's "Little Brother of the Wolf," pp. 312–317, and Jonathan Swift's "A Modest Proposal," pp. 332–341.

Premise is a reason in an argument. A formal argument consists of both a major premise and a minor premise. The conclusion follows necessarily from these premises. The following formal argument from Huxley's "Everyone Is a Scientist," p. 275, illustrates the nature of premises.

All hard and green apples are sour; *major premise*
This apple is hard and green; *minor premise*
Therefore this apple is sour. *conclusion*

See the introduction to "Reason in Argument," pp. 269–273.

Process Analysis as a principle of invention is the examination and discovery of relationships between the stages of a process and the process as a whole. This kind of invention usually involves dividing the whole process into major stages and the major stages into a clear sequence of individual steps, as in the Catton and Hayakawa examples on pp. 180–182. As a principle of design, process analysis suggests a *sequence* or arrangement of materials in an essay. Since the usual arrangement of materials in a process essay is chronological, such an essay usually has strong elements of *narrative* in it. See the introductions to "Process Analysis," pp. 180–183, and to "Extended Illustration," pp. 14–16.

Propaganda Devices are uses of language that cover up the lack of a solid factual basis for a position or the lack of sound reasoning behind a belief the writer is urging the reader to accept. They are often called informal fallacies. See *Bandwagon, Cardstacking, Hasty Generalizing, Namecalling,* and *Stereotyping.*

Purpose is the reason why a writer writes a given piece of writing—to influence or change the audience in a particular way. Sometimes writers aim to convince readers to believe the way they do on a specific issue or to take some specific action on a subject. At other times, they may simply want to explain a subject or to provide readers with new information about a subject. The purpose a writer has is reflected in the *thesis* of the piece of writing. See "An Introduction to Writing," p. xxviii.

Rational Appeal is the way in which writers arouse in readers a sense of the reasonableness of their argument. Writers accomplish this appeal through establishing clear and sound relations between facts, reasons, and conclusions. These logical connections are of two basic types: *deduction* and *induction.* See the introduction to "Reason in Argument," pp. 269–273.

Rebuttal is a systematic answer or counterproof that readers could make in response to an argument or part of an argument. Writers should anticipate these responses and speak to them in their arguments. See the introduction to "Argument," pp. 263–268, especially p. 267.

Selection is the process in writing of picking out from an experience, event, or subject those details that are most significant for the subject and most appropriate for the writer's purpose and the audience addressed. The writer's ability to select effective detail determines in large part how well the reader will understand the subject of a piece of writing—how well he or she can experience that subject (see, hear, touch, smell, taste, comprehend, understand it.) See the introduction to "Illustration," pp. 3–7.

Sequence is the order (in terms of time, space, or relative importance) in which items are presented in the finished paper and is thus an important principle of *design.* Determining what that order should be is related also to the principle of *invention.* See the introduction to "Extended Illustration," pp. 14–16; "Multiple Illustration," pp. 31–33; "Classification Analysis and Definition," pp. 139–141; "Process Analysis," pp. 180–183; and "Causal Analysis," pp. 223–228.

Simile is a statement that one thing is like another; e.g., "Bill is *like* an ox." See the introduction to "Simple Comparison and Contrast," pp. 69–71.

Simple Illustration is a brief illustration that is more than a single image but is not extended sufficiently to be a full-blown narrative or description. Simple illustrations usually function as a clarification or support for a single point in a larger piece of writing. See the introduction to "Simple Illustration," pp. 8–9.

Simple Comparison and Contrast is a brief pointing-out of the similarities and/or differences between two or more things. As such they form striking and vital parts of larger works. Rarely do simple comparison and contrast serve as the basis for a whole essay. In their basic form they are similes or metaphors, but they can also be analogies or symbols. See the introduction to "Simple Comparison and Contrast," pp. 69–71.

Sources for Writing are what writers draw upon in inventing or discovering their subject. These sources are often personal experience, memory, conversations, reading, etc. See "An Introduction to Writing," pp. xxvii–xxxiv, and the introduction to "Illustration," pp. 6–7.

Spatial Order is the arrangement of items into a coherent pattern moving from one point in space to another. See the introduction to "Extended Illustration," p. 14.

Speaker is the voice and presence of the writer that the readers hear and sense as they read a piece of writing.

Stereotyping is a propaganda device in which the writer avoids the issue at hand by putting all members of a class into one group: "We know that cooks are invariably drunks."

Style is the accumulation of choices the writer makes in wording, sentence structure, paragraphing, and overall design. These choices grow out of the writer's unique personality and out of his or her attitudes toward both the subject and the reading audience. See "An Introduction to Writing," pp. xxvii–xxxiv. Observe contrasting styles represented in this book: Mitford, pp. 206–212; Elbow pp. 183–186; McMurtry, p. 18; Huxley, pp. 273–282; Swift, pp. 232–241; etc.

Subject-by-Subject Structuring is one of the two common structural patterns of comparison and contrast writing. In this pattern, the writer first examines one subject fully. He or she then shifts to the other subject, pointing out how it is like or unlike the first. See the introduction to "Extended Comparison and Contrast," pp. 80–83.

Syllogism is a formal argument consisting of a major premise, a minor premise, and a conclusion. See the introduction to "Reason in Argument," pp. 269–273. In "Everyone Is a Scientist," p. 275, Thomas Henry Huxley uses the following syllogism as an example of deduction:

All hard and green apples are sour; *major premise*
This apple is hard and green; *minor premise*
Therefore this apple is sour. *conclusion*

The conclusion follows necessarily from the two premises; if both premises are true, the conclusion must also be true.

Symbol is a concrete image that represents something more than itself; very often it is a visual image standing in for a more abstract and non-material concept. For instance, reading Gwendolyn Brooks' "A Song in the Front Yard," pp. 74–75, we soon come to see that the front and back yards are symbols of two contrasting approaches to life. See the introduction to "Simple Comparison and Contrast," pp. 69–71.

Synthesis is the combining of parts into a coherent whole. It is an important element in *analysis*. See the introduction to "Analysis," pp. 135–138.

Thesis is the statement of the writer's central idea. This controlling idea will then be carried out in detail as the essay supports and develops that thesis. An example of a clearly stated thesis is the following: "A student unfairly accused of violating the parking regulations can win a case before the traffic judge by researching the subject thoroughly beforehand, observing several traffic court sessions, and explaining persuasively why receiving the traffic ticket was unfair." See "An Introduction to Writing," p. xxviii.

Tone is the distinctive attitude of the writer toward the subject and audience that is revealed in a piece of writing—serious, as in "Letter from Birmingham Jail," pp. 354–371; satiric, as in "A Modest Proposal," pp. 332–341; ironic, as in "The War Prayer," pp. 327–330; etc. The effective writers establish a tone that is appropriate to the purpose, the subject, and the audience of their writing.

Transition is the way in which a writer relates one topic or idea to another. It can be a word, phrase, sentence, or even a paragraph that makes it clear exactly what the relationship is between one topic and another. For example (itself a transition), Bruce Catton says: "Then, suddenly . . . ," (p. 100); Nora Ephron: "To give you another example . . . ," (p. 39); Langston Hughes: "Then I was left all alone . . . ," (p. 21); Ray Bradbury: "So, simply then, here is my formula" (p. 35). Thus, whether just a word (such as however, likewise, then), a whole phrase (on the other hand, on the whole, in other words), or a complete sentence or paragraph, transitions serve to make the author's movement from one idea to another a smooth and meaningful one. (See the introduction to "Extended Comparison and Contrast," p. 83).

Biographical Notes

CLEVELAND AMORY (b. 1917) became known as a chronicler of America's First Families with *The Proper Bostonians*, an account of Boston society, of which his own family is a part. An ardent conservationist and crusader for animal protection, Amory is president of the Fund for Animals.

ROBERT ANGUS (b. 1932), educated at Bucknell University, is a free-lance writer who has published widely on sound reproduction, tape recording, and other subjects. He lives in Canaan, Connecticut.

IMAMU A. BARAKA (b. 1934), formerly LeRoi Jones, is a writer and militant Black Nationalist. His writings attempt through artistic protest to expose social evils and force sweeping changes. Baraka became the scourge of many white liberals when he rejected them as enemies; but despite his inflammatory ideas, his literary talent is generally acknowledged.

RAY BRADBURY (b. 1920) has written, by his own estimation, over a thousand stories in addition to numerous novels and screenplays. Best known for his science fiction, his output is much too diverse to be stereotyped under any one category. He has received numerous awards and honors, including the Benjamin Franklin Award for the best story of the year in an American magazine—"Sun and Shadow."

J(ACOB) BRONOWSKI (1908–1974), a native of Poland, was educated at Cambridge, where both his literary and scientific interests manifested themselves. Though essentially a mathematician, Bronowski wrote extensively on broader subjects, attempting to establish philosophical bases for scientific research and exploring the nature of creative thought. He is best known to American audiences for his thirteen-part series *The Ascent of Man*, first shown on BBC television in 1973 and later repeated on PBS.

GWENDOLYN BROOKS (b. 1917), black American poet, is a native of Kansas now residing in Chicago. Among her numerous honors are the 1950 Pulitzer Prize for poetry and two Guggenheim awards.

WARREN S. BROWN (b. 1944), a psychophysiologist, was born and educated in California and is currently a member of the faculty of the School of Medicine, University of California at Los Angeles. His interests include research in the language functions of the human brain.

THOMAS CARLYLE (1795–1881) was a Scottish-born Victorian critic and historian. His best-known works are *The French Revolution* and *History of Frederic II of Prussia, Called Frederick the Great*.

RACHEL CARSON (1907–1964) was a marine biologist with the U.S. Fish and Wildlife Service. In her controversial *Silent Spring* (1962), she described the potentially dangerous effects the indiscriminate use of weed killers and insecticides has on human beings and wildlife.

BRUCE CATTON (b. 1899), an authority on the Civil War, is the author of books on the subject, including *Glory Road, A Stillness at Appomatox,* and *This Hallowed Ground.*

ROBERT COLES (b. 1929), Boston research psychiatrist and lecturer on education at Harvard, is an authority on problems of poverty and racial discrimination. His award-winning book *Children of Crisis: A Study of Courage and Fear* was based on an eight-year study of the civil rights struggle and presented a strong case for integrated schools.

AARON COPLAND (b. 1900), Brooklyn-born composer, lecturer, teacher, and author, won the Pulitzer Prize for Music in 1944 and has written for films, ballet, theater, and the concert hall. In such works as *Billy the Kid* and *Rodeo,* he has incorporated folk and jazz themes and evolved a uniquely American sound.

NORMAN COUSINS (b. 1912), editor of *Saturday Review,* is among the most distinguished living American men of letters. Author of many works on education and political and social issues, he has also served on numerous boards and committees. His books include *Modern Man is Obsolete* (1945), *The Religious Beliefs of the Founding Fathers* (1958), *The Last Defense in a Nuclear Age* (1960), and *The Celebration of Life* (1974).

JOAN DIDION (b. 1934) has been associate feature editor at *Vogue* since 1956. She is the winner of *Vogue*'s Prix de Paris and a Bread Loaf Fellowship in fiction and is the author of *Run River* (1963), *Slouching Towards Bethlehem* (1968), *Play It As It Lays* (1970), and *A Book of Common Prayer* (1977).

ANNIE DILLARD (b. 1945) is a contributing editor to *Harper's* magazine and columnist in *Living Wilderness.* Both poet and essayist, she is best known for her short prose pieces, both descriptive and meditative, that were collected into *Pilgrim at Tinker Creek* (1974)—the Pulitzer Prize-winner for nonfiction that year.

PETER ELBOW (b. 1935), a New Yorker, lectured in literature at M.I.T. and is now on the faculty of Evergreen State College. He is author of *Writing Without Teachers* (1973) and other works on teaching methods.

NORA EPHRON (b. 1941) has worked for the *New York Post, New York Magazine,* and *Esquire,* and has contributed to *Oui, McCall's,* and *Cosmopolitan* as well. Her *Crazy Salad* (1975) is a collection of her essays about women and has been well received. She is married to journalist and author Carl Bernstein.

JOSEPH FLETCHER (b. 1905), an Episcopal priest, lectures at the Danforth Seminary of the Harvard Business School. Associated with movements for abortion, voluntary sterilization, and planned parenthood, he has written several books, including *Morals and Medicine* and *Situation Ethics.*

ERICH FROMM (b. 1900), German-born psychoanalyst, has taught at universities in the United States and Mexico. Among his many books are *Psychoanalysis and Religion, Marx's Concept of Man, Beyond the Chains of Illusion, Escape from Freedom, The Sane Society,* and *The Crisis of Psychoanalysis.*

SAMUEL I. HAYAKAWA (b. 1906) has been a columnist, editor, book reviewer, professor of English, and president of San Francisco State University. He is now a U.S. Senator from California. His books include *Language in Thought and Action; Language, Meaning, and Maturity;* and *Symbol, Status, and Personality.*

LANGSTON HUGHES (1902–1967) was born in the Midwest and studied at Columbia and Lincoln universities. His use of the rhythms of blues and jazz music and his deep feeling for the American black experience run through all his work, including such collections of poetry as *The Big Sea* and *The Ways of the White Folks,* his five plays, and his short stories.

THOMAS HENRY HUXLEY (1825–1895) was the foremost advocate in England of Darwin's theory of evolution. He devoted himself to the question of man's origin and place in nature, the study of paleontology, and such writings as *Science and Culture* (1881) and *Evolution and Ethics* (1893).

SIR JAMES JEANS (1887–1946), English mathematician, astronomer, physicist, and author, is known for his work on the kinetic theory of gases and on radiations. He wrote several books popularizing science, including *The Universe Around Us, Through Space and Time,* and *The Mysterious Universe.*

THOMAS JEFFERSON (1743–1826) was governor of Virginia during the Revolutionary War and afterward served the new government in various capacities. In 1801 he became America's third president. Scholar, statesman, and liberal, he greatly influenced the political and intellectual life of the nation.

X. J. KENNEDY (b. 1929) is a poet, editor, critic, and English professor, presently at Tufts University. His books include *Nude Descending a Staircase* (1961), *Mark Twain's Frontier* (1963), *An Introduction to Poetry* (1966), and *Literature: An Introduction to Fiction, Poetry, and Drama* (1976).

MARTIN LUTHER KING, JR. (1929–1968) was born and raised in Atlanta, Ga., where he served as a Baptist minister and the president of the Southern Christian Leadership Conference until his assassination. Perhaps the foremost American civil rights leader of this century, King was dedicated to the nonviolent protest techniques of Gandhi. The Nobel Peace Prize was awarded to him in 1964. His writings include the books *Stride Toward Freedom, Strength to Love,* and *Why We Can't Wait.*

C(LIVE) S(TAPLES) LEWIS (1898–1963) was a British scholar, critic, essayist, novelist, and writer of children's books. The recurring concern of Lewis's work is to communicate a nondogmatic Christianity and an absolute morality to an audience of modern skeptics. His many books include *The Allegory of Love* (1936); *Out of the Silent Planet, That Hideous Strength,* and *The Screwtape Letters* (all 1946); *The Lion, the Witch, and the Wardrobe* (1950); *Mere Christianity* (1952); *The Four Loves* (1960); and *The Discarded Image* (1964).

LARRY MCMURTRY (b. 1936) writes about the ranching country of his native Texas. He is the author of *Horseman, Pass By,* and *Leaving Cheyenne,* which were brought to the screen as *Hud* and *Lovin' Molly.* His novel *The Last Picture Show,* a portrait of a dying Texas town, also became a major motion picture. His most recent novel is *Terms of Endearment* (1975).

ARNOLD J. MANDELL, M.D. (b. 1934) is a psychiatrist and neurochemist and a member of the Department of Psychiatry at the University of California at San Diego. His field of research is related behavior in animals and human beings. His publications include a novel, *The Nightmare Season* (1976).

KAORU MARUYAMA (b. 1899) is one of Japan's foremost contemporary lyric poets and intellectuals. Co-founder in 1933 of the Japanese poetry magazine *Four Seasons,* he is currently on the faculty of Aichi University.

ANDREW MARVELL (1621–1678) was an English poet and satirist. He is best remembered for his poems, including *To His Coy Mistress, The Emigrants in the Bermudas,* and *Thoughts in a Garden.*

ROLLO MAY (b. 1909) is a New York psychoanalyst and recipient of numerous awards for distinguished contributions to psychology. His books include *Meaning of Anxiety* (1950), *Man's Search for Himself* (1953), *Symbolism in Religion and Literature* (1960), *Psychology and the Human Dilemma* (1966), and *Love and Will* (1969).

JESSICA MITFORD (b. 1917) is an English writer now living in California. Her books include *The American Way of Death* (1963) a best-selling exposé of the burial business; and *Kind and Usual Punishment* (1973), a study of the American prison system.

WILLIE MORRIS (b. 1934) a native of Jackson, Mississippi, served as editor in chief of the *Texas Observer* and was the executive editor of *Harper's* magazine in New York until 1971. His memoir *North Toward Home* earned him a Houghton-Mifflin literary fellowship for nonfiction in 1967.

JOHN G. NEIHARDT (b. 1881), author, educator, and poet laureate of Nebraska by act of legislature, studied and lived among Omaha and Sioux Indians and later served with the U.S. Department of Interior, Bureau of Indian Affairs. His works include *A Cycle of the American West* and *Black Elk Speaks.*

FLORENCE H. PETTIT is a fabric designer, sculptor, and author who lives in Glenbrook, Connecticut. Her books include *How to Make Whirligigs and Whimmy Diddles and Other American Folkcraft Objects* (1972) and *Indigo Blues* (1974).

JOHN ROBINSON (b. 1908) grew up in New Jersey and received his college education at the University of California at Berkeley. An editor, photojournalist, and free-lance writer now living in the Seattle area, he has written numerous articles and books, including *Highways and Our Environment* (1971), which was selected as an American Ambassador book by the English-Speaking Union.

ANNE ROIPHE (b. 1935), a New York writer, is the author of *Up the Sandbox!* (1971), about the life of a housewife, which was made into a successful film. Her latest book, *Long Division* (1973), is the story of a woman driving with her 10-year-old daughter to Mexico for a divorce.

BERNARD RUDOFSKY (b. 1905) studied architecture and design in his native Austria. He wrote *Are Clothes Modern?* while directing costume research at the Museum of Modern Art in New York. His other works are *The Kimono Mind* and *Architecture Without Architects*.

CAROLINE SEEBOHM (b. 1940) describes herself as "an English writer living in New York." Educated at Oxford University, she is a senior writer for *House and Garden* magazine and also publishes frequently in *The New York Times* and the *New Statesman* of London. Her areas of interest are human behavior and health.

ROY C. SELBY, JR., M.D. (b. 1930) is a native Arkansan who was educated at Louisiana State University and the University of Arkansas Medical School. A neurosurgeon, he has published articles in medical journals in the fields of neurology and neurosurgery. Dr. Selby is now engaged in private practice in the Chicago area.

DOROTHY Z. SEYMOUR, former Editorial Specialist in Linguistic Study at Boston's Ginn and Company, taught reading to young children for seventeen years. She is the author of a group of children's readers and is now a free-lance editor, consultant, and contributor to educational journals.

GEORGE BERNARD SHAW (1856–1950), first employed as a London newspaper critic, became Britain's leading dramatist, applying classical techniques to modern subjects and awakening the social conscience of his age. His works include *The Devil's Disciple, Caesar and Cleopatra, Man and Superman, Major Barbara, Pygmalion,* and *Saint Joan.*

EARL SHORRIS (b. 1936), a Chicago native, has worked in journalism and advertising in Texas, California, and New York. Presently a contributing editor for *Harper's* magazine, he has written for *Atlantic Monthly, Ramparts, Esquire, Antioch Review,* and *New York Times*

Sunday Magazine. His books include *Ofay* (1966), *The Boots of the Virgin* (1968), and *The Death of the Great Spirit* (1971).

JONATHAN SWIFT (1667–1745), one of the greatest satirists in the English language, was an Anglican priest and long the Dean of St. Patrick's Cathedral in Dublin. His life-long subject matter—seen in his sermons as well as his verse and prose satires—includes attacks on immature sentimentality, on trust in human reason to solve problems exclusive of moral consideration, and on any institutuion that blunts the development of a moral sense. His books include *The Tale of a Tub* (1704) and *Gulliver's Travels* (1726).

THOMAS SZASZ, M.D. (b. 1920) is a Hungarian-born American psychiatrist, psychoanalyst, lecturer, and author. Currently a professor of psychiatry at the State University of New York Upstate Medical Center at Syracuse, his research interests include the epistemology of the behavioral sciences, the history of psychiatry, and psychiatry and law. His books include *Law, Liberty, and Psychiatry* (1963), *Ideology and Insanity* (1970), *The Second Sin* (1973), and *Heresies* (1976).

LEWIS THOMAS, M.D. (b. 1913) is president and chief executive officer of the Memorial Sloan-Kettering Cancer Center. An eminent physician, biologist, educator, and administrator, his series of essays entitled "Notes of a Biology Watcher" were first published in the *New England Journal of Medicine* and later collected to form *The Lives of a Cell: Notes of a Biology Watcher* (1974), which received a National Book Award in the following year.

JAMES THURBER (1894–1961) joined the staff of *The New Yorker* in 1927 and contributed to that magazine most of the humorous and ironic stories, essays, cartoons, fables and sketches of his Ohio boyhood that appeared later in his books. His other works include a memoir of *The New Yorker*'s Harold Ross and several children's books.

MARK TWAIN (1835–1910), novelist, journalist, and lecturer, was unsurpassed in his use of exaggeration, irreverence, and deadpan humor. He introduced colloquial speech into American fiction, drawing on his Missouri boyhood for such memorable books as *Tom Sawyer, Huckleberry Finn,* and *Life on the Mississippi.*

E. B. WHITE (b. 1899) left newspaper reporting to start *The New Yorker*'s "Talk of the Town" column and for five years also headed the "One Man's Meat" department of *Harper's.* In poems, sketches, essays, and stories, White comments humorously on urban and suburban anxiety and the complexity of modern family life.

VIRGINIA WOOLF (1882–1941), brilliant but unstable English novelist and critic, was part of the Bloomsbury group of artists and writers. She experimented with interior-monologue and stream-of-consciousness techniques in such novels as *Jacob's Room, To the Lighthouse, The Waves,* and *The Years.*

Index of Terms, Authors, and Titles

About the Authors

Forrest D. Burt, Professor of English at Texas A&M University, was born in Flora, Illinois; grew up in Illinois, Arizona, Texas, and California; and received his education at Wayland Baptist College (B.A.) and Texas Tech University (M.A., Ph.D.). His research and teaching interests are in Victorian literature, rhetoric and composition, and the English novel. He is presently Director of Freshman English at Texas A&M University.

E. Cleve Want, Associate Professor of English at Texas A&M University, is a native of Pine Bluff, Arkansas. He attended Hendrix College (B.A.), George Peabody College (M.A.), The Episcopal Theological Seminary of the Southwest (M.Div.), and Vanderbilt University (Ph.D.). His research and teaching interests are in Victorian literature, rhetoric and composition, and the Bible as literature. He is presently Director of the Undergraduate English Program at Texas A&M University.